W9-ACE-085

Critical Essays on
James Joyce's
Ulysses

Critical Essays on James Joyce's Ulysses

Bernard Benstock

G. K. Hall & Co. • Boston, Massachusetts

Library of Congress Cataloging in Publication Data

Critical essays on James Joyce's Ulysses / Bernard Benstock.
     p. cm. — (Critical essays on British literature)
   Includes index.
   ISBN 0-8161-8766-5 (alk. paper)
   1. Joyce, James, 1882-1941. Ulysses. I. Benstock, Bernard. II.
Series.
  PR6019.O9U636 1989
  823'.912 — dc19
                                             88-26866
                                             CIP

This publication is printed on permanent/durable acid-free paper
MANUFACTURED IN THE UNITED STATES OF AMERICA

CRITICAL ESSAYS ON BRITISH LITERATURE

The Critical Essays on British Literature series provides a variety of approaches to both the classical writers of Britain and Ireland and the best contemporary authors. The formats of the volumes in the series vary with the thematic designs of individual editors and with the number and nature of existing reviews, criticism, and scholarship. In general, the series represents the best in published criticism, augmented, where appropriate, by original essays by recognized authorities. It is hoped that each volume will be unique in developing a new overall perspective on its particular subject.

Bernard Benstock's collection of essays spans fifty-six years of *Ulysses* criticism, offering three sections that combine a few little-known and often polemic essays with major analyses of the novel at various junctures in the history of the book's criticism. The criticism begins with the early reaction of Carl Jung and follows through to the pioneering scholarship of Joyce's friends and others who first laid out the design of the book as a whole. The next section is devoted to the variety of criticism on a single representative chapter, Nausicaa. The final section deals with the new critical approaches to *Ulysses* that have appeared since 1970.

ZACK BOWEN, GENERAL EDITOR

University of Miami

CONTENTS

INTRODUCTION

In the Track of the Odyssean

Nothing rivals the experience of reading James Joyce's *Ulysses*, except for the series of experiences in rereading it. Yet the development of *Ulysses* criticism parallels the excitement of those rereadings for many who have become involved in the Ulyssean "process," the text undergoing changes effected by and effecting the changes in the criticism. To write the history of *Ulysses* criticism for the past seven decades no longer seems to be feasible, unless one audaciously undertook to publish a thin volume like those that appear as *A History of the World:* too much has happened in the constant addition to the vast shelves of books and articles about *Ulysses* to make for a containable history. A selection of essays reflecting "moments" in *Ulysses* criticism reveals something of the multifarious career of Joyce's book, high points (and an occasional low point) along the road. An incredible amount of nonsense has been written about *Ulysses*, most of which sinks to the bottom of the pond, but some of it has an uncanny durability. But valuable insights are often lost because of the transitory nature of literary criticism, or are simply absorbed into the assumed "givens" about the text. The score or so of essays collected in *Critical Essays on James Joyce's "Ulysses"* strives for diversity and historical longevity, bringing together isolated pieces that can for the first time be read as an entity, and assimilated individually by each reader.

These essays are assembled in three sections. The first takes its title from James Joyce's own colloquial phrase for the exegetical process, "What's This Here, Guvnor?" — and it allows for disparate observations of *Ulysses* as a complex text, from the large overview to the handling of a significant crux to a highly individualized reading of the book. The second, "Anatomies of 'Nausicaa,' " brings together several close examinations of that one chapter of *Ulysses*, as it was approached during those seven decades, as a "part of the whole." The third takes its point of departure from the 1970s, when new critical approaches of various sorts, nontraditional as well as traditional, ushered in a new generation of Joyce scholars, and is presented under the title "Future Indicative." These essays

1

form a sampler, but not a random sampling, a *part* of the history of *Ulysses* criticism that may be taken as a whole, a cross section instead of a survey.

BERNARD BENSTOCK

University of Miami

Part One

"What's This Here, Guvnor?"

Starting a fresh look at Joyce's *Ulysses*, that stately, plump book of 1922, through the eyes of the eminent psychiatrist Carl Jung, might seem bizarre, especially when one usually expects the commissioned pioneers, Stuart Gilbert and Frank Budgen. Writing in the early 1930s Jung had already had ample time to revise and refine his attitudes toward Joyce's disturbing novel, and had had access to the commentaries of Gilbert and Ernst Robert Curtius. "*Ulysses:* A Monologue" swings wildly from total rejection in its early pages to a positive acceptance of what Joyce had created, admittedly as a reaction to the enduring success of that controversial work. Jung's study stands as an unconscious barometer to the effects of *Ulysses* on the cultural world at large: it shifts from considering *Ulysses* as an aberration of its author to recognizing the book as diagnostic of the aberrations of the times.

The initial stress is on the negativeness of *Ulysses*, a reaction that Jung cannot separate himself from, although he finds ways to modify it. "Nothingness," he asserts; the book is "infernally nugatory" and "sheer negation." (That he finds only the last page of the book at all positive foreshadows his eventual focus on Molly, although at first he seems only aware of Bloom and Stephen.) "It seems to me now," he later contends, "that all that is negative in Joyce's work, all that is cold-blooded, bizarre and banal, grotesque and devilish, is a positive virtue for which it deserves praise." There is an important modification from a diagnosis of Joyce's "solipsistic isolation" to a reading of *Ulysses* as "a *document humaine* of our time."

Jung is indeed aware of his time, and from perspectives that are more extensive than those of a psychiatrist. As a literary critic he admits to a very traditional orientation that leaves him mystified and unresponsive to much that is modern, and it is understandable that he assumes *Ulysses* to be "surrealist" and "cubist." Nonetheless, he attempts to find the essence of what he considers a chaotic text, identifying its tone as "ironic, sardonic, virulent, contemptuous, sad, despairing, and bitter," and, in his realization that the author makes no attempt to be "agreeable," Jung acknowledges instinctively the modernist war against the "agreeableness"

3

mandated by Victorianism. As a product of its age and a reaction to it, *Ulysses* for Jung contains "an acute power of observation, a photographic memory for sense perceptions, a sensory curiosity directed inward as well as outward, the predominance of retrospective themes and resentments, a delirious confusion of the subjective and psychic with objective reality, a method of presentation that takes no account of the reader," and so on. The psychiatrist is never far from the center of Jung's observations, yet he is also aware of — and obviously more comfortable with — Joyce's sociological function, his "earnest endeavour to rub the noses of our contemporaries in the shadow-side of reality." We are immediately aware of the parallel here with George Bernard Shaw's letter to Sylvia Beach asserting that "In Ireland they try to make a cat cleanly by rubbing its nose in its own filth. Mr Joyce has tried the same treatment on the human subject."

No amount of rereading for Carl Jung in the 1930s would unearth any design other than chaos from the structure of *Ulysses*, although Gilbert had already provided him with an indication of tightly schematized patterns. A generation later, A. Walton Litz is as certain of a "design" in *Ulysses* as Jung had been of an absence of design. From Jung's perspective the gulf that separates Homer's Odysseus from Mr. Leopold Bloom is oceans-wide, yet as Litz scans the notesheets as well as the published text he considers "how much more important the Homeric background was for Joyce than it is to the reader," and he argues that the superimposition of Homeric material helps to create the epic in Joyce's novel. Jung understandably looks at the conventional novel for a guide to *Ulysses* and finds no resemblance; Litz hardly expects to find any, aware that "Joyce sacrificed many of the traditional unities of the novel." "The well-made novel of the nineteenth century," he reminds us, "founded on chronological action and composed of dramatic and expository passages . . . possessed a form which Joyce could no longer employ." In discerning "The Design of *Ulysses*," he re-creates the history of its composition in a way that provided scholarly underpinnings for literary critics in the last three decades, engendering the further explorations of Phillip Herring and Michael Groden. Litz finds Joyce's "principles of artistic selections" and the "rhythm of his prose" important to Joyce's creative process, assuring us (as Carl Jung never could) that "The search for internal consistency and harmony" was a constant Joycean concern and dominates the "order" of *Ulysses*.

The 1960s produced a diversified avalanche of Joyce scholarship and criticism, calling attention to the existence of a "Joyce Industry." The reaction against that industry can be noted in Anthony Cronin's essay in *A Question of Modernity*, where the sort of scholarship undertaken by Professor Litz is granted approval but the speculative critical approaches of other American professors, particularly the "symbol-hunters," are derided. Cronin stresses what several other Irish commentators have been stressing: the necessity of knowing Joyce's Ireland in order to know Joyce's *Ulysses*. Despite such immediate and local concerns, Cronin enters the international arena in evaluating the text, participating in the "higher criticism" that he debunks, in effect disputing Jung's view of the apocalyptic vision, scoffing at the "Homeric parallels" as "an elaborate ironic device designed to exhibit the decay of western civilisation and the emptiness and spiritual barrenness of the bourgeois, urban civilisation." Instead he identifies Joyce's Dubliners as lacking in bourgeois status and Ireland as relatively unindustrialized — a political issue that has resurfaced in the 1980s. Whereas Jung was quick to dismiss Bloom as of no consequence as a Ulysses ("very much unlike his ancient namesake . . . a passive, merely perceiving consciousness, a mere eye, ear, nose, and mouth"), Cronin insists that "If the adventures of the real Ulysses cast a dubious light on Bloom, Bloom in his turn casts an ambiguous light on his forerunner." Also, in contradistinction to the Jungian nugatory he feels that "*Ulysses* executes a complex movement of reconciliation and acceptance," that the creation of Leopold Bloom results in Joyce's "Multiple apotheosis," and that in the work we recognize the "worn, familiar, comical, shabby, eroded but not collapsed face of humanity." The Positive School of *Ulysses* commentary has a strong supporter in Cronin.

Apparently taking his cue from Litz, Cronin tackles the larger issue of the "form" of *Ulysses*, agreeing that "its plot is formless and does not give form to the book — it is not shaped to produce a series of dramatic sensations." Although a classification of the Joycean formative creation may still be in question, Cronin is convinced that "A new prose form has been achieved, free from the distortions of dramatic narrative, and not dependent for its intensity on dramatic confrontations and resolutions." What he emphasizes is the unusual assumption of *Ulysses* as a work of realism; it had of course been condemned in its early days, especially by Irish critics, as wallowing in the sloughs of Zolaesque naturalism, but Cronin shrugs off what he terms the "various confusions about 'naturalism' and 'realism' " — all the while contending that the "action" is "substantially and hypostatically real to begin with." His anchoring of the people and events in a real Dublin that he recognizes as his own allows for his view of the "substantive realism" of *Ulysses*. The Jungian characterization of Molly Bloom as the Great Mother ("who signifies the beginning and end of life") is bypassed here. For Cronin "Molly may or may not be Gea Tellus or the Great Earth Mother; she is certainly Bloom's wife."

Also characteristic of the criticism of the 1960s is the kind of close reading of the situation in *Ulysses* characteristic of John Z. Bennett's "Unposted Letter," published in a journal that does not necessarily specialize in Joyce studies, and consequently easily overlooked by Joyce scholars. Its impact, however, has not been lost on *Ulysses* commentary: it sets out to dispel "popular" (but largely unsubstantiated) notions about the

Blooms' marital and sexual problems. What is uncovered by Bennett may well be crucial to how we now read the text, and the care with which we do that reading.

A general scholarly journal like the *Bucknell Review* was certainly no unusual place to find an article on *Ulysses* like that of Bennett, but a publication sponsored by the Jewish Historical Society of England might seem somewhat outré, except that its title is *The Jews of Ireland, from Earliest Times to the Year 1910.* In his survey Louis Hyman devotes a chapter to Dublin Jews circa 1904 and locates among them a fictional one, Joyce's Leopold Bloom. Just as Bennett deals investigatively with the realistic situation *chez* Bloom from the internal evidence of Joyce's text, Hyman uncovers the realities beneath the creation of Bloom and even Molly, speculating from external evidence on the positioning of the fictional personages among their logical "progenitors." The Jewish elements of *Ulysses* have concerned Joyce commentators both for their "real" aspects, what was suspected about the small community into which Bloom could conceivably be related (and separated), and the assumed inconsistencies of so unlikely a relationship. Hyman has the authority of the historian and the daring of an investigative reporter, as well as the credentials of a local whose relative has a foothold in Joyce's text. Hyman may discover more Blooms and Blums in Joyce's city than the author would ever have need for his fiction, but he tracks them through many of the same sources used by James Joyce, so that like Walton Litz's reading of the completed text through the possibilities in Joyce's notes, Hyman reads Joyce's Dublin (and Triestine) sources comparatively.

By contrast Roy K. Gottfried reads the "syntax" of Joyce's text and investigates the unique approach to language and sentence construction that differentiates *Ulysses* from all other works of prose fiction, including Joyce's own. He analyzes the "paradox of every created sentence of *Ulysses*, the striking newness of its language transformed through an awareness of the order it manipulates," and finds in the grammatical structures a paradigm of Joyce's creative method, as well as a clue to the balance of chaos and order that governs the work. Gottfried builds on what Litz had uncovered, noting that "Joyce's method of composition, his brooding over the text, adding to it and aggrandizing it, as Litz's and more recent studies have shown, produces some noteworthy changes in the language." His linguistic analysis raises fundamental questions about *Ulysses*, including challenges to the existence of an omniscient narrator ("or authorial voice") in the "polyphonic narrative," and the differentiation between "character's monologue and just such an 'authorial' voice." Linguistic concerns have in many ways dominated the Joyce scholarship and criticism of the 1980s, and Gottfried's contribution qualifies him as a factor in the "Future Indicative" of *Ulysses* studies.

The six essays in the first part of this collection span almost half a century and are six varying answers to the "What's This Here, Guvnor?"

question, indicating something of the wide spread of intellectual concerns raised by Joyce's *Ulysses*. Diversity and individual perspectives have highlighted the historical range of developing criticism in this unusual area.

Ulysses: A Monologue

Carl Jung*

The Ulysses of my title has to do with James Joyce and not with that shrewd and storm-driven figure of Homer's world who knew how to escape by guile and wily deeds the enmity and vengeance of gods and men, and who after a wearisome voyage returned to hearth and home. Joyce's Ulysses, very much unlike his ancient namesake, is a passive, merely perceiving consciousness, a mere eye, ear, nose, and mouth, a sensory nerve exposed without choice or check to the roaring, chaotic, lunatic cataract of psychic and physical happenings, and registering all this with almost photographic accuracy.

Ulysses[1] is a book that pours along for seven hundred and thirty-five pages, a stream of time seven hundred and thirty-five days long which all consist in one single and senseless day in the life of every man, the completely irrelevant sixteenth day of June, 1904, in Dublin — a day on which, in all truth, nothing happens. The stream begins in the void and ends in the void. Is all this perhaps one single, immensely long, and excessively complicated Strindbergian pronouncement upon the essence of human life — a pronouncement which, to the reader's dismay, is never finished? Possibly it does touch upon the essence, but quite certainly it reflects life's ten thousand facets and their hundred thousand gradations of colour. So far as I can see, there are in those seven hundred and thirty-five pages no obvious repetitions, not a single blessed island where the long-suffering reader may come to rest; no place where he can seat himself, drunk with memories, and contemplate with satisfaction the stretch of road he has covered, be it one hundred pages or even less. If only he could spot some little commonplace that had obligingly slipped in again where it was not expected! But no! The pitiless stream rolls on without a break, and its velocity or viscosity increases in the last forty pages till it sweeps away even the punctuation marks. Here the suffocating emptiness becomes so

*From *The Collected Works of C. G. Jung,* trans. R. F. C. Hull, Bollinger Series XX, Vol. 15: *The Spirit in Man, Art, and Literature* (Princeton: Princeton University Press, 1966), 109–32. © 1966 by Princeton University Press. Reprinted by permission of Princeton University Press and Routledge & Kegan Paul.

unbearably tense that it reaches the bursting point. This utterly hopeless emptiness is the dominant note of the whole book. It not only begins and ends in nothingness, it consists of nothing but nothingness.[2] It is all infernally nugatory. As a piece of technical virtuosity it is a brilliant and hellish monster-birth.[3]

I had an uncle whose thinking was always direct and to the point. One day he stopped me on the street and demanded: "Do you know how the devil tortures the souls in hell?" When I said no, he replied: "He keeps them waiting." And with that he walked away. This remark occurred to me when I was ploughing through *Ulysses* for the first time. Every sentence rouses an expectation that is not fulfilled; finally, out of sheer resignation, you come to expect nothing, and to your horror it gradually dawns on you that you have hit the mark. In actual fact nothing happens, nothing comes of it all,[4] and yet a secret expectation battling with hopeless resignation drags the reader from page to page. The seven hundred and thirty-five pages that contain nothing by no means consist of blank paper but are closely printed. You read and read and read and you pretend to understand what you read. Occasionally you drop through an air-pocket into a new sentence, but once the proper degree of resignation has been reached you get accustomed to anything. Thus I read to page 135 with despair in my heart, falling asleep twice on the way. The incredible versatility of Joyce's style has a monotonous and hypnotic effect. Nothing comes to meet the reader, everything turns away from him, leaving him gaping after it. The book is always up and away, dissatisfied with itself, ironic, sardonic, virulent, contemptuous, sad, despairing, and bitter. It plays on the reader's sympathies to his own undoing unless sleep kindly intervenes and puts a stop to this drain of energy. Arrived at page 135, after making several heroic efforts to get at the book, to "do it justice," as the phrase goes, I fell at last into profound slumber.[5] When I awoke quite a while later, my views had undergone such a clarification that I started to read the book backwards. This method proved as good as the usual one; the book can just as well be read backwards, for it has no back and no front, no top and no bottom. Everything could easily have happened before, or might have happened afterwards.[6] You can read any of the conversations just as pleasurably backwards, for you don't miss the point of the gags. Every sentence is a gag, but taken together they make no point. You can also stop in the middle of a sentence — the first half still makes sense enough to live by itself, or at least seems to. The whole work has the character of a worm cut in half, that can grow a new head or a new tail as required.

This singular and uncanny characteristic of the Joycean mind shows that his work pertains to the class of cold-blooded animals and specifically to the worm family. If worms were gifted with literary powers they would write with the sympathetic nervous system for lack of a brain.[7] I suspect that something of this kind has happened to Joyce, that we have here a case of visceral thinking[8] with severe restriction of cerebral activity and its confinement to the perceptual processes. One is driven to unqualified admiration for Joyce's feats in the sensory sphere: what he sees, hears, tastes, smells, touches, inwardly as well as outwardly, is beyond measure astonishing. The ordinary mortal, if he is a specialist in sense-perception, is usually restricted either to the outer world or to the inner. Joyce knows them both. Garlands of subjective association twine themselves about the objective figures on a Dublin street. Objective and subjective, outer and inner, are so constantly intermingled that in the end, despite the clearness of the individual images, one wonders whether one is dealing with a physical or with a transcendental tape worm.[9] The tapeworm is a whole living cosmos in itself and is fabulously procreative; this, it seems to me, is an inelegant but not unfitting image for Joyce's proliferating chapters. It is true that the tapeworm can produce nothing but other tapeworms, but it produces them in inexhaustible quantities. Joyce's book might have been fourteen hundred and seventy pages long or even a multiple of that and still it would not have lessened infinity by a drop, and the essential would still have remained unsaid. But does Joyce want to say anything essential? Has this old-fashioned prejudice any right to exist here? Oscar Wilde maintained that a work of art is something entirely useless. Nowadays even the Philistine would raise no objection to this, yet in his heart he still expects a work of art to contain something "essential." Where is it with Joyce? Why doesn't he say it right out? Why doesn't he hand it to the reader with an expressive gesture — "a straight way, so that fools shall not err therein"?

Yes, I admit I feel I have been made a fool of. The book would not meet me half way, nothing in it made the least attempt to be agreeable, and that always gives the reader an irritating sense of inferiority. Obviously I have so much of the Philistine in my blood that I am naïve enough to suppose that a book wants to tell me something, to be understood — a sad case of mythological anthropomorphism projected on to the book! And what a book — no opinion possible — epitome of maddening defeat of intelligent reader, who after all is not such a — (if I may use Joyce's suggestive style). Surely a book has a content, represents something; but I suspect that Joyce did not wish to "represent" anything. Does it by any chance represent *him* — does that explain this solipsistic isolation, this drama without eyewitnesses, this infuriating disdain for the assiduous reader? Joyce has aroused my ill will. One should never rub the reader's nose into his own stupidity, but that is just what *Ulysses* does.

A therapist like myself is always practising therapy — even on himself. Irritation means: you haven't yet seen what's behind it. Consequently we should follow up our irritation and examine whatever it is we discover in our ill temper. I observe then: this solipsism, his contempt for the cultivated and intelligent member of the reading public who wants to understand,[10] who is well-meaning, and who tries to be kindly and just, gets on my nerves. There we have it, the cold-blooded unrelatedness of his mind which seems to come from the saurian in him or from still lower regions—conversation in and with one's own intestines—a man of stone, he with the horns of stone, the stony beard, the petrified intestines, Moses, turning his back with stony unconcern on the flesh-pots and gods of Egypt, and also on the reader, thereby outraging his feelings of good will.

From this stony underworld there rises up the vision of the tapeworm, rippling, peristaltic, monotonous because of its endless proglottic proliferation. No proglottid is quite like any other, yet they can easily be confused. In every segment of the book, however small, Joyce himself is the sole content of the segment. Everything is new and yet remains what it was from the beginning. Talk of likeness to nature! What pullulating richness—and what boredom! Joyce bores me to tears, but it is a vicious dangerous boredom such as not even the worst banality could induce. It is the boredom of nature, the bleak whistling of the wind over the crags of the Hebrides, sunrise and sunset over the wastes of the Sahara, the roar of the sea—real Wagnerian "programme music" as Curtius rightly says, and yet eternal repetition. Notwithstanding Joyce's baffling many-sidedness, certain themes can be picked out though they may not be intended. Perhaps he would like there to be none, for causality and finality have neither place nor meaning in his world, any more than have values. Nevertheless, themes are unavoidable, they are the scaffolding for all psychic happenings, however hard one tries to soak the soul out of every happening, as Joyce consistently does. Everything is desouled, every particle of warm blood has been chilled, events unroll in icy egoism. In all the book there is nothing pleasing, nothing refreshing, nothing hopeful, but only things that are grey, grisly, gruesome, or pathetic, tragic, ironic, all from the seamy side of life and so chaotic that you have to look for the thematic connections with a magnifying glass. And yet they are there, first of all in the form of unavowed resentments of a highly personal nature, the wreckage of a violently amputated boyhood; then as flotsam from the whole history of thought exhibited in pitiful nakedness to the staring crowd. The religious, erotic, and domestic prehistory of the author is reflected in the drab surface of the stream of events; we even behold the disintegration of his personality into Bloom, *l'homme moyen sensuel*, and the almost gaseous Stephen Dedalus, who is mere speculation and mere mind. Of these two, the former has no son and the latter no father.

Somewhere there may be a secret order or parallelism in the chapters—authoritative voices have been raised to this effect[11]—but in any case it is so well concealed that at first I noticed nothing of the kind. And even if I had, it would not have interested me in my helplessly irritated state, any more than would the monotony of any other squalid human comedy.

I had already taken up *Ulysses* in 1922 but had laid it aside disappointed and vexed. Today it still bores me as it did then. Why do I write about it? Ordinarily, I would no more be doing this than writing about any other form of surrealism (what is surrealism?) that passes my understanding. I am writing about Joyce because a publisher was incautious enough to ask me what I thought about him, or rather about *Ulysses*,[12] concerning which opinions are notoriously divided. The only thing beyond dispute is that *Ulysses* is a book that has gone through ten printings and that its author is glorified by some and damned by others. He stands in the cross-fire of discussion and is thus a phenomenon which the psychologist should not ignore. Joyce has exerted a very considerable influence on his contemporaries, and it was this fact which first aroused my interest in *Ulysses*. Had this book slipped noiselessly and unsung into the shades of oblivion I would certainly never have dragged it back again; for it annoyed me thoroughly and amused me only a little. Above all, it held over me the threat of boredom because it had only a negative effect on me and I feared it was the product of an author's negative mood.

But of course I am prejudiced. I am a psychiatrist, and that implies a professional prejudice with regard to all manifestations of the psyche. I must therefore warn the reader: the tragi-comedy of the average man, the cold shadow-side of life, the dull grey of spiritual nihilism are my daily bread. To me they are a tune ground out on a street organ, stale and without charm. Nothing in all this shocks or moves me, for all too often I have to help people out of these lamentable states. I must combat them incessantly and I may only expend my sympathy on people who do not turn their backs on me. *Ulysses* turns its back on me. It is unco-operative, it wants to go on singing its endless tune into endless time — a tune I know to satiety — and to extend to infinity its ganglionic rope-ladder of visceral thinking and cerebration reduced to mere sense-perception. It shows no tendency towards reconstruction; indeed, destructiveness seems to have become an end in itself.

But that is not the half of it — there is also the symptomatology! It is all too familiar, those interminable ramblings of the insane who have only a fragmentary consciousness and consequently suffer from a complete lack of judgment and an atrophy of all their values. Instead, there is often an intensification of the sense-activities. We find in these writings an acute power of observation, a photographic memory for sense-perceptions, a sensory curiosity directed inwards as well as outwards, the predominance of retrospective themes and resentments, a delirious confusion of the subjective and psychic with objective reality, a method of presentation that takes no account of the reader but indulges in neologisms, fragmentary quotations, sound- and speech-associations, abrupt transitions and hiatuses of thought. We also find an atrophy of feeling[12] that does not shrink from any depth of absurdity or cynicism. Even the layman would have no difficulty in tracing the analogies between *Ulysses* and the schizophrenic mentality. The resemblance is indeed so suspicious that an indignant reader might easily fling the book aside with the diagnosis "schizophrenia." For the psychiatrist the analogy is startling, but he would nevertheless point out that a characteristic mark of the compositions of the insane, namely, the presence of stereotyped expressions, is notably absent. *Ulysses* may be anything, but it is certainly not monotonous in the sense of being repetitious. (This is not a contradiction of what I said earlier; it is impossible to say anything contradictory about *Ulysses*.) The presentation is consistent and flowing, everything is in motion and nothing is fixed. The whole book is borne along on a subterranean current of life that shows singleness of aim and rigorous selectivity, both these being unmistakable proof of the existence of a unified personal will and directed intention. The mental functions are under severe control; they do not manifest themselves in a spontaneous and erratic way. The perceptive functions, that is, sensation and intuition, are given preference throughout, while the discriminative functions, thinking and feeling, are just as consistently suppressed. They appear merely as mental contents, as objects of perception. There is no relaxing of the general tendency to present a shadow-picture of the mind and the world, in spite of frequent temptations to surrender to a sudden touch of beauty. These are traits not ordinarily found in the insane. There remains, then, the insane person of an uncommon sort. But the psychiatrist has no criteria for judging such a person. What seems to be mental abnormality may be a kind of mental health which is inconceivable to the average understanding; it may even be a disguise for superlative powers of mind.

It would never occur to me to class *Ulysses* as a product of schizophrenia. Moreover, nothing would be gained by this label, for we wish to know why *Ulysses* exerts such a powerful influence and not whether its author is a high-grade or a low-grade schizophrenic. *Ulysses* is no more a pathological product than modern art as a whole. It is "cubistic" in the deepest sense because it resolves the picture of reality into an immensely complex painting whose dominant note is the melancholy of abstract objectivity. Cubism is not a disease but a tendency to represent reality in a certain way — and that way may be grotesquely realistic or grotesquely abstract. The clinical picture of schizophrenia is a mere analogy in that the schizophrenic apparently has the same tendency to treat reality as if it were strange to him, or, conversely, to estrange himself from reality. With the schizophrenic the tendency usually has no recognizable purpose but is a symptom inevitably arising from the disintegration of the personality into fragmentary personalities (the autonomous complexes). In the modern artist it is not produced by any disease in the individual but is a collective manifestation of our time. The artist does not follow an individual impulse, but rather a current of collective life which arises not directly from consciousness but from the collective unconscious of the modern psyche. Just because it is a collective phenomenon it bears identical fruit in the most widely separated realms, in painting as well as literature, in sculpture as well as architecture. It is, moreover, significant

that one of the spiritual fathers of the modern movement — van Gogh —
was actually schizophrenic.

The distortion of beauty and meaning by grotesque objectivity or
equally grotesque irreality is, in the insane, a consequence of the destruction of the personality; in the artist it has a creative purpose. Far from his
work being an expression of the destruction of his personality, the modern
artist finds the unity of his artistic personality in destructiveness. The
Mephistophelian perversion of sense into nonsense, of beauty into ugliness — in such an exasperating way that nonsense almost makes sense and
ugliness has a provocative beauty — is a creative achievement that has never
been pushed to such extremes in the history of human culture, though it is
nothing new in principle. We can observe something similar in the
perverse change of style under Ikhnaton, in the inane lamb symbolism of
the early Christians, in those doleful Pre-Raphaelite figures, and in late
Baroque art, strangling itself in its own convolutions. Despite their
differences all these epochs have an inner relationship: they were periods
of creative incubation whose meaning cannot be satisfactorily explained
from a causal standpoint. Such manifestations of the collective psyche
disclose their meaning only when they are considered teleologically as
anticipations of something new.

The epoch of Ikhnaton was the cradle of the first monotheism, which
has been preserved for the world in Jewish tradition. The crude infantilism
of the early Christian era portended nothing less than the transformation
of the Roman Empire into a City of God. The rejection of the art and
science of his time was not an impoverishment for the early Christian, but
a great spiritual gain. The Pre-Raphaelite primitives were the heralds of
an ideal of bodily beauty that had been lost to the world since classical
times. The Baroque was the last of the ecclesiastical styles, and its self-
destruction anticipates the triumph of the spirit of science over the spirit of
medieval dogmatism. Tiepolo, for instance, who had already reached the
danger zone in his technique, is not a symptom of decadence when
considered as an artistic personality, but labours with the whole of his
being to bring about a much needed disintegration.

This being so we can ascribe a positive, creative value and meaning
not only to *Ulysses* but also to its artistic congeners. In its destruction of
the criteria of beauty and meaning that have held till today, *Ulysses*
accomplishes wonders. It insults all our conventional feelings, it brutally
disappoints our expectations of sense and content, it thumbs its nose at all
synthesis. We would show ill will even to suspect any trace of synthesis or
form, for if we succeeded in demonstrating any such unmodern tendencies
in *Ulysses* this would amount to pointing out a gross aesthetic defect.
Everything abusive we can say about *Ulysses* bears witness to its peculiar
quality, for our abuse springs from the resentment of the unmodern man
who does not wish to see what the gods have graciously veiled from sight.

All those ungovernable forces that welled up in Nietzsche's Dionysian exuberance and flooded his intellect have burst forth in undiluted form in modern man. Even the darkest passages in the second part of *Faust*, even *Zarathustra* and, indeed, *Ecce Homo*, try in one way or another to recommend themselves to the public. But it is only modern man who has succeeded in creating an art in reverse, a backside of art that makes no attempt to be ingratiating, that tells us just where we get off, speaking with the same rebellious contrariness that had made itself disturbingly felt in those precursors of the moderns (not forgetting Hölderlin) who had already started to topple the old ideals.

If we stick to one field of experience only, it is not really possible to see clearly what is happening. It is not a matter of a single thrust aimed at one definite spot, but of an almost universal "restratification" of modern man, who is in the process of shaking off a world that has become obsolete. Unfortunately we cannot see into the future and so we do not know how far we still belong in the deepest sense to the Middle Ages. If, from the watch-towers of the future, we should seem stuck in medievalism up to the ears, I for one would be little surprised. For that alone would satisfactorily explain to us why there should be books or works of art after the style of *Ulysses*. They are drastic purgatives whose full effect would be dissipated if they did not meet with an equally strong and obstinate resistance. They are a kind of psychological specific which is of use only where the hardest and toughest material must be dealt with. They have this in common with Freudian theory, that they undermine with fanatical one-sidedness values that have already begun to crumble.

Ulysses makes a show of semi-scientific objectivity, at times even employing "scientific" language, and yet it displays a truly unscientific temper: it is sheer negation. Even so it is creative — a creative destruction. Here is no theatrical gesture of a Herostratus burning down temples, but an earnest endeavour to rub the noses of our contemporaries in the shadow-side of reality, not with any malicious intent but with the guileless naïveté of artistic objectivity. One may safely call the book pessimistic even though at the very end, on nearly the final page, a redeeming light breaks wistfully through the clouds. This is only *one* page against seven hundred and thirty-four which were one and all born of Orcus. Here and there, a fine crystal glitters in the black stream of mud, so that even the unmodern may realize that Joyce is an "artist" who knows his trade — which is more than can be said of most modern artists — and is even a past master at it, but a master who has piously renounced his powers in the name of a higher goal. Even in his "restratification" Joyce has remained a pious Catholic: his dynamite is expended chiefly upon churches and upon those psychic edifices which are begotten or influenced by churches. His "anti-world" has the medieval, thoroughly provincial, quintessentially Catholic atmosphere of an Erin trying desperately to enjoy its political independence. He worked at *Ulysses* in many foreign lands, and from all

of them he looked back in faith and kinship upon Mother Church and
Ireland. He used his foreign stopping-places merely as anchors to steady
his ship in the maelstrom of his Irish reminiscences and resentments. Yet
Ulysses does not strain back to his Ithaca — on the contrary, he makes
frantic efforts to rid himself of his Irish heritage.

We might suppose this behaviour to be of only local interest and
expect it to leave the rest of the world quite cold. But it does not leave the
world cold. The local phenomenon seems to be more or less universal, to
judge from its effects on Joyce's contemporaries. The cap must fit. There
must exist a whole community of moderns who are so numerous that they
have been able to devour ten editions of Ulysses since 1922. The book must
mean something to them, must even reveal something that they did not
know or feel before. They are not infernally bored by it, but are helped,
refreshed, instructed, converted, "restratified." Obviously, they are thrown
into a desirable state of some sort, for otherwise only the blackest hatred
could enable the reader to go through the book from page 1 to page 735
with attention and without fatal attacks of drowsiness. I therefore surmise
that medieval Catholic Ireland covers a geographical area of whose size I
have hitherto been ignorant; it is certainly far larger than the area
indicated on the ordinary map. This Catholic Middle Ages, with its
Messrs. Dedalus and Bloom, seems to be pretty well universal. There must
be whole sections of the population that are so bound to their spiritual
environment that nothing less than Joycean explosives are required to
break through their hermetic isolation. I am convinced that this is so: we
are still stuck in the Middle Ages up to the ears. And it is because Joyce's
contemporaries are so riddled with medieval prejudices that such prophets
of negation as he and Freud are needed to reveal to them the other side of
reality.

Of course, this tremendous task could hardly be accomplished by a
man who with Christian benevolence tried to make people turn an
unwilling eye on the shadow-side of things. That would amount only to
their looking on with perfect unconcern. No, the revelation must be
brought about by the appropriate attitude of mind, and Joyce is again a
master here. Only in this way can the forces of negative emotion be
mobilized. Ulysses shows how one should execute Nietzsche's "sacrilegious
backward grasp." Joyce sets about it coldly and objectively, and shows
himself more "bereft of gods" than Nietzsche ever dreamed of being. All
this on the implicit and correct assumption that the fascinating influence
exerted by the spiritual environment has nothing to do with reason, but
everything with feeling. One should not be misled into thinking that
because Joyce reveals a world that is horribly bleak and bereft of gods, it is
inconceivable that anyone should derive the slightest comfort from his
book. Strange as it may sound, it remains true that the world of Ulysses is a
better one than the world of those who are hopelessly bound to the
darkness of their spiritual birthplaces. Even though the evil and destruc-

tive elements predominate, they are far more valuable than the "good" that has come down to us from the past and proves in reality to be a ruthless tyrant, an illusory system of prejudices that robs life of its richness, emasculates it, and enforces a moral compulsion which in the end is unendurable. Nietzsche's "slave-uprising in morals" would be a good motto for *Ulysses*. What frees the prisoner of a system is an "objective" recognition of his world and of his own nature. Just as the arch-Bolshevist revels in his unshaven appearance, so the man who is bound in spirit finds a rapturous joy in saying straight out for once exactly how things are in his world. For the man who is dazzled by the light the darkness is a blessing, and the boundless desert is a paradise to the escaped prisoner. It is nothing less than redemption for the medieval man of today not to have to be the embodiment of goodness and beauty and common sense. Looked at from the shadow-side, ideals are not beacons on mountain peaks, but taskmasters and gaolers, a sort of metaphysical police originally thought up on Sinai by the tyrannical demagogue Moses and thereafter foisted upon mankind by a clever ruse.

From the causal point of view Joyce is a victim of Roman Catholic authoritarianism, but considered teleologically he is a reformer who for the present is satisfied with negation, a Protestant nourished by his own protests. Atrophy of feeling is a characteristic of modern man and always shows itself as a reaction when there is too much feeling around, and in particular too much false feeling. From the lack of feeling in *Ulysses* we may infer a hideous sentimentality in the age that produced it. But are we really so sentimental today?

Again a question which the future must answer. Still, there is a good deal of evidence to show that we actually are involved in a sentimentality hoax of gigantic proportions. Think of the lamentable role of popular sentiment in wartime! Think of our so-called humanitarianism! The psychiatrist knows only too well how each of us becomes the helpless but not pitiable victim of his own sentiments. Sentimentality is the superstructure erected upon brutality. Unfeelingness is the counter-position and inevitably suffers from the same defects. The success of *Ulysses* proves that even its lack of feeling has a positive effect on the reader, so that we must infer an excess of sentiment which he is quite willing to have damped down. I am deeply convinced that we are not only stuck in the Middle Ages but also are caught in our own sentimentality. It is therefore quite comprehensible that a prophet should arise to teach our culture a compensatory lack of feeling. Prophets are always disagreeable and usually have bad manners, but it is said that they occasionally hit the nail on the head. There are, as we know, major and minor prophets, and history will decide to which of them Joyce belongs. Like every true prophet, the artist is the unwitting mouthpiece of the psychic secrets of his time, and is often as unconscious as a sleep-walker. He supposes that it is he who speaks, but the spirit of the age is his prompter, and whatever this spirit says is proved true by its effects.

Ulysses is a *document humain* of our time and, what is more, it harbours a secret. It can release the spiritually bound, and its coldness can freeze all sentimentality — and even normal feeling — to the marrow. But these salutary effects do not exhaust its powers. The notion that the devil himself stood sponsor to the work, if interesting, is hardly a satisfactory hypothesis. There is life in it, and life is never exclusively evil and destructive. To be sure, the side of it that is most tangible seems negative and disruptive; but one senses behind it something intangible — a secret purpose which lends it meaning and value. Is this patchwork quilt of words and images perhaps "symbolic"? I am not thinking of an allegory (heaven forbid!), but of the symbol as an expression of something whose nature we cannot grasp. In that case a hidden meaning would doubtless shine through the curious fabric at some point, here and there notes would resound that had been heard at other times and places, maybe in unusual dreams or in the cryptic wisdom of forgotten races. This possibility cannot be contested, but, for myself, I cannot find the key. On the contrary, the book seems to me to be written in the full light of consciousness; it is not a dream and not a revelation of the unconscious. Compared with the *Zarathustra* or the second part of *Faust*, it shows an even stronger purposiveness and sense of direction. This is probably why *Ulysses* does not bear the features of a symbolic work. Of course, one senses the archetypal background. Behind Dedalus and Bloom there stand the eternal figures of spiritual and carnal man; Mrs. Bloom perhaps conceals an anima entangled in worldliness, and Ulysses himself might be the hero. But the book does not focus upon this background; it veers away in the opposite direction and strives to attain the utmost objectivity of consciousness. It is obviously not symbolic and has no intention of being so. Were it none the less symbolic in certain parts, then the unconscious, in spite of every precaution, would have played the author a trick or two. For when something is "symbolic," it means that a person divines its hidden, ungraspable nature and is trying desperately to capture in words the secret that eludes him. Whether it is something of the world he is striving to grasp or something of the spirit, he must turn to it with all his mental powers and penetrate all its iridescent veils in order to bring to the light of day the gold that lies jealously hidden in the depths.

But the shattering thing about *Ulysses* is that behind the thousand veils nothing lies hidden; it turns neither to the world nor to the spirit but, cold as the moon looking on from cosmic space,[13] leaves the comedy of genesis and decay to pursue its course. I sincerely hope that *Ulysses* is not symbolic, for if it were it would have failed in its purpose. What kind of anxiously guarded secret might it be that is hidden with matchless care under seven hundred and thirty-five unendurable pages? It is better not to waste one's time and energy on a fruitless treasure-hunt. Indeed, there *ought not* to be anything symbolic behind the book, for if there were our consciousness would be dragged back into world and spirit, perpetuating Messrs. Bloom and Dedalus to all eternity, befooled by the ten thousand facets of life. This is just what *Ulysses* seeks to prevent: it wants to be an eye of the moon, a consciousness detached from the object, in thrall neither to the gods nor to sensuality, and bound neither by love nor by hate, neither by conviction nor by prejudice. *Ulysses* does not preach this but practises it — detachment of consciousness[14] is the goal that shimmers through the fog of this book. This, surely, is its real secret, the secret of a new cosmic consciousness; and it is revealed not to him who has conscientiously waded through the seven hundred and thirty-five pages, but to him who has gazed at his world and his own mind for seven hundred and thirty-five days with the eyes of Ulysses. This space of time, at any rate, is to be taken symbolically — "a time, times and a half a time" — an indefinite time, therefore; but sufficiently long for the transformation to take place. The detachment of consciousness can be expressed in the Homeric image of Odysseus sailing the straits between Scylla and Charybdis, between the Symplegades, the clashing rocks of the world and the spirit; or, in the imagery of the Dublin inferno, between Father John Conmee and the Viceroy of Ireland, "a light crumpled throwaway," drifting down the Liffey (p. 239): "Elijah, skiff, light crumpled throwaway, sailed eastward by flanks of ships and trawlers, amid an archipelago of corks, beyond new Wapping street past Benson's ferry, and by the threemasted schooner *Rosevean* from Bridgwater with bricks."

Can this detachment of consciousness, this depersonalization of the personality, can this be the Ithaca of the Joycean Odyssey?

One might suppose that in a world of nothing but nothingness at least the "I" — James Joyce himself — would be left over. But has anyone noticed the appearance, among all the unhappy, shadowy "I"s of this book, of a single, actual ego? True, every figure in *Ulysses* is superlatively real, none of them could be other than what they are, they are themselves in every respect. And yet not one of them has an ego, there is no acutely conscious, human centre, an island surrounded by warm heart's blood, so small and yet so vitally important. All the Dedaluses, Blooms, Harrys, Lynches, Mulligans, and the rest of them talk and go about as in a collective dream that begins nowhere and ends nowhere, that takes place only because "Noman" — an unseen Odysseus — dreams it. None of them knows this, and yet all live for the sole reason that a god bids them live. That is how life is — *vita somnium breve* — and that is why the Joycean figures are so real. But the ego that embraces them all appears nowhere. It betrays itself by nothing, by no judgment, no sympathy, not a single anthropomorphism. The ego of the creator of these figures is not to be found. It is as though it had dissolved into the countless figures of *Ulysses*.[15] And yet, or rather for that very reason, all and everything, even the missing punctuation of the final chapter, is Joyce himself. His detached, contemplative consciousness, dispassionately embracing in one glance the timeless simultaneity of the happenings of the sixteenth day of June, 1904, must say of all these appearances: *Tat tvam asi*, "That art thou"—"thou" in a higher sense, not the ego but the self. For the self alone embraces the ego and the non-ego, the infernal regions, the viscera, the *imagines et lares*, and the heavens.

Whenever I read *Ulysses* there comes into my mind a Chinese picture, published by Richard Wilhelm,[16] of a yogi in meditation, with five human figures growing out of the top of his head and five more figures growing out of the top of each of *their* heads. This picture portrays the spiritual state of the yogi who is about to rid himself of his ego and to pass over into the more complete, more objective state of the self. This is the state of the "moon-disk, at rest and alone," of *sat-chit-ananda*, the epitome of being and not-being, the ultimate goal of the Eastern way of redemption, the priceless pearl of Indian and Chinese wisdom, sought and extolled through the centuries.

The "light crumpled throwaway" drifts towards the East. Three times this crumpled note turns up in *Ulysses*, each time mysteriously connected with Elijah. Twice we are told: "Elijah is coming." He actually does appear in the brothel scene (rightly compared by Middleton Murry to the Walpurgisnacht in *Faust*), where in Americanese he explains the secret of the note (p. 478):

> Boys, do it now. God's time is 12.25. Tell mother you'll be there. Rush your order and you play a slick ace. Join on right here! Book through to eternity junction, the nonstop run. Just one word more. Are you a god or a doggone clod? If the second advent came to Coney Island are we ready? Florry Christ, Stephen Christ, Zoe Christ, Bloom Christ, Kitty Christ, Lynch Christ, it's up to you to sense that cosmic force. Have we cold feet about the cosmos? No. Be on the side of the angels. Be a prism. *You have that something within, the higher self.*[17] You can rub shoulders with a Jesus, a Gautama, an Ingersoll. Are you all in this vibration? I say you are. You once nobble that, congregation, and a buck joyride to heaven becomes a back number. You got me? It's a lifebrightener, sure. The hottest stuff ever was. It's the whole pie with jam in. It's just the cutest snappiest line out. It is immense, supersumptuous. It restores.

One can see what has happened: the detachment of human consciousness and its consequent approximation to the divine—the whole basis and highest artistic achievement of *Ulysses*—suffers an infernal distortion in the drunken madhouse of the brothel as soon as it appears in the cloak of a traditional formula. Ulysses, the sorely tried wanderer, toils ever towards his island home, back to his true self, beating his way through the turmoil of eighteen chapters, and, free at last from the fool's world of illusions, "looks on from afar," impassively. Thus he achieves what a Jesus or a Buddha achieved, and what Faust also strove for—the overcoming of a fool's world, liberation from the opposites. And just as Faust was dissolved in the Eternal Feminine, so it is Molly Bloom (whom Stuart Gilbert compares to the blossoming earth) who has the last word in her unpunctuated monologue, putting a blessed close to the hellish, shrieking dissonances with a harmonious final chord.

Ulysses is the creator-god in Joyce, a true demiurge who has freed himself from entanglement in the physical and mental world and contemplates them with detached consciousness. He is for Joyce what Faust was for Goethe, or Zarathustra for Nietzsche. He is the higher self who returns to his divine home after blind entanglement in *samsara*. In the whole book no Ulysses appears; the book itself is Ulysses, a microcosm of James Joyce, the world of the self and the self of the world in one. Ulysses can return home only when he has turned his back on the world of mind and matter. This is surely the message underlying that sixteenth day of June, 1904, the everyday of everyman, on which persons of no importance restlessly do and say things without beginning or aim — a shadowy picture, dreamlike, infernal, sardonic, negative, ugly, devilish, but true. A picture that could give one bad dreams or induce the mood of a cosmic Ash Wednesday, such as the Creator might have felt on August 1, 1914. After the optimism of the seventh day of creation the demiurge must have found it pretty difficult in 1914 to identify himself with his handiwork. *Ulysses* was written between 1914 and 1921 — hardly the conditions for painting a particularly cheerful picture of the world or for taking it lovingly in one's arms (nor today either, for that matter). So it is not surprising that the demiurge in the artist sketched a negative picture, so blasphemously negative that in Anglo-Saxon countries the book was banned in order to avoid the scandal of its contradicting the creation story in Genesis! And that is how the misunderstood demiurge became Ulysses in search of his home.

There is so little feeling in *Ulysses* that it must be very pleasing to all aesthetes. But let us assume that the consciousness of *Ulysses* is not a moon but an ego that possesses judgment, understanding, and a feeling heart. Then the long road through the eighteen chapters would not only hold no delights but would be a road to Calvary; and the wanderer, overcome by so much suffering and folly, would sink down at nightfall into the arms of the Great Mother, who signifies the beginning and end of life. Under the cynicism of Ulysses there is hidden a great compassion; he knows the sufferings of a world that is neither beautiful nor good and, worse still, rolls on without hope through the eternally repeated everyday, dragging with it man's consciousness in an idiot dance through the hours, months, years. Ulysses has dared to take the step that leads to the detachment of consciousness from the object; he has freed himself from attachment, entanglement, and delusion, and can therefore turn homeward. He gives us more than a subjective expression of personal opinion, for the creative genius is never one but many, and he speaks in stillness to the souls of the multitude, whose meaning and destiny he embodies no less than the artist's own.

It seems to me now that all that is negative in Joyce's work, all that is cold-blooded, bizarre and banal, grotesque and devilish, is a positive virtue for which it deserves praise. Joyce's inexpressibly rich and myriad-faceted language unfolds itself in passages that creep along tapeworm fashion, terribly boring and monotonous, but the very boredom and monotony of it attain an epic grandeur that makes the book a *Mahabharata* of the world's futility and squalor. "From drains, clefts, cesspools, middens arise on all sides stagnant fumes" (p. 412). And in this open cloaca is reflected with blasphemous distortion practically everything that is highest in religious thought, exactly as in dreams. (Alfred Kubin's *Die andere Seite* is a country-cousin of the metropolitan *Ulysses*.)

Even this I willingly accept, for it cannot be denied. On the contrary, the transformation of eschatology into scatology proves the truth of Tertullian's dictums: *anima naturaliter christiana*. Ulysses shows himself a conscientious Antichrist and thereby proves that his Catholicism still holds together. He is not only a Christian but—still higher title to fame—a Buddhist, Shivaist, and a Gnostic (p. 481):

> (*With a voice of waves.*) . . . White yoghin of the Gods. Occult pimander of Hermes Trismegistos. (*With a voice of whistling seawind.*) Punarjanam patsypunjaub! I won't have my leg pulled. It has been said by one: beware of the left, the cult of Shakti. (*With a cry of stormbirds.*) Shakti, Shiva! Dark hidden Father! . . . Aum! Baum! Pyjaum! I am the light of the homestead, I am the dreamery creamery butter.

Is not that touching and significant? Even on the dunghill the oldest and noblest treasures of the spirit are not lost. There is no cranny in the psyche through which the divine afflatus could finally breathe out its life and perish in noisome filth. Old Hermes, father of all heretical bypaths, is right: "As above, so below." Stephen Dedalus, the bird-headed sky-man, trying to escape from the all too gaseous regions of the air, falls into an earthly slough and in the very depths encounters again the heights from which he fled. "And should I flee to the uttermost ends of the earth . . ." The close of this sentence is a blasphemy that furnishes the most convincing proof of this in all *Ulysses*.[18] Better still, that nosyparker Bloom, the perverse and impotent sensualist, experiences in the dirt something that had never happened to him before: his own transfiguration. Glad tidings: when the eternal signs have vanished from the heavens, the pig that hunts truffles finds them again in the earth. For they are indelibly stamped on the lowest as on the highest; only in the lukewarm intermediate realm that is accursed of God are they nowhere to be found.

Ulysses is absolutely objective and absolutely honest and therefore trustworthy. One can trust his testimony as to the power and nugatoriness of the world and the spirit. Ulysses alone is reality, life, meaning; in him is comprised the whole phantasmagoria of mind and matter, of egos and non-egos. And here I would like to ask Mr. Joyce a question: "Have you noticed that you are a representation, a thought, perhaps a complex of Ulysses? That he stands about you like a hundred-eyed Argus, and has thought up for you a world and an anti-world, filling them with objects without which you could not be conscious of your ego at all?" I do not know what the worthy author would answer to this question. Nor is it any business of mine — there is nothing to stop me from indulging in metaphysics on my own. But one is driven to ask it when one sees how neatly the microcosm of Dublin, on that sixteenth day of June, 1904, has been fished out of the chaotic macrocosm of world history, how it is dissected and spread out on a glass slide in all its tasty details, and described with the most pedantic exactitude by a completely detached observer. Here are the streets, here are the houses and a young couple out for a walk, a real Mr. Bloom goes about his advertising business, a real Stephen Dedalus diverts himself with aphoristic philosophy. It would be quite possible for Mr. Joyce himself to loom up at some Dublin street-corner. Why not? He is surely as real as Mr. Bloom and could therefore equally well be fished out, dissected, and described (as, for instance, in *A Portrait of the Artist as a Young Man*).

Who, then, is Ulysses? Doubtless he is a symbol of what makes up the totality, the oneness, of all the single appearances in *Ulysses* as a whole — Mr. Bloom, Stephen, Mrs. Bloom, and the rest, including Mr. Joyce. Try to imagine a being who is not a mere colourless conglomerate soul composed of an indefinite number of ill-assorted and antagonistic individual souls, but consists also of houses, street-processions, churches, the Liffey, several brothels, and a crumpled note on its way to the sea — and yet possesses a perceiving and registering consciousness! Such a monstrosity drives one to speculation, especially as one can prove nothing anyway and has to fall back on conjecture. I must confess that I suspect Ulysses of being a more comprehensive self who is the subject of all the objects on the glass slide, a being who acts as if he were Mr. Bloom or a printing-shop or a crumpled note, but actually is the "dark hidden Father" of his specimens. "I am the sacrificer and the sacrificed." In the language of the infernal regions: "I am the dreamery creamery butter." When he turns to the world with a loving embrace, all the gardens blossom. But when he turns his back upon it, the empty everyday rolls on — *labitur et labetur in omne volubilis aevum*.

The demiurge first created a world that in his vainglory seemed to him perfect; but looking upward he beheld a light which he had not created. Thereupon he turned back towards the place where was his home. But as he did so, his masculine creative power turned into feminine acquiescence, and he had to confess:

> All things ephemeral
> Are but a reflection;

The unattainable
Here finds perfection;
The indescribable
Here it is done;
The Eternal Feminine
Still draws us on.

From the specimen-slide far below upon earth, in Ireland, Dublin, 7 Eccles Street, from her bed as she grows sleepy at about two o'clock in the morning of the seventeenth of June, 1904, the voice of easy-going Mrs. Bloom speaks:

O and the sea the sea crimson sometimes like fire and the glorious sunsets and the figtrees in the Alameda gardens yes and all the queer little streets and pink and blue and yellow houses and the rosegardens and the jessamine and geraniums and cactuses and Gibraltar as a girl where I was a Flower of the mountain yes when I put the rose in my hair like the Andalusian girls used or shall I wear a red yes and how he kissed me under the Moorish wall and I thought well as well him as another and then I asked him with my eyes to ask again yes and then he asked me would I yes to say yes my mountain flower and first I put my arms around him yes and drew him down to me so he could feel my breasts all perfume yes and his heart was going like mad and yes I said yes I will Yes.

O *Ulysses*, you are truly a devotional book for the object-besotted, object-ridden white man! You are a spiritual exercise, an ascetic discipline, an agonizing ritual, an arcane procedure, eighteen alchemical alembics piled on top of one another, where amid acids, poisonous fumes, and fire and ice, the homunculus of a new, universal consciousness is distilled!

You say nothing and betray nothing, O *Ulysses*, but you give us the works! Penelope need no longer weave her never-ending garment; she now takes her ease in the gardens of the earth, for her husband is home again, all his wanderings over. A world has passed away, and is made new.

Concluding remark: I am now getting on pretty well with my reading of *Ulysses* — forward!

Notes

1. The quotations from *Ulysses* are in accordance with the 10th printing (Paris, 1928), a copy of which Jung owned and cited, though he evidently had seen *Ulysses* upon its first publication, 1922.

2. As Joyce himself says (*Work in Progress*, in *transition*): "We may come, touch and go, from atoms and ifs but we are presurely destined to be odd's without ends." [As in *Finnegans Wake* (1939), p. 455. Fragments were published 1924–38, under the title *Work in Progress*, in the monthly magazine *transition* and elsewhere. — EDITORS.]

3. Curtius *(James Joyce und sein Ulysses)* calls *Ulysses* a "Luciferian book, a work of Antichrist."

4. Curtius (ibid., p. 60): "A metaphysical nihilism is the substance of Joyce's work."

5. The magic words that sent me to sleep occur at the bottom of p. 134 and top of p. 135: "that stone effigy in frozen music, horned and terrible, of the human form divine, that eternal symbol of wisdom and prophecy which, if aught that the imagination or the hand of sculptor has wrought in marble of soultransfigured and of soultransfiguring deserves to live, deserves to live." At this point, dizzy with sleep, I turned the page and my eye fell on the following passage: "a man supple in combat: stonehorned, stonebearded, heart of stone." This refers to Moses, who refused to be cowed by the might of Egypt. The two passages contained the narcotic that switched off my consciousness, activating a still unconscious train of thought which consciousness would only have disturbed. As I later discovered, it dawned on me here for the first time what the author was doing and what was the idea behind his work.

6. This is greatly intensified in *Work in Progress*. Carola Giedion-Welcker aptly remarks on the "ever-recurring ideas in ever-changing forms, projected into a sphere of absolute irreality. Absolute time, absolute space" *(Neue Schweizer Rundschau,* Sept. 1929, p. 666).

7. In Janet's psychology this phenomenon is known as *abaissement du niveau mental.* Among the insane it happens involuntarily, but with Joyce it is the result of deliberate training. All the richness and grotesque profundity of dream-thinking comes to the surface when the "fonction du réel," that is, adapted consciousness, is switched off. Hence the predominance of psychic and verbal automatisms and the total neglect of any communicable meaning.

8. I think Stuart Gilbert *(James Joyce's "Ulysses,"* 1930, p. 40) is right in supposing that each chapter is presided over, among other things, by one of the visceral or sensory dominants. Those he cites are the kidneys, genitals, heart, lungs, oesophagus, brain, blood, ear, musculature, eye, nose, uterus, nerves, skeleton, skin. These dominants each function as a *leitmotif.* My remark about visceral thinking was written in 1930. For me Gilbert's proof offers valuable confirmation of the psychological fact that an *abaissement du niveau mental* constellates that Wernicke calls the "organ-representatives," i.e., symbols representing the organs.

9. Curtius, p. 30: "He reproduces the stream of consciousness without filtering it either logically or ethically."

10. Curtius, p. 8: "The author has done everything to avoid making it easier for the reader to understand."

11. Curtius, Stuart Gilbert, and others.

12. Gilbert, p. 2, speaks of a "deliberate deflation of sentiment."

13. Gilbert, p. 355 n.: ". . . to take, so to speak, a God's-eye view of the cosmos."

14. Gilbert likewise stresses this detachment. He says on p. 21: "The attitude of the author of *Ulysses* towards his personages is one of serene detachment." (I would put a question-mark after "serene.") P. 22: "All facts of any kind, mental or material, sublime or ridiculous, have an equivalence of meaning for the artist." P. 23: "In this detachment, as absolute as the indifference of Nature herself towards her children, we may see one of the causes of the apparent 'realism' of *Ulysses.*"

15. As Joyce himself says in *A Portrait of the Artist as a Young Man* (1930 edn., p. 245): "The artist, like the God of Creation, remains within or behind or beyond or above his handiwork, invisible, refined out of existence, indifferent, paring his fingernails."

16. Wilhelm and Jung, *The Secret of the Golden Flower* (1962 edn.), p. 57. [The picture is reproduced in *Alchemical Studies*, p. 33. —EDITORS.]

17. My italics.

18. This passage has been difficult to interpret, for the quotation could not be located

in *Ulysses*. Jung quoted the novel usually in English but here he uses German: " 'Und flöh' ich ans äusserste Ende der Welt, so . . .' der Nachsatz ist des Ulysses beweiskräftige Blasphemie." This may be a reference to the beginning of a speech of Stephen Dedalus in the Circe episode (p. 476): "What went forth to the ends of the world to traverse not itself. God, the sun, Shakespeare, a commercial traveller, having itself traversed in reality itself, becomes that self. . . . Wait a second. Damn that fellow's noise in the street. . . ." The "noise in the street" is a gramophone playing a sacred cantata, *The Holy City*. Professor Ellmann has suggested a back-reference here to Stephen's remark to Deasy in the Nestor episode (ch. 2): "That is God. . . . A shout in the street." Jung could also have intended a Biblical allusion; cf. Psalm 139: 7–9 (AV): ". . . whither shall I flee from thy presence? If I ascend up into heaven, thou art there: if I make my bed in hell, behold, thou art there. If I take the wings of the morning, and dwell in the uttermost parts of the sea . . ."

The Design of *Ulysses*   A. Walton Litz*

GROWTH OF A MASTERPIECE

Although *Ulysses* bears the date-line "Trieste-Zürich-Paris, 1914–1921" its origin lies in Joyce's early experiences, and a full history of its development would be a history of his artistic career to the age of forty. In 1917, with the novel well under way, Joyce told a Zürich friend, Georges Borach, of his early fascination with the *Odyssey*:

> I was twelve years old when we dealt with the Trojan War at school; only the *Odyssey* stuck in my memory. I want to be candid: at twelve I liked the mysticism in Ulysses. When I was writing *Dubliners*, I first wished to choose the title *Ulysses in Dublin*, but gave up the idea. In Rome, when I had finished about half of the *Portrait*, I realized that the Odyssey had to be the sequel, and I began to write *Ulysses*.[1]

The version of the *Odyssey* Joyce encountered at the age of twelve was Charles Lamb's *Adventures of Ulysses*, and the "mysticism" that he liked was probably Lamb's fusing of realistic action and symbolism, his attempt — announced in the Preface — to make the characters both human figures and figures denoting "external force or internal temptations".[2] Lamb's "mystical" view of the *Odyssey*, so unlike that of most nineteenth-century translators and critics, had a lasting influence on Joyce's imagination, proving to him that the Homeric plot could be recreated in the language of contemporary life and used as a foundation for symbolic actions. In 1922, shortly after the publication of *Ulysses*, he recommended that his Aunt Josephine (Mrs. William Murray) buy Lamb's *Adventures* as a guide to the novel, and every reader can profit from this advice.[3] In

*From *The Art of James Joyce* (London: Oxford University Press, 1961), 1–42. © 1961 by Oxford University Press. Reprinted by permission of the publisher.

contrast to the Victorian *Odyssey* of Butcher and Lang, Lamb's version helps us to understand the many similarities between the "internal temptations" of Ulysses and those of Leopold Bloom.

But although Ulysses was a "Favourite Hero" of the young Joyce,[4] the first evidence that he intended to write a story based on the wanderings of his hero dates from 1906, when he was twenty-four years old and working on *Dubliners*. On 30 September 1906 he wrote from Rome to his brother Stanislaus: "I have a new story for *Dubliners* in my head. It deals with Mr Hunter [a Dublin jew reported to be a cuckold, later one of the models for Bloom]." In November Joyce was still thinking of the story; then, on 6 February 1907, he notified Stanislaus that "*Ulysses* never got any forrader than the title."[5] The extreme personal difficulties the Joyce family encountered while living in Rome were obviously responsible in part for this neglect of *Ulysses*, but a further reason for delay is suggested by Joyce's remarks to Georges Borach. During his stay in Rome (July 1906–March 1907) Joyce realized that a full-length work based on the *Odyssey* "had to be the sequel" to *Portrait of the Artist* (then the half-completed *Stephen Hero*), and as a consequence the writing of the short story *Ulysses* was deferred. Additional evidence of this awakening to the possibilities of a modern "epic" may be found in those parallels between *Dubliners* and the *Odyssey* which have been detected by some critics. It is significant that these parallels are most tenuous in *The Dead*, the only story written after Joyce had abandoned his plan to make *Ulysses* a part of *Dubliners* and had foreseen a sequel to his autobiographical novel.[6]

Late in 1907 Joyce told Stanislaus that he wished to expand his story *Ulysses* into a short book, "a Dublin *Peer Gynt*"; it is not clear whether the short story was actually written at this time, or simply planned.[7] In any event nothing substantial came of the project, although between 1907 and 1914 Joyce maintained his interest in the *Odyssey*, carefully reading Homer and investigating the work of commentators such as Bérard.[8] He never lost sight of the potential "sequel" to *A Portrait*, and several manuscript fragments have survived which link *Stephen Hero* and *A Portrait* with *Ulysses*. Two of the fragments indicate that Joyce was working on a rudimentary version of the Martello tower scene while completing *Portrait*, but excluded it from his autobiographical novel in anticipation of the first chapter in *Ulysses*. These discarded passages show that the design of *Ulysses* was gradually developing in Joyce's mind while he completed *Portrait of the Artist*.

Early in 1914, with *Portrait* finished and appearing serially in the *Egoist*, Joyce turned his full attention to the problem of a sequel and began the monumental task which was to take him seven years. The total design of the new work was already far enough advanced in his mind that he could start by "setting down" what Herbert Gorman describes as "the preliminary sketches for the final sections."[9] Undoubtedly he wished to clarify some general problems of structure before concentrating on the early episodes. The nature of these "preliminary sketches" is difficult to determine, but presumably they contained material later included in the *Nostos* or close (the last three episodes). In June of 1920, with the *Circe* episode still unwritten, Joyce wrote to his literary agents, the English firm of Pinker & Son, that the "close of the book" was "already drafted."[10] Less than a month later he expanded upon this statement in a letter to Harriet Shaw Weaver: "A great part of the Nostos or close was written several years ago and the style is quite plain."[11] The amount of the *Nostos* previously written can be surmised from a passage in a letter sent to Frank Budgen late in 1920: "I am going to leave the last word with Molly Bloom, the final episode being written through her thoughts and tired Poldy being then asleep. *Eumeus* you know so there remains only to think out Ithaca in the way I suggest."[12]

These remarks would seem to indicate that *Eumaeus* was the first part of the *Nostos* to be fully conceived and outlined. Confirmation for this may be found in Gorman's statement that Joyce wrote *Circe* and *Eumaeus* "simultaneously," work on the partially constructed *Eumaeus* being a relief from the complexities of the Nighttown episode.[13]

These early "sketches for the final sections" raise the important question of the order in which Joyce wrote *Ulysses* and, later, *Finnegans Wake*. His approach to both works was "pictorial." In each case he attempted to visualize the general design of the work before completing individual episodes, and the process of composition did not correspond with the final order of the chapters; instead, he programmed his writing as his interests or the need for clarification dictated. He felt that only through a long process of revision and elaboration could a work of art achieve unified form. "The elements needed will only fuse after a prolonged existence together," he wrote in defence of his painstaking method of composition.[14] For Joyce revision provided an opportunity for exploration and discovery; it was a search for form. While constructing *Ulysses* and *Finnegans Wake* he often worked on several sections at the same time, allowing the development of one to illuminate the problems of the others. This method was made possible . . . by the unique form of Joyce's late work.

In the spring of 1914, with the "preliminary sketches for the final sections" of *Ulysses* behind him, Joyce called a temporary halt to the planning of *Ulysses* and began work on his play, *Exiles*, which occupied a large portion of his time until late 1915.[15] The writing of *Exiles* seems to have provided Joyce with a catharsis that was necessary before he could fully develop the design of *Ulysses*. In *Exiles* he exorcised the spectre of Ibsen, a dominant influence since the days at University College; but, more important, he dramatized in the play a personal experience of sexual jealousy, thus preparing the way for objective treatment of Bloom's jealousy and cuckoldry.[16] The writing of *Exiles*, like Stephen's laughter in the Library episode, enabled Joyce to "free his mind from his mind's bondage" (U 209).

Exiles completed, Joyce once again turned his full attention to *Ulysses* and began to compose the episodes in their final order, often working on two or three at once to promote their "fusion."[17] By June of 1915, when he and his family left Trieste for Zürich, he had begun the third episode, *Proteus*.[18] During the hard years of 1915 and 1916, while Joyce struggled for a living in the refugee city of Zürich, the writing of *Ulysses* still progressed. The design of the work seemed to exist as a single image in his mind, and no piece of information was too irrelevant to find its place in the comprehensive pattern.

As early as May of 1918 Joyce had conceived the basic structure of *Ulysses* in what was substantially its final form. On the 18th of that month he wrote to Harriet Weaver:

> I thank you for having transmitted to me the kind proposal of my New York publisher. Will you please write to him and say that I could not, for many reasons, undertake to deliver the entire typescript of *Ulysses* during the coming autumn. If the *Little Review* continues to publish it regularly he may publish as a cheap paperbound book the *Telemachia*, that is, the three first episodes — under the title, *Ulysses I*. I suggest this in case his idea be to keep the few persons who read what I write from forgetting that I still exist. The second part, the *Odyssey*, contains eleven episodes. The third part, *Nostos*, contains three episodes. In all seventeen episodes of which, including that which is now being typed and will be sent in a day or two, *Hades*, I have delivered six. It is impossible to say how much of the book is really written. Several other episodes have been drafted for the second time but that means nothing because although the third episode of the *Telemachia* has been a long time in the second draft I spent about 200 hours over it before I wrote it out finally.[19]

By the end of 1918 the first seven episodes had been published by the *Little Review* in tentative versions, and by the beginning of 1920 serial publication had reached the *Cyclops* episode. Meanwhile, Joyce had got as far as the thirteenth episode, *Nausicaa*, in his writing, with parts of *Oxen of the Sun* and the *Nostos* already drafted and material for the other episodes collected. It was at this point, and while writing the last five episodes, that he undertook "the great revision." One is tempted to compare this recasting of the earlier episodes with Henry James's revision of his early novels and tales for the New York Edition, but I think there is an important difference. James's revisions were, for the most part, elaborations and refinements of elements already present in the earlier versions: they seem to be logical extensions of the original intent. But Joyce's late revisions — as we shall see later — often ran counter to the intent of his earlier work. The early episodes of *Ulysses* were drafted in a style not far from that of *A Portrait*; but when Joyce returned to them in 1920 and 1921 he attempted radical alterations in their style and structure. In October of 1921, with parts of the novel already in proof, he wrote to Harriet Weaver concerning these late revisions: "*Eolus* is recast. *Hades* and the *Lotus-eaters* much amplified and the other episodes retouched a good deal. Not much change has been made in the *Telemachia* (the first three episodes of the book)."[20]

Joyce never stopped revising *Ulysses*, labouring unceasingly to give the novel a closer texture and more organic form. Every episode was subjected to an intensive process of revision; the extant drafts reveal massive alterations and augmentations. *Oxen of the Sun* and *Circe* seem to have given Joyce the most difficulty, as might be expected. "I wrote the *Circe* Episode nine times from first to last," he told a friend in January of 1921.[21]

As in the final stages of his work on *Finnegans Wake*, Joyce continued to augment and correct episodes until the moment of publication. Usually five or more sets of proof were required. In protesting to John Quinn against the sale of the *Ulysses* manuscript to A. S. W. Rosenbach, Joyce said: "It must be understood, however, that I will not write in any pages of the MS. to 'complete' it. The additions were made by me on printed proofs."[22]

The surviving sets of proofs for *Ulysses* were copiously corrected, the "emendations and additions exceeding sometimes 160 words on a single page."[23] *Ulysses* provides a perfect illustration of Paul Valéry's remark that a work of art is never finished, but only abandoned.

The burden of the evidence is that *Ulysses* was written "all of a piece." Many of the later episodes were planned and drafted early in the course of composition, while the episodes from *Calypso* to *Nausicaa* were considerably reworked during the years 1919–21 so that they would harmonize with Joyce's evolving aesthetic ideals. In his final revisions, Joyce sought to invest the earlier and plainer episodes with a complexity and richness of technique commensurate with that found in *Circe*, *Ithaca* and *Oxen of the Sun*. If we except *Penelope*, a late-comer and structurally a postscript, one might almost say that Joyce began to write *Ulysses* from both ends at once, meeting in the *Circe* episode where all the motifs are drawn together and transformed.[24] This same strategy was used again in the making of *Finnegans Wake*, and Joyce acknowledged it in a conversation with his friend August Suter. "I am boring through a mountain from two sides," he told Suter shortly after he began work on the *Wake*. "The question is, how to meet in the middle."[25]

THE LATE REVISIONS

The final stage in the growth of *Ulysses* marked a turning-point in Joyce's artistic development. It was during the last three years of composition (1919–21) that he wrote the intricate later episodes and revised the opening chapters, seeking to fuse the entire work into an organic whole. A close examination of the methods he employed at this time will demonstrate how far he had progressed from his earlier works, and will prepare the way for an understanding of those basic principles which governed the entire composition of *Finnegans Wake*.

By far the most extended and important descriptions of the manner in which Joyce constructed *Ulysses* are found in Frank Budgen's *James Joyce and the Making of "Ulysses."* Budgen was an intimate friend, and his book is a faithful record of Joyce at work. His account of the methods Joyce employed in resolving the formal problems posed by *Ulysses* provides an antidote to the sententious analyses of later critics such as Stuart Gilbert, who tend to over-emphasize the superficial order of the novel. Here, as a starting point, is a long passage describing Joyce at work in 1918–19.

> Joyce's method of composition always seemed to me to be that of a poet rather than that of a prose writer. The words he wrote were far advanced in his mind before they found shape on paper . . . he was a great believer in his luck. What he needed would come to him. That which he collected would prove useful in its time and place. And as, in a sense, the theme of *Ulysses* is the whole of life, there was no end to the variety of material that went to its building. Of the time detail of 1904 was none around him, but what he saw and heard in 1918 or 1919 would do just as well, for the shapes of life remain constant: only the dress and manners change. I have seen him collect in the space of a few hours the oddest assortment of material: a parody on the *House that Jack Built*, the name and action of a poison, the method of caning boys on training ships, the wobbly cessation of a tired unfinished sentence, the nervous trick of a convive turning his glass in inward-turning circles, a Swiss music-hall joke turning on a pun in Swiss dialect, a description of the Fitzsimmons shift.
>
> In one of the richest pages of *Ulysses* Stephen, on the seashore, communing with himself and tentatively building with words, calls for his tablets. . . . As far as concerns the need for tablets, the self-portrait was still like, only in Zürich Joyce was never without them. And they were not library slips, but little writing blocks specially made for the waistcoat pocket. At intervals, alone or in conversation, seated or walking, one of these tablets was produced, and a word or two scribbled on it at lightning speed as ear or memory served his turn. No one knew how all this material was given place in the completed pattern of his work, but from time to time in Joyce's flat one caught glimpses of a few of those big orange-coloured envelopes that are one of the glories of Switzerland, and these I always took to be storehouses of building material. The methods of making a multitude of criss-cross notes in pencil was a strange one for a man whose sight was never good. A necessary adjunct to the method was a huge oblong magnifying glass.[26]

Joyce laboured to a predetermined pattern; each fragment of material he gathered was marked for a specific place in the novel's general design.

The entire work, with all its complex internal allusions, seems to have developed in Joyce's mind as a single vast "image." Consequently, as Budgen points out, the "words he wrote were far advanced in his mind before they found shape on paper."

Budgen's description naturally raises the question of how Joyce organized and preserved the diverse materials of his novel: the answer is that they were collected in abbreviated form on a variety of note-sheets. Silvio Benco, writing of Joyce's visit to Trieste in 1919–20, provides the first eye-witness account of these notes: "He showed me the loose sheets on which he prepared the material of each episode, notes as to composition, quotations, references, ideas, essays in various styles. When the rough material was ready, he devoted himself to writing out the complete episode, and this he usually did in less than a month. Following this method, *Ulysses* had been begun in Trieste before the war, continued in Zürich, and now resumed in Trieste."[27]

These sheets were, in all probability, the classified repository for the fragments of material mentioned by Budgen. A number of the *Ulysses* note-sheets which have survived are marked with the names of the episodes to which they refer, and even the undesignated ones are concerned primarily with a single episode.[28] Evidently Joyce would sort out his fragmentary notes according to episodes and then copy them on to foolscap sheets or into notebooks, gradually building up a list of additions and insertions for each chapter.

We have already noted the "great revision" of earlier episodes which Joyce undertook while writing the final sections of his novel. Considering the complex patterns of association which bind *Ulysses* together, it was natural that as the novel expanded the author should wish to augment earlier chapters already published in the *Egoist* and *Little Review*. But Joyce's revisions went far beyond the alterations and additions of the conventional novelist. The entire novel was re-shaped, technical emphases were altered and a new aesthetic "direction" introduced. The remainer of this chapter will be primarily an assessment of this new "direction."

Joyce's letters of 1920–21 illuminate his use of the accumulated notes for early and late episodes. In a letter to Harriet Weaver, written on 12 July 1920, he commented on their function: "My intention is to remain here [in Paris] three months in order to write the last adventure *Circe* in peace (?) and also the first episode of the close. For this purpose I brought with me a recast of my notes and MS and also an extract of insertions for the first half of the book in case it be set up during my stay here."[29]

Later in 1920 Joyce again referred to these accumulated notes, in a letter to John Quinn:

> I began *Ulysses* in 1914 and shall finish it, I suppose, in 1921. This is, I think, the twentieth address at which I have written it—and the coldest. The complete notes fill a small valise, but in the course of continual changings very often it was not possible to sort them for the

final time before the publication of certain instalments [in the *Little Review*]. The insertions (chiefly verbal or phrases, rarely passages) must be put in for the book publication. Before leaving Trieste I did this sorting for all episodes up to and including *Circe*. The episodes which have the heaviest burden of addenda are *Lotus-eaters, Lestrygonians, Nausikaa* and *Cyclops*.[30]

These minor insertions mentioned by Joyce are consistent with the type of addenda found on the *Ulysses* note-sheets. The material of the note-sheets was used in an advanced stage of composition, either to augment an episode already in print or to expand a manuscript draft.

A year later (7 October 1921), during the last weeks of the writing of *Ulysses*, Joyce elaborated upon the use of these accumulated insertions in a letter to Miss Weaver:

> A few lines to let you know I am here again with MSS and pencils (red, green and blue) and cases of books and trunks and all the rest of my impedimenta nearly snowed up in proofs and nearly crazed with work. *Ulysses* will be finished in about three weeks, thank God, and (if the French printers don't all leap into the Rhône in despair at the mosaics I send them back) ought to be published early in November. I sent the *Penelope* episode to the printer as Larbaud wants to read it before he finishes his article for the Nouvelle Revue Française. The *Ithaca* episode which precedes it I am now putting in order. It is in reality the end as *Penelope* has no beginning, middle or end. I expect to have early next week about 240 pages of the book as it will appear ready and will send on. *Eolus* is recast. *Hades* and the *Lotus-eaters* much amplified and the other episodes retouched a good deal. Not much change has been made in the *Telemachia* . . .[31]

This is Joyce's first reference to the use of coloured pencils in the sorting process. While composing *Ulysses* he crossed out a number of notes in coloured pencil (usually red, blue, or green), either to indicate that these notes had been incorporated into the text or that he intended to use them at a certain stage in the process of composition. Although many of the notes slashed through in coloured pencil are not to be found in the finished novel, *none* of the uncrossed notes ever appear. I think one may safely conclude that Joyce transferred most of the lined-out notes either to a manuscript draft or a condensed list of insertions, but that many were eliminated in the last revisions. The function of the various colours is not completely clear: at times they indicate separate stages in the process of composition, while often they are used to differentiate among notes for two or more episodes appearing on the same sheet. For example, on a sheet where most of the notes are for *Ithaca* the insertions actually used in that episode are slashed in blue, while two notes which were used in the revision of earlier episodes are slashed in red.

Valery Larbaud, who began to write his famous article on *Ulysses* while Joyce was still revising the last sections of the novel, has described the note-sheets used by Joyce at that time.

> It [Joyce's text] is a genuine example of the art of mosaic. I have seen the drafts. They are entirely composed of abbreviated phrases underlined in various-coloured pencil. These are annotations intended to recall to the author complete phrases; and the pencil-marks indicate according to their colour that the underlined phrase belongs to such or such an episode. It makes one think of the boxes of little coloured cubes of the mosaic workers.[32]

Larbaud's description obviously applies either to the note-sheets under discussion or to similar compilations of rough notes. However, I would disagree with his statement that Joyce interlined (a more accurate term than "underlined") his notes in order to indicate their final positions in the novel; it seems more likely that they were crossed out at the time of their insertion into preliminary drafts of the episodes.

The comparison between Joyce's method of composition and that of the mosaic workers, which has been used by Budgen[33] as well as Larbaud, is strikingly appropriate. Joyce himself called the corrected galleys of *Ulysses* "mosaics."[34] He did not write *Ulysses* straight through, following the final order of the episodes. First it was necessary to determine the design of the novel, to visualize its characters and the course of the action, and this entailed putting scattered portions on paper in order to clarify them. Then, like the mosaic worker, Joyce collected and sorted material to fit the design. Finally, the fragments were placed in their proper positions through a process of rough drafts and revisions.

The evidence in favour of Joyce's having compiled and used the note-sheets late in the writing of *Ulysses* is substantial. The first mention of them is in the article by Silvio Benco previously cited, which refers to the period 1919–20; however, since comments by Joyce's friends on the years prior to 1918 are extremely rare, this carries little weight. More conclusive is the evidence of the notes themselves, most of which are of a nature that would occur in a late revision of the text: verbal insertions, cross-references, minor themes. Several of the notes can be assigned to a precise stage in the process of composition. The burden of this evidence is that the sheets were used (and probably compiled) sometime after 1919, when Joyce was writing the final episodes and augmenting the earlier ones. Many of the notes entered the text during the last-minute revisions of galley proof.

The typical note found on the *Ulysses* note-sheets is a minor verbal insertion designed to enrich the texture of the narrative. These verbal insertions are particularly common on the *Nausicaa*, *Penelope*, and — as might be expected — *Oxen of the Sun* sheets. The sentimental phrases for Gerty MacDowell's "namby-pamby jammy marmalady drawersy . . . style,"[35] the multitudinous events and fragments of conversation recalled by Molly in her closing reverie, the characteristic phrases for one imitated style or another—entries such as these make up the body of the *Nausicaa, Penelope,* and *Oxen* sheets. The left-hand column below contains a series of phrases transcribed from an *Oxen* note-sheet. The word "red" has been placed in square brackets after each phrase slashed by Joyce in red pencil; a heavy line indicates that one or more notes have been omitted. In the right-hand column are those sections from the opening of *Oxen of the Sun* affected by the notes, with the pertinent passages italicized. The first pages of *Oxen of the Sun* which appeared in the *Little Review* for September–December 1920 were included in the published novel without change; this suggests that Joyce wrote the later episodes of *Ulysses* directly into his final "complex" style, then revised the earlier episodes to harmonize with them.

a plan was by them adopted [red]

_____

was provided valiantly [red]

_____

in every public work it is to be considered [red]

terrestial orb [red]
with sapience endowed [red]

concealed from them were not
part of wisdom
    what pertains to [red]
    that no age be silent
        about your praises
not solely for the copiously moneyed [red]
scarcely or not even scarcely [red]
not sufficiently [red]

_____

aspect of the most distracting spectacles [red]

Certainly in *every public work* which in it anything of gravity contains preparation should be with importance commensurate and therefore *a plan was by them adopted* (whether by having preconsidered or as the maturation of experience it is difficult in being said which the discrepant opinions of subsequent inquirers are not up to the present congrued to render manifest) whereby maternity was so far from all accident possibility removed that whatever care the patient in that allhardest of woman hour chiefly required and *not solely for the copiously opulent* but also for her who *not* being *sufficiently moneyed scarcely* and often *not even scarcely* could subsist *valiantly* and for an inconsiderable emolument *was provided* (U 378).

Universally that person's acumen is esteemed very little perceptive concerning whatsoever matters are being held as most profitably by mortals *with sapience endowed* to be studied . . . (U 377).

Before born babe bliss had. Within womb won he worship. Whatever in that one case done commodiously done was. A couch by midwives attended with wholesome food reposeful cleanest swaddles as though forth-bringing were now done and by wise foresight set: but to this no less of what drugs there is need and surgical implements which are *pertaining to* her case not omitting *aspect* of all very *distracting spectacles* in various latitudes by our *terrestrial orb* offered together with images, divine and human, the cogitation of which by sejunct females is to tumescence conducive or eases issue in the high sunbright wellbuilt fair home of mothers when, ostensibly far gone and reproductitive, it is come by her thereto to lie in, her term up (U 378).

All those notes which Joyce marked in red are found in the text, inserted almost without change. Their function in reinforcing the deliberately stilted and archaic dialect of the prelude to *Oxen* is obvious. The episode must have been far advanced in Joyce's mind when he made these notes, as they are all stylistic additions to a particular section of the narrative. This process of deliberately "thickening" the existing narrative foreshadows the continuous revisions of *Work in Progress*, where the prose becomes denser and more complex with each successive revision.

Often the notes on a sheet bear little relation to each other except for the fact that they are intended for roughly the same part of an episode; take, for instance, this series of consecutive notes from a sheet labelled "*Ithaca*."

a donkey & trap [blue]   . . . a donkey with wicker trap or smart phaeton with good working solidungular cob (roan gelding, 14h)(U 699).

pleasant reflectio[n]s produce sleep [blue]   What pleasant reflection accompanied this action? The reflection that . . . (U 707).

simple interest at 5% of — LB in tree (jew) [red]   In 1885 he . . . in support of his political convictions, had climbed up into a secure position amid the ramifications of a tree on Northumberland road . . . (U 701).

rabbitry [blue]   A rabbitry and fowlrun . . . (U 699).

baronial hall, groaning table [green] MB spasm old clockface   Not to inherit . . . a baronial hall with gatelodge and carriage drive nor, on the other hand . . . (U 697).

space reversible time no [green]   an unsatisfactory equation between an exodus and return in time through reversible space and an exodus and return in space through irreversible time (U 713).

Joyce's synthesizing mind brought these stray fragments of material together in the dry, factual catechism of *Ithaca*. Unlike the notes for *Oxen of the Sun* cited above, these were not collected with their exact positions in *Ithaca* already determined; Joyce only knew what episode he wished to include them in, and they were worked into the text as opportunities for their use arose. In this case the different colours of pencil probably represent different periods of revision, various drafts of the episode.

More often than not, however, a series of notes will have a thematic unity even though the passages founded upon it are scattered in the final text. A good illustration is the following group of notes from a *Circe* sheet, all of which are slashed in blue pencil.

Sweetly hoarsely	Boylan murmurs "*Sweetly, hoarsely*," Molly "*Hoarsely, sweetly*" in the scene on pp. 552–53 of *Ulysses*.
Kiss the whip	
	"Mrs Bloom up yet?" Spoken to Bloom by
Mrs. Bloom	Boylan (U 551).
last articles	Bloom replies to Boylan: "I'm afraid not, sir, the last articles . . ." (U 551).
ask every 20 minutes	"Ask for that every ten minutes." Bello to Bloom (U 522).
touches the spot	"Touches the spot?" Bello to Bloom (U 529).

All these references are related to the scene where Bloom imagines himself assisting Blazes Boylan in his adulterous affair with Molly (U 551–53), and thus to the theme of male impotence. "Sweetly hoarsely," "Mrs. Bloom," and "last articles" are used in the same scene. "Ask every 20 minutes" and "touches the spot" appear — slightly transformed — in that section of *Circe* where Bella, metamorphosed into a male figure (Bello), dominates the female aspects of Bloom's personality (U 518ff.).

> BELLO
>
> Ask for that every ten minutes. Beg, pray for it as you never prayed before. (*He thrusts out a figged fist and foul cigar.*) Here, kiss that. Both. Kiss. (*He throws a leg astride and, pressing with horseman's knees, calls in a hard voice.*) Gee up! A cockhorse to Banbury cross. I'll ride him for the Eclipse stakes . . . (U 522).

The allusion to "Ride a cockhorse" points forward to Bloom's hallucinated vision of Boylan visiting Molly, where Lydia Douce cries: "Yumyum. O, he's carrying her round the room doing it! Ride a cock horse" (U 552). The theme of Bloom's impotence, his sexual "eclipse," is introduced again several pages after Bello rides him "for the Eclipse stakes." In the passage which incorporates the last note in the sequence ("touches the spot"), Bello derides Bloom as an inadequate cuckold (U 529).

The note not found in the published text of *Ulysses*, "Kiss the whip," is undoubtedly another reference to Bloom's impotence in the presence of more virile males. Perhaps it does reach the text, in a slightly changed form, when Bello "*thrusts out a figged fist and foul cigar*" to Bloom and says: "Here, kiss that. Both. Kiss" (U 522).

This grouping of related notes is typical of the *Ulysses* note-sheets. Although sometimes the notes on a sheet have no unity beyond the fact that they were gathered for a particular episode, more often Joyce assembled his material by themes and motifs, ultimately incorporating the notes into one or more scenes in the finished text. In this manner he achieved an extraordinary structural unity through a network of cross-references.

In compiling the note-sheets Joyce employed a form of associational shorthand to record the outlines of passages already visualized. A sequence such as "exhalations, see breath, telegraph wires," jotted down for *Ithaca* but never used, is characteristic: the words indicate an associational development that could form the basis of an extended passage. Similar cryptic patterns are found in Joyce's notes for *Exiles*, accompanied by elaborate explanations which are some indication of the vast amount of organized material represented by the abbreviated notes for *Ulysses*. For example, the skeleton sequence "Blister-amber-silver-oranges-apples-sug-arstick-hair-spongecake-ivy-roses-ribbon" is explained by Joyce as follows:

> The blister reminds her of the burning of her hand as a girl. She sees her own amber hair and her mother's silver hair. This silver is the crown of age but also the stigma of care and grief which she and her lover have laid upon it. This avenue of thought is shunned completely; and the other aspect, amber turned to silver by the years, her mother a prophecy of what she may one day be is hardly glanced at. Oranges, apples, sugarstick — these take the place of the shunned thoughts and are herself as she was, being her girlish joys. Hair: the mind turning again to this without adverting to its colour, adverting only to a distinctive sexual mark and to its growth and mystery rather than to its mystery. The softly growing symbol of her girlhood. Spongecake; a weak flash again of joys which now begin to seem more those of a child than those of a girl. Ivy and roses: she gathered ivy often when out in the evening with girls. Roses grew then a sudden scarlet note in the memory which may be a dim suggestion of the roses of the body. The ivy and the roses carry on and up, out of the idea of growth, through a creeping vegetable life into ardent perfumed flower life the symbol of mysteriously growing girlhood, her hair. Ribbon for her hair. Its fitting ornament for the eyes of others, and lastly for his eyes. Girlhood becomes virginity and puts on "the snood that is the sign of maidenhood." A proud and shy instinct turns her mind away from the loosening of her bound-up hair — however sweet or longed for or inevitable — and she embraces that which is hers alone and not hers and his also — happy distant dancing days, distant, gone forever, dead, or killed?[36]

Joyce used the associational technique which governs this passage in two ways: (1) to order the impressions and memories of his characters, and (2) to organize the heterogeneous raw materials of his art.

Often the most suggestive words or phrases on the note-sheets are elements in the "internal monologue" of a character, as in this sequence from a sheet containing notes for several episodes: "It seems history is to blame. nightmare. God noise in street, never let jews in, O'Rourke, left goal, Pyrrhus, Helen."

This is a recapitulation of the central elements around which Stephen's mind is oriented in the *Nestor* episode; he is haunted by memories of them for the remainder of the day, and they reappear again and again in his thoughts. In this note Joyce was reminding himself in capsule form of a scene to be kept fresh in Stephen's memory.

Many of the notes for *Ulysses* are "shorthand" notes in the sense that they were aimed at reminding Joyce of a fuller version already visualized. Expansion and elaboration are the most significant characteristics of Joyce's revisions. Often in the *Ithaca* episode an entire question-and-answer passage is the development of a single short note: the question "What pleasant reflection accompanied this action?" and its answer (U 707) can be traced to the abbreviated "pleasant reflections produce sleep." At their most elaborate the notes are merely rough outlines of the final version:

£5 reward, missing gent aged about 40 height 5, 8, full build, dark complexion, may have since grown a beard. Was dressed when last seen. Above will be paid for his discovery. (From an *Ithaca* note-sheet)	£5 reward lost, stolen or strayed from his residence 7 Eccles street, missing gent about 40, answering to the name of Bloom, Leopold (Poldy), height 5 ft 9 1/2 inches, full build, olive complexion, may have since grown a beard, when last seen was wearing a black suit. Above sum will be paid for information leading to his discovery. (U 712)

Details such as name, address, and colour of suit, the standard components of a "missing persons" notice, would have been superfluous in a note made by Joyce for his own use; they could be added later. Also added when he expanded the note were the suggestions of a "strayed animal" advertisement: "lost, stolen or strayed" and "answering to the name of Bloom."

The most interesting of Joyce's notes are those which illuminate the structure of the novel or the techniques of the various episodes. In the note-sheets he commonly refers to his characters by the names of their counterparts in the *Odyssey*. This is particularly noticeable on the *Eumaeus* sheets, where the Homeric allusions are richer than anywhere else. There are two possible reasons for this concentration in *Eumaeus*: (1) the episode was the first of the later chapters to be drafted, and Joyce seems to have relied more heavily on his Homeric parallels during the early stages of composition; (2) since the style of the episode is fatigued and murky to correspond with the moods of Bloom and Stephen, Joyce may have felt acutely the need for a supporting mythic structure.

However, only a fraction of the Homeric correspondences collected on the note-sheets appear in the text. In the following series, typical of the *Eumaeus* sheets, only four out of the eleven notes are slashed in pencil, and of these the only one I can definitely locate in *Ulysses* is non-Homeric: "Enoch Arden Face at the Window" (see U 608). Two others, "Ul. loses way in maze" and "Ul. wants to try wife first," apply roughly to the final version of the episode.

Ph. cease to convoy [slate gray]

Ul. loses way in maze [blue]

Pallos boosts her help

Ul. denies, upbraids her

She didn't want row with Neptune

Ul. wants to try wife first [slate gray]

Enoch Arden Face at the Window [slate gray]

Ul. recognises Ithaca

Kisses earth, shamrock clod

Pallos & Ul. hide treasure

Suitors 3 years round Pen

This series of notes served as a reminder of possible parallels between Bloom's return to Eccles Street and Ulysses's return to Ithaca. The first entry may refer to Joyce's acceptance of Victor Bérard's theory that the *Odyssey* is a "hellenization" of the "log" of a seafaring Semite, probably a Phoenician.[37] Ulysses is referred to as a Phoenician jew several times on the note-sheets.

The many Homeric parallels not included in the final text of *Ulysses* are significant, since they illustrate how much more important the Homeric background was for Joyce than it is to the reader. Invaluable to Joyce as a ready-made guide for the ordering of his material, the correspondences with the *Odyssey* do not provide a major level of meaning in the completed work. Ezra Pound was right in his early judgment of the Homeric framework: "These correspondences are part of Joyce's mediaevalism and are chiefly his own affair, a scaffold, a means of construction, justified by the result, and justifiable by it only."[38]

Among the notes which Joyce did *not* use, there are a number that shed light upon the novel's hidden relationships. For example, an unused note for *Penelope* illustrates the physiological basis of that episode: "rose-menses." Here the rose is a symbol of Molly's first love, the rose she wore in her hair "like the Andalusian girls" when she was "a Flower of the mountain" at Gibraltar (U 768); it is also the Rose of the Court of Love. But in Joyce's mind the rose was explicitly associated with menstruation.

The single word "Comus," found on one of the *Circe* note-sheets, illuminates Joyce's attitude toward the temptations of Nighttown: evidently he associated Bella Cohen with the evil tempter in *Comus*, Bloom and Stephen with the virtuous brothers. There is a striking parallel between the Comus myth and the story of Circe's temptations in the *Odyssey*. According to Milton, Comus was the son of Bacchus and Circe; and the herb Haemony, which is given to the brothers by the Attendant Spirit and protects them from evil, is analogous to the "Moly" Mercury gives Ulysses. Joyce must once have intended to include the Comus story as a minor motif in the *Circe* episode.

In a series of unused notes for *Oxen of the Sun* the following equation occurs: "Rudy = Mulvey." This coupling of Bloom's dead son with the young naval officer who was Molly's first lover adds a new ironic dimension to his grief. Similarly, a new parallel for the paternal relationship between Bloom and Stephen is given in the equation "Ul = W. Tell.," an unused note for *Ithaca*. Bloom, like William Tell, is the hero of an oppressed race, guided by love for his son.

Not only does the figure of Molly's first lover merge with the memory of her dead son, but Bloom sees his daughter Milly in Gerty MacDowell, the young girl on the beach in the *Nausicaa* episode: "Milly Nausikaa" appears in one of the unused notes for the episode. Bloom, like Earwicker after him, is unconsciously in love with his own daughter as a young reincarnation of his wife, and for this reason he is attracted to the "seaside" girl Gerty. Another reason to associate Nausicaa–Gerty with Milly is found in the latter's letter to Bloom, where she mentions Blazes Boylan's "song about those seaside girls" (U 66).

The union of Bloom and Stephen in *Eumaeus* is mentioned in a note for the episode: "Ul & Tel exchange unity." The note is crossed in blue pencil, a sign that Joyce found an adequate expression for this interchange. The catechism of *Ithaca* opens with a closely related question-and-answer: "What parallel courses did Bloom and Stephen follow returning? Starting united both at normal walking pace . . ." (U 650).

Joyce's exactitude in the use of concrete details and his dependence upon actual data, not so much for verisimilitude as for the satisfaction of his own scrupulous sense of artistic integrity, are illustrated by the rough map of Gibraltar which appears on one of the *Penelope* note-sheets. In order to refer accurately to Molly Bloom's birthplace, a city he had never visited, Joyce copied the important geographical points from a map and marked them on a sketch of his own. This sketch, which he obviously kept before him during the writing of the episode, includes a number of places mentioned by Molly in her closing monologue: "windmill hill" (U 747), "Europa point" (746 & 760), "firtree cove" (746 & 745), "OHaras tower" (745), "Catalan bay" (750), and the "Alameda gardens" (741, 747 & 768).

Joyce constructed each of the episodes with the same regard for realistic detail. Frank Budgen records that he "wrote the *Wandering Rocks* with a map of Dublin before him on which were traced in red ink the paths of the Earl of Dudley and Father Conmee. He calculated to a minute the time necessary for his characters to cover a given distance of the city."[39]

Joyce was always scrupulously accurate in his descriptions of Dublin. In 1920 he wrote to his aunt Josephine Murray asking for details of the steps and trees at the Star of the Sea church in Sandymount, the scene of the *Nausicaa* episode.[40] Apparently such inquiries were not unusual. The next year he wrote the same aunt asking her to confirm the possibility of Bloom's letting himself down into the area-way of 7 Eccles Street: "Is it possible for an ordinary person to climb over the area railings of no 7 Eccles street, either from the path or the steps, lower himself down from the lowest part of the railings till his feet are within 2 feet or 3 of the ground and drop unhurt. I saw it done myself but by a man of rather athletic build. I require this information in detail in order to determine the wording of a paragraph."[41]

In all his work Joyce depended upon the concrete details of the Dublin of his youth, whether collected by himself or others. His many notebooks, the *Epiphanies*, the notes for *Dubliners* and *Stephen Hero* printed by Gorman in his biography, the *Ulysses* note-sheets — all are evidence of this naturalistic foundation. It was inherent in Joyce's notion of "epiphany," the "showing forth" of character through a seemingly trivial action or detail of appearance, that he would need particular facts about the men and women who sat for his characters. However, his insatiable desire for concrete details — especially the minutiae of setting — went far beyond the actual needs of his art. His obsessive concern with realistic detail reveals his desperate need for principles of order and authority. Deprived of social and religious order by his self-imposed exile, and acutely aware of the disintegrating forces in modern European society, Joyce turned to the concrete details of place and character as one stable base for his writing. Like the elaborate ordering principles discussed by Stuart Gilbert in his *James Joyce's "Ulysses,"* the effects of which are manifest on every note-sheet, the details of Dublin life in 1904 were vastly important to Joyce during the making of *Ulysses*; but they are not essential to an understanding of the finished work. In so far as they obscure the central concerns of the novel they represent the price Joyce had to pay for his personal decisions.

The way in which the note-sheets kept the diverse elements of the novel clear in Joyce's mind is revealed in the handling of minor characters. Half of a double sheet containing notes for the *Circe* and *Cyclops* episodes is divided into squares numbered from 1 to 16, and under the appropriate numbers are listed the characters and a few of the important motifs introduced in each episode up to and including *Circe*. Not all the characters listed are of the living: "Rudy" appears under *Hades* because of his presence in Bloom's thoughts during the funeral. Similarly, "Elijah" and "Parallax" are two of the "characters" listed for *Lestrygonians*, and "Cranly" is a character in *Telemachus*. Since the table ends with an abbreviated enumeration of the characters in *Circe*, it is logical to suppose that it was compiled sometime in 1920, while Joyce was working on that episode. Most of the names on the sheet are slashed through in either blue or red pencil, although "Cranly," "Rudy" and "Parallax" are uncrossed. Perhaps Joyce wished to remember all the characters introduced in *Ulysses* prior to *Circe* so that he could be sure of incorporating them into that episode, where most of the novel's characters are brought together through the technique of metamorphosis.

Often it is possible to watch one of the novel's major motifs taking form on the note-sheets. While composing *Circe*, Joyce was constantly on the alert for analogies to "Moly," the magic herb of Mercury that gave Ulysses protection against Circe's wiles. First and most important the talisman is Molly herself, Bloom's constant love for his wife. But around this central identification Joyce constructed a network of correspondences including both physical objects and qualities of Bloom's personality. He jotted down equivalents for "Moly" as they came to him, and six different note-sheets yield an impressive list of the qualities and circumstances which save Bloom from the temptations of Bella Cohen's house and the fantasies of his own mind.

> Moly = absinthe, mercury [blue]
> Moly = chastity
> Change = Moly (narrow shoes) [blue]
> Moly — indifference [blue]
> Moly — beauty [blue]
> Moly — laughter [blue]
> Moly — satire [blue]
> Moly = conscience [blue]
> Moly = escape from poison [blue]
> Moly (Met-salt)

Speaking of the difficulty Joyce had in finding equivalents for "Moly," Frank Budgen comments:

> "Moly" was a harder nut to crack. What was the herb that conferred upon Ulysses immunity from Circe's magic, and thus enabled him to be of service to his companions? What was the "Moly" that saved Bloom from a surrender of his humanity? As a physical symbol Bloom's potato prophylactic against rheumatism and plague, inherited from his mother, would serve, but the real saviour of Bloom was a spiritual "Moly," a state of mind. Joyce wrote to me in 1920: "Moly is the gift of Hermes, god of public ways, and is the invisible influence (prayer, chance, agility, *presence of mind*, power of recuperation which saves in case of accident. This would cover immunity from syphilis — swine love).

. . . In this special case his plant may be said to have many leaves, indifference due to masturbation, pessimism congenital, a sense of the ridiculous, sudden fastidiousness in some detail, experience."[42]

The many "leaves" of "Moly" enumerated on the note-sheets are similar to those mentioned by Joyce in his letter to Budgen. The only mysterious entry is "Moly (Met-salt)," and the simplest explanation of it is that Joyce intended to introduce common table salt as a physical equivalent for "Moly." "Met" probably stands for "metamorphosis," the technique governing this identification and the entire episode as well.

Most of Joyce's notes which are not mere verbal insertions are reminders of motifs to be introduced or further developed. These notes, usually only a few words, were intended to remind Joyce of complex patterns of association already visualized and marked for specific positions in the narrative structure. The many notes of "Moly" provide a good example of this, although they are concerned primarily with one episode. A phrase slashed in red pencil on one of the *Circe* sheets, "3 Legs of Man," indicates the way in which these notes could represent a theme or motif running through several episodes. The heraldic device of the Isle of Man is the "Three Legs of Man," three flexed legs joined at the thighs, and the entry on the note-sheet refers specifically to that point in the Nighttown episode when the "*End of the World, a twoheaded octopus in gillie's kilts,*" appears "*in the form of the Three Legs of Man,*" (U 496). However, the Isle of Man is introduced in *Ulysses* as early as the *Hades* chapter through the figure of Reuben J. Dodd, solicitor and money-lender (U 92–93). Bloom tells his companions that Reuben's son dived into the Liffey to avoid being sent to the Isle of Man and away from the girl he loved. The scene in *Hades* establishes the Isle of Man as a symbol of isolation and sterility, and this central meaning is elaborated upon during succeeding episodes. Joyce's entry on the *Circe* sheet was simply a reminder that the emblem of the Isle of Man should appear in that episode as a climax to the chain of associations begun in the *Hades* chapter. It was the function of the note-sheets to assure that patterns and relationships already visualized by Joyce reached their fore-ordained positions in the text. Like the mosaic worker, he was continuously sorting and re-grouping his raw materials, assigning each fragment to its proper place in the general design. The mechanical nature of this process emphasizes the mechanical nature of those ordering principles which give *Ulysses* its superficial unity, and which sometimes obscure the deeper unity of the novel.

Joyce's revisions during the last three years of the making of *Ulysses* were so extensive that we must consult the earlier drafts if we are to view his artistic development in perspective. Any comprehensive treatment of *Ulysses* as a "work in progress" would involve detailed analysis of the many stages of development through which each episode passed, and would go far beyond the scope of this study. Indeed, Joyce's revisions were so extensive, and his elaborations so complex, that only someone intimately familiar with the novel and its intricate career can fully comprehend them.[43] Fortunately, however, Joyce's methods of composition remained constant from episode to episode, and only a few examples are needed to illustrate the pattern of his late work on *Ulysses*. I shall cite three passages at this point, and several others in subsequent chapters; more would be redundant. These passages, in connection with the previous discussion of the note-sheets, should convey a clear impression of the direction taken by Joyce's technical development during the period 1919–21.

The following passage of chauvinistic rhetoric, taken from an early draft of the *Cyclops* episode, is spoken by the pseudo-patriot Michael Cusack, known in the final version simply as "the citizen." It should be compared with the later version from the *Little Review* (Dec. 1919–Jan. 1920) printed immediately after it. The final version (U 320–22) is too long to be quoted in full, but it continues the process of elaboration evident in the *Little Review* version.

> —Blatherskite, says Cusack. Can you point to any other part of the wide world where the population has decreased to fifty per cent in fifty years under a civilized government? Where are the thirty millions of Irish should be here today instead of four? Where are our potteries and textiles, the finest in the world? Look at the beds of the Barrow and Shannon they won't deepen. Where is the other civilized government would leave us as treeless as Portugal with a million acres of marsh & bog to make us all die of consumption? Not a ship to be seen in our harbours, Queenstown, Kinsale, Galway, Killybegs, the third biggest harbour in the whole world. We had our trade with Spain and Europe before they were born and with the Flemings too. We had Spanish ale & wine in Galway, the winebark on the widedark waterway. First, they tried to slaughter us all, then to banish us, then to make us paupers and to starve us in the penal days, then to buy us as they buy everything else (when all fruit fails welcome haws) but they're as far off now as they were 700 years ago when they first came here and damnation well they know. But they'll know more than that and to their cost when the first Irish battleship is seen breasting the waves with the green flag at her helm.[44]

> —*Raimeis*, says the citizen. Where are the twenty millions of Irish should be here today instead of four? And our potteries and textiles, the best in the world! And the beds of the Barrow and Shannon they won't deepen with a million acres of marsh and bog to make us all die of consumption.
> —As treeless as Portugal we'll be soon, says John Wyse, if something is not [done] to reafforest the land. Larches, firs, all the trees of the conifer family are going fast. I was reading a report . . .
> —Save them, says the citizen, save the trees of Ireland for the future men of Ireland on the fair hills of Eire, O.

—Europe has its eyes on you, says Lenehan.

The fashionable international world attended en masse this afternoon at the wedding of the chevalier Jean Wyse de Nolan, grand high
chief ranger of the Irish National Foresters, with Miss Fir Conifer of
Pine Valley. The bride looked exquisitely charming in a creation of green
mercerised silk, moulded on an underslip of gloaming grey, sashed with
a yoke of broad emerald and finished with a triple flounce of darker
hued fringe, the scheme being relieved by bretelles and hip insertions of
acorn bronze. The maids of honour, Miss Larch Conifer and Miss
Spruce Conifer, sisters of the bride, wore very becoming costumes in the
same tone, a dainty *motif* of plume rose being worked into the pleats in
a pinstripe and repeated capriciously in the jadegreen toques in the form
of heron feathers of paletinted coral.

—And our eyes are on Europe, says the citizen. We had our trade
with Spain and the French and with the Flemings before those mongrels
were pupped. Spanish ale in Galway, the winebark on the winedark
waterway.

—And will again, says Joe.

—And with the help of the holy mother of God we will again, says
the citizen. Our harbours that are empty will be full again, Queenstown, Kinsale, Galway, Killybegs, the third largest harbour in the wide
world. And will again, says he, when the first Irish battleship is seen
breasting the waves with the green flag to the fore.[45]

The general pattern of revision that can be deduced from these
versions of the *Cyclops* passage holds true for most of Joyce's late work on
Ulysses. Three points should be noted:

(1) Although a selective process is still discernible, Joyce searching for
the *mot juste* and attempting to record with absolute fidelity the speech
rhythms of his characters, the majority of the revisions are *expansive* in
nature. The original version provides a general outline of the situation,
and establishes the realistic foundations; then, by a process of elaboration
or accretion, this original outline is filled in and amplified.

(2) Almost every major element in the final version can be traced to
some "seed" in the original draft. Joyce followed a conventional process of
association in expanding these "seeds."

(3) The formal "correspondences" which characterize each episode of
Ulysses and are carefully tabulated in Stuart Gilbert's study (in this case
the technique of "gigantism" and the inserted parodies) are usually a result
of Joyce's late work on the episode. Here the elaborate parody of the
coniferous wedding stems from a single sentence in the first version, the
citizen's complaint that Ireland has been left "as treeless as Portugal."

The tendency of Joyce's late revisions is apparent in the growth of a
short passage from the *Nausicaa* episode. Three stages in its development
are reflected in a notebook which dates from 1919–1920[46] Here is the
original version: "A lonely lost candle climbed the air and broke and shed
a cluster of violet and one white stars. They floated fell: and they faded.

And among the elms a hoisted linstock lit the lamp at Leahy's terrace. Twittering the bat flew here and there."

Subsequent marginal insertions and interlinear changes produced this expanded text: "A lost long candle wandered the sky from Mirus bazaar in aid of Mercer's hospital and broke drooping and shed a cluster of violet and one white stars. They floated fell: they faded. And among the elms a hoisted linstock lit the lamp at Leahy's terrace. Twittering the bat flew here and there."

Another marginal note, apparently of a later date than the others, introduced the following sentence after "Leahy's terrace": "By the screens of lighted window, by equal gardens a shrill voice went crying plaintively: *Evening Telegraph, extra edition Result of the Gold Cup races* and from the door of Dignam's house a boy ran out and called."

Finally, after several more revisions, the passage reached *Ulysses* in this form:

> A long lost candle wandered up the sky from Mirus bazaar in search of funds for Mercer's hospital and broke, drooping, and shed a cluster of violet but one white stars. They floated, fell: they faded. The shepherd's hour: the hour of holding: hour of tryst. From house to house, giving his everwelcome double knock, went the nine o'clock postman, the glowworm's lamp at his belt gleaming here and there through the laurel hedges. And among the five young trees a hoisted linstock lit the lamp at Leahy's terrace. By screens of lighted windows, by equal gardens a shrill voice went crying, wailing: *Evening Telegraph, stop-press edition! Result of the Gold Cup race!* and from the door of Dignam's house a boy ran out and called. Twittering the bat flew here, flew there. (U 372)

The growth of this passage provides a beautiful illustration of Joyce's method. Principles of artistic selection are still at work, and Joyce's care for the rhythm of his prose is everywhere evident. The alteration of "elms" to "five young trees" intensifies our visual sense of place; "flew here, flew there" is greatly superior to "flew here and there" as a description of the bat's darting flight. The search for the *mot juste* is reflected in the first sentence, where Joyce rejected "climbed" and then "ascended" before choosing "wandered" as the correct equivalent for the candle's motion. All these changes are reminiscent of a conversation recorded by Frank Budgen:

> I enquired about *Ulysses*. Was it progressing?
> "I have been working hard on it all day," said Joyce.
> "Does that mean that you have written a great deal?" I said.
> "Two sentences," said Joyce.
> I looked sideways but Joyce was not smiling. I thought of Flaubert.
> "You have been seeking the *mot juste*?" I said.
> "No," said Joyce. "I have the words already. What I am seeking is

the perfect order of words in the sentence. There is an order in every way appropriate. I think I have it."

"What are the words?" I asked.

"I believe I told you," said Joyce, "that my book is a modern Odyssey. Every episode in it corresponds to an adventure of Ulysses. I am now writing the *Lestrygonians* episode, which corresponds to the adventure of Ulysses with the cannibals. My hero is going to lunch. But there is a seduction motive in the Odyssey, the cannibal king's daughter. Seduction appears in my book as women's silk petticoats hanging in a shop window. The words through which I express the effect of it on my hungry hero are: 'Perfume of embraces all him assailed. With hungered flesh obscurely, he mutely craved to adore.' You can see for yourself in how many different ways they might be arranged."[47]

But although Joyce maintained the care for rhythm and precision of phrasing that characterized his earlier revisions of *Dubliners* and *A Portrait*, his late work on *Ulysses* was primarily elaborative, the accretion of motifs and the addition of intricate ordering patterns. The major changes in the passage from *Nausicaa* are expansive rather than selective. The addition of the reference to Mirus bazaar connects the passage with several others in *Ulysses*; and the alteration of "in aid of" to "in search of funds for" accomplishes a slight change in our view of the enterprise.[48] Another addition, the sentence describing the rounds of the "nine o'clock postman," not only reinforces the tone of the passage but establishes the hour, an essential part of Joyce's elaborate *schema*. However, the most important expansion involves the Gold Cup race, one of the novel's important *leitmotifs*. Bloom's accidental involvement with the race has become part of his sense of alienation; moreover, the victory of "Throwaway" over "Sceptre" may be seen symbolically as a defeat for fertility. Bringing with it this double sense of social and sexual frustration, the motif is ideally suited for this point in the *Nausicaa* episode, when Bloom's mind is filled with thoughts of Molly, Blazes Boylan, and his recent onanism.

In the evolution of this passage from *Nausicaa* we see how Joyce managed to unify *Ulysses* through a network of interlocking motifs and cross-references. Like a mosaic worker, he began with the basic outlines of his work and elaborated upon them, gradually establishing through a succession of detailed additions the extraordinary symbolic and realistic unity of the novel. In a sense the process of composition parallels the process which we follow as readers: a gradual accretion of details which finally form themselves into related patterns. To trace the evolution of an episode is to re-enact our own gradual apprehension of the work.

One more example of Joyce's method is needed to reinforce my point, this time an extract from Leopold Bloom's interior monologue in *Nausicaa*. Only the first and last versions are printed, omitting several interme-

diate stages of revision. In the final text I have italicized all those phrases
or sentences which are present in some form in the original version.

> That's very strange about my watch. Wonder is there any magnetic
> influence between the person because half past four was about the time
> he. Yes, I suppose, at once. Half past I remember looking in Pill lane.
> Also that now is magnetism. Dress up and look and suggest and let you
> see and see more and defy you if you're a man to see that, legs, look,
> look. and. Tip. Have to let fly.[49]

> *Very strange about my watch.* Wristwatches are always going
> wrong. *Wonder is there any magnetic influence between the person*
> *because that was about the time he. Yes, I suppose at once.* Cat's away
> the mice will play. *I remember looking in Pill lane. Also that now is*
> *magnetism.* Back of everything magnetism. Earth for instance pulling
> this and being pulled. That causes movement. And time? Well that's the
> time the movement takes. Then if one thing stopped the whole ghesabo
> would stop bit by bit. Because it's arranged. Magnetic needle tells you
> what's going on in the sun, the stars. Little piece of steel iron. When you
> hold out the fork. Come. Come. Tip. Woman and man that is. Fork and
> steel. Molly, he. *Dress up and look and suggest and let you see and see*
> *more and defy you if you're a man to see that and, like a sneeze coming,*
> *legs, look, look and if you have any guts in you. Tip. Have to let fly.* (U
> 367)

Here the expansive nature of Joyce's late revisions is clearly revealed.
The original version is almost a shorthand record of Bloom's associative
process; successive revisions gave substance to these associations and bound
together the themes of magnetism, time, and sexual attraction. At the
same time, minor alterations and additions enhanced the characteristic
idiom of Bloom's thoughts. The evolution of the passage exemplifies that
"slow elaborative patience" which the young Stephen thought "classical,"
and which is the hallmark of Joyce's mature method.[50]

ORDER

It was inevitable that *Ulysses* should undergo extensive revision and
elaboration as Joyce prepared the novel for final publication. Substantial
changes in the earlier episodes were necessitated by the introduction in
later chapters of new motifs and further details of characterization.
Furthermore, Joyce's aesthetic ideals were considerably altered while
Ulysses was "in progress," and in the last stage of composition he sought to
harmonize the form of the earlier episodes with the complexity he had
achieved in drafting later sections. His method of characterization, which
depended upon the accretion of thousands of minor details, meant that no
section was ever "finished." The search for internal consistency and
harmony was unending.

However, Joyce's reworking of the earlier sections went far beyond these predictable expansions and alterations. When one reads the versions of the early episodes published between 1918 and 1920 in the *Egoist* and *Little Review* one is struck immediately by the absence of many of those elaborate "correspondences" documented by Stuart Gilbert and outlined by Joyce on a chart he circulated among his friends.[51] The familiar *schema* of the novel — the correspondence of each episode to a particular organ, colour, symbol, and art, and the casting of each episode in a distinctive style — is absent from the earlier versions. One of Joyce's major aims in revising the earlier episodes of *Ulysses* was to impose this elaborate pattern of correspondences upon them, to transform the entire novel into an "epic" work.

By the time Joyce had reached mid-point in the drafting of *Ulysses* (*c.* 1919) the "correspondences" for each episode were in the foreground of his mind. They are referred to constantly in his notes, and he was obviously conscious of them in the final stages of composition. While working on the *Oxen of the Sun* episode, which takes place in a Lying-In hospital during the birth of a child, Joyce consulted an elaborate chart which recorded the characteristics of the human foetus at every stage in its development.[52] This enabled him, while working on the episode, to establish correspondences involving the growth of the foetus, the evolution of the English language, the geological development of the earth, and the progress of *Ulysses* up to that point.[53] This complex scheme was gradually woven into the episode and became an integral part of its substance: indeed, it *is* the substance. But when Joyce returned to the earlier episodes and attempted to impose similar schemes upon them, he was less successful. I think this accounts for the impression most of us have while reading *Ulysses* that many of the "correspondences" in the earlier sections lie on the surface and hardly participate in the essential life of the episodes.

When one views the making of *Ulysses* in perspective, it is seen to embody Joyce's entire development from the techniques of *Dubliners* and *A Portrait* to those of *Finnegans Wake*. The earliest versions of the opening episodes were composed in the manner he employed while transforming *Stephen Hero* into *Portrait of the Artist;* but the principles which governed his work in 1920 and 1921 did not differ greatly from those he followed in writing *Finnegans Wake*. Anyone versed in the methods of the *Wake* will find the late elaborations of *Ulysses* familiar ground. During the writing of *Ulysses* Joyce's techniques and aesthetic ideals underwent a profound change. Of course one can argue — and with some justification — that the extreme techniques Joyce employed in finishing *Ulysses* are foreshadowed in the style and structure of his earlier works. But the notion of a technical revolution seems closer to the truth than that of evolution, for in the space of three or four years he travelled most of the distance from *Dubliners* to *Finnegans Wake*.

These rapid changes in Joyce's technical aims are reflected in the radical alteration of his method of composition. The late work on *Ulysses* reveals a process almost the opposite of that which transformed *Stephen Hero* into *Portrait of the Artist*. In revising *Stephen Hero* Joyce exercised a rigorous selectivity, discarding the multiple events and elaborate expository passages of the earlier work in favour of a few scenes of "epiphanies" which embody the essential characteristics of Stephen's development. The richness of the earlier work was sacrificed in favour of intensity, and in accordance with Joyce's shifting attitude toward his own youth. But the revisions of *Ulysses* undertaken during the last years of its composition were seldom selective. They were almost entirely expansive, and the economy Joyce exercised in achieving isolated effects was overshadowed by the incessant elaborations. The ideal of dramatic compression that governed the recasting of *Stephen Hero* was replaced by an ideal of inclusiveness. In one of his early notebooks, dating from 1904, Joyce jotted down the phrase "centripetal writing."[54] His early revisions of *Dubliners* and the autobiographical novel *were* "centripetal," turning in upon a few dramatic situations. But the revisions of *Ulysses* were centrifugal, moving further and further away from the conventional centres of action. Fortunately the human forces of Bloom and Stephen, and the momentum established in the early chapters, kept the revisions of *Ulysses* from completely overshadowing the *données* of each episode. But in *Finnegans Wake*, where the process of revision was intensified and carried out over a much longer period of time, one often finds crucial elements in the first drafts which have been totally obscured by the time the final version is reached.

This movement from "centripetal" to "centrifugal" writing during the evolution of *Ulysses* mirrors a general change in Joyce's artistic stance. A process of selectivity harmonizes with his early notion of the "epiphany," which assumes that it is possible to reveal a whole area of experience through a single gesture or phrase. In shaping the *Portrait* Joyce sought continually to create "epiphanies," and to define Stephen's attitudes by a stringent process of exclusion; later in his career he attempted to define by a process of inclusion. The earlier method implies that there is a significance, a "quidditas," residing in each thing, and that the task of the artist is to discover this significance by a process of distillation. In the later method it is the artist who creates the significance through language. Thus in the *Portrait* a single gesture may reveal a character's essential nature; but in *Finnegans Wake* Humphrey Chimpden Earwicker's nature is established by multiple relationships with all the fallen heroes of history and legend.

It seems appropriate at this point to seek for the reasons behind Joyce's growing interest in formal — almost mechanical — designs. What rationale can we provide for the elaborate patterns of analogy characteristic of each episode, patterns which often (as in *Oxen of the Sun*) seem grotesquely over-elaborate? To what extent is the *schema* of the novel an essential adjunct to the human drama?

First it must be acknowledged that the "epic" proportions of *Ulysses* are absolutely dependent on the major Homeric analogues and, to a lesser extent, on the other ordering frames. But can we justify these intricate elaborations solely on this ground? I do not think so; at least two other factors must be considered.

One of these is Joyce's increasing preoccupation with linguistic experimentation, his desire to stretch the potentialities of English prose in all directions. This desire was bound up with a sheer delight in verbal manipulation, a delight which permeates these remarks to Frank Budgen concerning *Oxen of the Sun:*

> Am working hard at *Oxen of the Sun*, the idea being the crime committed against fecundity by sterilizing the act of coition. Scene: Lying-in-hospital. Technique: a ninepart episode without divisions introduced by a Sallustian-Tacitean prelude (the unfertilized ovum), then by way of earliest English alliterative and monosyllabic and Anglo-Saxon ("Before born the babe had bliss. Within the womb he won worship." "Bloom dull dreamy heard: in held hat stony staring.") then by way of Mandeville . . . then Malory's *Morte d'Arthur* . . . then a passage solemn, as of Milton, Taylor, Hooker, followed by a Latin-gossipy bit, style of Burton/Browne, then a passage Bunyanesque . . . After a diary-style bit Pepys-Evelyn . . . and so on through Defoe-Swift and Steele-Addison-Sterne and Landor-Pater-Newman until it ends in a frightful jumble of pidgin English, nigger English, Cockney, Irish, Bowery slang and broken doggerel. This procession is also linked back at each part subtly with some foregoing episode of the day and, besides this, with the natural stages of development in the embryo and the periods of faunal evolution in general. The double-thudding Anglo-Saxon motive recurs from time to time ("Loth to move from Horne's house") to give the sense of the hoofs of oxen. Bloom is the spermatozoon, the hospital the womb, the nurse the ovum, Stephen the embryo.
>
> How's that for High?[55]

But beyond the function of the *schema* as an essential vehicle for Joyce's themes, and as a vehicle for his restless experimentation, we must acknowledge its function as the source of "neutral" but controlling designs. In his attempt to compose an epic of a single day, and to record the internal as well as the external lives of his characters, Joyce sacrificed many of the traditional unities of the novel. The well-made novel of the nineteenth century, founded on chronological action and composed of dramatic and expository passages (Henry James's "drama" and "picture"), possessed a form which Joyce could no longer employ. In 1919, while part of *Ulysses* was being serialized in the *Little Review* and the *Egoist*, Virginia Woolf defined Joyce's break with traditional forms of expression:

> . . . he is concerned at all costs to reveal the flickerings of that innermost flame which flashes its messages through the brain, and in order to preserve it he disregards with complete courage whatever seems to him adventitious, whether it be probability, or coherence or any other

of these signposts which for generations have served to support the imagination of a reader when called upon to imagine what he can neither touch nor see.[56]

Here is a clear recognition that Joyce consciously rejected those traditional "supports" which provided order for both author and reader; but Virginia Woolf does not describe the radical innovations which replaced them. In his attempt to bring the effects of poetry to the novel, to "internalize" the narration and record various levels of consciousness, Joyce needed as many formal orders as possible to encompass and control his work. And as conventional representation decreased in importance toward the end of *Ulysses*, the need for other patterns increased. The multiple designs Joyce wove into *Ulysses* provide a stable scaffold for the reader, but the "support" they gave to Joyce may have been even greater. Most criticism of *Ulysses* is founded on the assumption that the essential life of the novel lies in the elaborate scheme of correspondences which Joyce revealed to his early commentators; but anyone who has examined his worksheets will realize that many of the correspondences represented for Joyce a kind of "neutral" order. They provided frames which could control his diverse materials without merging into them. Deprived of the traditional orders of home, country and religion, Joyce had a desperate and rather untidy passion for order of any kind. All sorts of mechanical systems are used on the note-sheets to organize the diverse elements. While writing the last episode Joyce kept a sketch-map of Gibraltar before him, not because there is a complicated use of geographical detail in Molly's monologue but because the map provided Joyce with fixed points of reference. Similarly, there are many more Homeric references on the *Ulysses* note-sheets than ever made their way into the text, and we are forced to conclude that the parallel with the *Odyssey* was more useful to Joyce during the process of composition that it is to us while we read the book. Time and again he spoke of the comfort he derived from the narrative order of the *Odyssey*: it provided him — in his own words — with fixed "ports of call."[57] The major parallels between the wanderings of Mr. Bloom and those of Ulysses are an important dimension of the novel, but in working out the trivial details of the Homeric correspondence Joyce was exploring his own materials, not preparing clues for future readers.

We have already seen the care Joyce took during the course of composition to define the various qualities symbolized by "Moly," the magic herb which saves Ulysses from Circe's magic. But are we as readers expected to discover and relate to each other the multiple equivalents enumerated on the note-sheets? Probably not. In this case, as in so many others, the detailed working-out of a "correspondence" was primarily for Joyce's benefit, a part of the rigid discipline he had to undergo in order to control his disparate materials. Many of these detailed schemes lurk in the background of the novel, like the discarded scaffolding of a building which reflects its external form but tells us little of the essential nature. It would be a grave mistake to found any interpretation of *Ulysses* on Joyce's *schema*, rather than on the human actions of Stephen, and Molly, and Mr. Leopold Bloom.

Notes

1. Georges Borach, "Conversations with James Joyce," trans. Joseph Prescott, *College English*, XV (March 1954), 325. Borach is recalling a conversation of 1 August 1917.

2. W. B. Stanford, *The Ulysses Theme*, Oxford, 1954, pp. 186–87. Stanford was the first to discover that Joyce had to read the first seven chapters of Lamb's *Adventures of Ulysses* in 1893–94 while preparing for the Intermediate Examination in English. See his useful studies of Joyce's early contact with the *Odyssey* in *Envoy*, V (April 1951), 62–69, and *The Listener*, XLVI (19 July 1951), 99, 105. Kevin Sullivan has also examined Joyce's reading of Lamb in *Joyce among the Jesuits*, New York, 1958, pp. 94–98.

3. *Letters*, 193. JJ to Mrs. William Murray, 10 Nov. 1922.

4. Gorman, 45. At Belvedere College Joyce wrote an essay on Ulysses as "My Favourite Hero."

5. Gorman, 176. See also Ellmann, 238–39. The versions quoted here are based upon my reading of the original letters (now in the Cornell University Library).

6. See Richard Levin and Charles Shattuck, "First Flight to Ithaca," in *James Joyce: Two Decades of Criticism*, ed. Seon Givens, New York, 1948, pp. 47–94. Levin and Shattuck argue for a deliberate parallel with the *Odyssey* embracing all fifteen stories, but their reasoning is forced when they reach *The Dead*. For the date of *The Dead*, see Ellmann, 252 ff.

7. Ellmann, 274–75.

8. Richard Ellmann, "The Backgrounds of *Ulysses*," *Kenyon Review*, XVI (Summer 1954), 342.

9. Gorman, 224. It is interesting to note that when Joyce began to write *Finnegans Wake*, nine years later, he also started by sketching in passages which ultimately were incorporated in the work's later episodes.

10. E. L. A., "James Joyce to His Literary Agents," *More Books* (Boston), XVIII (Jan. 1943), 22. Letter of 22 June 1920.

11. *Letters*, 143. JJ to HSW, 12 July 1920.

12. *Letters*, 152. JJ to FB, 10 Dec. 1920.

13. Gorman, 268.

14. *Letters*, 128. JJ to HSW, 20 July 1919.

15. *Letters*, 104–05. JJ to John Quinn, 10 July 1917. Joyce began making notes for *Exiles* in Nov. 1913.

16. See Ellmann, Chap. XVII.

17. For a detailed chronology of Joyce's work on *Ulysses*, see Appendix C [in *The Art of James Joyce*].

18. Gorman, 230.

19. *Letters*, 113. Ultimately the middle section contained twelve episodes.

20. *Letters*, 172. JJ to HSW, 7 Oct. 1921.

21. *Letters*, 156. JJ to John Quinn, 7 Jan. 1921.

22. *Letters*, 209–10. JJ to John Quinn, 5 Feb. 1924.

23. Slocum, 142, item E. 5. f.; from the private catalogue of Edward W. Titus,

describing the set of proofs in his possession. See the entire Slocum and Cahoon description of the proofs, pp. 141–43. Some of the proofs were used by Joseph Prescott in the preparation of his unpublished doctoral thesis, "James Joyce's *Ulysses* as a Work in Progress," Harvard University, 1944. Professor Prescott is now preparing a detailed study of Joyce's work on *Ulysses*.

24. In a letter of 22 June 1920 Joyce seems to indicate that *Circe* was the last episode to be drafted. See *Letters*, 141.

25. Frank Budgen, "James Joyce," in *James Joyce: Two Decades of Criticism*, ed. Seon Givens, New York, 1948, p. 24.

26. Budgen, 175–77.

27. Silvio Benco, "James Joyce in Trieste," *The Bookman* (New York), LXXII (Dec. 1930), 380.

28. The note-sheets referred to in this chapter were given to Miss Harriet Weaver in 1938 by Paul Léon, presumably at the direction of Joyce. They are now in the British Museum. For a full description of the note-sheets, see Appendix A. A more technical discussion of the notes — including the problem of their date — will be found in my article on "Joyce's Notes for the Last Episodes of *Ulysses*," *Modern Fiction Studies*, IV (Spring 1958), 3–20.

29. *Letters*, 142.

30. Slocum, 138, item E. 5. a.

31. *Letters*, 172.

32. "The *Ulysses* of James Joyce," *Criterion*, I (Oct. 1922), 102.

33. Budgen, 178.

34. *Letters*, 172.

35. *Letters*, 135. JJ to Frank Budgen, 3 Jan. 1920.

36. *Exiles*, ed. Padraic Colum, New York, 1951, pp. 119–20.

37. See in this connection Stuart Gilbert's *James Joyce's "Ulysses,"* New Edn., London, 1952, pp. 85–87, where M. Bérard's theories concerning the authorship of the *Odyssey* are summarized.

38. *Literary Essays of Ezra Pound*, ed. T. S. Eliot, London, 1954, p. 406. From the "Paris Letter" to *The Dial*, June 1922.

39. Budgen, 124–25.

40. *Letters*, 135. JJ to Mrs. William Murray, 5 Jan. 1920.

41. *Letters*, 175. JJ to Mrs. William Murray, 2 Nov. 1921.

42. Budgen, 236–37. See also *Letters*, 147–49.

43. A forthcoming study of the *Ulysses* MSS. by Professor Joseph Prescott of Wayne State University will do much to fill this need.

44. From an early fragment of the *Cyclops* episode now in the Lockwood Memorial Library, University of Buffalo (La Hune 256). The MS. dates in all probability from 1918.

45. *Little Review*, VI (Dec. 1919), 60; and VI (Jan. 1920), 53. Several obvious misprints have been silently corrected. Joyce never saw the proofs for those episodes which appeared in the *Little Review*, and the American printer occasionally deleted passages which he considered "obscene." The *Little Review* versions of the early episodes are substantially the same as those found in the Rosenbach MS. (see Appendix A); most of the discrepancies between the *Little Review* and the Rosenbach MS. may be accounted for by the lack of scrupulous proof-reading.

46. From a MS. version of the last half of *Nausicaa* now in the Cornell University Library, p. 32. It probably dates from early 1920.

47. Budgen, 20.

48. For other references to "Mirus bazaar" see U 180, 251, 473, 563. The alteration from "aid" to "search" occurred on the proof-sheets; see Joseph Prescott, "Stylistic Realism in Joyce's *Ulysses*," *A James Joyce Miscellany: Second Series*, ed. Marvin Magalaner, Carbondale, 1959, p. 18.

49. From Cornell *Nausicaa* MS. p. 28.

50. See *Stephen Hero*, ed. Theodore Spencer, New Edn., New York, 1955, p. 97.

51. Several versions of this *schema* are available: see Gilbert, *James Joyce's "Ulysses,"* p. 41, and Hugh Kenner, *Dublin's Joyce*, Bloomington, 1956, pp. 226–27. The most complete reproduction of the *schema* will be found in *A James Joyce Miscellany: Second Series*, p. 48.

52. One version of this chart is now in the Cornell collection; a more detailed version, with verbal annotations, is among the *Ulysses* note-sheets in the British Museum.

53. See A. M. Klein's brilliant analysis of the episode, *Here and Now*, I (Jan. 1949), 28–48.

54. Gorman, 136.

55. *Letters*, 138–39. JJ to Frank Budgen, 13 March 1920.

56. Virginia Woolf, "Modern Fiction," *The Common Reader: First and Second Series*, New York, 1948, p. 214.

57. *Letters*, 204.

The Advent of Bloom   Anthony Cronin*

It has become the fashion to assume, when discussing what *Ulysses* is about, that it is about its own technique. Of course many books are primarily concerned with their own technique. The majority of dramatically constructed novels, whose action consists of an organised, interlocking, self-sustaining, artificially contrived sequence of events, are not so much about life as about their own dramatic technique. But *Ulysses* is not so constructed. There is drama in its action as there is drama in every day, but event does not factitiously control or create the nature of further event as it does in most fiction; and if *Ulysses* can be said to have a plot, its plot is formless and does not give form to the book — it is not shaped to produce a series of dramatic sensations for purposes aesthetic or otherwise; it has no conclusion in event, only a termination in time; it is not resolved by a neat regroupment of the characters in their sexual relationships, nor by mayhem on Joyce's part, since nobody dies, or commits suicide, or is murdered to bring the book to a close.

However, it would seem that this mere absence of a complicated, technical machinery of dramatic causation has given rise to the impression that the form the book does have conceals vast mysteries and profundities of intention. The propagators of this idea belong mostly to the nowadays dominant school of academic, pseudoscientific, semeiological and herme-

*From *A Question of Modernity* (London: Secker & Warburg, 1966), 58–96. Reprinted by permission of A. D. Peters & Co. Ltd.

neutical criticism, and, however much their "interpretations" may differ, in their general agreement about methods of interpretation they now form a majority bloc of opinion and are so active as to render Joyce the outstanding victim of these methods.

It has long been notorious (though many early readers remained understandably oblivious of the fact) that *Ulysses* is partly organised round an elaborate system of correspondences and basic motifs. Each section corresponds more or less to an episode in the *Odyssey*; some employ multiple references to a particular colour; all but one to a particular organ of the body; each has a basic "symbol," though the actual meaning of the word in this context may puzzle some of us. There exists even a famous "schema" which Joyce drew up illustrating all this and presented to Mr. Herbert Gorman, though he subsequently objected very strenuously to its publication.

The common demand for esoteric meanings in *Ulysses* has fed voraciously on the details of the "schema," on the Homeric and other parallels and on Joyce's multiplicity of allusion and reference: it has been assumed that, hidden within this labyrinth, is the key to what he "meant," what the book is really "about." And not only have the basic analogies and correspondences been so enucleated and construed, but, not content with what is admittedly there, the higher criticism has turned each page into a jungle of symbol and reference, so that in the interests of semeiology, and on the most dubious grounds, the ordinary physical, substantive reality, the living world of the book has been almost entirely denatured. The function of the various techniques of narration employed (catechism, narcissism, incubism, etc., to use Joyce's own amusing terminology) has been wistfully debated as a key to the meaning of the whole; the action itself has been held to have symbolic or allegorical significances (the difference is not always clear to the unenthusiastic mind) which go far to rob it of any simple human significance at all. Thus the taking of a cup of cocoa becomes, because cocoa is "mass-produced," "the sacrifice of the mass." Galileo-Bloom gets into bed with Venus, both goddess and planet; and in the Ascot Gold Cup, Sceptre, "the phallic favourite, loses to Throwaway, the outside who represents infertility." Such circumlocuities of intention on Joyce's part are not quite inconceivable, of course, but one is entitled to ask whether, if Sir William Bass's great mare had recovered from the effects of winning four classics in 1902 and had won the Gold Cup of 1904, the symbolism would have been reversed. Or would Joyce have left the race out altogether? If he had, his picture of Dublin on the day of such an event would be remarkably incomplete.

Besides the Homeric parallels, the colours, the organs of the body and the basic symbol of each episode, there are what might be called other extensions of situation: biblical, biographical, historical, classical, etc. Thus Bloom is not only Ulysses, but he is also Shakespeare; he is sometimes apparently, Christ; and, in my own opinion, he is definitely the Holy

Ghost. And there are certain recurrent images, phrases and themes such as, besides the aforementioned Gold Cup Race, Mr Deasy's letter, the jingle of Boylan's sidecar and Bloom's bed, the blind piano tuner, etc. With the possible exception of Nosey Flynn's snuffle these have naturally been accorded the status of significant symbols. One eminent authority's explanation of what lies behind the innocent-seeming foot and mouth disease reads as follows (W. Y. Tindall in *James Joyce: His Way of Interpreting the Contemporary World*):

"Continual allusions to cattle and their disorders [in fact the foot and mouth disease, often a feature of the Irish scene, is the only one mentioned] establish the foot and mouth disease, the subject of Mr Deasy's letter to the press, as a significant theme. In the maternity hospital, cattle serve as an obvious symbol of fertility, and foot and mouth disease, the trouble with cows [foot and mouth disease affects also bullocks, which of course are sterile anyway], becomes a symbol of infertility and Dublin's distemper." That foot and mouth also function on a Freudian level (foot as male and mouth as female) corroborates their meaning in this context. As "bullockbefriending bard" Stephen champions fertility or art against the sterility all round him.

Most of the exegesis concerned simply shows the higher criticism of to-day to be the old Browning Society in disguise: great writers have great messages which need deciphering and a great work has a great inner meaning which can operate on us in paraphrase. The judicious interpretation of symbol and correspondence can prove *Ulysses* to be "important" in terms of its inner "message" or "meaning," neo-Thomist, neo-Freudian, mythopoeic, metempsychotic or what not. It has proved perfectly easy to reduce it to the merest and dullest of allegory. Thus besides the neo-Freudian interpretation of the use that is made of "cattle and their disorders" may be put another critic's neo-theological interpretation of an incident in the cabman's shelter (Mr J. Mitchell Morse in *The Sympathetic Alien: James Joyce and Catholicism*). Stephen, we are told, "rejects the inefficacious sacrament of the cabmen's shelter ('something in the shape of solid food . . . a bun, or so it seemed' and 'what was temporarily supposed to be called coffee')" and this incident is the climax of the book because, though he "does have many social sins on his conscience — almost the whole catalogue of *ayenbite of Inwyt* . . . he is absolved from them by . . . refusing to take communion. That is the act of renunciation that purifies and frees the artist in him." What happened in fact was that Bloom ventured "to plausibly suggest to break the ice" a cup of coffee and a roll for Stephen. When they were brought he was preoccupied with his theory that the proprietor of the stall was Skin-the-Goat, the famous assassin of Lord Frederick Cavendish, so he silently pushed the cup of "what was temporarily supposed to be called coffee" and the "rather antediluvian specimen of a bun" over to his companion. Some ten pages later he breaks off a discourse on Bacon's authorship of the plays of

Shakespeare to say—"Can't you drink that coffee by the way? Let me stir it and take a piece of that bun. It's like one of our skipper's bricks disguised. Still, no one can give what he hasn't got. Try a bit." Couldn't Stephen be contrived to get out his mental organs, for the moment refusing to dictate further!

This "reading" of Mr Mitchell Morse is illuminating in several respects. First, the reluctance to take the matter further: why, if the bun is the host, is it "like one of our skipper's bricks disguised" (the sailor who was on the *Rosevean* "from Bridgwater with bricks")? If this game is started it should be kept up on the assumption that Joyce was consistent. Second, the puzzling refusal to explain why, when on the very next page he is urged to "have a shot at it now" Stephen does take "a sip of the offending beverage." And if the offending beverage, the coffee of the cabman's shelter, is part of the sacrifice of the mass, what becomes of the other explainer's "mass-produced" cocoa, which Stephen and Bloom share a little later in Eccles Street? Where the one eminent exegetist sees Stephen refusing to participate in the sacrifice of the mass in the cabman's shelter, the other sees Stephen and Bloom celebrating it a little later on in Eccles Street. The untutored reader, who may well find a sufficient delight in either episode without the aid of such hermeneutics, will doubtless feel that it is not in fact incumbent on him to decide whether it is the coffee or the cocoa which is the blood of Christ; but it is perhaps worth remarking that there may be some confusion on somebody's part, whether Joyce's or his critics', as to what precisely is a symbol.

A symbol is presumably something that, when contemplated, will reveal mysterious depths of meaning; and it will, presumably, have some aura of suggestion about it to begin with. The mass-produced cocoa, and the temporarily-agreed-on coffee, may be signs or emblems; *Ulysses* may be a work of boring algebra; but although the proponent of the cocoa suggests that it was while existing on that humble beverage in Paris that Joyce came to value it, there would seem to be certain inescapable aesthetic difficulties about erecting it into a symbol. In other words, if this is the kind of thing *Ulysses* is about, the ordinary apparatus of aesthetic perception, however alert and sensitive, will not do; what is needed to "find out what it is about" is a curiosity like a process server's. The semeiologists and exegetists universally fail to see that any attempt to approach a work of art through a series of acts of mere intellectual comprehension is stultifying. There is a joy in apprehension, but this laborious deciphering is not it, and has only the effect of reducing the world of *Ulysses* to some monstrous enchanted fairyland where everything turns out to be masquerading as something else. Those who are adept at telling us what Joyce was up to are singularly unable to give us any valid and satisfying *aesthetic* reason why he should be up to it; if this is what he was up to, his mind was that of a puzzle setter, not that of a great literary artist. As Pound says about the Homeric parallels, "any blockhead can trace them," but not any blockhead can give us a convincing aesthetic reason why they should be there.

The Homeric framework is in fact pretty loose: the chronology of the *Odyssey* is not followed at all, and Joyce is more than arbitrary in deciding what he will or will not use. It remains obscure why some episodes should have basic colour motifs and others none; and why the first three should have no organ of the body motif. That the symbol of the Lotus Eater's episode (the one in which Bloom buys the soap, goes into the church and thinks about his bath) should be the eucharist, may be an ironic comment about the effect of that sacrament on the faithful; but since the Eolus or Cave of the Winds episode takes place in a newspaper office, and that of the Sirens in the bar of a hotel, it cannot be held to be either very esoteric or very significant that the symbol of the one should be an editor, and of the other, barmaids.

The commonest explanation of the Homeric parallels is that they are an elaborate ironic device designed to exhibit the decay of western civilisation and the emptiness and spiritual barrenness of the bourgeois, urban civilisation with which Joyce is supposed to be concerned. That he did exploit his framework for ironic purposes is undoubtedly true, but a certain elephantine coarseness of irony would be implied if the whole thing were simply a huge long joke at the expense of Dublin, the twentieth century and Leopold Bloom. What irony there is may be directed both ways. If the adventures of the real Ulysses cast a dubious light on Bloom, Bloom in his turn casts an ambiguous light on his forerunner. Joyce believed that a great deal of life had never got into heroic literature. But in general his ironic effects are subtler than any that could be produced by mere comparisons, either way. Nor has it been demonstrated that he brooded as much about the decline of the west as some critics, themselves addicted to certain views about that phenomenon, would have us believe. Dublin was not then, any more than it is now, typical of "modern urban civilisation" and, whatever the characters of *Ulysses* may be, they are not "modern industrial man," or even modern urban man, or typical middle-class man or anything else. Bloom, in spite of his nine hundred pounds' worth of Canadian scrip, is scarcely respectable enough to stand in for the bourgeoisie. Of his companions at the funeral, Martin Cunningham, the most eminent, has a wife who pawns the furniture every Saturday; Tom Kernan is a habitual drunkard who has been seriously injured when falling down the lavatory steps of a public house; Simon Dedalus is a jobless bankrupt whose only occupation is the praising of his own past; Jack Power keeps a barmaid under mysterious circumstances. The deceased himself has recently lost his job through that failing which is, according to Simon Dedalus, who ought to know, "many a good man's fault." And of Simon Dedalus's friends and companions of the afternoon session in the Ormond, neither Bob Cowley, who has two bailiffs "prowling round the house trying to effect an entrance," nor Ben Dollard of the *basso profundo*, a wealthy businessman who has been reduced by Bass's Number One Ale to living in a doss-house, could be taken as representative material for a thesis on bourgeois material civilisation unless that thesis were a temperance tract: any more surely than could jingle jaunty Blazes Boylan; Lenehan ("that toucher") who earns a dubious living on the fringes of racing journalism; J. J. O'Molloy ("Gambling. Debts of honour. Reaping the whirlwind."); the Citizen ("waiting for what would drop from the sky in the way of a drink"), Hynes ("a decent fellow when he has it but sure like that he never does"), the editor of the *Freeman* himself ("sad case . . . incipient jigs"); or indeed any of the other characters, from McCoy, Nosey Flynn and The Nameless One down to "the former Gumley," reduced by drink to the status of night watchman, or Corley who borrows half a crown from Stephen for a kip for the night. If this is the plight of modern urban middle-class man it is indeed a parlous one; if this material is an epitome of the state of modern urban civilisation, the said civilisation's ills are odder (though perhaps simpler) than one had thought.

But a common misconception about *Ulysses* is that its characters are a cross-section of middle or lower-middle class Dublin. They are in fact splendidly typical of a certain kind of Dubliner, but not even in a city so small as Dublin could they all, or nearly all, be so well acquainted with each other unless they had a bond or an activity in common. That activity is song. With the exception of Stephen's medical friends practically every character is connected with that world of semi-professional, semi-amateur concert and operatic singing which flourished in Dublin, a city then, and to a much lesser degree still, devoted to vocal music, a world still, though moribund, by no means defunct. In habit and in speech they are also typical members of the drinking classes; but it is as well, where generalisations are concerned, and to get the picture of Dublin straight, to remember that they know each other largely because they belong to a particular circle whose bond was song. Joyce and his parents belonged to this and, apart from the students, Father Conmee and the company in the library, it furnishes the cast of the book.

Not very oddly perhaps, Ezra Pound and T. S. Eliot both came quite early on to much the same conclusion about the Homeric parallels; Pound when he said that "these correspondences are part of Joyce's mediaevalism, and are chiefly his own affair, a scaffold, a means of construction, justified by the result, and justifiable by it only"; and Eliot, in his review of *Ulysses* in *The Dial*, November 1923, when he concluded that the mythical extensions were "a way of controlling, of ordering, of giving a shape and a significance to the immense panorama of futility and anarchy which is contemporary history." There is a difference between the two descriptions, but in essence they are the same: the Homeric parallels, like much else, are a constructive and controlling device. Like much else they have perhaps achieved an exaggerated importance because Joyce insisted on talking about his work only in terms of the structural devices that sustained it. In a recent examination of Joyce's working methods an intelligent scholar, Mr A. Walton Litz, points out that "the many Homeric parallels not included in the final text of *Ulysses* are significant, since they illustrate how much more important the Homeric background was for Joyce than it is to the reader." He goes on to show that the elaborate correspondences of the "schema" are absent from the early versions of the book and he justly adds:

> In his attempt to bring the effects of poetry to the novel, to "internalize" the narration and record various levels of consciousness, Joyce needed as many formal orders as possible to encompass and control his work. And as conventional representation decreased in importance toward the end of *Ulysses*, the need for other patterns increased. The multiple designs Joyce wove into *Ulysses* provide a stable scaffold for the reader, but the "support" they gave to Joyce may have been even greater. Most criticism of *Ulysses* is founded on the assumption that the essential life of the novel lies in the elaborate scheme of correspondences which Joyce revealed to his early commentators; but anyone who has examined his worksheets will realise that many of the correspondences represented for Joyce a kind of "neutral" order. They provided frames which could control his diverse materials without merging into them. Deprived of the traditional orders of home, country and religion, Joyce had a desperate and rather untidy passion for order of any kind. All sorts of mechanical systems are used on the note-sheets to organise the diverse elements . . . there are many more Homeric references on the *Ulysses* note-sheets than ever made their way into the text, and we are forced to conclude that the parallel with the *Odyssey* was more useful to Joyce during the process of composition than it is to us while we read the book. Time and again he spoke of the comfort he derived from the narrative order of the *Odyssey*: it provided him — in his own words — with fixed "ports of call." The major parallels between the wanderings of Mr. Bloom and those of *Ulysses* are an important dimension of the novel, but in working out the trivial details of the Homeric correspondence Joyce was exploring his own materials, not preparing clues for future readers.

Of course, Joyce used his controlling patterns, as any form may be used, to find further illuminations of his material. Part of the function of form, for the writer, is that it is itself suggestive. Both the Homeric parallels and the less important correspondences provided Joyce with new ironies and insights as he went along — the use that he makes of the organs of the body, the human heart in the funeral sequence for example. A fruitful technique is itself creative, an organism which will not only help to control, but to develop and to extend the limits of vision, and Joyce's structural devices, the *Odyssey* and the other correspondences, do this. To say that they remain primarily technical devices is not to demean them. The imagination will not function without a framework of some sort. Joyce was dispensing, among other things, with plot in the ordinary sense of the word, the mechanism, the sustaining device that provides the reason for the existence of the majority of novels and the form for nearly all of them, which largely decides when they should begin, how they should progress and when they should end, and dictates to a considerable extent what objects should be mentioned, what scenes described, what characters introduced. He had to find his "ports of call"; he had to find, indeed he did find, a framework which would not only control his material and give it unity, but provide the all-important scaffold for the imagination as well. Nor indeed should it be forgotten that in every use of form as well as in every extension of allusion there is an element of play, that element of play which paradoxically deepens the being of a work of art and without which the composition of works of art on the scale of *Ulysses* would scarcely be possible.

II

The attempt to reduce the physical reality of the world of *Ulysses* to a series of hieroglyphs ignores the references to symbolic or metaphysical intentions in art which Joyce himself made. There is a curious passage in *Stephen Hero* in which we are told that Stephen "even thought of explaining the audacities of his verse as symbolical allusions. It was hard for him to compel his head to preserve the strict temperature of classicism." And in *A Portrait of the Artist as a Young Man*, Stephen specifically rejects in so many words any aesthetic based on symbolism (and incidentally formulates a post–Cézanne aesthetic of great exactness). Speaking of Aquinas's use of the word *claritas* he admits that it had baffled him for a long time and goes on:

> It would lead you to believe he had in mind symbolism or idealism, the supreme quality of beauty being a light from some other world, the idea of which the matter is but the shadow, the reality of which it is but the symbol . . . the artistic discovery and representation of the divine purpose in anything or a force of generalisation which would make the aesthetic image a universal one, make it outshine its proper conditions. But that is literary talk. . . . When you have apprehended that basket as one thing and have then analysed it according to its form and apprehended it as a thing you make the only synthesis which is logically and esthetically permissible. You see that it is that thing which it is and no other thing. The radiance of which he speaks is the scholastic *quidditas*, the *whatness* of a thing.

Nor would the treatment meted out to George Russell and his theory that "art has to reveal to us ideas, formless spiritual essences" in *Ulysses* suggest that Joyce's purposes were symbolic, at least in so far as that word suggests a metaphysical intent, or that any great change of mind had taken place between the writing of the *Portrait* and the writing of *Ulysses*.

It has been suggested that in the use of Homer, Joyce desired to give his work epic dimensions; and that in his use of physiology and the arts, etc., his purpose was primarily encyclopaedic, that he wished *Ulysses* to enclose as many human preoccupations and to include as much erudition and general information as possible. This latter would also be an idea hard to justify on mere aesthetic grounds; but there is no doubt that the complicated interplay between his material and its intentional extensions of reference does enlarge *Ulysses* in the sense of increasing the universality of the action. But this would have been a dangerous game to play if the action were not substantially and hypostatically real to begin with. Most Joyce criticism tends to rob the ordinary surface reality of the book of this substantive realism.

Many of the "significant themes," the recurring motifs, are perfectly natural and important details whose justification and necessity are plain. The names of Dublin landmarks which the characters have to pass and re-pass have been credited with obscure symbolical depths as if Joyce had made up the whole city out of his head: if he had picked other landmarks one supposes that they would have been turned to good purpose by the commentators also. What Professor Tindall calls "continual allusions to cattle and their disorders," meaning the foot and mouth disease, are not necessarily intended as pointers to Freudian symbol, and an ineffably clumsy one at that. They constitute apt natural detail, a source of some superb comedy, and an element in the comic technique by which such figures as Mr Deasy and the editor ("J. J. O'Molloy, about to follow him in, said quietly to Stephen: I hope you will live to see it published.") are made real. Above all it is a perfect piece of grotesquery with which to shackle Stephen and it contributes a good deal to our knowledge of him: he takes an amount of trouble over the letter and risks a little humiliation; he blushes when he hands it over. In his own mind it is an ironic reminder of his situation, the "bullockbefriending bard" who is reminded by Lynch that so far only "a capful of light odes can call your genius father"; and in the reader's consciousness it may stand not as a symbol but simply as an associational reminder of his wasteful, uncreative days. It will be seen that in interpreting it as a symbol for Stephen's championship of fertility or art against the sterility all round him, Professor Tindall has not only indulged himself in totally unwarrantable Freudian assumptions but has actually gone directly contrary to the plain reading of the text as well. Like all the other recurring themes, echoing, re-echoing and reappearing in various places at various hours of the day, it contributes to the unity and to the living texture of the whole book and to our feeling for the city and its common preoccupations. And like some others, the Gold Cup for example, which is first in the debatable future and then in the irrevocable past, it serves beautifully to remind us of the actual passage of the day. When late at night in the coffee stall we find that the letter is actually in the paper with Bloom "a bit flabbergasted at Myles Crawford's after all managing the thing," the whole long day is thrown into perspective behind us. And these repetitions also serve to remind us of the people who are off stage and of other specific moments in time; they are part of our developing consciousness and knowledge of the people and the milieu of the book.

Judging from the work of some of his commentators, to attempt to seek secondary, hermeneutic purposes on Joyce's part is often to miss the real nature of his achievement. To anyone who knows Dublin, the recurring theme of the Ascot Gold Cup will seem perfectly natural and right; and it is certainly very illuminating. It serves to emphasise Bloom's isolation among his fellow citizens and their suspicions of him (they have it both ways: he is accused not only of being a "whiteyed kaffir . . . that never backed a horse in anger in his life" but of secretly backing the winner and "then sloping off with his five quid without putting up a pint of stuff like a man"). It increases Bloom's stature (he and Davy Byrne, the moral publican, are above such frivolities, but he condemns nobody else for indulging in them). There may or may not be a pun to connect Bloom's masturbation on the strand and his abandonment of his wife to Mulligan with the names of the winner and the much-backed Sceptre, but in that case why does Mulligan himself back Sceptre? The Gold Cup is abundantly justified by the light it throws on Bloom; it would be justified anyway even by the light it throws on Nosey Flynn, Davy Byrne and the company in Barney Kiernan's. And it would be more than worth its weight in gold were it only for the fact that it is the cause of such consummate abuse of Bloom. The commentators speak as if the ability to invent the pun were more remarkable than the ability to invent the comedy. If the pun does exist, it is not a very remarkable stroke aesthetically, though it may exhibit Joyce's cleverness; on the other hand the human use that is made of the Gold Cup is superb.[1]

Those who are intent on turning *Ulysses* into mere anagram and allegory are perhaps so because they are incapable of appreciating the "profane joy" with which ordinary mundanities are invested in it. Perhaps too they are unsympathetic towards the kind of life which in large part it portrays; incapable of savouring, for example, the citizen's language as Joyce himself savours it, to some extent even uninterested in the primary satisfactions we derive from language and the representation of life. Whatever Joyce's secondary purposes may have been, whatever elaborations of technique and allusion he indulges in, that is not where the true greatness of the book lies. Mr. Bloom may be Shakespeare; what is important to us is that he is Bloom. The fact that he is not only Odysseus but Shakespeare and Sinbad the sailor as well, does not account for his fascination: as if Joyce's talents lay simply in the ability to invent more and more "meaningful" parallels. Nor is the worth of the book to be suggested by explaining what it is really "about," as if Joyce was a nostrum vendor, a mystic or a philosopher. What the book is "about" may be important in the sense that every writer may have to be judged by the *quality* of his vision as well as by his ability to express it, though this is a debatable point which would require a lot of definition. It is irrelevant, if we mean by what it is "about" a mere attitude hidden in the hermeneutics which, if discovered, would only have the force of an attitude and not the force of art. To speak of the quality of a man's vision is not to speak of the worth of his mere, paraphrasable opinions about history or religion or our place in the cosmos: an ideology which could be discovered and exclaimed over like that of any other fashionable sage. Every recorded statement we have exhibits Joyce's total contempt for abstract ideas, his cheerful and not at all hag-ridden scepticism about religion, his indifference to the profundities of the new psychology. A good deal of confusion exists about the nature of his vision; he has been accused of everything from sentimentality, to indifference, to rage; but before asking what his book is about it is equally, if not more important, to enquire into the almost totally neglected question of what in fact it is.

III

What it is can perhaps be seen more clearly by a preliminary examination of what it is not. It is to begin with unlike almost any other novel ever written. Almost all other novels are patterned dramatically. They are concerned not only with a situation, but with a situation that unfolds itself, a plot, which progresses through a chain of causation, often involving coincidence, frequently violence or at least death. Life in such books is to a greater or lesser degree subordinated to event. We get little or no static living, but only those events which contribute more or less to the main stream. Irrelevancies may be included but they are usually said to have had some influence on the behaviour of the characters in the crises of event. Life has to be contained within the pattern of event; it is therefore neater and smaller than real living. The events, being patterned, are also neater than the events in life, which have usually no pattern. Plot events are dialectic, being explainable in terms of each other, whereas events in life are frequently isolated and inexplicable, or, if explicable, they are so only in terms of an infinite conglomeration of factors which would stretch outside the book. The events out of which the pattern of event is made are both more clear-cut and more probable than the events in life, though the pattern as a whole is usually highly improbable.

The justification for this patterning in most serious works is presumably more than the amusement of the reader with a good story, the satisfaction of his aroused curiosity, or the gratification of his delight in violence or intrigue. The justification, if there is one, must rest both on the negative claim that much is allowable in letters that does not obtain in life, like speaking in iambic pentameters; and on the positive claim that the dramatic arrangement of life in a book is a means of producing pity, terror, catharsis or any other emotion that it is proper to feel in the presence of a work of art. The latter claim rests on the assumption that an artificial arrangement of life in a pattern of event and a curtailment of life in the interests of a pattern of event can be a source of aesthetic satisfaction.

Still the falsification of life remains. We may say that this falsification is tacitly admitted between the writer and the reader, just as a composer of opera tacitly agrees with the audience that people do not communicate by singing at each other; it exists all the same. There is no such falsification of life in *Ulysses*. Of course *Ulysses* is not just a "slice of life," as it was once assumed to be, though even as a slice of life, if that were conceivable, it would still be very great. (Samuel Beckett has said that Joyce thought it was perhaps "over-constructed": some of the commentators seem to suggest that it is constructed to the exclusion of everything but the construction and is the "greater" for that.) But the necessary limitations of Joyce's form do not result in a falsification of life as do those of the ordinary novel of self-sustaining event. In *Ulysses*, for the first time in fiction, life could be almost completely itself. Where in the novel of event each picture, each person, each happening, each thought has to be subordinated to the over-all pattern, in *Ulysses* they are allowed their own importance. Nothing is a mere turning point in the narrative, a mere link in a chain of causation, a puppet called upon to give the story a twist or a push. Though there is event—there is a good deal of real drama in the episode of the funeral carriage: the stony silence with which, as Irish Catholics believing in the last sacraments, his companions greet Bloom's assertion that sudden death is the best, and the unfortunate reference to suicide—it has its own right to exist independently. Conversation, anecdote, thought, desultory impression, image and happening are freed at last from their long subordination to plot. They do not have to play a part; or to suffer drastic curtailment because they are counted as irrelevant. Of course they have to have some significance: *Ulysses* would be a terrifying monstrosity if they had not. Each is, in fact, an epiphany, to use Joyce's own term, of greater or lesser importance; but their importance is not that of mere contributing factors to a story. This is the texture of life, not the artificiality of contrived event; and, as a result, *Ulysses* is a prose work much of which one can read as one does a poem, for the epiphanies and the words themselves, not for the sake of a story to which they contribute, though they do, of course, contribute to the total impression the book makes.

Succeeding in this, Joyce has succeeded in eliminating the underlying falsehood of the novel. Though there may be a tacit agreement between the reader and the writer that things do not happen as the novel suggests, that they are not so isolated, nor clear-cut, nor interlocked, nor dramatic; and that most of life is composed of experiences which do not serve the novelist's purposes, there nevertheless remains a residual feeling on the reader's part that things ought to be like this, that fiction is in some way better than fact, a feeling that is bad for fact, for living, and, one might add, bad for fiction too. The various confusions about "naturalism" and "realism" do not help matters. Zola, the great prophet of naturalism, is full of the most preposterous melodrama. Nor, for all that we hear about the influence or non-influence of *Ulysses*, has the novel, even the so-called serious novel, altered very much, if at all, in this respect: event is still preponderant at the expense of texture.

But alone with this liberation of ordinary living from the shackles of plot, goes an enormous extension of the range of life included. If one of the simplest but most important functions of the writer is to extend the recorded area of human experience, Joyce has flung the frontiers further out than any writer of this century — and it is to the particular honour of this century that whole new tracts of human experience, never before explored, have been brought under the amending and meliorating rule of the artist's compassion. Whatever his secondary purposes may have been, whatever intertwining strands of meaning and experience *Ulysses* contains, whatever the point of the story, if there is a point, all his statements go to show that Joyce considered it a major, indeed *the* major part of his vocation as a writer to speak the truths that had never before been spoken. As his brother points out, he was a realist and an extremist who had had the advantage over most writers of having to conduct his after-dinner discussions about life in a country in which the dinner itself was often lacking. From the time when he told Stanislaus that "he had no doubt that most artists, even the greatest, belied the life they knew," so that "literature . . . was a parody of life" and came to believe, according to Stanislaus, that "the poetry of noble sentiments, the romantic music, and the dramatic passions, with a dominant love theme, which culture offered him as a true poetic insight into the universal problems of human life, did not fit in with life as he knew it" — his primary purpose as an artist was clear. He ended his first adolescent manifesto with a quotation from Ibsen: " 'What will you do in our society, Miss Hessel'? asked Rorlund — "I will let in fresh air, pastor,' answered Lona." And in *Ulysses* itself he writes of the "secrets, silent, stony" which "sit in the dark palaces of both our hearts: secrets weary of their tyranny: tyrants willing to be de-throned."

Part of this process was technical: ordinary living had to be freed from the distortions of plot, from the skimping and twisting essential in the novel of event, of men and women in dramatic conflict, so that it could achieve its own entelechy. But along with this liberation from the tyranny of narrative went a tremendous extension of the amount of life included. Joyce includes so much that had never been included in art before, of man not only in his basic sexuality but in his basic sordidity as well, that he must stand as one of the great liberators of the human spirit from the tyranny of its own secrets. And not only did he bring such things within the scope of expression; he brought them, which is more important, within the scope of art.

IV

A man's message is his way of seeing. Instead of asking whether Bloom will or will not get his breakfast in bed in the morning, and what if anything, is the significance of the meeting between Bloom and Stephen, it is perhaps better to ask what spirit pervades and informs *Ulysses*. The mood of a book should operate on the reader more surely and a great deal more subtly than anything that could be described as its message.

"The theme of *Ulysses* is simple," says Mr Richard Ellmann in his book, *James Joyce*, "casual kindness overcomes unconscionable power." Mr Harry Levin in *James Joyce*, however, will have nothing to do with such calendar mottoes. He thinks that the book offers no hope and no comfort, that there is only the author's creative intensity, beating down "like an aroused volcano upon an ancient city, overtaking its doomed inhabitants in forum or temple, at home or at brothel, and petrifying them in the insensate agonies of paralysis." (Incidentally it is difficult to make out from Mr Levin's celebrated study whether he enjoyed reading the book or not.) Mr Hugh Kenner thinks the book is a gargantuan, ironic machine, and he favours the dilemma of Modern Industrial Man, the dead remains of classical and Christian civilisation being incapsulated in the speech of the characters, whose language is the language of eighteenth-century Dublin, in order to show how the mighty are fallen. That the language of the nameless narrator of the Cyclops episode is the language of eighteenth-century Dublin one is inclined to doubt. It is sufficiently obvious that neither he nor the citizen are Industrial Men, or industrious men either, for the matter of that. Many people have found the book terrible. George Orwell believed that it was "the product of a special vision of life, the vision of a Catholic who has lost his faith. What Joyce is saying is, 'Here is life without God. Just look at it!' " (Apart altogether from whether we really feel that Joyce is saying anything like this when we read the book, it is perhaps worth remarking here that though all the evidence goes to show that he was a cheerful sort of unbeliever it is rather to be doubted whether, as Mr Eliot has pointed out to the present author, anybody brought up as an Irish Catholic could ever, deep in his being, envisage the world as "godless.") Mr William Empson thinks that Bloom's isolation and Stephen's megalomania are so monstrous that, if the book is to be bearable, it must have a happy ending. He thinks Joyce meant to indicate that Stephen went to bed with Molly, the first woman not a whore he had ever been to bed with, and that this not only produced an enormous improvement in his character, but was the means of restoring conjugal relations between the Blooms.

All this disagreement would seem to suggest that there is a deep inherent difficulty in deciding what are the values of the book, even, let us say, to put it perfectly simply, in deciding whether it is a cheerful book or a very gloomy one.

The values with which we are surrounded in life are, so to speak, concentric: near at hand are those of the parental, or, later, the human circle in which we move, outside them the values of society and beyond that again what are alleged to be the values of God or of the grave. Before discussing his larger vision it would be as well to see whether Joyce accepts, rejects, endorses or modifies the ordinary close-at-hand values of society and it is perhaps instructive to compare him with a famous, and in many ways remarkable, novelist who is said to have attacked them. Thackeray's *Vanity Fair* is an instructive contrast in several respects. *Vanity Fair* is ostensibly an attack on society, on high society for its unwarrantable scorn for all beneath it, on a universally uncharitable attitude towards poverty and misfortune, on the hypocrisy that abounds on all levels of the social ladder and the cheating, dishonesty, calculation and toadying that it masks, in particular on the Victorian marriage-mart as a form of respectable prostitution. Yet the book itself is deeply involved with society also. Thackeray assumes that his readers are normal middle-class people with normal middle-class values, though they are evidently supposed to be better-hearted than he thinks the world is in general. If he is hard on society he is even harder on Becky. Her father, the Soho painter, is treated just as we would expect such an arty, "dissolute" character to be treated for the benefit of such an audience. The counterweights in the book, feminine virtue as exemplified by Amelia and masculine decency, honesty and kindliness as represented by Dobbin are, frankly, in an adult world, ridiculous. Much play is made of Amelia's innocence, gentleness and charitableness as an example to us all, but as a moral yardstick this is nursery nonsense, for if she had been born in a slum these virtues would have had to undergo considerable modification, probably for the better: as she is in the book, Amelia and her virtues, so-called, are simply the product of upbringing, education and good middle-class shelter. Again the contrast between Dobbin and the others is altogether jejune as a matter of serious morality, for Dobbin's virtues depend on his money: indeed the exercise of his vaunted virtues is generally simply an exercise of his money. An even more fundamental flaw in the book is Thackeray's complete acceptance of the struggle for money, for success, for rank and position as important and interesting in itself. It is not simply that the world finds it so and therefore he must write about it: but that he finds it so himself and expects us to do so as well. Generally speaking he is hopelessly, and to a large extent unconsciously, involved with the majority of the values of society. When we ask ourselves who his ideal reader would be, we are forced to conclude that it would be somebody like Amelia herself, a gently brought up girl who accepted the so-called values of innocence and decency as alternatives to those of the world.

Thackeray quite obviously expects the reader to share his beliefs, his prejudices and his values: his book is written in the assurance that there is a common ground and that it is quite easily reached by people of goodwill. Joyce does not seem to have any prejudices, whatever about values or beliefs. As far as can be seen, initially at least, what he expects from the reader is only a level of literacy and a freedom from atavistic reaction to sexual abnormality, dirt, drink, dishonesty, failure (how failure sets Thackeray off, one way or the other!) and all societal obstacles to admiration or compassion, or at least a cool regard. The people of *Ulysses* are a pretty battered lot. Debt, drink, idleness afflict practically all of them, Stephen included. Bloom is not idle, but he is not very industrious either, and his record of false starts and lost jobs in Cuffe's, Wisdom Hely's, Thom's and elsewhere certainly amount to failure, a failure from which only the nine hundred pounds and the insurance policy inherited from his father protect him. Parts of his past, the making up to Mrs Riordan, for example, or the suggestion to Molly that she should pose in the nude for the rich dilettantes in Merrion Square, are not very creditable in terms of the sort of values we imbibe from Thackeray or indeed any of the writing of the past. Nor would the rest of the people in the book appear, by these standards, very prepossessing. The three old men who foregather in the Ormond would not have much to say for themselves in most courts of judgment of life. Ben Dollard of the bass baritone has squandered his substance and reduced himself to penury; Bob Cowley is in the hands of the bailiffs, Simon Dedalus's daughters are near starving while he drinks. Yet there seems to be nothing much on their consciences that a ball of malt and a bar of a song will not amend. Is Joyce's attitude towards them condemnatory, compassionate or indifferent? Are we supposed to admire them as they evidently to some extent admire themselves?

The first thing one is forced to conclude is that if *Ulysses* is an examination of hell, or futility, or an unredeemed decay, or anything else of that nature — which it is frequently alleged to be — it presents some very curious characteristics. Here is a passage from *Stephen Hero* which is an illuminating contrast to the tone of *Ulysses*. Stephen has gone to the Adelphi Hotel to look for Cranly. He finds him in the billiard-room and sits down beside him to watch the game:

> It was a three-handed game. An elderly clerk, evidently in a patronising mood, was playing two of his junior colleagues. The elderly clerk was a tall stout man who wore gilt spectacles on a face like a red shrivelled apple. He was in his shirt-sleeves and he played and spoke so briskly as to suggest that he was drilling rather than playing. The young clerks were both clean-shaven. One of them was a thickset young man who played doggedly without speaking, the other was an effervescent young man with white eyebrows and a nervous manner. Cranly and Stephen watched the game progress, creep from point to point. The heavy young man put his ball on the floor three times in succession and the scoring was so slow that the marker came and stood by the table as a reminder that the twenty minutes had passed. The players chalked their cues oftener than before and, seeing that they were in earnest about finishing

the game, the marker did not say anything about the time. But his presence acted upon them. The elderly clerk jerked his cue at his ball, making a bad stroke, and stood back from the table blinking his eyes and saying "Missed that time." The effervescent young clerk hurried to his ball, made a bad stroke and, looking along his cue, said "Ah!." The dogged young man shot his ball straight into the top pocket, a fact which the marker registered at once on the broken marking-board. The elderly clerk peered for a few critical seconds over the rim of his glasses, made another bad stroke and, at once proceeding to chalk his cue, said briefly and sharply to the effervescent young man "Come on now, White. Hurry up now."

The hopeless pretence of those three lives before him, their unredeemable servility, made the back of Stephen's eyes feel burning hot. He laid his hand on Cranly's shoulder and said impetuously:

"We must go at once. I can't stand it any longer."

If this is hell, and it is, we are out of it in *Ulysses*. There is no one in *Ulysses* whose life is a hopeless pretence or who presents an aspect of unredeemable servility. Indeed there is scarcely anyone who does not bear himself with panache, with gaiety, with scurrility or with pride. Bloom, though insulted, certainly feels no inferiority. And it is instructive to compare the mood of the portraiture in *Ulysses* with Joyce's treatment of the same people in *Dubliners*. It comes as something of a shock to realise that the Ignatius Gallagher whose scoop we hear about in the *Freeman's Journal* office is the vulgarian who appeared from London in "A Little Cloud." The Lenehan of *Ulysses* is a great deal less insufferable (and more cheerful) than the Lenehan who hangs about while Corley extracts money from the slavey in "Two Gallants." Martin Cunningham, Jack Power, McCoy, Tom Kernan are all treated harshly and satirically in the earlier book but with what almost amounts to gentleness in the later. But the strangest blossoming concerns someone who had appeared only in the *Portrait* and *Stephen Hero*. Simon Dedalus now at last attains those legendary dimensions that the *Portrait* had grudgingly hinted at. He is given size, humour, style and pathos; it is made quite clear that he retains his daughter's amused affection even though he refuses her the money he proceeds to spend in the Ormond; and his song in that place is given its full worth of beauty. We see him well away now on his downward path, in the glory of his scandalous autumn, and we leave him in full voice.

Joyce openly enjoys his material in *Ulysses* and grants it a worth which, for any but satirical purposes, is denied to it in *Dubliners*. I have no wish to suggest that the book is Pickwickian or that Simon Dedalus is a first cousin of the Cheeryble brothers; nor that the book presents a happier view of experience simply because it is funnier than *Dubliners* or the *Portrait*. But the humour of *Ulysses* can scarcely be other than sympathetic, for the simple reason that most of it is made by the characters themselves. It is their tongues and imaginations, the vitality of their language, the grotesquery of their wit which, as much as anything else, draw us back to the book and make it, whatever else it may be, one of the funniest in the language.

And there can hardly be any question but that Joyce enjoys them just as they enjoy themselves. The Citizen is well aware that he is giving a performance, albeit straightfaced, and he is certainly enjoying himself. In *Dubliners* the comedy is of a kind that gives Joyce and the reader bitter and mordant amusement — the asinine conversation about the doctrine of infallibility in the story, "Grace," for example — but which the characters themselves can hardly be said to share. *Dubliners* may be comic; it is anything but humorous. If the man who wrote *Dubliners* has looked upon the Gorgon's head, the man who wrote *Ulysses* has certainly not been turned to stone.

And it is often forgotten how much of *Ulysses* explores the lives of people other than simply Bloom and Stephen: when Joyce's narrowness of scope as a novelist is complained of, it should be remembered how skilfully and often how movingly he touched in the whole background of a minor character's life: Martin Cunningham's wife, J. J. O'Molloy's attempts to borrow money, the Dignam household, Mrs Breen's marriage, Father Conmee's complacency, Zoe's patter. Hundreds of such details, flitting across Bloom's mind or emerging from some conversation, evoke, seldom without compassion, the lives of a dozen others.

The people of *Ulysses* are not a cross-section of the bourgeois world: they are Joyce's father's world, that narrow world of drink and song, of debt and redemption, of vulgarity, wit and seedy gentility that his father inhabited. It is through singing that they are, for the most part, acquainted; and Joyce himself loved song. "The humour of *Ulysses* is his; its people are his friends. The book is his spittin' image," he said to Louis Gillet after his father's death. And, apart from their feeling for song, the people of *Ulysses* are by no means without their virtues: their ready understanding of misfortune, their willingness to help each other beat the rap, their refusal to judge each other by the standards of mere respectability are apparent. *Ulysses*, says Mr Harry Levin in his book, *James Joyce: A Critical Introduction*, is an epic "entirely lacking in the epic virtues of love, friendship and magnanimity," but he seems to be forgetting or ignoring something deeply important in the characters' attitude to each other:

> For a few days tell him, Father Cowley said anxiously.
>
> Ben Dollard halted and stared, his loud orifice open, a dangling button of his coat wagging brightbacked from its thread as he wiped away the heavy shraums that clogged his eyes to hear aright.
>
> What few days? he boomed. Hasn't your landlord distrained for rent?
>
> He has, Father Cowley said.
>
> Then our friend's writ is not worth the paper it's printed on, Ben

Dollard said. The landlord has the prior claim. I gave him all the
particulars. 29 Windsor Avenue. Love is the name?

That's right, Father Cowley said . . . But are you sure of that?

You can tell Barabbas from me, Ben Dollard said, that he can put
that writ where Jacko put the nuts.

He led Father Cowley boldly forward linked to his bulk.

Filberts I believe they were, Mr Dedalus said, as he dropped his
glasses on his coatfront, following them.

And along with their readiness to help, however desultory, idle or
unreliable it may be, they have a gaiety and courage in face of their own
usually well-deserved misfortunes, which is part of an attitude to life that
may at bottom be weak and self-deceiving, but which also augurs a
certain generosity and recklessness of spirit not markedly characteristic of
the bourgeois world. Apart from Stephen's student friends and the
librarians these people are all, or nearly all, failures of one kind or
another. Even the editor of the *Freeman* is, according to Ned Lambert, a
"sad case" of "incipient jigs." That Joyce should have thought an exposure
of their limitations and weaknesses worth the full weight of so much of the
book is inconceivable. Many judgments on the people of *Ulysses* seem to
proceed from a sort of upset liberalism or shocked Protestantism which
finds them and their humour an outrage, but these judgments are
certainly not shared by Joyce himself. Yeats was nearer the mark when he
agreed that *Ulysses* was "cruel" but added that it was "our Irish cruelty,
and also our kind of strength." A great deal of the humour of these people
is admittedly cruel, but then it is *Galgenhumor,* the product of misfortune, and those who find it too cruel would probably find most Irish
humour so, from Lever's to Samuel Beckett's, and might profitably even
take a closer look at some of the humour of Somerville and Ross.

The confusion of morality with mere respectability which is almost
endemic in the English mind is entirely absent in Joyce, and the vulgarity
of judgment by mere status is entirely absent from his book. The people of
Ulysses, though they belong, very roughly speaking, to a certain social
class, form an almost completely classless community. Though the realities
of money and survival are known to them, the irrelevancies of the social
structure are not important to Joyce. Nor does *Ulysses* contain any
lingering traces of a morality — sexual, social, monetary or hygienic —
unconsciously adopted from respectable society and silently assumed to be
held in common with the respectable reader. Joyce has shifted the process
of judgment of human behaviour altogether away from that governed
merely by social reflex. And this is one of the ways in which he is a
specifically modern writer, reflecting the real consciousness of our time;
for whatever else may be said about it, and with all its vulgarities, its
violences, its half-baked caricatures of serious creative purposes on its
head, ours is a time of liberation from merely societal values. That his
book is in large part governed by this spirit of tolerance and liberation is

all the more remarkable in that it is populated not by artists or anarchists or beats or professional rebels of one kind or another, but by some of the outwardly ordinary people of Dublin in 1904. It is as if the lid had been pulled off ordinary society to reveal the falsity of the lie that people are divided into the respectable and the criminal: to reveal in all its outrageousness the unbiddable eccentricity, weakness, humour and unreliability of men.

V

But if, as is suggested, the dominant humour, the spirit that pervades and informs the book, is sympathetic, it would seem an odd sort of book about Dublin for the young man we know as Stephen Dedalus to have written in after life. And we are surely meant to understand that Stephen did write the book we are reading. Indeed, as we shall see later, his forthcoming authorship is referred to in it. If the book is tolerant, if it is more than tolerant, and is, in some sort, a celebration of its material, it is admittedly hard to imagine Stephen Dedalus maturing to write it, for we know from the *Portrait* what Stephen Dedalus thought of the Dublin of his youth. But it is possible that we are meant to be surprised; that part of Joyce's point is that we should be surprised.

We can easily imagine Stephen going on to write books of other kinds: something rather Paterish perhaps, or like those passionate novels of dedication by D'Annunzio which the young Joyce admired even more than he admired Flaubert's. Something in the neo-Baudelairean fashion of the *fin de siècle* is not altogether unlikely or, to be more generous, something as original and as terrible as a new *Saison en enfer*. It would certainly have been difficult to predict that after he had described his revolt in the *Portrait*, and the world from which he revolted in *Dubliners*, and gone on to the justification and triumph of revolt and severance, it would take the form of a humorous, but by no means caustic celebration of the goings on in the world he had left: Miss Douce snapping her garter for the benefit of Blazes Boylan, the Citizen's monologue, the meditations of Father John Conmee, the singing in the Ormond, Gerty MacDowell exposing her drawers for the delectation of Leopold Bloom, Lenehan's story about "what star is that, Poldy?"—the whole conception of the saintly Leopold himself. In other words, a celebration of everything from which he had revolted. The creation of Leopold Bloom certainly seems an odd final triumph and climax after all that aesthetic flag-waving, more especially if the attitude of his creator to him and to his fellow Dubliners is neither ironic, vengeful nor despairing. And it will perhaps seem even odder if we compare the draft *Stephen Hero* with the unfinished *Portrait* of the same young man, for Stephen Dedalus is made certainly, and it seems deliberately, less likely than his prototype Stephen Hero to be the eventual author of *Ulysses*. The differences in this respect between the draft and the finished book are at first sight puzzling; but they are also instructive, and they cast light on *Ulysses*.

The *Portrait* is, of course, technically far more sophisticated than its predecessor. The two signs of technical mastery — the absence of overt description and formal explanation — have been achieved, while *Stephen Hero* is full of explanation, description and emphasis. The pacing of the finished book is admirable while the judgment of pace in the fragment is atrocious.

Yet, and this is the odd thing, the eye behind *Stephen Hero* often seems colder, more ironic and more sophisticated than the eye that drew the *Portrait*. Whereas the *Portrait* is a huge advance in sophistication of technique and the handling of material, the youthfulness and romanticism of its subject are heightened, rather than the reverse. All Stephen's crises and relationships are handled much more coolly, not to say cynically in *Stephen Hero*, than they are to be later on in the *Portrait*. His attitude to his parents is much more fully and humorously conveyed; his feelings about Emma are much more cynically and perceptively elaborated than in the later book, where they are reduced to a cipher of romantic love. And there are instructive contrasts in the handling of certain episodes. One concerns the girl whom Stephen encounters wading in the stream at Dollymount Strand just after he has decided to reject the claims of the Church and feels for the first time the sensuous, pagan beauty of the world. Though the account of the episode itself is missing from the fragment, there is an unmistakable reference to it. In the *Portrait* Stephen had seen a girl, her legs bared to the hips, her face "touched with the wonder of mortal beauty . . . and when she felt his presence and the worship of his eyes her eyes turned to him in quiet sufferance of his gaze, without shame or wantonness." At length, Stephen turned away from her and suddenly set off across the strand . . . "singing wildly to the sea, crying to greet the advent of the life that had cried to him." The reference to the episode in *Stephen Hero* strikes a different note. Here Stephen is described as going to exactly the same spot to stare at the children and the nurses (presumably the "gay lightclad figures of children and girls" of the *Portrait*: "He used to stand to stare at them sometimes until the ash of his cigarette fell onto his coat but, though he saw all that was intended, he met no other Lucy: and he usually returned to the Liffey side, somewhat amused at his dejection and thinking that if he had made his proposal to Lucy instead of to Emma he might have met with better luck." This is rather different from, "Her image had passed into his soul for ever and no word had broken the holy silence of his ecstasy" of the *Portrait*: at least he found out her name.

We are on a lower, more mundane plane of reality in *Stephen Hero* than we are to be later on in the finished book. In fact the *Portrait*, with its exalted Stephen, its impressionist background, its shadowy cast behind the brilliantly lit central figure and its successions of dramatic monologues, is written in a mood of dramatic zeal and enraptured fervour which seems odd in a man who was recasting a much more casual, homely and cynical work of his adolescence, and which is much further from the principles of detached classicism he had already formulated.

Another illuminating instance concerns Stephen's apostasy. The famous conversation with Cranly at the close of the *Portrait* is duplicated in *Stephen Hero*, but the tone of it is altogether different. Where in the *Portrait* the suggestion is not so much disbelief as Satanism, "I will not serve," in *Stephen Hero* Stephen states quite plainly that he no longer believes; and his attitude in general is more human, more forthright and lacking in the Jesuitical subtleties which add a perverted prestige to the attitude of Stephen Dedalus.

> . . . Look here, I cannot talk on this subject. I am not a scholar and I receive no pay as a minister of God. I want to live, do you understand . . . I don't care whether I am right or wrong. There is always that risk in human affairs, I suppose . . . the whole affair is too damn idiotic. Give it up. I am very young. When I have a beard to my middle I will study Hebrew and then write to you about it . . . You urge me to postpone life—till when? Life is now—this is life: if I postpone it I may never live.

For some reason then, between the abandonment of the draft shortly after he left Ireland and the beginning of serious work on the *Portrait* in 1909, Stephen became a much more sombre, single-minded and heroic figure with a faint suggestion of incense and sulphur about him, and his relations with the world became less haphazard, human, and comic. The world itself became a grimmer adversary while the world of beauty to which the soul aspired became more sensuous and more ecstatic. The reason, I suggest, becomes clearer if we put out of our heads the common, if curious, notion that Joyce wrote only about what happened to him up to the age of twenty-two. Suppose he intends to show us that it is surprising that the youthful Joyce matured to write *Ulysses*, that he is congratulating himself on the danger he has passed, and commenting on what has happened to him in the interval. In order to do this most clearly it would be necessary to exaggerate the youthful romanticism and aestheticism of Stephen; and this, between *Stephen Hero* and the *Portrait*, is what he did. It would be necessary for us also to assume that he had, while writing *A Portrait of the Artist as a Young Man*, some more or less definite glimmerings of the temper, form and dominant attitudes of the later book—that it would be, by contrast to the work of revolt, a work of acceptance. All the evidence shows that the idea of *Ulysses* was conceived in Joyce's mind at the same time as *A Portrait of the Artist* was begun; that it grew as the *Portrait* progressed and that he was ready to begin it immediately after the *Portrait* was finished: *that the two are, to all intents and purposes, one book.* So that whatever shifts of emphasis in the final version of the *Portrait* are to be accounted for, the reason most probably lies in the design of the two books as a whole. At a certain point in *Ulysses*, Buck Mulligan makes an interesting reference to the book itself.

> Buck Mulligan bent across the table gravely.
>
> They drove his wits astray, he said, by visions of hell. He will never capture the Attic note. The note of Swinburne, of all poets, the white death and the ruddy birth. That is his tragedy. He can never be a poet. The joy of creation . . .
>
> Eternal punishment, Haines said, nodding curtly. I see. I tackled him this morning on belief. There was something on his mind, I saw. It's rather interesting because Professor Pokorny of Vienna makes an interesting point out of that.
>
> Buck Mulligan's watchful eyes saw the waitress come. He helped her to unload the tray.
>
> He can find no trace of hell in ancient Irish myth, Haines said . . . The moral idea seems lacking, the sense of destiny, of retribution. Rather strange he should have just that fixed idea. Does he write anything for your movement?
>
> He sank two lumps of sugar deftly longwise through the whipped cream. Buck Mulligan slit a steaming scone in two and plastered butter over its smoking pith. He bit off a soft piece hungrily.
>
> Ten years, he said, chewing and laughing. He is going to write something in ten years.
>
> Seems a long way off, Haines said, thoughtfully lifting his spoon. Still, I shouldn't wonder if he did after all.

Ten years, almost to the month, after than conversation, *Ulysses* was begun in Trieste. They had not in fact driven his wits astray, by visions of hell or otherwise, but I think we are meant to realise that it had been a pretty near thing. Mulligan's "Attic note" here is far too close to Stephen Hero's "classic temper" to be mere coincidence. Joyce was writing among other things his own epic, and with him everything had, like justice, not only to be done, but to be seen to be done. The point in elevating Stephen Dedalus, in making him more limited and more satanic, is evidently to show the dangers that he ran and to make his ultimate triumph in achieving the "classic temper" more plain. Joyce is congratulating himself on having attained it, "a temper of security and satisfaction and patience" which acknowledges that "as long as this place in nature is given us it is right that art should do no violence to the gift." And he is pointing out the dangers Stephen Dedalus ran of succumbing to "the romantic temper . . . an insecure, unsatisfied, impatient temper which sees no fit abode here for its ideals." Mr Empson is right. The book has a happy ending. Stephen not only wrote it, but he wrote it in a particular way, looking back in a particular way from the standpoint of what then he was. It is significant that Stephen Hero's praise of the classic temper is omitted from the *Portrait*, as is his curious reference to the romantic, idealistic side of his nature as "the monster in him." And his clear-cut realisation that the failure to reconcile the world as it is, with the ideal world of the imagination, is, "however disguised or expressed, the most utter of pessimisms," is not allowed to jar on Stephen's self-communings in the completed book:

> The spectacle of the world which his intelligence presented to him with every sordid and deceptive detail set side by side with the spectacle of the world which the monster in him, now grown to a reasonably heroic stage, resented also had often filled him with such sudden despair as could be assuaged only by melancholy versing. He had all but decided to consider the two worlds as aliens one to another—however disguised or expressed, the most utter of pessimisms—when he encountered through the medium of hardly procured translations the spirit of Henrik Ibsen.

VI

It is striking how clearly Joyce, in his own career, sums up the *fin de siècle* and its immediate aftermath, the advent of modern literature. There is an aesthetic revolt. A brave, proud, Satanic but "languid" young man scorns the world as it is and rejects its paths in favour of his own right to follow and create an ideal beauty. The *fin de siècle* artist turns his back on the meanness, squalor and ignobility of the world. Then suddenly in the aftermath we find modern art as never before concerned with that world and attempting to bring all that very squalor within its compass: within, that is to say, in some way or other, the compass of "beauty."

Stephen is right to revolt against and abandon the Dublin he knew, and the parental environment into which he had been born. While remaining personally within it he was unlikely to accomplish much. "When the soul of man is born in this country there are nets flung at it to hold it back from flight. You talk to me of nationality, language, religion. I shall try to fly by those nets." Physically and spiritually of course he did. *Ulysses* is in no sense a double apostasy. Its author is not finding sustenance or illumination in the spiritual values of its characters. But he is in their human value, and in their human reality. In the Proteus episode, while Stephen is communing with himself on the strand, contemplating a visit to his uncle, he reflects on his family. We hear, in this reflection, his real, "consubstantial father's voice" for the first time, commenting on his in-laws: "O weeping God, the things I married into. The drunken little costdrawer and his brother, the cornet player. Highly respectable gondoliers. And skeweyed Walter sirring his father, no less. Sir. Yes, sir. No, sir. Jesus wept: and no wonder by Christ." And Stephen imagines also his uncle's greeting:

> Sit down or by the law Harry I'll knock you down.
> Walter squints vainly for a chair.
> He has nothing to sit down on, sir.
> He has nowhere to put it, you mug. Bring in your Chippendale chair.
> Would you like a bite of something? . . . the rich of a rasher fried with a

herring? Sure? So much the better. We have nothing in the house but backache pills.

And he reflects: "Houses of decay, mine his and all. You told the Clongowes gentry you had an uncle a judge and an uncle a general in the army. Come out of them, Stephen. Beauty is not there." Yet, if the purpose of Stephen's revolt, and, in whatever sense, the purpose of the artist, was the creation or extraction of some form of beauty, and if *Ulysses* was the justification of that revolt and the fulfilment of that purpose, then beauty must lie there, even in those "houses of decay" which are its subject. If, to put it simply, the book was his father's "spitting image," it is in the contemplation of that image that beauty must lie.

Ulysses executes a complex movement of reconciliation and acceptance: towards the world of its author's father, towards the "sordid and deceptive" world of ordinary living; and, because the self, having abandoned the heroic lie, is now seen to be part of that world, towards the self as well. For Stephen and, ultimately, because art achieves the general through the particular instance, for us, they are one and the same. He had been tempted to reject the world of mundane, sordid and deceptive detail, as well as his father's houses of decay, in favour of an ideal beauty. That to reject the mundanities and sordidities of this world is also to reject a great deal of the self, every human being knows, in whom "the monster" who favours the ideal has not grown to dominatingly "heroic proportions." It was through the concept and the creation of Leopold Bloom that Joyce, with many characteristic ironies and subtleties, but also with an immense simplicity, achieved the multiple apotheosis he desired.

"There is," says Lenehan, "a touch of the artist about old Bloom. He's a cultured allroundman, Bloom is. . . . He's not one of your common or garden . . . you know . . . There's a touch of the artist about old Bloom."

There is indeed, for "As we . . . weave and unweave our bodies, Stephen said, from day to day, their molecules shuttled to and fro, so does the artist weave and unweave his image." And a few pages later we are reminded of another Jewish character in the same young man's assertion that Shakespeare "drew Shylock out of his own long pocket."

There are many parallels between Bloom and Stephen just as there are many resemblances between Bloom and the mature Joyce. Boylan stands in relation to Bloom as Mulligan does to Stephen: accenting his isolation, making a mockery of his attitudinisings, representing a worldly glitter and a sexual flamboyance which neither Bloom nor Stephen possesses: "Wit. You would give your five wits for youth's proud livery he pranks in. Lineaments of gratified desire."

To a large extent, though not nearly to the same extent as Stephen, Bloom rejects the values of the society within which he moves. Both are humiliated; both are excluded, partly by choice and partly by force. Both are infidels, though both are concerned with and coloured by the ancient faiths within which they were nurtured. Both of them have deep and complex feelings about the histories of their races and their ancestral religions; but, nevertheless, to both of them history is a nightmare from which one must struggle to awake. Both have reason to feel remorse about the dead.

But their contrasts in resemblance are no less interesting than the resemblances themselves. Whereas Stephen is almost overwhelmed by his remorse, Bloom recovers his balance comparatively easily. In the brothel Bloom finds the thought of his ancestral background a source of strength; Stephen finds the thought of his merely another source of remorse. Parallel to Stephen's dramatic defiance of convention and society runs Bloom's comic, often shaken, often degraded, seldom dignified, never wholly triumphant, but still stubborn, courageous and, in the main, successful attempt to achieve the same end: to be oneself. But Bloom has merely to remain himself, whereas Stephen has to become. Confronted like Stephen by mockery, assault, the temptations of the flesh, Messianic ambition and remorse, Bloom, unlike Stephen, has attained to a certain magnanimity.

In general, where we find a resemblance, in circumstance or personality, between the two, and when we see its end, we can say that the difference is that Bloom is more mature than Stephen and seems to body forth — with some irony of course and some caricature, but nonetheless fairly faithfully — the differences between Stephen and the mature Joyce.[2]

But Bloom had to be made inclusive not only of the circumstantial Joyce, but of the human nature that Joyce and all men shared. If the pretences to heroism were to be stripped away and *Ulysses* was to be the first great masterpiece of unheroic literature; if Bloom was to survive as the first great anti-hero, standing in for all unheroic men, including the self, if the "silent secrets" sitting in the dark palaces of all men's hearts which were "weary of their tyranny" were to be dethroned, the avatar had to be subjected to and his power of survival tested against the most open and the most cruel tests.[3]

This frequently ridiculous, often humiliated man is seen in every possible intimacy and exposed to every possible nuance of contempt. He is put to flight by physical threats; he is cuckolded; he masturbates before our eyes; most of the atavisms born of fear and shame by which we are accustomed to react to others and judge ourselves are flouted. Nor does Joyce spare him his humour. From the episode of John Henry Menton's hat to the silly questions about Gibraltar in the coffee stall, he is exposed to it. Even such ambiguous qualities as his wariness at fence sometimes desert him in favour of a boyish and ridiculous vanity for the truth. And the cruellest cut of all is reserved till last. Molly may or may not be Gea Tellus or the Great Earth Mother; she is certainly Bloom's wife. She knows him through and through and she spares him nothing. If she remembers his romantic insistence on Howth Head, she also remembers his peculiar request in Harold's Cross Road. Joyce's purpose in ending the book with Molly's monologue has been much debated; yet it seems fairly obvious that if his purpose was the total exposure of Bloom, and the exposure of him in the most candid light, no tribunal could equal in intimate knowledge and ultimate frankness the thoughts of his woman.

Yet the remarkable thing is that in some way Bloom survives all this, even Molly's inquisition, though shakily as usual. "Let them go and get a husband first that's fit to be looked at," Molly says of the Miss Kearneys; and she recognises that he is in some sense or other superior to his mockers: " . . . theyre a nice lot all of them well theyre not going to get my husband again into their clutches if I can help it making fun of him then behind his back I know well when he goes on with his idiotics because he has sense enough not to squander every penny piece he earns down their gullets and looks after his wife and family goodfornothings . . ."

Her final "yes" may or may not have the allegorical implications her admirers have read into it; it may or not be a "yes" to life; it is certainly a repetition of her original acceptance of Bloom.

Nor does the reader withhold his assent, as the long book draws to a close and we get to know Bloom through intimacies of body and soul to which no other character in literature had ever previously been subjected. Joyce set out to show man in a light he had never been seen in before; to expose him to a gaze more omnipresent and more exacting than any to which he had ever previously been exposed. He weighted the circumstances against his man; he put him in situations which normally arouse only our contempt; he exposed him to the jibes of the cruellest wits in Europe; he brought the elaborations of his own irony gleefully to bear upon him. Yet it is the measure of his success in his ultimate purpose that the man not only survives but survives triumphantly, as the first great hero of unheroic literature; that he arouses not only our compassion and sympathy, our affection and humorous understanding, but, before his long chapter of humiliations is over, our profoundest respect.

That Bloom's own qualities, often overlooked by criticism, and always derided by the other characters, had something to do with this miracle we must admit; though they are certainly not the whole story. He is at least averagely kind. He performs, for example, most of what are known in Catholic theology as "the corporal works of mercy" during the day: he visits the sick, comforts the afflicted, buries the dead, shelters the homeless, etc. Though no combatant, he can bring himself to assert vital truths in the teeth of the opposition.

> But it's no use, says he. Force, hatred, history, all that. That's not life for men and women, insult and hatred. And everybody knows that it's the very opposite of that that is really life.
> What? says Alf.
> Love, says Bloom. I mean the opposite of hatred.

And he pays for this, and for similar pronouncements, in more ways than one. It is typical of Joyce's method that it is the enunciation of this simple and terrible truth that brings down upon him Hynes's cruel and brilliant sneer about his own abilities as a lover — "I wonder did he ever put it out of sight" — just as it is his display of learning in Lenehan's story of coming home beside Molly in the sidecar which exposes him to the jibe, so amusing to the teller that he momentarily collapses with laughter, about "that's only a pinprick."

His own humour, his irony, his subtlety and his intelligence are, in general, easy to underestimate. His mind only works in clichés in the coffee stall scene when he is tired, and it does not seem to have been noticed that he is here making a mistaken attempt to impress Stephen as a sort of literary man and thinker. What he utters are the clichés of editorial journalism, particularly provincial journalism of a sort that is written in Ireland to this day, though it was probably more widespread everywhere in 1904. It is just the sort of language we might expect Bloom to use in order to impress Stephen intellectually at the beginning of their acquaintance. (The general unpopularity of this extremely funny and engaging section of the book with critics who are not particularly well acquainted with Ireland, may stem from their lack of recognition of the precise kind of language he is talking.) Before that, as Dr. S. L. Goldberg has pointed out (he is very good on Bloom's process of thought, suggesting that his stream of consciousness, far from being "jellyfish," is actually composed of illuminating and rewarding epiphanies), Bloom's quiet ability to think for himself, his equanimity without insensitivity, above all, perhaps, his combination of moral seriousness with a generally humorous, caustic, but tolerant cast of mind are remarkable enough. Joyce's purpose would not have been well-served either if Bloom had been merely the sort of stupid, acquiescent, bumbling mediocrity which earlier criticism often made him out to be. It was necessary that he should be deprived of certain dignities and exposed in certain lights, that he should be the opposite of Napoleonic and often the apotheosis of the foolish, but it would not have done, either, to make him out merely a dull cretin. In his kindness and his gropings after better things he is surely as human as in his *niaiseries*. Joyce had to be fair twice over.

Nor is he dull in any other sense. The fact that he is not a scurrilous wit like most of the others, that he is grave and quiet in demeanour and talks seriously when he believes the issues are serious, should not disguise the fact that his mind has a constant and perhaps predominantly humorous cast:

> All kinds of places are good for ads. That quack doctor for the clap used to be stuck up in all the greenhouses. Never see it now. Strictly confidential. Dr Hy Franks. Didn't cost him a red like Maginni the dancing master self advertisement. Got fellows to stick them up or stick them up himself for that matter on the q.t. running in to loosen a button. Fly by night. Just the place too. POST NO BILLS. POST 111 PILLS. Some chap with a dose burning him.

But it must be repeated that it is in no way primarily because of his intellectual or moral qualities that Bloom so arouses our interest and so commands our affection. (It should not, really, except to critics, be necessary to prove that he does the latter: no character in contemporary fiction has such a widely variegated personal following.) I mean my Ulysses to be a good man, said Joyce to Frank Budgen right enough; and we can see that he is, however strange the definition of goodness might seem by orthodox standards, but it is not this in the end. When we ask what it is, we are forced ultimately I think to recognise that here is the familiar: the worn, familiar, comical, shabby, eroded but not collapsed face of humanity. In his vulnerability, his weakness, his secrecies, his continuous but uncertain ability to remain upright, his clinging to as few props, his constantly threatened dignity, Bloom commands that affection in the midst of comedy which we give to our own image, stained and worn as it is. Joyce has given him an almost infinite complexity as well; because the book is technically, for all its faults, a *tour de force*, we learn about Bloom as we learn about nobody else in fiction while we go along. And his creator has also breathed life into him and surrounded him, on this one day, with a world masterfully rich in the comic and in living detail. But his ultimate triumph was to extract this ordinary poetry of humanity from him; and it is a strange one, for his creator was Stephen Dedalus, that well-known aesthete.

VII

Joyce's movement, as he was subsequently to demonstrate at length, was circular. By "the commodious vicus of recirculation" one came back to where one started, to the father and the race. He had, in particular (as, it is alleged, has all humanity in general) a fallen father, "foosterfather." The fall began in the dark wet winter of Parnell's downfall and death, when John Joyce began that long downward progress in which the instincts of a dandy and a gentleman, a Corkman and a coaster, a whiskey-drinking "praiser of his own past" were to consort oddly with, and to succeed only in accelerating, that decline into "squalor and insincerity" of which Stephen Hero speaks. The two falls, Parnell's and his Parnellite father's, were for ever after symbolically one in Joyce's mind. He was to harmonise them humorously and to entwine them with all other falls and fathers in *Finnegans Wake*. In *Ulysses* he has achieved out of the resentments and limitations of adolescence, even out of the justified attitudes of revolt and the judgments he was entitled to make about his spiritual and carnal inheritance, an attitude of compassion, tolerance and delight, which returns to that inheritance what it gave him: pride, humour, a love of song, a sense of style and a knowledge of the obverse of these coins, the degradations, the inescapable Irishnesses of life. The contrast between Stanislaus's attitude to his father, as expressed in *My Brother's Keeper*, and

Joyce's is almost a parable of the difference between the viewpoint of the good man and the artist. The one is a judgment, harsh, clear and unforgiving. The other is an acceptance.

Yet, important though this movement was for Joyce — this achievement, like Shakespeare (according to Stephen), of the spiritual paternity of his own father — it is not the whole story. Like "the greyedauburn Shakespeare," walking in Fetter Lane Joyce was "weaving and unweaving his own image" and seeing himself as he then was "by reflection from that which then I shall be"; and he was also attempting to incorporate and to redeem aspects of our common humanity which had never been incorporated victoriously into literature before. It is here that Leopold Bloom enters, contrasted in his humility yet his continuing, if comic, integrity, with Stephen Dedalus; the self-image transmuted into an Irish Jew with ancestry somewhere in central Europe, with "a touch of the artist" and yet without the artist's redemption from the conditions of ordinary living. For Bloom does represent ordinary living, though isolated and set apart. He is pragmatic, yet a visionary; mean and careful, yet often in trouble out of generosity or fineness of spirit; betrayed and betraying, yet loyal after his fashion in the primary instances of love; ridiculous, yet dignified; spat upon, yet victorious; sensitive yet complacent, with the complacency which turns out in the end to be one of humanity's great defences, a clinging to the moment and the necessities of the moment, a form of continuing courage. All this adds up to the inescapable Jewishness of life. Bloom is not heroic, in the old sense. Nor is he abysmal, in the old sense, as any character in literature with certain of his characteristics would have had to be before him. In him, for the first time, our unpromising, unpoetic, unheroic image is found to have surprising possibilities for pride and for poetry.

The greatness of *Ulysses* is partly technical.[4] A new prose form has been achieved, free from the distortions of dramatic narrative, and not dependent for its intensity on dramatic confrontations and resolutions. Yet it has intensity: a matter of language, of density of life, of immediacy of texture, in a word, of poetry. That the texture is yet "ordinary" proves that intensity, poetry, resides here too, its extraction being a matter of language and of the pitch of interest with which the ordinary is contemplated and then evoked.

In this sense it can hardly be otherwise than "on the side of life," ordinary, continuing life, as against dogmatisms of one kind or another. Such poetry cannot avoid possessing, in Coleridge's word, geniality; and if this were all that were to be said it would still be enough. Poetry is enough. The book does not have to be "about" anything, except, of course, Leopold Bloom.

Yet over such a large area, an uncoloured contemplation and evocation of life is tantamount to impossible. There remains the question of the author's vision. One cannot prove syllogistically that the temper of the book is what Joyce called "the classic temper," that it is an act of acceptance and an act of *pietas*. One can only appeal to the reader's response to its abounding humour, its creative zest, its ability to anneal the spirit (all of which are inseparably bound up with its poetry and its "geniality"); and one can only try, as I have tried, to show that Joyce meant it to be received in this way and that, in part, he wrote a saga about a young man who achieved this classic temper. It is not necessary to seek profundities of meaning in *Ulysses*. Criticism has performed no service for Joyce by the suggestion that we must unravel the book before we can understand it; and that patience, skill and drudgery in unravelment are the primary qualities required of its ideal reader. They are not the sort of qualities commonly found in those most remarkable for receptivity and generosity of response to art or anything else. The suggestion that they are essential is part of the academic claim to indispensability – let alone usefulness – which has followed in our time as a result of the vesting of academic interests in literature. Yet it is also the duty of the critic to seek to interpret a book in the spirit in which it is written. Whether the facts that *Ulysses* is partly a strange act of *pietas* on Joyce's part; that Bloom, as well as being plain Leopold Bloom of Eccles Street, is a mediator between the artist and mankind; or that the book is a work of abounding comedy, full of "profane joy," make it greater than if it were a work of hatred and disgust, is a question difficult to answer. We can only fruitfully say that all great works of art are full of intensity, and that there is not therefore so much difference between opposing visions as criticism may be tempted to suggest.

It is certain, however, that if we can describe *Ulysses* in this way we claim it to be more important than it would be if the whole enormous structure had been raised in support of some theory about metempsychosis, some illumination of comparative myth, or some conviction about the decline of Western man. It is in the redemption of our common and ordinary humanity from its own "deceits and sordities," and the totality as well as the poetic intensity of its statement of the conditions of ordinary living, that its originality and its importance for us lies. More than any other book *Ulysses* marks the end of heroic literature, and with the advent of Bloom man takes on a new poetic interest for his complex mundanity rather than as an actor of greater or lesser strength and tragic resonance. The resonance is there, and the tragedy as well as the triumph, but they are otherwise revealed. In no previous work, to take but one of his characteristics, had a "good" man been shown who was not altogether "normal" sexually.

We are rightly suspicious of the notion of progress, but there is a sense in which there is progress in the arts. We cover more ground, we say what has not been said; partial and limited like the visions of other artists of other eras though ours may be, we extend both the ordinary recorded area of human experience and the reclaimed area of poetic compassion; and we in our time have been honest. *Ulysses* has faults, of eccentricity, of mere display, of mechanical thoroughness. Yet in the way it encompasses ordinary living and the way it gives to much that had been denied it the intensity and texture of poetry, *Ulysses* is a landmark, perhaps the most important single event in the great break-through that has been achieved in this century.

Notes

1. Joyce seems to think it was a Handicap; a fact which casts a dubious light on his encyclopaedism. It is, of course, a weight-for-age race.

2. Bloom is of course important also, as an instrument of Joyce's return to his father's world, though it is also true that he emphasises his differences from it. He, who "knows your old fellow" is also "middler the Holy Ghost," the third person of the blessed Trinity, mediator between the son and his consubstantial father's world. This theme is made so plain and is so constantly returned to that to suggest it as a central motif in the book is not to indulge in any arcane exegesis. It is not necessary for any of the three characters to become other than they are, in order that we may grasp Bloom's middle position between Dublin and Trieste, between the father and his associates in Ireland and the artist in the Austro-Hungarian empire — where, incidentally, old Virag, Bloom's father, was born. Joyce came to delight in the existence and the creative possibilities of his father's world, but he did not desire to be part of it. Hence his hero is Bloom, the common man who is also the outsider, the Dubliner who is also a stranger.

3. There is a sense in which Bloom stands in for all humanity: like Kafka's K, Chaplin's tramp or Beckett's old man. Endlessly interesting, unmistakably real though he is in the personal detail which is piled up, he is yet sufficiently outside his immediate environment to take on a certain universality. His position is ambiguous in several respects. Though no anarchist, he is at least a failure. He stands far enough outside the society to present a contrast and suggest, however comical it may be, a conflict: in this he again resembles K, anxious to co-operate but denied the opportunity, or Chaplin's tramp, gazing wistfully at the lighted ballroom, or Beckett's old men who are anonymously fed and maintained in their solitude. That Bloom should be Odysseus, Sinbad the sailor, the wandering Jew and whatnot, may help to confer this universality upon him. It is done in more important ways by a series of carefully arranged ironies and ambiguities in his personal position: orphaned son and bereaved father, worldly wise and yet a failure, Irish and non-Irish, husband yet cuckold, faithful and faithless.

4. *Ulysses* and *The Waste Land*, published so near together in time, began in English that attempt to find new forms to accommodate more images in a new relationship, which remains characteristic of much of the most interesting work of this century, though not always of the most praised.

Unposted Letter:
Joyce's Leopold Bloom

John Z. Bennett*

In the Nausicaa episode of *Ulysses*, as Leopold Bloom rests upon his rock, already weary of his "very fatiguing day," he takes up a bit of stick and begins to write in the sand yet another of the book's innumerable "riddling sentences": "I AM A . . . ." But there is no more room, and the all-important "other word" is never added (p. 375).[1]

Bloom's critics of forty years, however, have supplied it indefatigably, and he has been made manifest in an astonishing variety of persons and attributes. He is Odysseus, or Christ (or a parody of Christ, or an unrealized Christ), or he is Adam, or the Flesh, or the Lion-as-Vegetable, or the Common Man in Isolation, or Everyman Afoot, and so on through transmutations as imaginative as those he suffers in Nighttown, until he becomes at last, inevitably, a mere Robot.

Everyone understands that Joyce's artistic method — that of "manipulating what at first sight seems to be mere physical detail into dramatic symbolism"[2] — requires, invites, even dares such archetypal readings. But it may well be wondered whether, in such a plethora of solutions, it is not gratuitous to worry the puzzle further. Bloom himself rejects the effort and rubs away his letter to Gerty MacDowell: "Hopeless thing, sand. Nothing grows in it. All fades" (p. 375). Furthermore, as Mr. R. M. Adams has remarked, there is a very real danger of vitiating criticism by "treating *Ulysses* as an enigma, not a novel."[3]

If the problem could be left at that, all would be well, no doubt. But the work *is* an enigma: even its most confident explicators have a curiously predictable tendency to begin in certitude and order only to end in frantic and fragmented pursuits of details through its interminable mazes. After all, merely as far as Bloom himself is concerned, who *was* Phil Gilligan? And what was the quarrel about meadowland evaluations at Cuffes? And if at long last we have discovered where Moses was when the lights went out, still who is M'Intosh, that "once prosperous cit" who "loves a lady that is dead" (pp. 420, 437)? And *do* fish ever get seasick (p. 372)?

The number of such questions may eventually be raised to Bloom's own version of infinity, that is, to the 9th power of the 9th power of 9; but what is worse, such is Joyce's cunning, we cannot tell whether any problem is major or minor until all have been made relevant in the ultimate harmony of the book. We cannot, with Bloom, rub the sentence out.

The purpose of this study, therefore, is to confront yet once again the riddle of Leopold Bloom, generally as it is relevant to his "personal" role in the novel, and specifically as it is posed by his relationship to Molly, or, as

*From the *Bucknell Review* 14, No. 1 (1966):1–12. Reprinted by permission of the *Bucknell Review*.

it is stated in the inimitable style of Martha Clifford, whoever she is: "Are you not happy in your home you poor little naughty boy?" (p. 76).

It would seem that nothing could be more obvious than the answer to this question: dishonored, betrayed, a servant to the woman who treats him with scorn or indifference, Bloom is a very unhappy man in his home. His marriage is on the rocks, and indeed it has been for many years. What is not so apparent, however, especially in the symbolistic readings of Bloom, is why the marriage has foundered. On the contrary, such readings tend to obscure Bloom's identity as a "husband" in the novel, and particularly to obviate the literal and very real pain he suffers in being Poldy the Cuckold. Yet it is quite clear, for instance, that from the moment Bloom first sees Boylan's "bold hand" until he escapes into sleep, if indeed he does escape, the agony of his wife's latest infidelity is never dulled.

And to say that Bloom transcends these betrayals in the "equanimity" of knowing that adultery is no worse than a host of other sins creates more difficulties than it resolves. It is only in the dehumanized technic of Ithaca that such a judgment is possible; but then human problems also become entirely meaningless when they are so reduced to weights and measures. And furthermore, Bloom's equanimity looks very much like that same "inertia" which keeps him from deserting the house entirely (p. 713).[4]

In all justice, it may be argued, as many critics do, that the marriage of Leopold and Molly is not yet an absolute loss. There is still a kind of fondness between them. For Leopold, Molly in violet petticoats is still worth the horrendous and humiliating effort to get a modicum of sober sense out of Myles Crawford. And from Molly's point of view, it is pleasant to hear Poldy stumbling up the stairs with her breakfast; and, regarding his explanations of esoteric matters, if his efforts "leave us as wise as we were" (p. 729), "still he knows a lot of mixed up things" (p. 728).

But these values are ambiguous, ironically measuring, as well, Bloom's weakness and Molly's tyranny. There is little rapport, not to say faith between them. The meek Leopold is an incorrigible Don Juan, in thought if not always in deed: among the conquests in the bedroom of his brain are the lady at the Grosvenor, the girl in Eustace Street settling her garters, another running up the stairs at Greene's, as well as Lotty Clarke, Mrs. Mirian Dandrade, Bridie Kelley, Josie Powell "that was," Gerty MacDowell, Mary Driscoll, Martha Clifford, and forty-four other applicants for the job of assisting a gentleman in the literary business of exchanging obscene letters.

And Molly it would seem (aside fom her novels and her erotic reveries embracing thoughts of priests, Negroes, drunken sailors, violent assault by unknown men, and so on) has committed adultery with virtually every man Leopold knows and with a goodly number whom neither he nor Molly can even name.

Mr. Adams has questioned whether we are to take this estimate of

Molly's lovers seriously. While granting the nymphomaniac tone of Molly's thoughts, he demonstrates that before Boylan it is quite possible she had no adulterous relations with any of the "suitors," save possibly Bartell D'Arcy (p. 730).[5]

This opinion seems to be borne out by Bloom's own reactions to Boylan. It is true, for instance, that he thinks of various men in erotic relation to Molly — as Val Dillon, Lenehan, Father Farley, the gentleman with the opera glasses in the Gaiety Theatre, and others — but the irritation in these thoughts seems mild compared with his agony concerning Boylan's advent.

Furthermore, as opposed to the other affairs, the liaison with Boylan has a clear and definite history. Molly, apparently unknown to Leopold, has first seen Boylan in the D.B.C., where the communication of the "bold eye" together with a bit of foot-eroticism was first effected (p. 729). But to Bloom's knowledge, and correctly, their first formal introduction occurred when "The full moon was the night we were Sunday fortnight . . . Walking down by the Tolka" (p. 165), that is, 29 May 1904,[6] the night May's band played Ponchielli's "Dance of the Hours" (pp. 69, 165, 368, 518, 725).

It was during the walk by the Tolka River that Boylan signalled the immemorial question upon Molly's hand and received her inevitable response. The date is very significant, for, as will be substantiated more fully, it was on this night of 29 May 1904, that Molly and Bloom last had sexual relations (p. 725).[7]

Yet the following morning Molly asks the fateful question about Boylan, and Bloom is overwhelmed: "No use humming then" (p. 69). The judgment implicit in Molly's behavior is obvious: Bloom is an inadequate lover. And the choice of the "usurper" is being announced. This fact is perfectly clear to Leopold, so much so that within the succeeding weeks he will send Milly away to Mullingar, a move which Molly understands for what it really means, and indeed actually approves of (p. 751).

The ascendancy of Boylan then becomes a constant and pervasive agony in Bloom's consciousness.[8] But whether Blazes is the literal-first or imaginative-latest in the series of Molly's infidelities, the marital betrayal, fact or fiction, is real to Leopold. And indeed perhaps its most sinister aspect is that it calls forth in him a profound pessimism, a sense of the "useless," the hopeless, a feeling of the unalterable futility of effort. Feelings of despair are dominant in Bloom's notions of Fate, Kismet, the circular stream of life: "Think you're escaping and run into yourself" (p. 370), in the recurring thought that "all is lost," even becoming objectified in the watch that stops, "just when he and she" (p. 370).

Bloom's end is in its origins: love began as musical chairs and charades; or, as Molly says, "staring at one another for about 10 minutes as if we met somewhere" (p. 756). It ends in jangling quoits, met him pikehoses, and a literal Rip Van Winkle-Bloom. "Me," says Bloom, remembering with fervor and eloquence the great moment of the Howth Hill picnic, "and me now" (p. 173). The same memory leads to Molly's much considered "Yes"; but for Leopold it is only "Stuck, the flies buzzed" (p. 174).

Admittedly, this view of the Blooms' marital situation and of the primal importance of Molly's infidelity makes an assumption regarding Leopold's viability as a lover which has not been generally urged. Mr. Adams, for example, on the basis of the evidence (pp. 720–21) in *Ulysses*, agrees with the opinion that for ten years Molly "has been deprived of all sexual contact with her husband."[9] If this is so, then of course there is justification for Molly's treatment of Leopold.

The passage in question asserts of Leopold and Molly: "complete carnal intercourse, with ejaculation of semen within the natural female organ, having last taken place . . . 27 November 1893 . . . there remained a period of 10 years, 5 months and 18 days during which carnal intercourse had been incomplete, without ejaculation of semen within the natural female organ."[10] The important term in this commentary is *incomplete*, a term which does not imply continence, but on the contrary suggests rather some form of sexual congress brought to "unnatural" termination, or, in other words, a form of contraception, and specifically that form known as *coitus interruptus*.

Obviously such an interpretation assumes that Bloom is sexually potent, a power also not always granted him by his less generous critics, and not without reason. Bella-Bello Cohen, for instance, accuses him in these terms: "What else are you good for, an impotent thing like you?" (p. 528).

But surely Bloom's response to Gerty MacDowell on Sandymount cancels this objection. And certainly Molly's evidence gives no support to the libel; for it is the speculation regarding *what* woman Leopold has been with, not whether he has been with one, that sets her entire monologue in motion: "Yes because he never did a thing like that before as ask to get his breakfast in bed with a couple of eggs . . . yes he came somewhere Im sure by his appetite anyway love its not or hed be off his feed thinking of her so either it was one of those night women . . . or else if its not that its some little bitch or other he got in with somewhere or picked up on the sly" (pp. 723–24).

Facile as Molly is at proving both sides of an argument with the same bit of evidence, the assumption of Bloom's potency is not controverted by her ambiguous response to his evident "appetite." Furthermore, in the process of "syllogizing" she reveals a significant fact: "Yes because he couldnt possibly do without it that long so he must do it somewhere and the last time he came on my bottom *when was it the night Boylan gave my hand a great squeeze going along by the Tolka* (p. 725, italics mine). This date, as has been shown, is 29 May 1904, not 1894. It would seem evident, then, that the Blooms have indeed had sexual congress through the decade since 1894, but relations carried on under some form of contraception, presumably *coitus interruptus*.

This hypothesis might explain in part why Molly is so dissatisfied with Bloom as a lover. Whether correct or not, sexologists have long asserted that *coitus interruptus* is a technique of dubious value. Dorothy D. Bromley, for instance, reports that "Urologists are particularly severe in their condemnation of *coitus interruptus* as the cause of various functional and nervous disorders in men. . . . But there is no doubt that the practice often causes nervous disturbances in women."[11]

Molly, it will be recalled, will not sleep with the lights out (p. 748), and as for Bloom's technique as a lover "he ought to give it up now at this age of his life simply ruination for any woman and no satisfaction in it pretending to like it till he comes and then finish it off myself anyway" (p. 725). And "Im not an old shrivelled hag before my time living with him so cold never embracing me . . . a woman wants to be embraced 20 times a day" (p. 756); "he wont let you enjoy anything naturally" (p. 756); and, finally, "its all his own fault if Im an adulteress" (p. 765).

Furthermore, Bloom carries in his pocketbook a "French letter" (pp. 364, 757), the term being an old euphemism for the contraceptive sheath, or, as it is called elsewhere in *Ulysses*, the "preservative." Bloom has a supply of these sheaths in the locked drawer of his desk—a drawer which Molly has thoroughly investigated, of course. They were ordered, it appears, from the same London establishment from which Bloom secured the obscene postcards (p. 706), an association which suggests "perversion," and indeed Bloom himself says of the French letter, "cause of half the trouble" (p. 364). Needless to say, however, any form of contraception in Catholic Dublin would be considered immoral, and this is especially true of *coitus interruptus*, for it is also a true form of onanism.[12]

Lastly, it is evident that Molly herself employs yet another contraceptive technique: "So much the better in case any of it wasnt washed out properly" (p. 727).

Unpleasant as this sort of investigation certainly is, it nonetheless re-orders any view of Bloom's "sin against fertility," as W. Y. Tindall puts it,[13] and makes Bloom's motivations even more puzzling. If the nature of the "sin" is clear, then the more urgent question is why, in the face of such devastating consequences, and from no real physical necessity, does he continue to commit it?

In an answer to this question it may be of value to attempt a survey of the Blooms' courtship and marriage.

Their romance, which had begun at Dillon's in musical chairs and vocal solos, was continued at Luke Doyle's in charades, developed in Poldy's love poetry and erotic letters (p. 732), took the form of Bloom's perversity concerning drawers—but then bloomers were *named* after Mr.

Bloom (p. 746) — and was physically consummated on Howth Hill, presumably, on the 8th of September, 1888, Molly's 18th birthday (pp. 720–21).

They were married a month later on the 8th of October, 1888. Millicent, the daughter, was born on the 15th of June, 1889, though there is no evidence that the augury of Milly in 1888 either hastened the marriage or was a source of trouble between Leopold and Molly. On the contrary, Milly was, from Padney Socks to Silly-Milly, a great joy to Bloom. It is the vision of Milly which frees his mind from the wasteland of Agendath (p. 61), and perhaps from the horrific advent of the beasts, the murderers of the sun, in the lying-in hospital (p. 407). And Molly, too, though characteristically changeable in her attitude, admits that Milly is like herself and rightly belongs in the general female conspiracy against Bloom: when Milly breaks the little statue of Narcissus, Molly has it repaired without telling Leopold (p. 751).

Even so, it is evident in Milly's reports of Bannon and the picnic they are to take on Monday that the pattern of loss is about to be repeated, and with regret Bloom understands that Milly too is slipping away from him.[14]

At this point it would be assuring if the various removals of the Blooms through the years of their marriage could be determined accurately. However, as Mr. Adams has shown, it is impossible to untangle the Blooms' affairs.[15] It is certain that in the early days of their marriage they continued on friendly terms with old acquaintances — the Dillons, Mastianskys, Moisels, and Citrons. "Pleasant old times," Bloom reflects (p. 60). And Molly recalls with undiminished pleasure the irritation she was able to give Josie Powell by becoming Mrs. Bloom (pp. 728–29).

Through these years, 1888 to 1894, Bloom was working for Wisdom Hely, "a traveller for blotting paper," as Ned Lambert contemptuously puts it (p. 105). But if Bloom was not particularly successful in impressing Hely with his advertising schemes, he certainly was "happy in his home" during this period.

> Happy. Happier then. Snug little room that was with the red wallpaper, Dockrell's one and ninepence a dozen. Milly's tubbing night. American soap I bought: elderflower. Cosy smell of her bathwater. Funny she looked soaped all over. Shapely too. Now photography.
> (p. 153)

But in 1894 Bloom lost the job at Hely's, and he and Molly moved, evidently to Holles Street, where they were "on the rocks" and Bloom was reduced to peddling Molly's hair (p. 363), and she herself to selling clothes and playing the piano in the Coffee Palace (p. 378).

Mr. Adams has pointed out that Bloom's memory of the decade since 1894 is very hazy, notably lacking in detail, while his recollections of the years through 1894 are remarkably clear and rich in events.[16] Bloom, like anyone else, seeks to avoid the remembrance of events that were painful or humiliating (his characteristic formula is to change the subject by fertile association with something harmless); and, therefore, his fuzziness or downright suppression of memory concerning the decade since 1894 suggests that the "trauma" in his marriage occurred in that year. And indeed a calamity did befall the Blooms in the winter of 1893–94, namely, the death of their newborn son, Rudy.

All was well until then, and Bloom was a proud and solicitous expectant father. "Got big then. Had to refuse the Greystones concert. My son inside her" (p. 88). He remembers going down to the pantry at night to get Malaga raisins for Molly, "before Rudy was born" (p. 149). And one of the Bloom-jokes enjoyed by the drunken heroes at Kiernan's is told by Ned Lambert (in the dyed suit): "you should have seen Bloom before that son of his that died was born. I met him one day in the south city markets buying a tin of Neave's food six weeks before the wife was delivered" (p. 332).

The Blooms last had what would be called "normal," not to say "moral" marital relations on 27 November 1893. Rudy was born a month later on 29 December 1893, and died eleven days following, on 9 January 1894 (p. 720). It is significant, surely, that this is the date from which has been calculated the ten-year period of the so-called sexual denial of Molly.

The death of Rudy was a catastrophe of the first order for Leopold and Molly. Bloom did not cease, in all the intervening years, to mourn the lost son. Rudy is always just at the fringes of his consciousness.

Mrs. Thornton, he remembers, "knew from the first poor little Rudy wouldn't live. Well, God is good, sir. She knew at once. He would be eleven now if he had lived" (p. 66). And hearing Simon Dedalus' tirade against Mulligan, Bloom thinks, "Full of his son. He is right. Something to hand on. If little Rudy had lived. See him grow up. Hear his voice in the house. Walking beside Molly in an Eton suit" (p. 88). Later, in the Hades episode, he thinks, "a dwarf's face mauve and wrinkled like little Rudy's was. Dwarf's body, weak as putty, in a whitelined deal box" (p. 94). In the cemetery he calls to mind the location of his own burial plot, where his mother lies, and little Rudy (p. 109). And Ben Dollard's rendition of "The Croppy Boy" forces the comparison: "I too, last my race. Milly young student. Well, my fault perhaps. No son. Rudy" (p. 280).

As Sir Leopold, he grieves for the "only manchild which on his eleventh day on live had died," and recalls that "the good lady Marion . . . was wondrous stricken of heart for that evil hap and for his burial did him on a fair corselet of lamb's wool . . . lest he might perish utterly and lie akeled" (p. 384). Molly remembers this as well: "I suppose I oughtnt to have buried him in that little woolly jacket I knitted crying as I was" (p. 763).

Nonetheless, back of this grief there is a curious ambiguity in Bloom's feelings, a sense not only of loss but also of personal failure as a man, a sense even of guilt. "Our. Little. Beggar. Baby. Meant nothing. Mistake of nature. If it's healthy it's from the mother. If not the man" (p. 94).[17]

At the moment, a funeral coach bearing the body of a child has just passed, and, therefore, it is clear that Bloom is thinking generally about infant mortality — a question he chooses to discuss later at the lying-in hospital. But the thought turns strangely into a kind of dreadful folk-logic, which, whether he believes it or not, is a superstition he has had to live with: if the child is sickly, or if the child dies, the failure is in the nature of the father. Molly appears to agree with this logic: "that have a fine son like that theyre not satisfied and I none *was he not able to make one it wasn't my fault*" (p. 763, italics mine).

The phrases of Bloom — "dwarf's mauve face," "mistake of nature," "Mrs. Thornton knew at once," "poor little Rudy," — when paralleled by Molly's "whats the use of going into mourning for what was neither one thing nor another" (p. 759), suggests that Rudy was not only sickly, but perhaps malformed, and therefore that Bloom, in the context of the superstition, has real reason not only for grief but also for guilt and for feeling that a judgment has been passed on his manhood.

Perhaps now the "logic" of Bloom's trauma can be formulated: having failed so horrifically in procreation, Bloom fears the risk of another child, with all its attendant possibilities of death; but this rejection of "something to hope for, not like the past you can't have back" (p. 101) paralyzes him as a viable and virile paterfamilias.

This too is the meaning of the accusation which is made against him in the voice of Carlyle in Oxen of the Sun. Indeed the principal subject of the episode is that of human fertility; and the major human crime in this regard is "Copulation without population!" (p. 416). Therefore, the praise of Theodore Purefoy is the curse of Leopold. "In her lay a Godframed Godgiven preformed possibility which thou has fructified with thy modicum of man's work" (p. 416). For all its ludicrous bombast and echo of a drunken Stephen, the judgment has the ring of truth; and as for Bloom, "Has he not nearer home a seedfield that lies fallow for the want of a ploughshare?" — this hypocrite who is "his own and his only enjoyer" (p. 402)? And he must hear Stephen hysterically yet quite ironically assert that the thunder is the voice of the God Bringforth, passing damnation on all who have refused to realize the godpossible by the use of the Preservative Killchild (p. 389). Later, in Circe, Bloom will be accused by Purefoy: "He employs a mechanical device to frustrate the sacred ends of nature" (p. 482). And it should be noted that the black mass in honor of "Dog" is performed by the spoiled priests under the preservative umbrella (p. 583).

Allowing for extravagance and for the hallucinatory character of these scenes, the personal evidence of Leopold and Molly nonetheless confirms their essential truth and makes it clear that the death of Rudy was indeed the crisis in their lives which was not then and has not yet been resolved. "Twenty-eight I was," says Bloom. "She was twenty-three when we left Lombard street west something changed. *Could never like it again after Rudy*" (p. 165, italics mine). And in sad echo, Molly recalls: "I knew well Id never have another our 1st death too it was *we were never the same since*" (p. 763, italics mine).

Indeed they were not. The move from Lombard Street led merely to the inevitable pattern of successive removals and multitudinous jobs which has brought them to Eccles Street and an "Unfurnished apartment to let."

If, as it appears, Bloom's reaction to the death of his son has left him caught in a net of grief and guilt, in fact, one with his father, with Mrs. Sinico, with the "once prosperous cit," even with Athos, the dog, in "the love that kills" (p. 113), it remains to be considered whether any salvation has been effected by his odyssey. And this question most obviously centers on the vision of Rudy which occurs at the conclusion of Circe.

Mr. Stuart Gilbert has maintained that the vision is "a tranquil close after the bestiality," and this calm is the signal that the "wave-worn mariner who, riding out a tempest mad with magic, has made at last the haven where he would be."[18] Whether this means that Bloom has "worked through" his own psychic difficulties and has identified "would be" with what yet "could be" is uncertain. It is true that at one point during the day he has thought of the possibility of having another child: "Too late now. Or if not? If not? If still?" (p. 280). And even Molly considers it, though, it must be admitted, with undisguised scorn: "yes thatd be awfully jolly" (p. 727).

But it is more likely that Mr. Gilbert, like Mr. Tindall and all subsequent critics who have emphasized the "paternity motif" in *Ulysses*, intends to say that the mystical estate of fatherhood is about to be conferred on Bloom in the person of Stephen Dedalus and that the vision of Rudy is not more than its sign and seal.

And, indeed, the correspondences are remarkable, in that the vision of Rudy seems to be a complex of elements from Stephen's own experience as well as from Leopold's. For instance, it is Stephen who has thought of himself as a "changeling," as Rudy is described: thinking of Dublin in Viking times, Stephen imagines the "horde of jerkined dwarfs . . . I moved among them on the frozen Liffey, that I, a changeling, among the spluttering resin fires" (p. 46). Bloom and Molly both recall seeing Stephen at Dillon's long ago, "in his lord Fauntleroy suit and curly hair like a prince on the stage" (pp. 414–15, 664, 759). Bloom has imagined Rudy in an Eton suit, and has himself appeared so dressed in his memory of his own father (p. 431). The lamb Rudy carries probably derives from the woolly jacket Molly knitted. The ruby and diamond buttons recall Stephen's response to jewelry (p. 238), though Bloom also has had associations enough with "ruby" and has even thought of diamonds: "Jewels. Diamonds flash better" in the dusk (p. 369). As for the glass shoes, Stephen wears "a Buck's castoffs" (p. 50), and both Stephen and Bloom have been uncomfortable in ill-mended socks (pp. 208, 88). Rudy is reading the Hagaddah, and ironically, we learn later that Bloom's father's Hagaddah has been marked with the old gentleman's glasses at the prayers for Passover (p. 708). The bronze helmet is curious: perhaps it suggests the gear of knighthood, as Rudy is Sir Leopold's son; or perhaps it is a grim jest, continuing the medics' obscenities regarding the French *capotes*. The violet ribbon on Rudy's ivory cane calls to mind Molly's violet garters (p. 362) and Bloom's purple ones (p. 696). And the cane itself may be a transmutation of Stephen's "familiar" and of Bloom's stick from the beach.

Nonetheless, such a synthesis is not fully convincing; a vision of Rudy is hardly a surprise in the world of Circe. Bloom has thought of Rudy all through the day, and the vision's meaning, aside from being an inevitable idealization, is not clear. Like so many of Joyce's symbols, this one seems indeterminable, ambiguous — as easily the symbol of the irretrievably lost as of the hope conceivably found. At best this ambiguity suggests only that choices are still available to Bloom.

And in fact changes are indicated — not monumental, but significant. Leopold has ordered breakfast in bed, a remarkably bold move for a man who has been a servant for so many years — a bold move, and one undertaken in the most obvious and the most likely field of action.

But, as always, whether Molly will comply is not for mere man to say. "Hopeless thing, sand." A hopeless thing, too, is the task of governing Molly Bloom.

Notes

1. All page references to *Ulysses* are to the Modern Library Edition (New York, 1946).

2. Caroline Gordon and Allen Tate, *The House of Fiction* (New York, 1950), p. 279.

3. *Surface and Symbol: The Consistency of James Joyce's "Ulysses"* (New York, 1962), p. 33.

4. For interesting "objections" to Joyce's science, see Adams, p. 181 ff.

5. Adams, p. 37.

6. C. R. Cheney, ed., *Handbook of Dates for Students of English History* (London, 1955), Table 13, p. 108.

7. This is a period of 18 days, evidently another example of Joyce's use of the "closed field" as hypothecated by Hugh Kenner in "Art in a Closed Field," *Virginia Quarterly Review*, XXXVIII (Autumn 1962), 604.

8. For further evidence of Boylan's intrusions, see pp. 61, 62, 63, 69, 74, 76, 91, 101, 122, 151, 152, 165, 170, 172, 180, 256, 260, 262, 268, 276, 363, 368, 375, 410, 518, 529, 550, 560, 561, 609, 626, 631, 634, 635, 638, 639, 717.

9. Adams, pp. 37–38.

10. This is evidently also a "Jesuit jibe." Compare Father Conmee's speculations regarding the first Countess of Belvedere and her husband's brother: " . . . if she had not committed adultery fully, *eiaculatio seminis inter vas naturale mulieris*" (p. 220).

11. *Birth Control: Its Use and Misuse* (New York, 1934), pp. 70, 72; Sigmund Freud, in 1894, "The Justification of Detaching from Neurasthenia a Particular Syndrome: the Anxiety-Neurosis," *Collected Papers* (London, 1948), I, 88; Victor W. Eisenstein, *Neurotic Interaction in Marriage* (New York, 1953), p. 112.

12. *Ibid.*, p. 67.

13. *James Joyce: His Way of Interpreting the Modern World* (New York, 1950), p. 115.

14. Bannon gives this relationship a sinister turn when he decamps from Burke's apparently because he has learned that Bloom is "Photo's Papli" (p. 416).

15. Adams, pp. 186–189.

16. *Ibid.*, p. 188.

17. Rudy was conceived under characteristic Bloomian conditions, in Raymond Terrace and at an open window overlooking two dogs copulating in the street. Both Leopold and Molly attest to this report, though evidently Molly did not see the "sergeant grinning up" (pp. 83, 763). It is one of the many curious coincidences of the book that the singer to whom Molly hurls a coin is a militaryman-beggar who is described as one who "jerks, growls, and bays" (p. 222).

18. *James Joyce's "Ulysses"* (New York, 1955), p. 348.

Some Aspects of the Jewish Backgrounds of *Ulysses*   Louis Hyman*

On 7 October 1904, James Joyce left Dublin for good (returning only in 1909 and 1912 for brief visits), a voluntary exile, as Yeats[1] wrote of him in 1923, "in flight from the objects of his hatred, bearing in mind always in minute detail, even to the names over the shops, the Dublin that he hated but would not forget." His novel *Ulysses*, begun in 1914, was published in Paris in 1922 by a young American, Sylvia Beach. Everyone now knows that it records events in the lives of three main characters on an average day in Dublin, 16 June 1904; that it succeeds in its pervasive symbolism in presenting an exhaustive critique of contemporary society as reflected in the doings of the Irish capital on that day; that the chief figures in it, Leopold Bloom, the middle-aged Irish-Jewish advertising canvasser, his voluptuous wife, Molly, the young writer, Stephen Dedalus, correspond to the Homeric trio, Ulysses, Penelope, and Telemachus. The novel puts Dublin in a conspicuous charting on the map of contemporary world literature.

Apart from that of Bloom, the baptised Irish Jew, the names of authentic members of the Dublin Jewish community who lived on the south side of the city in St. Kevin's Parade, Lombard Street West, and in and about Lower Clanbrassil Street appear in the novel. In the *Circe* episode, when Bella Cohen,[2] the "madam" of the brothel which Dedalus visited, threatens Bloom and commands that he should sign his will, die, and be buried in the shrubbery jakes, he bursts into tears:

(Bloom, broken, closely veiled for the sacrifice, sobs, his face to the earth. The passing bell is heard. Darkshawled figures of the circumcised, in sackcloth and ashes, stand by the wailing wall.[3] M. Shulomo-

*From *The Jews of Ireland* (Dublin: Irish University Press, 1972), 167–92.

witz,[4] *Joseph Goldwater,*[5] *Moses Herzog,*[6] *Harris Rosenberg, M.
Moisel,*[7] *J. Citron,*[8] *Minnie Watchman,*[9] *O. Mastiansky,*[10] *the Reverend
Leopold Abramovitz,*[11] *Chazen. With swaying arms they wail in
pneuma over the recreant Bloom).*

THE CIRCUMCISED: (In a dark guttural chant as they cast dead sea
fruit upon him, no flowers.[12]) Shema Israel Adonai Elohenu Adonai
Echad.

Bella Cohen, who appears in the records simply as Mrs. Cohen,[13] was
a real person, occupant in 1890 of 82 Mecklenburg Street, in the heart of
Dublin's then "red-light" district, and in 1904 still living at the same
address, which by then was officially called 82 Tyrone Street. The one-
eyed Moses Herzog fits into the *Cyclops* episode and the name of Citron
appealed to Joyce because it spoke for the traditional fruit of the Jewish
festival of Tabernacles, commemorating the wanderings of the Israelites in
the desert, and thus a symbol of the Wandering Jew. Bloom's tailor,
George Robert Mesias,[14] of 5 Eden Quay, was a native of Russia and
appears in a parade of false messiahs in the *Circe* episode. In the Census of
Ireland, 1901, he is listed as a widower of the Jewish persuasion, aged 36,
lodging at the home of Hoseas Weiner in Clontarf West. A tall and
handsome man, he married Elsie Watson as his second wife, on 5
November 1901 at Clontarf Presbyterian Church. The names of the other
Dublin Jews, of whom one at least is made a friend of Leopold Bloom in
his youth, were taken from *Thom's Directory* for 1905, a source book of
Ulysses, because their names suited the Jewish themes in the novel and
were introduced into the narrative to show that they comprised a part of
Dublin's contemporary population, for one aspect of *Ulysses*, and a major
one at that, is the presentation of the city in 1904.

One English Jew appears in *Ulysses* in the person of Dr Hy Franks, a
quack doctor who had posters stuck up in greenhouses and urinals offering
treatment for venereal diseases. "All kinds of places are good for ads"[15] is
Bloom's observation on Franks' promotional activities. In the *Circe*[16]
episode Lipoti Virag,[17] Bloom's grandfather, unscrews his ibis-head which
is carried out crying "Quack" of the pox doctor advertised on the fly bill.
Henry Jacob Franks,[18] born in Manchester in 1852, arrived in Dublin in
1903 after deserting his Turkish-born wife Miriam (née Mandil) and their
four children.

Several persons, some Dubliners, others Italian, Greek, and Hungarian, helped Joyce to complete his hero; Joyce was rarely content to fasten a
major character to a single individual. The first of the Dublin models for
Bloom was a tall, dark-complexioned clerk named Alfred H. Hunter, who
was rumoured a cuckold. Richard Ellmann was misled by Stanislaus Joyce
into believing that Hunter was a Jew.[19] The son of William H. Hunter,
shoemaker,[20] Alfred, lodging at the home of a Mrs. Ryan, of 2 Oxford
Road, Rathmines, was married in the Catholic Church of Our Immaculate Lady of Refuge, Rathmines,[21] on 1 February 1898 to Margaret

Cummins, daughter of Michael Cummins, bricklayer, and Anne Cummins, stationer, of 32 Castlewood Avenue, Rathmines,[22] a few doors away from No. 23 where James Joyce lived from 1884 to 1887.[23] After their marriage, the Hunters lived in Clonliffe Road near Ballybough Road.[24] In 1899 Hunter had an office at 1 Clare Street in the building occupied by W. A. Gilbey, wine merchant, and A. Leslie and Co., house and land agents and surveyors,[25] and next door to Marcus J. Bloom, dentist, and father of Joseph Bloom, also dentist, of 2 Clare Street, an authentic character in *Ulysses*. Hunter's name appears in the *Freeman's Journal* of 14 July 1904 in a list of mourners attending the funeral of Matthew Kane, a friend of James Joyce's father and a model for Martin Cunningham in the novel.[26] Joyce had met Hunter only twice and on 3 December 1906 asked his brother Stanislaus, and afterwards his aunt, Josephine Murray, to obtain all the details about him that they could. He had intended writing a short story for *Dubliners* called "Ulysses," describing the day's wanderings of Hunter about Dublin, but on 6 February 1907 he wrote that "Ulysses never got any forrader than the title."[27] On the night of 22 June 1904, Joyce was involved in an incident which he adapted in *Ulysses* and after which Hunter played a notable part. Joyce was badly beaten up by a young man to whose girl-friend he had made overtures, apparently unaware that the young woman had an official escort. He was left in the street with "black eye, sprained wrist, sprained ankle, cut chin, cut hand"[28] and was rescued by Hunter,[29] who took him home and, as Joyce makes Leopold Bloom minister to Stephen Dedalus in the *Eumaeus* episode after he had rescued him from Nighttown, "bucked him up generally in orthodox Samaritan fashion."[30]

The figure of the cuckolded Jew occupied Joyce's mind for the next 14 years. On one of his visits to Dublin, in 1909 or 1912, he may have been intrigued by the story of an Irish Jew whose wife had been unfaithful to him during his absence in foreign parts. On 8 November 1889, Joseph Blum (*sic*), draper, of 20 Oakfield Place, Dublin, son of Jonas Blum, dealer, of the same address, was married by certificate at the Registrar's Office, Cork,[31] to Sarah Levy, born in or about 1870,[32] of 68 Hibernian Buildings, daughter of Joseph Levy (1838–1936), a great wit, beadle of the Cork synagogue, Councillor of the Cork Chovevei Zion (Lovers of Zion) Tent in 1893[33] and, as a native of Tavrig, among the first Lithuanian Jewish settlers in that city. After a stay of four years at 64 Hibernian Buildings where two daughters, Bertha in 1891 and Dora in 1892, were born, Blum, now spelling his name Bloom, returned to Dublin and lived in a cottage at 3 Blackpits, off Lower Clanbrassil Street. There his wife gave birth to three sons: Myer in 1894, Eli in 1895 and Solomon in 1898. In the birth certificate of his son Eli he is described as an agent. In or about 1900, Bloom decided to seek his fortune in South Africa and, like the enigmatic sailor from Carrigaloe, in Queenstown (now Cobh), in the County of Cork, mentioned in the *Eumaeus* episode,[34] and Joyce's Leopold

Bloom, left his wife a grass widow.[35] Sarah, completely assimilated in Irish mannerisms and speech, is reputed to have become the mistress of a Jewish lodger, by whom she had a daughter. One can imagine Sarah saying to herself as Molly did in the *Penelope* episode, musing about her adultery with Blazes Boylan, "anyhow its done now once and for all with all the talk in the world about it people make."[36] Deserted by her husband, alienated from her parents and ostracised by the community, Sarah, who is remembered by her contemporaries for her good looks,[37] was hard put to it to maintain her family on her own and moved to a tenement house in 3 Bishop Street, opposite Jacob's Biscuit Factory, to whose girl workers she sold drapery on the weekly payments system.[38] Dora was sent in 1900 to her grandparents' home in Cork and emigrated to America in 1908. On board ship she met and married a fellow-emigrant, a Liverpool musician.[39] After two years her two younger brothers, Eli and Solomon, followed her to the United States. Living in very straitened circumstances. Sarah and her eldest teenage daughter are reputed to have turned to prostitution.[40] An old lady,[41] a native of Dublin, recalls, some months before her marriage on 20 February 1907, seeing Sarah and her daughter apparently soliciting at the corner of Earl Street, near Nelson's Pillar. Laurence Elyan, a native of Cork and a retired Irish civil servant, now (1971) resident in Jerusalem, recollects, as a boy, reading for old Joseph Levy, in 1914, a letter from Sarah of 3 Bishop Street, Dublin, appealing for money.[42] It is believed that Bertha who, like fairhaired, slimsandalled Milly Bloom,[43] is described by a contemporary[44] as tall and fair-haired and who, in 1911, worked as an assistant in a stationer's shop,[45] was befriended by and taken care of by the Salvation Army at whose rallies she is reported to have sung.[46] Her brother Myer worked first as a library clerk[47] and later as a book-seller at Eason's.[48] It may be mentioned that Solomon Levy (died *circa* 1910), Sarah's brother, was a great lover of light operas which he used to hum continually.[49] The five children of May (Michele), her sister, were all musically inclined and organised themselves into a private band which played at family functions. About 1920, Sarah, after a short stay in Belfast, is said to have emigrated to America together with her daughter Bertha and son Myer. Joyce was anxious to know from A. J. Leventhal, then a young graduate of Trinity College, Dublin, who visited him in Paris in 1921, whether the Blooms still lived in the South Circular Road district, although he did not mention any particular person of that name. Leventhal recalls that Joyce's interest in the Blooms was more than casual and that he was relieved to hear that they had died or left the city.[50]

Joseph Bloom's sister, Bassa[51] (1870–1941), blue-lipped, of plumpish build and highly rubicund complexion, was usually clad in a one-piece dress and a shabby brown coat; of dubious repute,[52] dishevelled and invariably carrying an umbrella, she used to roam the Jewish district mumbling maledictions.[53] Her father Jonas or Jone, popularly known as Yonah, moved in 1892[54] to 38 Lombard Street West,[55] Leopold Bloom's address in 1893–4, until his death in 1912. A kindly and witty man with a gentle smile, neatly groomed with a trimmed red beard, he wore a frock-like coat and a silk hat of the period. Mrs. Rebecca Ita Isaacson (1889–1970), while visiting her grandfather Nisan Moisel of 20 Arbutus Place, a character in *Ulysses*, recalls, as a schoolgirl in 1902 or 1903, seeing Jonas Bloom with saddened eyes and hands folded behind his back, following his pregnant spinster daughter as she walked slowly up and down Oakfield Place, a cul-de-sac opposite their home.[56]

A son or nephew of Jonas was Jacob Bloom, dealer, of 1 St. Michael's Terrace, Blackpits, who, on 30 May 1899, married Matilda, sister of Rudolph Burack, a witness at the marriage and a brother-in-law of the Louis Wine of 33 Wellington Quay. It was Wine's antique shop that Leopold Bloom, in the *Sirens* episode[57] passes on his way to the Ormond bar, bearing the volume *Sweets of Sin* which he had purchased for Molly in the bookshop[58] in the cubbyhole partitioned from the main shop at 26 Wellington Quay[59] rented by a Dublin Jew, Aaron Figatner of 6 Seapoint Terrace, Irishtown.[60] Leopold Bloom, passing the jeweller's shop, read Figatner's name and asked himself why he always thought his name was Figather: "Bloom whose dark eye read Aaron Figatner's name. Why do I always think Figather? Gathering figs I think."[61] Lionel Marks, a brother-in-law of John Michael Higgins,[62] was the second witness at Jacob Bloom's marriage and kept the antique shop at 16 Upper Ormond Quay where Leopold Bloom in the *Sirens* episode[63] sees in the window a picture of Robert Emmet, the Irish rebel, whose dying words, which have a carminative effect on him, he tries to recall. Jacob Bloom, whose occupation is given in his children's birth certificates as a brass-finisher, worked as a plumber. He had five children: Bertha Jenny, born at John Street, Sligo, in 1900, Sarah at 59 Lombard Street West, Dublin, in 1901, Fanny, at No. 77 in 1903, Mayer William at 4 Brainboro', off Greenville Terrace, in 1905, and Rachel at the same address in 1907. One of his children is said to have married out of the faith and the family emigrated to America after the First World War.[64]

Another member of the Bloom clan who lived in Dublin contemporaneously with Joyce was Isaac Blum (*sic*),[65] leather merchant, of 3 Desmond Street, off Lombard Street West, whose wife Daisy, née Liknaitzky, gave birth to a daughter Gladys Margaret on 23 December 1903. Daisy, who converted to Catholicism, was a music teacher in Dublin in 1909.[66] It is possible that Joyce knew of her and derived some of the characterisation of Molly from her.

Isaac Blum was a son of Solomon (Zalman) Bloom, who lived at 3 Desmond Street, a two-storey house, from 1903 to 1905 when his name appears in the records as the occupant.[67] Solomon who was a cousin of Jonas arrived in Dublin in or about 1893, living at 36 Martin Street, where his daughter Leah married Isaac Rouf, pedlar, son of Nakman (*sic*) Rouf, carpenter, on 1 March 1895. The marriage certificate records Solomon's occupation as a butcher. In 1895 Solomon moved to 98 Lower Clanbrassil Street,[68] where his daughter Ida married Aaron Freedman, draper, of 5 Walworth Road, on 9 June 1897. Now trading as a draper, he moved in 1901 to 6 Lombard Street West, where he lived for two years.[69] On 15 March 1904, his daughter Johanna Blum (sic) of 3 Desmond Street was married to Israel A. Weiner, general draper of 26 Victoria Street, who, as a new immigrant and pedlar in drapery in 1901, boarded with the Bloom family.[70] In 1905, Weiner was the manager of a loan office at 15 Fleet Street and lived at 25 Ashfield Road, Ranelagh.[71] The Mrs. Bloom who lived at 1 Chelmsford Road, Ranelagh from 1908 to 1915[72] could have been Johanna's mother who is known to have moved to Ranelagh.[73]

Solomon Bloom had two sons, Joseph born in 1885 who worked as a framemaker and David born in 1888 who was a draper's assistant.[74] Two other members of the Bloom clan, Simon and Bernard, were sons of another Solomon, who was a brother of Jonas and who, on arriving in Dublin, lived in Armstrong Street, near Harold's Cross Bridge, now Robert Emmet Bridge in the vicinity of Upper Clanbrassil Street, not far from the home of the Murrays, Joyce's grandparents. In 1910, Simon was involved in the murder of a girl who worked in a photographer's shop in Wexford;[75] she had jilted him and he had vainly planned a double suicide. Simon was exonerated on mental grounds and, after some time in an institution, left for America.[76] The incident presumably gave Joyce, who was on a visit to Ireland in 1909, the idea of establishing Bloom's daughter as an apprentice in a photographer's shop.[77]

Bernard (Benny) (1881–1966), who is described in the Census of Ireland, 1901, as a traveller, was popularly known as "Bloom the canvasser." Armed with religious pictures, he could walk ten to twenty miles a day in the streets of Dublin to solicit customers at a shilling a head for coreligionists trading on the weekly payments system, one of whom was Israel Citron, a friend of Leopold Bloom in Ulysses. An amiable man, ever ready to do a favour, with an instinctive knack of rounding up prospective clients, he could organise four to eight "weeklies" a month and never run out of them. He had a touch of the Wanderlust and yet an inner serenity, an apparent contradiction in his personality. A veteran of the Boer War, 1899–1902, for which he volunteered in the year 1901, he recalled to an old friend[78] the night marches, where soldiers had to chew tough, sun-dried biltong. Under the command of General Botha, he is said to have taken part in the South-West African expedition[79] which forced the Germans to capitulate in July 1915. In South Africa he worked as a waiter[80] in a hotel and as a bookie's runner placing bets on a commission basis for residents of the hotel. He claimed to have owned a goldmine in South Africa, but in Dublin, whither he returned in 1916, apart from canvassing, he eked out a living by purchasing old jewellery and gold. Always in financial straits, he would borrow from one acquaintance to pay another. Very fond of a drink, his favourite haunt was Fitzpatrick's pub at the corner of Donovan's Lane and Lower Clanbrassil Street in the vicinity of Blackpits and St. Kevin's Parade. Perhaps Joyce had him in mind when he made Leopold Bloom an advertisement canvasser. This Bloom was a man of simple tastes who loved to play billiards and cards; he never lost his temper, but when bested he could bear a grudge and brood alone for days. A "mousey" man,[81] about five feet five inches in height and eight stone in weight, he was full of boundless energy, yet restrained and withdrawn through some pain suffered in earlier life. Reputed a roué and nicknamed "Knee-trembler" by his cronies, he wore a smart check suit and sported a gold pin in his tie.[82] Time touched him gently and in his eighties he had the face and bearing of a man of fifty; even in old age he wore his hat at a rakish angle. Zoe Higgins, one of the harlots in Bella Cohen's establishment, calls Leopold "little mousey"[83] and he is referred to in the *Cyclops* episode as a "bloody mouseabout . . . with his argol bargol."[84]

One of the "weekly men," as they were commonly called in Ireland, was Pesach Bloom,[85] in no wise connected with the other Dublin Blooms or Blums; he came from Shavil, in Lithuania, in 1882 and traded for many years on the weekly payments system in County Wicklow. He died on 10 June 1903, aged 49, some three months after being hit[86] by a falling slate during the cyclone, popularly known as "The Big Wind,"[87] that swept Dublin on 26–27 February 1903, laying low so many of the sturdiest oaks in the Phoenix Park. On 16 June 1904,[88] Zelig (or Zelick) (1880–1910), Pesach's second son,[89] appeared as a witness in the "Canada swindle case," mentioned in both the *Aeolus* and the *Cyclops* episodes in *Ulysses*,[90] in which a Jew, recently arrived from Germany, had swindled prospective emigrants. The bogus emigration agent was a man named James Wought, confectioner and tailor, whose aliases included Saphiro, Spiro and Sparks; he was charged with obtaining twenty shillings from Benjamin Zaretzky of Leeds, through a press advertisement offering to procure a passage to Canada for him. Zelig Bloom, of 49 A Lower Clanbrassil Street, also interpreted the evidence of Anna Cohen, who spoke in Yiddish and kept a "lodging house for Jews" at the same address where the accused stayed for some time. This could be the factual background for Joyce's making Leopold Bloom's father reside at 52 Clanbrassil Street when Leopold was still a schoolboy.[91] Another Bloom family, whose connection with the other Dublin Blooms is unknown, was that of Eli J. Bloom, pedlar, of 6 Martin Street, whose daughter Malkah (Molly) married Himan (*sic*) Watchman, dealer of 24 Martin Street, on 5 October 1897. In Cork,[92] the minister of the congregation during 1896–1902 was the Rev. Eli Bloom, who arrived in Ireland after ministering for one year to the Jewish community at Wrexham in Denbyshire, Wales.[93] On leaving Cork he ministered to the Merthyr Tydfil community for forty years.[94]

Another Bloom (Blum) family of German origin had been resident in Dublin since 1840, and one of its descendants, Joseph Bloom, who appears as an authentic character in *Ulysses*,[95] was, in 1911, a bachelor and lived in the home of his mother Catherine at 10 Tritonville Road, Sandy-mount,[96] not far from where Joyce's aunt, Josephine Murray, lived for many years.[97] In the same house lived Joseph's sisters, Florence and Beatrice, both listed in the Census of Ireland for 1911 as professors of music. A renowned wit, Joseph practised dentistry, like his father, Mark J. Bloom, at 2 Clare Street, in 1903 and 1904. Mark (1846–1894?) who, like Joyce's Leopold, became a Catholic on marriage, was the son of Joseph Blum, toy importer and commission agent, and was a foundation member of the Dublin Dental Hospital in 1876.

The mere concept of the Irish Jew raised a laugh in the Ireland of Joyce's day. Edward Raphael Lipsett[98] (1869–1921), a Dublin Jew, journal-ist, novelist, and playwright, wrote impressions of the Jews in Ireland in 1906, under the pen-name of Halitvack:

> There is an invisible but impassable barrier between Jew and Christian — a barrier which the one party will not, and the other cannot, break through. You cannot get one native to remember that a Jew may be an Irishman. The term "Irish Jew" seems to have a contradictory ring upon the native ear; the very idea is wholly incon-ceivable to the native mind . . . Irish Jews feel that if they spoke of each other as Jewish Irishmen, it would meet with a cutting cynicism from the natives that the two elements can never merge into one, for any single purpose . . . There is undoubtedly a mutual estrangement be-tween the Jews and the Irish. The Jews understand the Irish little; the Irish understand the Jews less. Each seems a peculiar race in the eyes of the other; and, in a word, the position of Jews in Ireland is peculiarly peculiar.

Lipsett's impressions may have truly represented the situation of the Jews in the unsympathetic social climate of Ireland at the turn of the century, at best grudgingly neutral to them and at worst openly hostile, and it may well be that an awareness of that situation of aliens detached from the Irish world around them, living in an Irish exile, never wholly accepted by their fellow-countrymen, prompted Joyce in introducing the themes of isolation, exile, and alienation in *Ulysses* and in designing the novel as he did.

Further light is thrown on the relations between the Irish and Jews in the Dublin of the early twentieth century by letters in the Anglo-Jewish press from two Jewish students of Trinity College at the beginning of the year 1909 on the controversial topic of the establishment of Zionist societies at British universities. E(dward) L(ipman) (1887–1965), a classi-cal scholar, medical student, friend of Arthur Griffith[99] and later a member of the Irish literary circles of the day, in his counter-arguments writes this:

> . . . we are asked to establish a society that would lead to a more open state of separation than exists at present. Many college friends of

mine, men devoid of bigotry and prejudice, lovers of the Jewish race and believers in our superiority, have complained of our exclusiveness and non-intercourse with themselves. We cannot blame them . . . ; the dislike of strangers, the objection to those whose ideals are different from our own, is inherent in most men. "While in Rome, live as the Romans" ought to be our motto. We should identify our interests with those of our fellow-countrymen and at times even subordinate our own, provided that we do not violate any real principles. All this applies to Ireland and Irishmen and from what we know of human nature to Englishmen likewise. I object to the establishment of any such society as the above for the same reasons that I objected to the formation of a Jewish "Home Rule" party in Ireland, because it is bound to spread ill-feeling and distrust instead of cordiality and good comradeship. I hope no one will imagine that this letter possesses any assimilative tendencies as no one would deplore this more than the writer who is somewhat conceited in his pride of race.[100]

In the second letter,[101] Hyman Edelstein,[102] a classical scholar and later Canadian poet and prose-writer, writes:

> I, born in Ireland, am a *true* Englishman[103] [*sic*] of the Jewish faith. A *true* Irishman once said to me, "Arra, sure an' yer a— Jewman."[104] A *true* Scotchman would like to salute his Jewish fellow-countryman in his own brogue. I know a *true* Englishman would dispute my frantic zeal to be known as an Englishman, call me "Sheeny" and other patriotic names. This is confirmed by Christian friends who recognise that I, having a distinct history, literature, language, and country, compared to all which those of all other nations, dead or living, are as dross, cannot feel exactly as they when they proudly talk of Brian Boru and of Nelson, no matter how much I may admire these heroes. On the other hand, they gladly confess they felt as I do when I talk of Moses, our kings, warriors, psalmists, prophets and philosophers. For which reason, I am most seriously thinking of asking these Christian friends—*true* Englishmen, Welshmen, Scotchmen and Irishmen, to appeal in the Jewish press that all British University Jews should form with them a "British Zionist League." This would give the lie to our pretensions with a sublime vengeance. But later on, the "Jewish World" with all its anti-Nationalist correspondents, having read the chapter titled "Revelations" in George Eliot's "Daniel Deronda," will agree with Spinoza that "there is no reason why the Jews should not again be a *chosen* nation."

But Joyce often thought of his own Irish people as having many points in common with the Jews as regards both their character and their destiny. In his monumental biography of Joyce, Richard Ellmann describes "the similarity of the Jews and the Irish" as a favourite topic of Joyce's conversation.[105] They were alike, he declared, in being impulsive, given to fantasy, addicted to associative thinking, wanting in rational discipline; these are made qualities of Bloom's mind. When a young Jewish student from Harvard wrote to him to praise *Ulysses* but complain of its treatment of the Jews, Joyce, surprised and much upset at the resentment aroused in some of his Jewish friends at the portrayal of Bloom, replied that he was in complete sympathy with the Jews.[106] He further asserted that, in making the protagonist of *Ulysses* Jewish, he had put the Jew on the map of European literature, and in the spring of 1939 he told his friend, Frank Budgen, that he had already helped 16 Jews to escape from Nazi territory to Britain.[107] In the autumn of 1940, soon after the promulgation of antisemitic laws in German-occupied France, he once remarked to his friend, Maria Jolas,[108] one of his Paris circle, "Antisemitism is one of the easiest prejudices to foment." He showed deep sympathy for the Jews and often spoke of his own affinity for them as a wandering, persecuted people. Although Jews, according to Budgen,[109] irritated him at times and at others bored him, he greatly admired their close family ties. "I sometimes think," he once said to his friend in Paris, "that it was a heroic sacrifice on their part when they refused to accept the Christian revelation. Look at them. They are better husbands than we are, better fathers and better sons."[110] And again he remarked, "A Jew is both king and priest in his own family."[111]

As Joyce divined when he made Bloom the hero of *Ulysses*, the Jew is the twentieth century symbol for Everyman. "Bloom," as R. P. Blackmur[112] has excellently put it, "is the wanderer, the movement and enterprise in Man, the thing immortal in society which persists from form to form. He is Everyman in exile, the exile in every man." David Daiches,[113] in his article "James Joyce's Jew," remarks: "his fellow Dubliners, though most of them respect his human kindness and dependability, see him as in some degree an outsider. His efforts to achieve real communication with his fellows are never wholly successful. Being an Irish Jew, he both belongs to Dublin and does not belong. He is both a Dubliner and an exile in Dublin. In exploring the paradox of Bloom's both belonging and being isolated Joyce is exploring a central paradox of the human condition as he sees it; *all* men are in a sense exiles . . . And at the same time all men belong to a community . . . Gregariousness and a sense of inner loneliness coexist in all men. In Joyce's symbolic sense all men are Jews.[114] In making his hero a Jew Joyce was emphasizing the fact that the complete man always includes the exile."[115] Robert M. Adams[116] believes that Bloom's Jewish character was a symbol into which Joyce tried to project, not only his own social reflections about modern Man, but some rather intimate and complex psychic responses of his own. Herbert Howarth[117] attributes the Jewish theme to Joyce's desire to elaborate on the Celtic commonplace of associating Ireland with Israel. In terms of Israel, the Irish thought of themselves as the Children of Israel, with England as the Egypt of the Pharaohs and the deliverance from English tyranny as their Exodus. As early as 1748, Dr. Charles Lucas[118] (1731–71), distinguished Irish patriot, who frequently contributed articles to the *Freeman's Journal*[119] over the signature of "A Citizen" or "Civis," declared that the imposition of laws made in a "strange, a foreign Parliament," without their consent or knowledge, placed the Protestant Irish under a more severe bondage than the Israelites suffered in Egypt. The Citizen in the *Cyclops* episode refers thus to the starving peasants that left Ireland for America during the potato famine of 1846: "those that came to the land of the free remember the land of bondage."[120] Professor MacHugh in the *Aeolus* episode[121] recites from memory John F. Taylor's moving speech on the Irish language delivered at a meeting of the University College Law Students' Debating Society on 24 October 1901, comparing young Ireland in revolt against British rule with young Moses in revolt against Egyptian; comparing also the lures of the two mighty civilisations, the British and Egyptian, rejected by proud young Ireland and by proud young Moses alike. Influenced, perhaps, by the researches of the French Homeric scholar, Victor Bérard,[122] who argued for Semitic impacts on the Greek epic, Joyce "with a characteristic leap of insight made of his Ulysses a Jew" — the words are George Steiner's[123] — and remarked to his friend, Frank Budgen[124]: "There's a lot to be said for the theory that the *Odyssey* is a Semitic poem." In his plan of *Ulysses* sent to Carlo Linati (1878–1949) as early as 1920, Joyce wrote: "It is an epic of two races (Israelite-Irish) and at the same time the cycle of the human body as well as a little story of a day (life)."[125] He himself dubbed the novel the "farced epistol to the hibruws."[126]

In an early essay, Yeats drew a comparison between Ireland and Judaea at the time of the birth of Christ and also wrote that the Irish race, transformed by a national art, would become "a chosen race, one of the pillars that uphold the world." In his *History of Ireland*,[127] written originally in Irish, Geoffrey Keating (c.1570–c.1644) describes how the founder of the modern Irish race, Milesius, son of Breogan, traced his genealogy through 22 Gaelic names and 13 Hebrew names "passing through Japhet and Adam." The Irish were an Israelitish tribe who had wandered through Scythia (where their king, Fenius Farsaigh, had inaugurated a great language school) across Europe through Spain into Ireland.[128] The names of his brothers, who helped him to subdue the country, were recorded in Irish topography. This passage stimulated the ingenuity of Joyce, who, in the *Ithaca* episode,[129] jokingly introduced analogies between Jewish and cultural history which other Irish writers took seriously:[130]

> What points of contact existed between these languages and between the people who spoke them?
>
> The presence of guttural sounds, diacritic aspirations, epenthetic and servile letters in both languages: their antiquity, both having been taught on the plain of Shinar 242 years after the deluge in the seminary instituted by Fenius Farsaigh, descendant of Noah, progenitor of Israel, and ascendant of Heber and Heremon, progenitors of Ireland: their archeological, genealogical, hagiographical, exegetical, homilectic, to-ponamoastic, historical and religious literature comprising the works of

rabbis and culdees. Torah, Talmud (Mischna and Ghemara), Massor, Pentateuch, Book of the Dun Cow, Book of Ballymote, Garland of Howth, Book of Kells: their dispersal, persecution, survival and revival: the isolation of their synagogical and ecclesiastical rites in ghetto (S. Mary's Abbey)[131] and masshouse (Adam and Eve's tavern): the proscription of their national costumes in penal laws and Jewish dress acts:[132] the restoration in Chanan David of Zion and the possibility of Irish political autonomy or devolution.

Though it was in Trieste[133] and Zurich that Joyce mainly came in contact with Jews who helped him to write about the Jewish and Zionist themes in *Ulysses* and to round out the character of Bloom, his acquaintance with members of the Jewish faith and their problems may have begun much earlier in Ireland. As a boy, he may have heard his father, a Corkman, speak at the dinner table of the anti-Jewish outbursts in Cork in 1888 and 1894,[134] the latter of which occurred only three months after he had visited the city. He met, as we saw,[135] the Sinclair twin-brothers in 1903 to discuss the project of establishing a weekly newspaper in Dublin, and a year later he obtained financial help from one of them before his departure, or hegira, as he called it, from Ireland. He closely followed the divorce case of Morris Harris,[136] grandfather of the Sinclairs. He knew the family of Marcus Tertius Moses,[137] whose great-grandfather became a convert to Christianity in Dublin in 1785. The Moses family had a crest of a cock reguardant proper and its motto in Hebrew "I crow till I die," stamped on the flap of their envelopes. Marcus Tertius Moses, famed for his charity, was a wholesale tea merchant and agent[138] at 14 Eustace Street, Dublin, but resided at Liskeard, Delgany, in County Wicklow, and must have been acquainted with Joyce's father when he lived in Bray. In the *Circe* episode, Bloom recalls a day in 1890, soon after his daughter Milly was weaned, when they "all went together to Fairyhouse races, was it? . . . I mean Leopardstown," and on the return journey "coming along by Foxrock in that old fiveseater shanderadan of a waggonette . . . Molly was laughing because Rogers and Maggot O'Reilly were mimicking a cock as we passed a farmhouse and Marcus Tertius Moses, the tea merchant, drove past us in a gig with his daughter, Dancer Moses was her name, and the poodle in her lap bridled up. . . ."[139] Joyce must also have known Philip Moisel,[140] who married the daughter of a Church of Ireland minister, of Kingsland Parade, and whose father, Nisan Moisel[141] of 20 Arbutus Place, informed Bloom of the ritual quality of the citrons. Joyce heard of Philip's death in South Africa in about 1903 and refers to him in the *Ithaca* episode as one of Bloom's former companions who lived in Heytesbury Street and died of pyemia. He also knew of the pregnancy of Philip's stepsister-in-law, who is made to go walking with Molly Bloom just before Milly is born. He may have met the one-eyed bibulous Moses Herzog[142] in one of Dublin's bars or have heard of him from the collector of bad debts, one of his many

Dublin acquaintances, who appears in *Ulysses* as the nameless narrator in the *Cyclops* episode.

Joyce must have heard of the discussions which John Francis Byrne (1879–1960), his confidant and closest friend at University College and later a journalist in the United States,[143] had with a fellow-member in the Sackville Chess Club, small, dark, black-bearded Abraham Moses Zaks (1863–1932) of 25 St. Kevin's Parade, at whose home Byrne often dined.[144] Zaks, who was ordained a rabbi, eked out a livelihood by running a small junk-shop off Redmond's Hill. Widely read and self-educated in the classics and mathematics, he enjoyed nothing in life more than an argument. The Sackville Chess Club had been formed in the autumn of 1902 among former patrons of the Dublin Bread Company restaurant (D.B.C.), including Israel Citron, for whose drapery trade "Bloom, the canvasser" solicited customers, the same Citron in *Ulysses* at whose home Molly and Leopold Bloom spent some "pleasant evenings." Joyce may have derived the details of Bloom's memories of the Jewish quarter in which he lived as a boy and as a young man from Byrne's descriptions of the evenings that he records spending with his Jewish friend, Zaks, and to which Citron may also have been invited. Joyce, in his solitary peregrinations through the city for seven or eight hours on end, must have enjoyed his game of finding equivalents in Dublin for his Homeric parallels and must have been happy to have come across the one-eyed Moses Herzog, neighbour of Zaks and Citron, whom he introduced into the *Cyclops* episode without mentioning that blemish, as he made his way round Dublin peddling his groceries. Together with Byrne or by himself, he must have visited the Jewish quarter[145] on the south side where Herzog and most of the other Jewish characters of *Ulysses* lived. He may have heard of the series of public lectures on the aims and objects of the Zionist movement given in January 1900 in Dublin, Cork, Limerick and Belfast by Leopold Greenberg (1862–1931), close personal friend of Theodor Herzl and editor (1907–1931) of the London *Jewish Chronicle:* it was reported in the Anglo–Jewish[146] and possibly in the local Irish press. Byrne, one of the best chess players in Ireland at the time, is likely to have mentioned the meetings of the Dublin Young Men's Zionist Association — Zaks was its President — in which his chess colleagues, David Baker,[147] who played first board for the Clontarf Chess Club, and Philip (d. 1932), his brother, champion of Ireland in the Tailteann Chess Tournament of 1924 and All-Ireland champion in 1927–29, were active. It is safe to assume that, on Joyce's return to Dublin in 1909, Byrne told him of his lecture on "The Life of Spinoza,"[148] on 26 January 1908, to the Dublin Young Men's Zionist Association at 57 Lombard Street West, and of the reactions of the audience[149] when he read out the writ of excommunication. It is more than reasonable to suppose that Joyce read either the *Freeman's Journal,* the *Irish Truth,* or the *All-Ireland Review,* which reported in detail one of the rare outbursts of antisemitism in Ireland in 1904,[150] a boycott of Jewish merchants in Limerick that was followed by some violence, and which has been described as having some influence on *Ulysses*.[151] In making a Jew protagonist of his novel, Joyce was, as Valery Larbaud and Richard Ellmann believe, not acting as a propagandist for better treatment of minorities but, as Marvin Magalaner suggests, may rather have wished to establish a frame of reference against which the reader might place the attitude of Jew and non-Jew towards each other in the Ireland of that period. The Limerick affair and the ensuing discussion in the press may have given him the background of tension that he was seeking. Joyce could not have been unaware of the researches which his friend, John Wyse Power, was doing on the history of the Jews of Ireland. Joyce was back in Dublin in July 1909,[152] a few months after Power had spoken to the Jewish Literary and Social Club on the subject.[153] Power may have drawn his attention to an item in *Notes and Queries* of 11 May 1867, in which a correspondent, discussing the persecution of the Jews in Europe, remarks: "It is said that in Ireland the Jew never was persecuted! Was it from a more exalted view of civil and religious liberty, or because the Jew was an absentee from that country? I am inclined to think that the Jew was a non-resident in Ireland until late years."[154] This may well be the source of the conversation between Stephen Dedalus and Garrett Deasy, with Deasy joking that Ireland had never persecuted the Jews only because she never let them in.[155] Another source might be the curt entry of 1079 in the Annals of Inisfallen, with which Joyce was familiar, regarding the cold reception of a small delegation of Jews pleading to secure the right of entry into Ireland for their coreligionists.[156]

When Joyce began writing *Ulysses* in Trieste in 1914, he was at a distance of some ten or fifteen years from Dublin, but what he saw or heard in 1912 or 1914 would do just as well. Among the Jewish intellectuals whom he met in Trieste there was Moses Dlugacz[157] (1884–1943); they had a common interest in literature and etymology, music and philosophy. The son[158] and grandson of Ukrainian rabbis and himself an ordained rabbi[159] in his fifteenth year, Dlugacz became Joyce's [160] pupil in English on his appointment in 1912 to the post of chief cashier in the local Cunard Line office. The English lessons continued till the outbreak of the First World War, when the English shipping office had to close down. During the war years Dlugacz traded as a provision merchant[161] with a small store in Via Torrebianca. Among other provisions he sold cigarettes, alcoholic drinks, sweetmeats, cheese, dried fruits, nuts, and pickled cabbage, and, in a small way, he was a wholesale[162] supplier of cheese and meat products to the Austrian army fighting on the Austro-Italian front along the Isonzo River. Dlugacz tried to win over to the Zionist[163] cause all Jews and Gentiles with whom he came in contact; no doubt he tried to make a convert of Joyce, who, discussing the Irish revival with Padraic Colum in

1903, remarked contemptuously "I dislike all enthusiasms,"[164] and who seems in this instance, too, to have remained unsympathetic. Dlugacz organised and voluntarily directed courses in Hebrew[165] and Jewish history for the Triestine Jewish youth, and perhaps gave Hebrew lessons to Joyce, who is reported to have studied the language. When A. J. Leventhal[166] visited Joyce in Paris in 1921,[167] Joyce showed him some of the Hebrew words in *Ulysses*, but refused to credit Leventhal's suggestion that there was some confusion between the Spanish and German transliterations — an error that persists in the published text. Before the departure of his visitor, Joyce sat down at the piano and played and sang the Hebrew song, "Hatikvah," the Zionist national anthem, the first distich of which Leopold Bloom chanted to Stephen Dedalus in the *Ithaca* episode.[168] A member of the Board of the "Ufficio Palestinese," the local representative of the Jewish Agency for Palestine, which was established in 1918 to organise the departure of Jews for Palestine, Dlugacz advocated the foundation of a shipping company for their transportation, and attended the XII Zionist Congress in Carlsbad in 1921[169] This is the factual background for the translation of Moses Dlugacz to Dublin in 1904 as the ferret-eyed proprietor of a pork-butcher's shop in Upper Dorset Street with Zionist propaganda on his counter, one of the few "adopted" Dubliners in *Ulysses* and the only shopkeeper mentioned in the novel who is not listed in *Thom's Directory* for 1905. This also explains the description "Enthusiast"[170] applied to Dlugacz by Bloom when leaving the butcher's shop.

All the figures in the *Cyclops* episode are antisemitic, with the partial exception of John Wyse, or John Wyse Nolan, in real life John Wyse Power (d. 1926). On 13 February 1909, he lectured on "The Jews of Ireland in the Middle Ages"[171] to the Jewish Literary and Social Club at 57 Lombard Street West, under the chairmanship of Maurice Solomons, J.P.,[172] father of Edwin, Bethel, and Estelle, and Honorary Consul for the Austro-Hungarian Empire, whose name appears in *Ulysses*;[173] the vote of thanks was proposed by the Rev. Abraham Gudansky,[174] father of District Justice Herman Good, seconded by Joseph Edelstein,[175] and supported by Bernard Fox (later Judge Bernard Fox, C.B.E., Recorder of Belfast). It was John Wyse Nolan who, in Barney Kiernan's bar, mentions that Bloom advised the leaders of the Sinn Fein nationalists on conspiratorial strategy, a statement later confirmed by Martin Cunningham.[176] As Bloom is leaving the bar with Martin Cunningham, Power, and Crofton, to visit Paddy Dignam's widow, the Citizen follows them outside and shouts antisemitic insults. Bloom responds by naming great Jews of history and reminding him that Christ was a Jew: "Mendelssohn was a jew and Karl Marx and Mercadante and Spinoza. And the Saviour was a jew and his father was a jew . . . Your God was a jew. Christ was a jew like me."[177] Bloom's bold rejoinder to the fanatical nationalist recalls the words of Timothy M. Healy, K.C.,[178] M.P., first Governor-General of the Irish Free State, in

praise of the Jewish people, when speaking in the case of William O'Brien
v. Devlin and others. On that occasion, he reminded his Police Court
audience that the Saviour was a Jew and the Virgin a Jewess.[179]

In the *Cyclops* episode Joyce, to whom the one-eyed-two-eyed dichotomy was very important, introduces an authentic one-eyed Dublin Jew,[180]
Moses Herzog. Herzog, popularly known in Yiddish, or judisch,[181] Joyce's
way of writing it, as "Moshe with the left eye," was a compulsive drinker,
like the bibulous narrator of the *Cyclops* episode himself, and was
notorious for slipping out of St. Kevin's Parade synagogue for a drink
during the protracted services of the High Festivals.[182] Near the opening of
the episode, the garrulous narrator encounters Joe Hynes and, just before
they decide to enter Barney Kiernan's, he explains that he is working as a
collector of bad debts and is trying to get a payment of three shillings a
week from foxy Michael E. Geraghty,[183] "an old plumber," of 29 Arbour
Hill, who was charged by the law and ordered to pay the weekly
instalment for a large order of sugar and tea provided by Moses Herzog
who lives "over there near Heytesbury Street." The narrator tells how
Geraghty has rebuffed him, saying that, if Herzog pursues him for the
money, he will summon the Jewish pedlar for trading without a licence,
and then the narrator mocks at Herzog complaining in broken English of
not being paid for his groceries: "I had to laugh at the little jewy getting
his shirt out. 'He drink me my teas. He eat me my sugars. Because he no
pay me my moneys?' " The narrator's mockery recalls a popular verse of
the period which is of interest as throwing light on the occupation of the
Lithuanian immigrant Jews at the turn of the century: —

> 'Two shillies, two shillies, the Jewman did cry,
> For a fine pair of blankets from me you did buy;
> Do you think me von idjit or von bloomin' fool,
> If I don't get my shillie I must have my vool.

This verse[184] was adapted as a battle-cry by the young non-Jews of the
lower end of Lombard Street West, in their gang warfare against their
young Jewish neighbours of Oakfield Place and the upper end of Lombard
Street. But the Jewish boys were not daunted by invective and stones and
responded spontaneously, if somewhat priggishly, with the following
parody:

> Two pennies, two pennies, the Christian did shout,
> For a bottle of porter or Guinness's stout;
> My wife's got no shawl and my kids have no shoes,
> But I must have my money, I must have my booze.

Herzog, the Jewish pedlar, is clearly fated never to collect his debt,
just as Joe Hynes is unlikely to repay the three shillings which he borrowed
from Leopold Bloom in the episode of the *Lestrygonians*. The Herzog-
Geraghty interpolation serves as a light-hearted correspondence to the
more serious Homeric parallelism with Herzog[185] as Polyphemus and

Geraghty as Ulysses, wriggling out by cunning from the "cave" of his Herzogean Cyclops and the hands of the law. Harold Fisch[186] believes that Herzog has clearly been conflated in this incident with "ben Bloom Elijah," the mock-epic hero of the *Cyclops* episode and of the novel. Both, he says, are victims of xenophobia; both are "robbed and plundered": the words are used by Bloom in the bar, but they apply to the position of Herzog. David S. Galloway[187] puts it thus: ". . . Bloom's thematic relationship to Moses Herzog is strongly reinforced: both are aliens, Jewish exiles in Irish Dublin and both are owed 'debts' by society which it is unlikely they will ever collect."

In 1915, when his friend, Ottocaro Weiss, commented on the possibility of a Jewish State, Joyce remarked:[188] "That's all very well, but believe me, a warship with a captain called Kanalgitter and his aide named Captain Afterduft would be the funniest thing the old Mediterranean has ever seen." His attitude to Zionism is seen in the "Zion-Palestine" motif,[189] which is among the most persistent of symbols in *Ulysses*. It appears for the first time when Bloom goes out in the morning to Dlugacz's butcher shop to buy a pork kidney for breakfast and finds on his counter pieces of wrapping-up newspaper, perhaps a little too obviously placed there by Joyce.[190] One of these pages, adorned with an advertisement photograph of an early Zionist farm[191] which Bloom paints in words, presented a prospectus for building new settlements in Palestine: "He took up a large page from a pile of cut sheets. The model farm[192] at Kinnereth on the lakeshore of Tiberias. Can become ideal sanatorium.[193] Moses Montefiore. I thought he was. Farmhouse, wall around it, blurred cattle cropping, He held the page from him: interesting: read it nearer, the blurred cropping cattle, the page rustling. . . ."

Walking back home, he looks again at the wrapping and considers another advertisement of a plantation company for recultivating Palestine, making a mental note of its main points. Under the strong monetary impression of the prospectus,* Bloom apparently summarises rapidly from a German original, retaining some of the German phraseology in his English version:

> "Agendath Netaim:[194] planter's company.[195] To purchase vast sandy tracts from Turkish government and plant with eucalyptus trees. Excellent for shade, fuel and construction. Orangegroves and immense

---

*A hint of the prospectus is found in the contract signed in 1913 between "Agudath Netayim" (a variant transliteration) of Palestine, represented by Arnold Kretchmar-Israeli, and the South African Zionist Federation for the establishment of a farm on about 600 dunams near Hadera, which would be planted with almonds and olives. The cost of the farm was to be about £4,500 and the contract stipulated that it be paid off in six instalments of £750 each. The farm was to be divided into 150 portions, the value of each to be £30, and the societies were asked to pay for their portions in instalments of £5 a year. At the end of the six years, the Federation informed its societies, "the Company will hand over to us a farm ready planted, which will have a revenue, and which will be entirely our own property." See Marcia Gitlin, *The Vision Amazing: The Story of South African Zionism* (Johannesburg, 1950), pp. 158–9.

melonfields north of Jaffa. You pay eight marks and they plant a dunam for you with olives, oranges, almonds or citrons. Olives cheaper: oranges need artificial irrigation. Every year you get a sending[196] of the crop. Your name entered for life as owner in the bank of the union. Can pay ten down and the balance in yearly instalments. Bleibtreustrasse, 34, Berlin, W. 15.[197]

Nothing doing. Still an idea behind it."[198]

Leopold Bloom muses about various things — cattle, olives, citrons that he and his wife Molly used to enjoy. "Citron" recalls other Jewish exiles like himself, poor Citron[199] of St. Kevin's Parade, and Moisel[200] or Arbutus Place and cither-playing Mastiansky:[201]

> Oranges[202] in tissue paper packed in crates. Citrons too. Wonder is poor Citron still alive in Saint Kevin's parade. And Mastiansky with the old cither. Pleasant evenings we had then. Molly in Citron's basketchair. Nice to hold, cool waxen fruit, hold in the hand, lift it to the nostrils and smell the perfume. Like that, heavy, sweet, wild perfume. Always the same, year after year. They fetched high prices too Moisel told me. Arbutus place: Pleasant street: pleasant old times. Must be without a flaw, he said. Coming all that way:[203] Spain, Gibraltar, Mediterranean, the Levant. Crates lined up on the quayside at Jaffa, chap ticking them off in a book, navvies handling them in soiled dungarees . . .

A cloud slowly covers the sun and, in a grey horror which sears his flesh, Bloom's mind turns to a sudden vision of modern Palestine and the Dead Sea and he thinks of the sufferings of the Jewish-people, their dispersal after the conquest of Judaea and their ceaseless wanderings: "A barren land,[204] bare waste. Volcanic lake, the dead sea: . . . Brimstone they called it raining down: the cities of the plain: Sodom, Gomorrah, Edom. All dead names. A dead sea in a dead land, grey and old. Old now. It bore the oldest, the finest race. . . . The oldest people. Wandered far away over all the earth, captivity to captivity. It lay there now. Now it could bear no more. Dead: . . . Desolation."

The surname Mastiansky is, as we have seen, a misprint for Masliansky, and Masliansky, a personal acquaintance of Bloom in earlier days but seemingly cut off from him by apostasy, could be identical with Philip Masliansky, who in 1896 lived at 2 Martin Street, in 1899–1900 at 63 Lombard Street West[205] and from 1901–1906 at 16 St. Kevin's Parade. On 8 October 1896, as Phinchas (sic) Masliansky, he married Florra Leanse (or Lyons) at the Adelaide Road synagogue.[206] *Thom's Directories* record him as Phinis (sic) Mosliansky in 1899 and 1900, as P. Masliansky in 1901 and as P. Mastiansky in 1902–1906. Although qualified as a shochet (ritual slaughterer), he earned his livelihood by peddling drapery. A handsome man with a small pointed beard and endowed with a fine singing voice, Philip, aged about 30 in 1904, was the son of Moses Masliansky, a native of Slutzk in the province of Minsk, Hebrew teacher, beadle of the Chevrah Tehillim synagogue in Lombard Street West, and a committee member of the Dublin Reading and Debating Association in 1898.[207] His half-sister, Doreen, while still in her teens, helped her father by teaching the Yiddish language and songs to the young Dublin Jewish girls of the time. His stepmother had a lyrical soprano voice and entertained her family and her neighbours by singing popular Jewish melodies from Abraham Goldfaden's[208] operettas *Bar Cochba, Die Zauberin (The Witch),* and *Shulamith* or *Daughter of Zion,* which were very popular in Dublin in the first decade of the century.[209] This might have inspired Bloom's "pleasant evenings" at home of Citron,[210] with Mastiansky playing the cither. Joyce may well have heard of the musical Masliansky family from his friend John F. Byrne, who spent many an evening, as noted,[211] dining with Abraham Moses Zaks at 13 St. Kevin's Parade. Zaks could well have invited members of the neighbouring Masliansky family to entertain, with exotic and sentimental folksongs, his Gentile guest, who writes[212] of himself that, at the close of the nineteenth century, he was even fonder of music than his music-loving friend, James Joyce. About 1906, Moses, Isaac and Philip Masliansky, with their families, left for New York to join their cousin, Zevi Hirsch Masliansky[213] (1856-1943), Zionist leader and great Yiddish folk-orator, and their descendants are now (1971) living in Seattle.[214]

Moisel of Arbutus Place is identical with the ninety-year-old Nisan Moisel[215] (1814-1909), with whose two sons and their families Bloom was acquainted and from whom he obtained the information about the ritual quality and price of citrons. Trading as a greengrocer and poultry dealer, Moisel lived first in Kingsland Park Avenue and later at 20 Arbutus Place, a cul-de-sac off Lombard Street West, not far from No. 38, where Bloom lived in 1893.[216] By his first wife, Sarah Rivah Newman, sister of the Rev. Louis Newman,[217] of No. 39, who died on 14 July 1904,[218] he was the father of Elyah Wolf Moisel[219] (1856-1904), whose wife, Basseh (née Hodess), gave birth to a daughter, Rebecca Ita, on 28 June 1889, thirteen days after Molly Bloom's daughter, Milly, was born: "Funny sight two of them together, their bellies out. Molly and Mrs. Moisel. Mothers' meeting,"[220] Bloom reflects in the episode of the *Lestrygonians.* By his second wife, Haya, Nisan was the father of Philip Moisel, popularly known as Orkeh, who, about 1892, married the daughter of a Church of Ireland minister, of Kingsland Parade, and resided in Heytesbury Street. Towards the close of the century, he emigrated to South Africa and died there about 1903. Shortly afterwards, his widow moved back to her parents' home. One of her sons, a tall, broad-shouldered man, who spoke with a marked brogue, was an authority on classical music and became the proprietor of "The Gramophone Stores," at 6 Johnston's Court, off Grafton Street, whose owner was listed in *Thom's Directory* for 1960 as C. Moiselle.

Throughout the long day, Bloom, though nominally a Catholic, still has the exilic yearnings of a Jew for his ancient homeland. He thinks of the sun traversing the sky from morning to evening: "Fading gold sky. A mother watches from her doorway. She calls her children home in their dark language,"[221] reminding us of Rachel mourning for her children. In one of his many moments of introspection and retrospection, he reveals his memories in the section headed "AND IT WAS THE FEAST OF PASS-OVER" in the *Aeolus* chapter, when he goes to the newspaper office to see about an advertisement, looks at the typesetter "neatly distributing type," and thinks:

> Reads it backwards first. Quickly he does it. Must require some practice that. . . . Poor papa with the hagada book, reading backwards with his finger to me. Pessach. Next year in Jerusalem. Dear, O dear! All that long business about that brought us out of the land of Egypt and into[222] the house of bondage [the "into" here is unconscious and Joyce's irony; Bloom is out of Egypt, the land of bondage, but has found new bondage in his "freedom"] alleluia. Shema Israel Adonai Elohenu. No, that's the other. Then the twelve brothers, Jacob's sons. And then the lamb and the cat and the dog and the stick and the water and the butcher and then the angel of death kills the butcher and he kills the ox and the dog kills the cat. Sounds a bit silly till you come to look into it well. Justice it means but it's everybody eating everybody else. That's what life is after all.[223]

But Bloom is the reluctant exile who accepts life as it is in Dublin in 1904; the message from the plantations of "Agendath Netaim" and the model farm on the lake-shore of Kinnereth delivered to Bloom, the Irish Jew in exile, through the agency of Dlugacz, the Zionist butcher, is consigned that night to the flames by Bloom,[224] the prospective Irish country gentleman. His is Homer's creed, the politician's "art of the possible";[225] in Dublin and Cork, there were not a few Jews who, like Bloom, dreamt of the Orient but, unlike him, thought there was "something doing" in Palestine and made plans to settle there.

Notes

1. Ellmann, *James Joyce*, p. 706 footnote.

2. *Ulysses*, p. 655 (544).

3. Even Dublin had its Wailing Wall in 1904. The story is told of Mrs. Bessie Light (d. 1916), an old Jewish lady in Dublin, who insisted on coming regularly to see each of her grandsons off as they left, in succession, at the turn of the century for South Africa, from the North Wall of the River Liffey, whence Joyce also made his hegira. The old lady would bemoan her fate near a pole at the wharf popularly known by the Irish porters as the "Wailing Wall." Letter to me from Mrs. J. S. Bloom, of Seattle, 1 June 1968.

4. M. Shulomowitz is probably identical with the M. Shmulovitch (d. 1940) who appears in *Thom's Directory* for 1905 as secretary of the Jewish Library at 57 Lombard Street West; as Isaac Myer Shmulowitz, he was the Dublin correspondent of the London Hebrew weekly, *Hayehudi*, who left for South Africa in 1904. See *Hayehudi*, 15 October 1904. Shmulowitz returned to Ireland some years later and settled in Cork, where he married Anne, daughter of the Rev. Meyer Elyan, Minister of the Cork congregation.

5. Joseph Goldwater lived at 77 Lombard Street West, and Harris Rosenberg at No. 63. At the close of the nineteenth century, the Dublin Hebrew Young Men's Association met at the

Rooms at 77 Lombard Street West, its officials in 1899 being Honorary Secretary, I. M. Shmulowitz, Committee, Isaac Shein (d. 1931), M. Chitron (sic) -Light, H. Greentuch, and Solomon Bloom. See *Jewish World*, to March 1899. Morris Citron (d. 1931) was Honorary Secretary of the Dublin Jewish Literary and Social Club in 1905-6. See Jewish Year Book 5666 (1905-6).

6. Moses Herzog, after whom Saul Bellow's *Herzog* is almost certainly named, was a one-eyed bachelor who left for South Africa in 1908. His sister-in-law Marion Rachel, wife of Isaac Herzog, had died on 8 March 1900, at the age of fifty six. Herzog lived at 13 St. Kevin's Parade, a few doors away from Citron and Mastiansky, and traded as an itinerant grocer. His name appears three times in the *Cyclops* episode. See *infra*, pp. 186–187.

7. M. Moisel, who appears thus in *Thom's Directory* for 1904 and 1905, is probably a misprint for N. Moisel, the "Nisan" Moisel who told Bloom about the price and quality of citrons. See *infra*, pp. 188, 190.

8. J. Citron, who appears thus in *Thom's Directory* for 1905, is a misprint for I[srael] Citron (1876-1951) who lived at No. 17 and not at 28 St. Kevin's Parade. See *Thom's Directory* for 1905 and *Ulysses*, p. 156 (122). See also *infra*, pp. 174, 188. He was a brother of the Morris Citron referred to in note 5 above.

9. Minnie Watchman, my great-aunt, is recorded in *Thom's Directory* for 1905 as the tenant of 20 St. Kevin's Parade, as her husband, Jacob Leib, was in Dundalk in 1904 setting up a business. She wrongly appears in the *Directory* with the prefix "Mr," and Joyce, by including her name in the list of the circumcised, was probably having his own little private joke on the *Directory*. For similar errors noted in the *Directory*, see J. F. Byrne, *Silent Years*, p. 154.

10. O. Mastiansky is probably a misprint for P. Mastiansky, who according to *Thom's Directory* for 1905, lived at 1ö St. Kevin's Parade. He is supposed to be the same person as Julius Mastiansky, who figures in *Ulysses* as one of Molly Bloom's lovers (see p. 863 (731)) and one of the former friends of Bloom with whom he had discussions on various subjects in 1892 and 1893 (see p. 778 (667)). The name Mastiansky, which is unknown in the Dublin Jewish community of the time, is a misprint for Masliansky (see *infra*, p. 189).

11. The Reverend Leopold Abramovitz, Chazen, is identical with Abraham Lipman Abramovitz (d. 1907), Reader of the Lennox Street synagogue. An ordained rabbi, he arrived in Dublin in 1887 and served the community as shochet (ritual slaughterer), chazan (reader), mohel (circumciser) and Hebrew teacher. See his obituary in the London Hebrew weekly, *Hayehudi*, 10 October 1907. See also *infra*, p. 193. He was the grandfather of Robert Kahan (1893–1951), a Dublin civil servant and a keen student of Joyce.

12. By excluding flowers, Joyce showed his familiarity with orthodox Jewish custom, which forbids the placing of flowers on graves. See A. J. Leventhal, "The Jew Errant," *The Dubliner*, Vol. 2, Spring 1963, No. 1, p. 21.

13. *Thom's Directories*, 1890–1905.

14. *Ulysses*, pp. 139 (110), 617 (487); Census of Ireland, 1901.

15. *Ibid.*, p. 193 (153).

16. *Ibid.*, p. 638 (523).

17. Bloom's father, Rudolph, who came from Hungary, anglicised his family name Virag, which means "flower" in Hungarian, as Bloom.

18. Letters to me from Mrs. Mabel Rothband, 14 November 1963, and Mrs. Dorothy H. Goldstone, 8 February 1969. Franks was a great-grandson of Isaac Franks, married in Dublin in 1781 and a grandson of Jacob Franks, who died in Dublin in 1846. See *supra*, p. 301, note 13.

19. See Ellmann, *James Joyce*, pp. 238, 778, note 38.

20. Marriage Certificate B 5 42 No. 156 at the General Register Office, now changed to Oifig an Ard-Chláraitheora, Custom House, Dublin.

21. The marriage of John Joyce to Mary Jane Murray took place at the same church on 5 May 1880. See Ellmann, *op. cit.*, p. 17.

22. *Thom's Directory*, 1899.

23. Ellmann, *op. cit.*, p. 23.

24. *Letters of James Joyce* [vol. I] ed. Stuart Gilbert (London, 1957), p. 174.

25. *Thom's Directory*, 1899.

26. See R. M. Adams, *op. cit.*, p. 62.

27. Gorman, Herbert. *James Joyce* (London, 1941), pp. 176–177.

28. *Letters of James Joyce*, [vol. 1], p. 55, C. P. Curran, *James Joyce Remembered* (London, 1968), pp. 48–49 and Ellmann, *Ulysses: A Short History*, pp. 707–708, appended to the first Penguin edition of *Ulysses*, 1968.

29. It may be of interest to record that a Leopold Andrew Walshe Hunter graduated as a B. A. at the Summer Commencements of Trinity College, Dublin, in 1904.

30. *Ulysses*, p. 704 (613).

31. Letter to me from Mr. D. Sexton, Deputy Registrar of Marriages, etc., Cork Health Authority, 9 April 1969.

32. In her marriage certificate at the General Register Office, Custom House, Dublin, Sarah is recorded as "a minor." 1870 was the year of Molly Bloom's birth.

33. See *Palestina:* Chovevei Zion Quarterly, No. 6, December 1893.

34. *Ulysses*, p. 719 (624).

35. In the Census of Ireland, 1911, Sarah Bloom is described as a widow.

36. *Ulysses*, p. 875 (740).

37. Interview with Mrs. Janie Davis and Mrs. Rebecca Miller, 1969.

38. Letter to me from Samuel Garber, 16 March 1970.

39. Letter to me from Philip Sless, 8 January 1970.

40. Letter to me from S. H. Leventhal, 17 September 1968.

41. Interview with Mrs. Rose Spiro, formerly Mrs. Rose Yodaiken, 1969.

42. Interview with Laurence Elyan, 1968.

43. *Ulysses*, pp. 74 (61), 653 (542).

44. Letter to me from Samuel Garber, 12 August 1970.

45. Census of Ireland, 1911.

46. Interview with Mrs. Rebecca Isaacson, 1969.

47. Census of Ireland, 1911.

48. Letter to me from Samuel Garber, 16 March 1970.

49. Interview with Joseph Birkhan, 1969.

50. Letter to me from A. J. Leventhal, 19 November 1969.

51. In the Register of the Dolphin's Barn Cemetery she appears as Bassa Bloom but her death certificate records her as Sarah Bloom, housekeeper of 36 Victoria Street.

52. Interview in 1968 with Mrs. Rachel Grossman (1885–1969), former resident of Jerusalem, and daughter of Rabbi Isaac Meyer Yosselson of Dublin; letter to me from Arthur Robinson, 19 July 1968, formerly of 36 Lombard Street West and now resident in Johannesburg.

53. Letter to me from Max Nurock, 28 July 1968.

54. *Thom's Directories*, 1892–1912. In the directories from 1892 to 1984 he appears as T. Bloom and from 1895 to 1911 as J. Bloom.

55. For some oddities of *Ulysses'* time-pattern see Adams, *Surface and Symbol*, pp. 186–187, where he refers to Joyce's inconsistency in making the Blooms live in Lombard Street

West early in 1893, moving them to Raymond Terrace early in March of the same year, making them live in the City Arms Hotel at 54 Prussia Street late in the year 1893 and early in 1894 and recording them as still in Lombard Street West in 1894.

56. Memorandum of Mrs. Rebecca Ita Isaacson, 23 July 1969.

57. *Ulysses*, p. 331 (258).

58. J. F. Byrne in his *Silent Years: An Autobiography with Memoirs of James Joyce and Our Ireland* (New York, 1963), pp. 18–19, was misled in regarding as a Jew "the bookseller of *Sweets of Sin*," Josh Strong, who is unnamed in *Ulysses* and from whom Bloom purchased for himself *Aristotle's Masterpiece* which Molly called the "Aristocrat's Masterpiece." See *Ulysses*, pp. 303–304 (236–237), 686 (586), 913 (772).

59. J. F. Byrne, *op. cit.*, p. 19, has the following note referring to the occupant of the main shop of 26 Wellington Quay which some years before had been occupied by Simon Marks: "(It) was rented by one Figatner, another wealthy Jew and jeweler. Fig was altogether a different character from Josh. He had the reputation of being well versed in Oriental languages. I was told he had lectured in those languages in Trinity College, this I never verified. He always wore a black hat, frock coat, flamboyant waistcoat with a gold chain like a hawser, and spats. Somewhere around 1894, he was married to a young Irish girl, daughter of the caretaker of the local Workmen's Club on Wellington Quay. In *Ulysses*, Chapter XV, Josh Strong and Figatner are referred to, the former as "the bookseller of " '*Sweets of Sins*.' "

60. *Thom's Dublin Directory*, 1895.

61. *Ulysses*, p. 334 (259).

62. A. J. Leventhal spoke with Joyce of the Jewish families mentioned in *Ulysses*, of one with the incongruous name of Higgins, whom Joyce had related to Bloom. See *supra*, p. 143 and Ellmann, *James Joyce*, p. 527.

63. *Ulysses*, p. 375 (290).

64. Interview with Mrs. Leah Gruson, 1969.

65. At the close of the nineteenth century there lived in Dublin an Isaac Bloom who was apparently non-Jewish. On 27 February 1898, Thomas Edward Bloom, soldier of Richmond Barracks, son of Isaac Bloom, painter, married Elizabeth Gillespie of 34 Denzille Street at the Roman Catholic Church of St. Andrew's. A son John was born in the Coombe Hospital on 28 May 1898.

66. Ellmann, "The Backgrounds of *Ulysses*," *The Kenyon Review*, Vol. xvi, Summer 1954, No. 3, p. 381.

67. *Dublin Directories*, 1904–1905.

68. *Ibid.*, 1895; see Ellmann, *James Joyce*, p. 17 and footnote.

69. *Ibid.*, 1901–1903.

70. Census of Ireland, 1901.

71. *Dublin Directory*, 1905.

72. *Dublin Directories*, 1908–1915.

73. Interview with Mrs. Rebecca Isaacson, 1969.

74. Census of Ireland, 1901.

75. Letter to me from S. H. Leventhal, 27 October 1968; interview with Mrs. Leah Gruson, 1969; Ellmann, *James Joyce*, p. 386.

76. Interview with Mrs. Rebecca Isaacson, 1969. This information came to her from Hannah Berman, resident in Dublin at the time.

77. *Ulysses*, p. 198 (156).

78. Letter to me from Philip Ordman, 25 September 1968.

79. Interview with Mervyn Hool, 1969.

80. Letter to me from Philip Ordman, 4 March 1969.

81. Interview with Mrs. Rebecca Ita Isaacson, 1967.

82. Letter to me from Dr. Ivor Citron, 12 October 1969.

83. *Ulysses*, p. 599 (475).

84. *Ibid.*, p. 436 (336).

85. Pesach is Hebrew for Passover; he had never anglicised his name. In the 1901 Census his name appears as Paisax.

86. Letter to me from Mrs. J. S. Bloom, 21 August 1968.

87. See *Ulysses*, p. 518 (396); letter to me from Max Nurock, 8 December 1968 and *Ulysses*, p. 174 (138).

88. See the *Evening Mail*, 16 June 1904, *Evening Telegraph*, 16 June 1904, *Freeman's Journal*, 17 June 1904 and 12 July 1904, reporting that Wought was sentenced to twelve months with hard labour. The case was heard in the Southern Court before Mr. Swifte, K. C., and not before the Dublin Recorder, Sir Frederick Falkiner, whom Joyce intentionally introduced.

89. Robert Bloom (born 1876), eldest son of Pesach, emigrated to Seattle, America, in 1897 and later settled in Fairbanks, Alaska, during the Gold Rush (see Mrs. Robert (Jessie S.) Bloom, "The Jews of Alaska," in the *American Jewish Archives*, Vol. XV, No. 2, November 1963). He and his wife now (1971) reside in Seattle. Pesach's younger son, Nathan Meyer (1888–1944), joined his brother in Alaska in 1906. In the First World War he was a member of the Alaskan contingent in the American Army and on his discharge moved to South Africa to join his brother Solomon (1885–1966), who emigrated to Johannesburg in 1905 and was nicknamed "Pat" because of his pronounced brogue.

90. *Ulysses*, pp. 162 (127), 417 (322).

91. *Ibid.*, p. 852 (723).

92. *Jewish Year Book*, 5657–5662: 1896–1903. On 7 February 1899, Alfred Bloom, soldier of Old Barracks, Fermoy, County Cork, son of Samuel Bloom, stoker of the Royal Navy, deceased, married Margaret McAuliffe of Fermoy. This Bloom family was apparently of non-Jewish origin.

93. *Jewish Year Book*, 5657: 1896–1897.

94. See *Jewish Chronicle*, 14 April 1969, p. 43.

95. *Ulysses*, pp. 322 (250), 582 (455).

96. Census of Ireland, 1911.

97. Adams *Surface and Symbol*, p. 62.

98. *Jewish Chronicle*, 21 December 1906. A native of Lithuania and son of a rabbi, Lipsett, anglicised from Lipschitz, emigrated to Ireland, where he became a journalist, writing for the *Dublin Daily Mail* and the London *Jewish Chronicle*, in which he published a series of sketches of life in a mythical Lithuanian village which he called "Pavenda." His novel *Didy*, published in 1912, is mentioned in the Rev. Stephen J. Brown's *Ireland in Fiction* (Dublin 1916), p. 147. Lipsett married a Gentile, is said to have turned convert and missionary, and left for New York in 1908. See *Jewish Chronicle*, 25 November 1921.

99. In a letter dated 27 January 1969, A. J. Leventhal writes: "There is a story (he [Edward Lipman] told me himself) about his returning to Dublin on leave during the First World War, towards the end of it, and entering the "Bailey" in Duke Street where Griffith and his friends used to meet. He was in the R.A.M.C. dressed as an officer. He was coldly received by the occupants of the pub and quickly left. He had hardly covered 50 yards when he was overtaken by a panting Griffith who said he had not noticed him when he came in and rushed to tell him that his uniform in no way interfered with his friendship. I don't think Lipman ever met Joyce but he was very friendly with Frank Budgen and treasured a copy of the latter's work on Joyce."

100. *Jewish World*, 1 January 1909.

101. *Ibid.*, 15 January 1909.

102. See Appendix X(b), pp. 362–363.

103. Unlike Edelstein, Bloom in *Ulysses* stands up for his own Irishness, and calls himself an Irishman not only in public as in the *Cyclops* episode:

"What is your nation if I may ask, says the citizen."
"Ireland, says Bloom. I was born here. Ireland,"
but also in his deepest and most inward thoughts.

104. E. R. Lipsett, using the pen-name of "Halitvack," has the following remarks on the term "Jewman": "They have coined here a term which is nowhere else in circulation. Nowhere else is the term 'Jewman' known; here we hear nothing else, and infrequently we see it, too. It is a piece of vulgarity that has crept into print unconsciously; though instances are not lacking where it has been pushed in on purpose. Often have I seen the 'Jewman' staring up from placards in the street. The bill on the editor's board is not made up by the creeping process. Often, too, one may hear the 'Jewman' drop informally from the lips of highly-placed personages and officials." "Halitvack," *loc. cit.* A. J. Leventhal (born in Dublin in 1896), in an article, "What it Means to be a Jew" published in *The Bell*, edited by Séan O'Faoláin, Vol. 10, No. 3 (June 1945), p. 209, writing on the significance of the term "Jewman" to him while still in his 'teens, remarks: "I did not know that this was a word current only in Ireland, where the English variants 'sheeny' and 'Jewboy' had never found a home. 'Jewman' was obviously formed on the analogy of Frenchman, Englishman, etc., and in parts of the country one can still hear 'Russianman.' The term was not, in the first instance, pejorative. I have even heard a mother teach a babe in arms his first lesson in racial differences by pointing me out as a Jewman. Synge was the first writer to print the word . . . in *The Playboy of the Western World* [1907]." (A. J. Leventhal later became a university lecturer and a dramatic and art critic. See Appendix X(b), p. 285).

105. Ellmann, *James Joyce*, pp. 407–8.

106. *Ibid.*, p. 722.

107. See Frank Budgen, "James Joyce," in *James Joyce: Two Decades of Criticism*, edited with a new introduction by Seon Givens (New York, 1963), p. 23. This article originally appeared in *Partisan Review*, March–April, 1941.

108. Interview with Maria Jolas, 1966.

109. Frank Budgen, *loc. cit.*, p. 23.

110. Frank Budgen, "James Joyce," *Horizon*, III, February 1941, p. 107.

111. Ellmann, *James Joyce*, p. 384 footnote.

112. "The Jew in Search of a Son," in the *Virginia Quarterly Review*, xxiv, 1948, p. 109.

113. *Jewish Chronicle Quarterly Supplement*, No. 1, 25 December 1959, p. 2.

114. The following pertinent and authentic story illustrating native Irish wit is worth recording here. In the 1870s, the Rev. Philipp Bender, Minister of the Dublin congregation, took a party of friends to the lovely Glen of the Dargle, near Bray, County Wicklow. A car was hired for the day. Paddy, the driver, was a typical Irish wit and got on very well with the Jewish cleric, who was himself a born humourist. At the end of the day's hire, Mr. Bender, who was the soul of generosity, gave the driver, on behalf of himself and his friends, a sovereign above the required fare. The astonished recipient assured his benefactor that he knew him for a "rale gintleman" as soon as he had set eyes upon his features, and Mr. Bender thought that he might improve the occasion by a gentle lesson on Jewish generosity. "See, Pat," said he, "have you ever had such a tip before?" "No, your honour," was the reply. "Well, then," said Mr. Bender, "remember that you have been employed by Jews." "Jews, is it?" was the immediate pious exclamation, "*would to Christ ivery wan was Jews*" (My italics – L. H.)

115. For the symbolic significance of Jewishness in the American context see Albert

Goldman, "Boy-Man Schlemiel," in *Explorations,* ed. by Murray Mindlin with Chaim Bermant (London, 1967), pp. 5–7, where reference is made to Leopold Bloom.

116. R. M. Adams, *op. cit.,* p. 106.

117. Herbert Howarth, *The Irish Writers* (1880–1940), p. 24.

118. See Webb, *Compendium of Irish Biography* and *Dictionary of National Biography, s.v.* Lucas, Charles; see also J. T. Gilbert, *A History of the City of Dublin,* iii, p. 39.

119. See *Ulysses,* p. 176 (139).

120. *Ibid.,* p. 428 (330).

121. *Ibid.,* pp. 179–81 (141–3).

122. Victor Bérard, *Les Phéniciens et l'Odyssée* (Paris, 1902–3, 2 tomes); see also Gilbert, *James Joyce's Ulysses,* pp. 54–5 *et passim.*

123. See essay by George Steiner, "Homer and the Scholars," in *Language and Silence* (London, 1967), pp. 209–210.

124. Frank Budgen, *James Joyce and the Making of "Ulysses"* (Bloomington, 1960), p. 170.

125. *Letters of James Joyce,* ed. Gilbert, p. 146.

126. See *Finnegans Wake,* p. 228.

127. See Book I, sec. xv. Keating's book was translated into English by Father Patrick S. Dinneen (1860–1934) and published in 1908 for the Irish Texts Society.

128. See *op. cit.,* pp. 136–7.

129. See *Ulysses,* pp. 806–7 (688–9).

130. See *supra,* pp. 1–2 and Douglas Hyde, *A Literary History of Ireland* (Dublin, 1899), p. 48, quoted by Howarth, *op. cit.,* p. 260.

131. See *supra,* p. 105.

132. *Dublin Evening Telegraph,* 15 February 1909, for a report of a lecture on "The Jews in Ireland in the Middle Ages," by John Wyse Power, friend of Joyce, who dwelt with much pleasure on the fact that Daniel O'Connell himself, a kinsman of the Joyce family, had the obsolete Statute "De Judaismo," which prescribed a special dress for Jews, formally repealed in 1846; see also G. F. Abbott, *Israel in Europe* (London, 1907), p. 323.

133. See Ellmann, *op. cit.,* pp. 280–283 *et passim.*

134. See *infra,* pp. 221–223.

135. See *supra,* p. 149.

136. See *supra,* p. 148.

137. See *supra,* p. 63.

138. See *Thom's Directory* for 1905.

139. *Ulysses,* pp. 577–8 (448–9).

140. See *infra,* pp. 190–191.

141. See *infra,* p. 190.

142. See *infra,* pp. 186–187.

143. Byrne tried to assist Zaks in finding employment in New York when his Jewish friend emigrated to the United States in 1911. Letter to me from Jacob G. Zaks of New York, 18 October 1962.

144. *Silent Years,* p. 182.

145. James Joyce, *Portrait of the Artist as a Young Man* (new edition, London, 1942), p. 206.

146. *Jewish World,* 19 January 1900.

147. *Silent Years,* p. 179. David Baker, who later moved to Leeds, was Vice-

Commander of the Dublin Chovevei Zio (Lovers of Zion) in 1900. See *Hayehudi*, 1 November 1900.

148. *Silent Years*, pp. 183–84 and *Jewish World*, 31 January 1908.

149. Messrs. Joseph Edelstein, Philip Wigoder, Philip Baker, Moses Leventhal, Jacob Zlotover and Falk Ginsberg took part in the discussion that followed Byrne's lecture.

150. See *infra*, pp. 212–217.

151. See Marvin Magalaner, "The Anti-Semitic Limerick Incidents and Joyce's 'Blooms-day' in *PMLA* (December 1953), LXVIII, pp. 1219–23.

152. Ellmann, *James Joyce*, p. 285.

153. See *infra*, p. 185.

154. *Notes and Queries*, 3rd ser. xi., p. 377.

155. *Ulysses*, p. 44 (36).

156. See *supra*, p. 3.

157. Interview in 1966 with his widow, Mrs. Rachele Dlugacz, and his daughter, Mrs. Hemda Sassover, now (1971) resident in Haifa.

158. See David Daiches, "James Joyce's Jew," *Jewish Chronicle Quarterly Supplement*, 25 December 1959, pp. 2–3, where Dlugacz is regarded as a highly improbable and wholly imaginary character. R. M. Adams, *Surface and Symbol*, pp. 101, 215, regards him as a renegade Hungarian Jew whose name seems to have been adopted from that of a Polish historian, Jan Dlugosz (1415–80). Richard Ellmann makes no mention of him in his monumental biography of James Joyce.

159. Dlugacz's rabbinical diploma dated 21 Sivan (June) 1898, and signed by Rabbi Israel Shevach Lerner, Head of the Beth Din (Ecclesiastical Court) of the community of Dinevitch, in the Ukraine, is in the possession of his widow.

160. Joyce, who had his wife, Nora, painted by the Triestine artist Tullio Silvestri, in 1913, inscribed the portrait, at the suggestion of Dlugacz, with the words "Mora ma bella" from the Song of Solomon, 1, 5. Dlugacz was presented with an autographed copy of *Dubliners* soon after its publication on 15 June 1914. Interview with Mrs. Hemda Sassover.

161. Interview in Trieste in 1966 with Giuseppe Fano, Director of the "Ufficio Palestinese," of Trieste, in 1918 and one of Joyce's creditors in 1912 for stationery requisites. See *Letters of James Joyce*, ii, p. 299.

162. Interview in 1966 with Arthur Freud, Hebrew pupil of Dlugacz in Trieste in 1912, now (1971) resident in Jerusalem.

163. Interview in 1966 with Arrigo Barac (formerly Blitz), Hebrew pupil of Dlugacz in 1918 in Trieste, now (1971) resident in Haifa.

164. See Ellmann, *James Joyce*, p. 140.

165. Letter from Alessandro Levi-Minzi, of Trieste, 10 February 1966.

166. See *supra*, p. 171 and *infra*, p. 285.

167. Ellmann, *op. cit.*, p. 527; see *supra*, p. 171.

168. *Ulysses*, p. 807 (689).

169. Stenographisches Protokols Der Verhandlungen des XII Zionisten Kongresses In Karlsbad von 1 bis 14 September, 1921 (Berlin, 1922), p. 6.

170. *Ulysses*, p. 83 (68).

171. See *supra*, p. 289, note 18.

172. See *infra*, pp. 196–197.

173. *Ulysses*, p. 328 (254).

174. See *infra*, p. 200.

175. See *infra*, p. 201.

176. *Ulysses*, p. 436 (337).

177. *Ibid.*, pp. 444–5 (342).

178. Healy, Parnell's lieutenant, staunchly stood by his leader in the O'Shea divorce scandal after Parnell had been repudiated by Davitt, Gladstone and the Church hierarchy. Healy, using Mosaic imagery commonly applied to Parnell, declared that the leader should not be abandoned "within sight of the Promised Land." Later Healy joined Parnell's opponents, whereupon the nine-year-old James Joyce wrote a poem denouncing Healy under the title, "Et Tu Healy?" In his attitude to Jews, Healy was not consistent either. In 1914, some time after the O'Brien-Devlin case, when appearing in the District Courts on behalf of licensed traders, he publicly attacked Sir Matthew Nathan, the Under-Secretary for Ireland, as a German Jew.

179. See *Jewish Chronicle*, 27 November 1914.

180. Interview with Mrs. Rebecca Ita Isaacson, 1967. The story is told of Moses Herzog that when a matchmaker tried to marry him off to an unattractive lady he is alleged to have replied: "Even one eye wants to see something decent."

181. See "Joyce's Notes on the End of *Oxen of the Sun*," edited by Alan M. Cohn, *James Joyce Quarterly*, Vol. 4, Number 3, Spring 1967, pp. 195–6.

182. This information came to Mrs. Isaacson from Simon Eppel, one of Herzog's Dublin contemporaries.

183. *Ulysses*, pp. 376–8 (287–8).

184. A. J. Leventhal, *What it Means to be a Jew*, loc. cit., p. 209.

185. See Harry Blamires, *The Bloomsday Book* (London, 1966), pp. 121–2.

186. "The Hero as Jew: Reflections on 'Herzog,' in *Judaism*, vol. 17, Number 1, Winter 1968, p. 42.

187. "Moses-Bloom-Herzog: Bellow's Everyman," in the *Southern Review*, Winter 1966, Vol. ii. New Series. January 1966, Number 1, pp. 65–6.

188. Ellmann, *op. cit.*, p. 408.

189. For more on the significance of the East in Bloom's thought, see Gilbert, *James Joyce's "Ulysses,"* pp. 43, 135–6, 143–5; Leo Shapiro, "The 'Zion' Motif in Joyce's *Ulysses*," in *Jewish Frontier*, xiii, No. 9 (September 1946), pp. 14–16.

190. See S. L. Goldberg, *The Classical Temper: A Study of James Joyce's "Ulysses"* (London, 1961), p. 258.

191. *Ulysses*, pp. 70–1 (59).

192. The farm at Kinnereth, commonly called the "training farm," was founded by the Palestine Land Development Company on 8 June 1908, to train Jews as agricultural workers and to prove that a farm employing Jewish workers could be profitable. It was to serve as a model (hence "model farm") for similar projects to be established later. The farm being completely isolated, the wall and an iron gate were built to ward off the attacks of hostile Bedouin and fellahin in the neighbourhood.

193. The Palestine Land Development Company also circularised a prospectus in German from its Berlin address at Bleibtreustrasse 34/35. This two-paged prospectus could have been one of the large pages of cut sheets with the photograph of the model farm at Kinnereth which Joyce contrived as piled on Dlugacz's counter. The prospectus announced the establishment of a Jewish Garden City in Palestine; it also proposed the erection of a sanatorium to utilise the sulphur springs in the vicinity. The project on the lake shore of Kinnereth was first broached by Theodor Herzl in his book *Altneuland* and would be, the prospectus comments, the realisation of Herzl's dream. This, therefore, could be the factual background for Bloom's speculation on the originator of the scheme above.

194. "Agudath Netaim" (Company of Plantations), the original Hebrew form of "Agendath Netaim" (planter's company) as it appears in *Ulysses*, is anachronistically referred

to in the novel, as it was still one year from its foundation. It was established in Palestine only in the summer of 1905 by Aaron Eisenberg, of Rehovoth. Incorporated as a Turkish company under the name of "Societé Ottomane de Commerce, d'Agriculture, et d'Industrie," its aim was to save the prospective settler the initial hardships involved in setting up a farm by itself buying land, developing it and planting trees for him. "Agudath Netaim" laid out such plantations, between 1905 and 1914, at Hefzibah, near Hadera, at Rehovoth, near Jaffa, and at other places. In 1906, Professor Otto Warburg of Berlin, as a member of the Zionist Executive, then known as the "inner-Actions Committee," founded a plantation company called "Pflanzungsverein 'Palästina' " which, in Palestine, was sometimes referred to as "Agudath Netioth" or "Agudath Netaim, Erez Israel" but which never used the Hebrew designation as its letter-head. There was no official connection between the Berlin company and Eisenberg's "Agudath Netaim" but there was a very friendly relationship between them. Thus, in a brochure entitled "Die Anlage von Pflanzungen in Palästina" published by Warburg's department in or about 1909 and republished in 1912, small capitalists who intended to start a plantation in Palestine were advised to carry out the work through "Agudath Netaim." This is the sort of brochure which Joyce may have seen in the home of one of his Triestine Jewish friends.

195. As the Hebrew word "Netaim" is plural, the possessive form of its English equivalent should be "plantations'."

196. A small amount of almonds was sent annually by the plantation company to its shareholders so as to establish a real link between them and their plantation in Palestine.

197. Bleibtreustrasse, 34, the Berlin address of "Agendath Netaim" in the novel, does not appear in any of the voluminous records pertaining to Eisenberg's "Agudath Netaim" preserved in the Central Zionist Archives in Jerusalem, and was apparently borrowed by Joyce from one of the advertisements or prospectuses of the Palestine Land Development Company, the Immobiligesellsch, Palästina m.b.H. ("Palestine Real Estate Corporation, Ltd.") or the Tiberia Land-u. Plantagengesellsch.m.b.H. ("Tiberias Land and Plantation Corporation, Ltd.") which had their Berlin offices at 34, Bleibtreustrasse, W. 15, because it fitted in with the themes of infidelity and betrayal in *Ulysses*.

198. *Ulysses*, p. 72 (60).

199. See *supra*, p. 168.

200. *Ulysses*, p. 73 (60) and *infra*, p. 190.

201. See *infra*, p. 190.

202. *Ulysses*, pp. 72-3 (60-1).

203. See the London Hebrew weekly, *Hayehudi*, 4 October 1900, where its Dublin correspondent, Isaac Myer Shmulowitz, reported the arrival in Dublin of several hundred citrons from Gan Shmuel, Palestine.

204. *Ulysses*, p. 73 (61).

205. Philip's brother, Isaac, appears in *Thom's Directory* for 1902 as Isaac Maslidusky (*sic*) of 63 Lombard Street West.

206. MS. Register of Marriages of the Dublin Hebrew congregation from 15 April 1891 to 25 February 1914, p. 16, No. 31.

207. Interview in 1968 with Mrs. Rachel Grossman (1885-1969), former resident of Jerusalem and daughter of Rabbi Isaac Meyer Yosselson of Dublin.

208. See A. Z. Idelsohn, *Jewish Music* (New York, 1948), pp. 447-453 and Ruth Rubin, *Voices of a People* (New York and London, 1963), pp. 270-271.

209. In or about 1902 *Bar Cochba* was produced at the Abbey Theatre by the Dublin Amateur Operatic and Dramatic Society with Mr. L. Briscoe taking the title role, Mr. Antanovski as Pappus, the dwarf intriguer, and Miss Minnie Cohen as Dinah. *Shulamith* was produced at the Abbey Theatre in June 1908. See *Jewish World*, 19 June, 10 July 1908. In May 1910, the Operatic and Dramatic Society produced *Die Zauberin* at the Abbey Theatre under

the directorship of the Rev. Simon Steinberg, Reader of the Lombard Street West synagogue, formerly professor and musical director of the Berlin Academy of Music, who later emigrated to South Africa. See *Jewish World*, 20 May, 8 July 1910.

210. *Ulysses*, pp. 70–1 (60–1).

211. See *supra*, p. 182.

212. *Silent Years*, p. 65.

213. Zevi Hirsch Masliansky was the Hebrew teacher of Chaim Weizmann, first President of the State of Israel (see *Trial and Error*, Illustrated Edition of the Autobiography of Chaim Weizmann, London, 1950, pp. 39, 42). By a remarkable coincidence, of which Joyce would have been delighted to know, he was a boyhood friend of Aaron Eisenberg, founder of the plantation company "Agudath Netaim" in Palestine, whose prospectus Bloom picked up in the Dublin butcher shop of Moses Dlugacz, and Dlugacz, as a Zionist, was present at the XII Zionist Congress in Carlsbad in 1921 which the Rev. Hirsch Masliansky also attended. See *supra*, p. 185.

214. Letter to me from Mrs. Shulamit Schwartz Nardi, 6 January 1970.

215. Interview with his granddaughter, Mrs. Rebecca Ita Isaacson (née Moisel), in 1967.

216. See R. M. Adams, *Surface and Symbol*, pp. 186–7, for chronological inconsistencies concerning Bloom's residence at Lombard Street West.

217. The Rev. Louis Newman, shochet of the St. Kevin's Parade synagogue, was the father of Arthur Newman (1874–1968), prominent communal worker in the first half of the century.

218. See the London Hebrew weekly, *Hayehudi*, 21 July 1904.

219. See *infra*, p. 347.

220. *Ulysses*, p. 204 (162).

221. *Ulysses*, p. 68 (57).

222. See Irene Orgel Briskin, "Some New Light on 'The Parable of the Plums' " in the *James Joyce Quarterly*, Vol. 3, No. 4, Summer 1966, p. 247 footnote 20.

223. *Ulysses*, p. 155 (122). See Joseph Prescott, "Notes on Joyce's *Ulysses*," in *Modern Language Quarterly*, vol. XIII (June 1952), p. 152; Arnold Goldman, *The Joyce Paradox*, pp. 130–2.

224. *Ulysses*, p. 830 (707).

225. See W. B. Stanford, "Ulyssean Qualities in Joyce's Leopold Bloom," in *Comparative Literature*, vol. V., No. 2 (Spring 1953), p. 136; see also Gilbert, *James Joyce's Ulysses*, p. 366.

Joycean Syntax as
Appropriate Order

Roy K. Gottfried*

> The third part of grammar is Syntax, which shows the agreement and right disposition of words in a sentence. A sentence is an assemblage of words, expressed in proper order, and concurring to make a complete sense.
>
> — Lindley Murray, *English Grammar*

> He then recollected the morning littered bed etcetera and the book about Ruby with met him pike hoses in it which must have fell down sufficiently appropriately beside the domestic chamberpot with apologies to Lindley Murray.
>
> — *Ulysses*

As a fatigued and drunken Stephen listens to Bloom at the cabman's shelter, "he could hear, of course, all kinds of words changing colour like those crabs about Ringsend in the morning, burrowing quickly into all colours of different sorts of the same sand where they had a home somewhere beneath or seemed to."[1] The reader of *Ulysses* has a similar if not quite synaesthetic response to the language of the novel: even in these few sentences he sees words change, not color, but position and place. Prepositional phrases are repeatedly strung together ("about Ringsend in the morning"; "of different sorts of the same sand") while adverbs alternate with prepositions: "they had a home somewhere beneath." The sentence shifts ground abruptly, breaking off with a verb phrase that seems to undo the simile constructed: "like crabs . . . or seemed to." Parts of speech burrow like those crabs throughout the syntax of this sentence, and their alteration is a most prominent feature.

Such movement and rearrangement of parts are the most noticeable features of any sentence in the large novel. Rhythm, rhyme, and sound patterns are also important features, as all contribute to texture and sense, but the syntactic changes are the most striking. The parts of speech which burrow through the syntax of the sentence are perhaps less like crabs than like Hamlet's "enginers," sappers actually undermining the order of the sentence with appropriately explosive results. Recognizable grammatical elements are scrambled in startling ways. "Mr Best entered, tall, young, mild, light. He bore in his hand with grace a notebook, new, large, clean, bright" (186). Beyond the poetics of rhythm and rhyme in this sentence, there is a strategy; by moving the object, *notebook*, to the end of the predicate, thus putting the prepositional phrases in between and out of the way, a long string of adjectives can be built. That string would hardly have

*From *The Art of Joyce's Syntax in "Ulysses"* (Athens: University of Georgia Press, 1980), 1–24. © 1980 by the University of Georgia Press. Reprinted by permission of the publisher.

room had normal order been followed; rearrangement of syntax makes some very useful breeches.

The results of this engineering are prevalent throughout the text, and every part of speech can be the means for a new explosive arrangement. The process of displacement gives concrete status to the nouns as grammatical objects in this sentence: "All watched awhile through their windows caps and hats lifted by passers" (88); while compression of verbs can make for a comic effect in this: "plunging his knife into her until it just struck him that" (642). Displacement gives an air of anticipation to every sentence, and this following adverb is made possible by a proleptic glance at the description of its object: "[he] moved slowly frogwise his green legs in the . . . water" (21).

As every part of speech is a means for disordering and re-ordering, it is no surprise to find a sentence completely undermined, a reversed and razed image of normal order: "From drains, clefts, cesspools, middens arise on all sides stagnant fumes" (433).

The features of syntactic displacement are observable in the language of every chapter. In a book of "eighteen different points of view and . . . as many styles," as Joyce wrote to Harriet Shaw Weaver,[2] these features of manipulation might be the common denominator of all the chapters and characters. The example which began this chapter was the narrator of "Eumaeus." Stephen's monologue is certainly unmistakable and different. "Me sits there with his augur's rod of ash, in borrowed sandals, by day beside a livid sea, unbeheld, in violet night walking beneath a reign of uncouth stars" (48). Such touches as the archaic and inverted "rod of ash" and the pathetic fallacy "uncouth stars" are its chief marks of recognition. Yet his monologue is no less noticeable for its changes: phrases intrude here in different positions as each refers backward and forward. The adjective *unbeheld* in the center refers back to the ungrammatical *me*, subject of the sentence; the phrase "by day" is adverbial and modifies the verb *sit*. The prepositional phrase "in borrowed sandals" refers back to the subject, but "in violet night" refers to the participle that follows it, *walking*. In turn, that participle modifies the subject at the beginning of the sentence. Throughout even this self-consciously poetic sentence there is the careful transformation of syntax into a shifting and a striking new form.

Bloom's monologue, so characteristic of him and so different from Stephen's, also evidences these features. "The far east. Lovely spot it must be: the garden of the world, big lazy leaves to float about on, cactuses, flowery meads, snaky lianas they call them" (71). Here what seems to be a series of nouns is interposed between two predicates, "leaves to float on" and "lianas they call them." Bloom depicts Molly thus: "Looking at me, the sheet up to her eyes, Spanish, smelling herself" (84). Each phrase describes his wife, but each has a different grammatical construction. Long sentences become entangled as they are ordered in Bloom's mind:

"Windy night that was I went to fetch her there was that lodge meeting on about those lottery tickets after Goodwin's concert" (156). The *there* is not an adverb modifying *fetch* but rather a pronoun, subject of the sentence "there was that lodge meeting." *After* refers not to the time of that meeting but rather refers all the way back to when Bloom "went to fetch"; it skips over the lodge and the lottery, the secrets of Bloom's life. Prepositions brought together collide: "meeting on about."

The omniscient narrator, or authorial voice, is an entity of some question in the polyphonic narrative of *Ulysses*. Yet all his voices are characterized consistently by the unique configuration of syntax. Bloom's "eyes sought answer from the river and saw a rowboat rock at anchor on the treacly swells lazily its plastered board" (153): the placing of the two prepositional phrases gives a suggestion that the verb *rock* is intransitive ("he saw a rowboat rock"); yet the insertion of the noun phrase at the end makes the verb transitive and thrusts back into the sentence with the requirements of grammar (and it also reveals the presence of the artist's hand in ordering). Similarly, the delay caused by the intrusion of various phrases in this sentence suggests the control of the narrative voice: "Moving through the air high spars of a threemaster, her sails brailed up on the crosstrees, homing, upstream, silently moving, a silent ship" (51). Even a declarative sentence of encyclopaedic cataloguing demonstrates a change in syntactic order: "From Six Mile Point, Flathouse, Nine Mile Stone follow the footpeople with knotty sticks, salmongaffs, lassos" (572).

Distinguishing in the text between character's monologue and just such an "authorial" voice is a continual problem in the interpretation of *Ulysses*. Much is to be gained by determining the transfer of points of view; yet in order to do so, one must first recognize the basic elements that make them so similar and hard to distinguish from one another. As the above examples illustrate, all parts of the text share common characteristics at the level of syntax. The disorder and rearranging, features obtaining regardless of speaker, are precisely what unites character and narrator and creates a common ground between them. The jumbled order of a sentence brings the internal and external of the novel into tangency. In pushing the prepositional phrase "to the yard" to the end of the following sentence, away from the verb it modifies, Joyce creates an opening in the line that allows for the change in perspective and gives him the opportunity to combine two viewpoints. (It also, incidentally, gives the phrase a sly ambiguity.) "A man and ready he drained his glass to the lees and walked, to men too they [goddesses] gave themselves, manly conscious, lay with men lovers, a youth enjoyed her, to the yard" (176–77). The last phrase, prepositional, belongs to the narrator's third person "he . . . walked"; Bloom's thoughts about the sex lives of goddesses intervene in the gap. The reordered syntax of *Ulysses* enables both character and narrator to be united: it is the common area of their respective presences in the text. Moreover, the syntax is the means by which they can also be distinguished.

As might be apparent from the previous cursory examples, there is something unique, fundamental, and pervasive about the syntax of *Ulysses*. It is unlike that of Joyce's earlier works, and in some measure unlike that of his last. The very opening of the novel presents a language clearly operating with its own sense of linguistic order in which adverbs and adjectives share prominence with the subject of the sentence—even with, as in this case, a character: "Stately, plump Buck Mulligan"; "Halted, he peered"; "Solemnly, he came." Such particlarities of a changed syntactic order can be observed in all forms of language within the text.

The novel's recreation of spoken forms, its oral dimension, is informed by the unique character of its syntax. Sentences such as "snails out of the ground the French eat" (174), or "sun's heat it is" (175), which have been called an "Irish type of sentence,"[3] display the propensity for altering normal order. A direct object and a predicate nominative, respectively, are replaced, pushed to the opening of the sentence, and illustrate the features of Joyce's manipulated syntax.

Much as with the recreation of oral speech, so too the novel's recreation of written language illustrates the features of syntactic manipulation. A boldface headline in "Aeolus" gives prominence to a prepositional phrase, then follows it with a pronoun: "WITH UNFEIGNED REGRET IT IS WE ANNOUNCE . . ." (118).

Joyce's mode of composition, his brooding over the text, adding to it and aggrandizing it, as Litz's and more recent studies have shown,[4] produces some noteworthy changes in the language. Here are two parts at different stages of writing, first an early typescript and second the final text in the novel (intermediate stages of composition have been suppressed).

> —As it were, in the peerless panorama of bosky grove and undulating plain and luscious pastureland, steeped in the translucent glow of our mild Irish twilight . . .

> —As 'twere, in the peerless panorama of Ireland's portfolio, unmatched, despite their wellpraised prototypes in other vaunted prized regions, for very beauty, of bosky grove and undulating plain and luscious pastureland of vernal green, steeped in the transcendent translucent glow of our mild mysterious Irish twilight . . . (125)

The changes are all made with the obvious intent of inflating the text—the chapter is "Aeolus," its art windy rhetoric—"peerless panorama of Ireland's portfolio." Yet the changes result in a very clear syntactic manipulation. Prepositions are separated from their antecedents: "portfolio . . . of," "unmatched . . . for"; adjectives separated from their nouns: *unmatched* from *panorama, steeped* from any number of possibilities. It could hardly be argued that Joyce's mode of composition is the result of his ordering of syntax; but it is probably not the cause either: the early text also demonstrates the manipulation. (For example, it already separates *panorama* from *steeped* and thus possibly explains the development of the later text.) Even in its composition, one finds Joyce's language ordered and disordered.

Sentences are opened to syntactic displacement and aggrandizement in the final stage of the printed text itself. On one page in "Wandering Rocks" there is the following simple sentence: "Mr Kernan, pleased with the order he had booked, walked boldly along James's street." One page later a mutation of this appears in all the newness of its altered syntax: "From the sundial towards James's Gate walked Mr Kernan pleased with the order he had booked for Pulbrook Robertson boldly along James's Street, past Shackleton's offices" (239). Starting with a prepositional phrase — the place, after all, Kernan starts from — the sentence inverts the order of subject and verb; then goes through an adjective phrase describing Kernan as pleased and an adverb describing the way he walked; and finally ends with two other prepositional phrases.

This manipulation of sentence parts, this refashioning of syntactic order, are the essential qualities of the Joycean sentence. Each and every sentence in the large novel is, in fact, a potential illustration of these features. Although a description of each sentence would be a difficult, almost impossible task, and several works address themselves to such a catalogue,[5] it is not the weight of the evidence that is discouraging (whenever was magnitude an obstacle to Joyce's readers?); the problem lies rather in the fact that any listing of sentences would merely enumerate incidences and accumulate statistics. The noticeable quality of every Joycean sentence suggests something beyond examples of original and creative language. *Ulysses* abounds in such sentences as "Waiting always for a word of help his hand moved faithfully the unsteady symbols" (28), and each sentence is subject to an artistic process which not only achieves the striking originality which is any particular example but which also, given the consistency of the disordering, suggests more than the sentence itself. That quality of something beyond mere lexical engineering or accumulated statistic is worthy of consideration. Joyce wrote too carefully and conscientiously not to give any thought to the effect of each part; he risked the publication of *Dubliners* to preserve the integrity of his own choice. In a long exchange with Grant Richards over, among other issues, the word *bloody* in several stories, Joyce showed not only his pride in art but also his sense of that art's effect: "The word, the exact expression I have used ['He'd bloody well put his teeth down his throat,' from 'A Boarding House'], in my opinion the one expression in the English language which can create on the reader the effect which I wish to create."[6] What is true of a word in *Dubliners* can hardly be less true of the words in *Ulysses*; an episode recounted by Frank Budgen makes Joyce's awareness of his artistic choice abundantly clear: " 'You have been seeking the *mot juste?*' (Budgen asked). 'No,' said Joyce. 'I have the words already. What I am seeking is the perfect order of the words in the sentence. There is an order in every way appropriate.' "[7] That appropriate order is clearly the order of syntax readapted so as to be appropriate to Joyce. It is more than shining creativity; it has a studied purpose and effect. An exploration of the syntax of *Ulysses* without the restrictions of statistics has the flexibility and the latitude to explore what is effective and appropriate.

The intentional twists and turns of syntax, which create all the transformed constructions, are illustrative of certain characteristics of the Joycean sentence: a freedom within bounds, an extension of certain expected patterns of syntax to the limit of their rules, but not beyond. Joyce's language has a two-sided effect, one which explodes language into new forms while still relying on the normal, expected order to render the new creation sensible.[8] The language is characterized by a tacit acceptance of the ordering rules of syntax while using those same rules to twist sentences into new images. Joyce makes his own "appropriate" way, as he says, "with apologies to Lindley Murray." Yet while the Dedalian craftsman beats the syntactic connections between his words to airy thinness, those connections remain strong and supplely effective. In every sentence, shifting series of phrases form agile connections in the language, thin but tenacious threads of meaning spun by the syntax and pulled by the artful repositioning. For Joyce, style was a matter of proper words in improper places: each sentence is pulled between the order of syntax and the freedom of newly created forms.

While sentences range in degree from order to openness, there is present within each sentence the sense of order which is the purpose of syntax. In the connections of proper form there is the suggestion of control and limit. Participles interspersed with active verbs fix precisely the movement of this sentence: "He fitted the book roughly into his inner pocket and, stubbing his toes against the broken commode, hurried out towards the smell, stepping hastily down the stairs with a flurried stork's legs" (65).

The alternation of phrasing and diction give the following paragraphs a vibrancy oscillating between the poles of appropriate creativity and proper order. Aided by alliteration, in a chapter whose "art" is music, this is a syntactic theme played with variations. "Miss Kennedy sauntered sadly from bright light, twining a loose hair behind an ear. Sauntering sadly, gold no more, she twisted twined a hair. Sadly she twined in sauntering gold hair behind a curving ear" (258). Words appear in different forms, moving from verb to participle and back: *twining* changes to *twined* while *sauntered* changes to *sauntering*. The same adverb changes its referent: "sauntered sadly . . . sadly she twined." The participial phrase in each sentence appears in a different position: at end, beginning, and middle, respectively. The loose interplay of words and the alternation of parts are ultimately held in order by the form of syntax and yield a rhythmic tension of opposition.

The result of such creative disordering within syntactic structure is a motion of changing parts, and this can yield such sentences, grammatically correct but misleadingly meandering, as "It will (the air) do you good, Bloom said, meaning also the walk, in a moment" (660). Yet the disordering can also result in the freedom of artistic variety. "He foresaw his pale body reclined in it at full, naked, in a womb of warmth, oiled by scented melting soap, softly laved" (86). The sentence alternates prepositional phrases referring to the bathtub — "in it," "in a womb of warmth" — with adjectives referring to the object of the sentence, the body — "naked," "reclined," "oiled by," "softly laved."[9] The result is a moving lexical surface, fraught with the pull of order and disorder, proper form and appropriate, creative form.

The reason for Joyce's abuse within use of syntax lies chiefly in the fact that he wants both to give and to take. For all his anomalous creations of language, he needs the normal order of syntax not only to show off these creations to advantage, but also to render them understandable; as Lindley Murray claims, it is order that makes "a complete sense." Joyce draws attention to syntactic rules in one sentence in order to defy them in the next. The language of *Ulysses* is a freedom within bounds, a freedom which takes its definition, as all freedoms do, from the order it makes free with. It relies on the limits of order to give it its creative opportunities.[10] *Ulysses* is a balance of formal experimentation with existing orders (forms of the novel, forms of sentences); and for all its being a supposed training ground for *Finnegans Wake*,[11] it distinguishes itself clearly, and in nothing more clearly than in its language. Normal syntax is there, a pattern which contains the vibrant language of the novel, just as a map of Dublin's streets would contain the voyages of an epic hero.

This two-sided attitude was possible because Joyce instinctively and actively recognized the paradoxical nature of language. Conscious of words even from his youth, a teacher of English and a speaker of three foreign tongues, he sensed two essential concurrent features of language. One is the very determined and fixed aspect dictated by the patterns of syntax. A sentence with the subject in the third person singular must, if it is to be understood, have the verb in the appropriate person; if that verb is transitive, the rules require that it be accompanied by a direct object, and so on until the closing period, when presumably all the requirements are met. The immediate effect of syntax is evident especially to one who tries to speak a foreign language: sentences move, indeed unroll themselves until they reach their end. This movement is language's second feature, closely aligned with and actually inseparable from the first; sentences move around, changing directions in a shifting looseness while they complete and in order to complete the requirements of syntax. While fixed, the sentences are free; while loose, they are constrained.

Such a contention also suggests that the defining terms of Joyce's linguistic creativity are closely related, indeed interdependent. Each term takes its presence and meaning from the other, and both are necessary to describe Joyce's art. In the rhythmic example from "Sirens," cited earlier, it was evident that the characteristic license and order of the sentences were relative that one sentence was defined by the text: "Miss Kennedy sauntered sadly from bright light, twining a loose hair behind an ear. Sauntering sadly, gold no more, she twisted twined a hair" (258).

Joyce's repatterning is present throughout the text: it consists of his twisting and reshaping of syntax according to his own sense of what is appropriate order. Thus he constantly establishes the general features of his disordering and repatterning within the span of any several sentences encountered. Take as a most obvious example the opening of the novel, where the reader is first exposed to the language of *Ulysses:* "Stephen suffered him to pull out and hold up on show by its corner a dirty crumpled handkerchief" (4). The two infinitive phrases are followed not by their object, nor by one prepositional phrase ("on show"), but by two, by way of increasing grammatical anticipation and finally resolving it. This so evident syntactic manipulation is Joyce's creative deviation from what one would consider normal syntactic form.

Yet that deviation in the face of normal order becomes, in its own turn, a standard or basis — if one will, a norm — for further experimentation and creative disruption by Joyce.[12] All of the language of his text is at one and the same time an order and a disorder in scales various to each other: having created his own deviations, Joyce uses them as a new order from which to work further transformations.

Such interdependence is possible because Joyce is never absolutist, but ever careful to balance and offset any series of options, to keep them open, in flux, paradoxical, and poised. Similarly, the terms of order and appropriate disorder used here to describe what is so characteristic of Joyce's syntax are not absolute. Rather, interdependent as they are, they take their meaning in contrast to and in context with one another. Like Bloom and Molly in bed, their positions are determined "relatively to themselves and to each other" (737). The terms indicate the range of possibilities in both the deviations and the normative constructions; being interrelated and offset, they emphasize the different potentials of a language always twisted and refashioned.

> Richie, admiring, descanted on that man's glorious voice. He remembered one night long ago. Never forget that night. Si sang *'Twas rank and fame:* in Ned Lambert's 'twas. Good God he never heard in all his life a note like that he never did *then false one we had better part* so clear so God he never heard *since love lives not* a clinking voice ask Lambert he can tell you too.
> Goulding, a flush struggling in his pale, told Mr Bloom, face of the night, Si in Ned Lambert's, Dedalus' house, sang *'Twas rank and fame.*
> He, Mr Bloom, listened while he, Richie Goulding, told him, Mr Bloom of the night he, Richie, heard him, Si Dedalus, sing *'Twas rank and fame* in his, Ned Lambert's house.
> (267–77)

Here, in the span of three paragraphs whose subjects are nearly identical, the relativity of Joyce's linguistic poles is evident. The first paragraph approximates a normal order of syntax: "He remembered"; "in Ned Lambert's 'twas"; "Good God he never heard." The sentences are nearly complete grammatical forms and are clearly ordered. The last phrases are somewhat abrupt, as the entire paragraph is clearly manipulated to render the immediacy of spoken language and the interruption of song in the next room.

The second paragraph blends the phrases of music with those of narrative, by making the echoes of the song grammatically part of the sentences: "Goulding, a flush"; "Bloom, face." The two clauses, "Goulding told," "Si Dedalus . . . sang," are set loose, not subordinated or joined. The effect of the manipulation of song and syntax — while in the service of the theme and technique of the chapter — provides a loosened surface which is rich with intonation, rhythm, and suggestiveness. By opening up the syntax, the potentials for construction and the possibilities for meaning are increased.

The third paragraph insists on an order of language as studied and maniacal as the language in a grammar book. Every pronoun as subject and object is listed, with the referents additionally supplied. The effect is to stress the rules of grammar, to insist on the order and system inherent in language which the preceding paragraphs manipulate to such purpose.

The three paragraphs descend, on the page and in some scale, down to a very tightened order of language which Joyce can exploit. The first paragraph might even be called a norm or average for Joyce: it is manipulated to render allusions as well as thoughts and conversations, and is grammatically clear but with gaps that open up the syntax. The middle paragraph takes language further, untying syntax into parataxis, suppressing grammatical connections, taking language towards all possible and appropriate variations. That paragraph illustrates the freedom of language and the openness of meaning; but clearly its freedom is constituted in relation to the other paragraphs around it and to the language of the novel. It is a freedom not absolute but relative, just as the control of the third paragraph is tightened and ordered in relation to that freedom.

The definition of these principles is made additionally relative by their context within the novel, where they appear and what they stress. As mentioned earlier, the styles that vary from chapter to chapter ultimately have their common denominator in the language being manipulated, but the terms of that manipulation are similarly open to adaptability and variety.

The result of the syntactic relativity is to yield both variety and order, freedom and fixity. Every deviation from normal syntactic order opens up increasingly the vast potentials that are in language. A sentence such as the following can only be a product of a language potentially open to variety: "[He] heard warm running sunlight and in the air behind him friendly words" (10). The rhythmic variety is achieved by the displacing of the prepositional phrase. There is here a similarity between Joyce's sentence and a line of Hopkins's "The Windhover": "in his riding/Of the rolling level underneath him steady air." Chronology does little to support a sense of indebtedness: Stephen could not have read Hopkins in 1904, and if Joyce later did, the fact is not known. Yet the similarity has its cause deeper than borrowings. In both writers there is a sense of stress caused by the order of language and the variety possible in playing off that order. Hopkins's "sprung rhythm" of instress is achieved by altering words from their expected metrical order. Joyce's appropriate language is made up of a release of words from the bonds of their normal syntactic order. In both men, there is the recognition of an existing order, and the tension which results in the opening up of that order to new forms and possibilities.

The language of *Ulysses* can be seen as using the characteristics of a syntax both open and closed to a particular purpose, setting them up against each other in a subtle tension. The various sentences described above stress the two factors clearly: they have a grammatical comprehension achieved by and within the prescribed freedom of the sentence parts. It is the free motion of the sentences which carries the stream of language along (as well as the "stream of consciousness" and even the narrative itself); it is the order of syntax which restrains and banks its course.

And indeed such channelled expression may be the only possible kind. There is a point at which, without order, thought and communication can no longer exist. Nietzsche appears only in some of Joyce's short-lived youthful fury and some jokes in *Ulysses*, but he expresses the necessity of order in language and thought in a way quite close to Joyce's silent assent and artful maneuvering: "Wir hören auf zu denken, wenn wir es nicht in dem sprachlichen Zwange tun wollen. . . . Das vernünftige Denken ist ein Interpretieren nach einem Schema."[13] ("We cease to think when we do not wish to think in linguistic constraints. Logical thinking is an exposition according to a pattern.") This is an admission of the need for a certain restriction ("Zwang") to make thought and communication possible. There is as well an expression of intent, even conscious desire, to work within those restrictions — *wollen*. Concomitant with this willingness there is a recognition of a freedom of interpretation and a variety possible within that system. These terms speak to the dual nature of the Joycean sentence. A freedom of movement and an awareness of the need for systems which bind and confine, these are characteristics of Joyce's life no less than of his life's work of art.

Joyce is the exile who left Dublin only to see it more clearly. There can hardly be a freedom of the *non serviam*, if there is no established religion to serve; nor is free thought (of which Stephen considers himself the "horrible example") possible without a dogma. Joyce's brother Stanislaus remarked astutely: "The interest that my brother always retained in the philosophy of the Catholic Church sprang from the fact that he considered

Catholic philosophy to be the most coherent attempt to establish . . . an intellectual and material stability. In his own case, however, freedom was a necessity: it was the guiding theme of his life. He accepted its gifts and its perils as he accepted his own personality, as he accepted the life that produced him."[14] As in God's universe in *Paradise Lost,* the order is set to give man his choice: he is thus free, to choose and to fall; or, like the artist Dedalus, free to choose, to fly, and to fall. A freedom within bounds, a chaos amid order, this is the discord out of which Joyce makes the concord of the novel. There is the overall order of hours, places, organs, arts — the schemes Joyce gave to Linati and Gilbert — which seem inadequate to the book's myriad details and minute complexity; and in their inadequacy lies some measure of their usefulness, for without the original plan, the order, the pattern, no such cornucopia could be possible.[15] Joyce's was a mind which acquiesced to pattern, a mind medieval or Catholic, or both; plans and systems were not uncongenial to it. It needed the pattern to have the whole, to test the limits which it would then go up to, fill to the brim. The *Odyssey* itself may be a poor guide to the novel, but for Joyce it was the skeleton on which he could flesh out his art. A medieval Catholic mind had many prescribed plans, yet from such plans come the limitlessness of the *Divine Comedy* or the Cathedral of Chartres.

At the heart of Joyce's creativity lies the enigma that he must have limits in order to transgress them, set up schemes only to undo them. The order he makes for himself must be appropriated as well as appropriate; he must use all forms so as to create his own art. Order defines the limits to which he must go. He accumulates specific details about particular places and persons in Dublin to render the most cosmic perspective in which those very details lose meaning; conversely, he follows the outlines of a universal myth in order to render the most precise account of an event in a certain place and time. Joyce must use and master all the techniques of the nineteenth century artist to be the most original of the twentieth: he masters naturalism in order to turn his book towards symbolism. Paradoxes abound in *Ulysses* because of the particular nature of Joyce's creativity: the novel is pan- and myopic, specific and general, ordered and chaotic. At the base of all this lies the paradox of every created sentence of *Ulysses,* the striking newness of its language transformed through an awareness of the order it manipulates.

In a letter to his brother in 1905 Joyce says of himself, "The struggle against conventions in which I am at present involved was not entered into by me so much as a protest against these conventions as with the intention of living in conformity with my moral nature."[16] That moral nature was certainly a difficult and contradictory one, the few times it displayed itself directly, yet Joyce recognizes that his is a nature which does not exist merely to flay conventions for the sake of flaying, but a nature profoundly concerned with finding its own way amid and among them.

Joyce the model student, the young artist, lived within system and order. Synge saw the young man as "obsessed by rules"; and even his lonely but vast reading at night in Paris libraries showed a desire for "formalism."[17] His Jesuit school training was planned centuries before, and Joyce followed it well. Jesuit teaching may not have given him a respect for religion, but it did teach him "the order of words" and a strong sense of syntax and grammar.[18]

One classroom exercise at Belvedere was a translation of an ode of Horace. The ten-year-old Joyce was careful to locate the correct parts of his translation in a most effective way. The Latin reads; "Fies nobilium tu quoque fontium, / me dicente cavis impositam ilicem / saxis, unde loquaces / lymphae desiliunt tuae" (3. 13). Joyce translated: "be of the noble founts! I sing / The oak tree o'er thine echoing / Crags, the waters murmuring." While heralding the postured formality of his own poetry, this piece of juvenilia is quite creative in its correctness: separating the adjective from its noun by means of the line break, Joyce makes it enact the form of a cliff. This simple exercise evidences a sensitivity for the expressive character and the plastic quality of the written line, both within the constraints of translation. Kevin Sullivan, who relates this incident, claims that the translation demonstrates "a sense of language that was to mature into genius."[19] As an adult writer Joyce would continue to exploit language's plastic qualities to the fullest, as in a sentence where the subject outrides the syntax as the characters on horses are said to do: "In the saddles of the leaders, leaping leaders, rode outriders" (248). Indeed, this sense of language is the same in the schoolboy assignment as in the mature novel: it is expressive form created through the manipulation of words.

For the Jesuits, Joyce also wrote an essay entitled "The Study of Languages" in which he noted that "both in style and syntax there is always present a carefulness, a carefulness bred of the first implantings of precision."[20] Joyce acknowledged this studied precision and even prided himself on it. To Stanislaus he wrote, "Would you be surprised if I wrote a very good English grammar some day?"[21] As a description of Joyce's attitude to language, Ellmann's comment is typical: "At a time others were questioning the liberties he took with English, Joyce was conscious only of its restraints upon him."[22] But being aware of restrictions by no means implies not accepting them; Joyce's "moral nature" may have been egotistical, but it could also be accommodating, and it was precise. To the mob of Russelite mystics Joyce takes a counterstance not only of Aristotelean exactness, the dagger definitions, but also syntactical exactness: "I, who dishevelled ways forsook / To hold the poets' grammar book" ("The Holy Office"). Joyce's was a pride luciferean in rebellion, bred of his knowledge and power to use language and to use it well, which means also to misuse it intelligently. T. S. Eliot claimed that there could be no real blasphemy without there being a deep understanding of the object, and as true as this may be of Joyce's Catholicism, it is no less true of his language in *Ulysses*. It is a language so precise in its use and deviations as to insist on all the rules in the poet's grammar book. Joyce considered *Ulysses* as being written, for all its uniqueness, in a "wideawake language, a cutanddry grammar."[23] To call such sentences as "perfume of embraces all him assailed" or "with hungered flesh obscurely, he mutely craved to adore" (168) cut-and-dry is to insist intelligently and not perversely on the rules they lovingly affront.

Whether Joyce was influenced by any specific linguistic theories during the many years of writing *Ulysses* is largely a matter of conjecture. A general work which was to change thinking about language, Saussure's *Cours de linguistique générale*, was printed in 1916, although Joyce had not read it before finishing *Ulysses*.[24] While in Paris, writing *Work in Progress*, Joyce attended several lectures by a French Jesuit.[25] Mary Colum, who attended with Joyce, describes one of these occasions:

> Abbé Jousse was lecturing in Paris. He was a noted propounder of a theory that Joyce gave adherence to, that language had its origin in gesture — "In the beginning was the rhythmic gesture," Joyce often said.
>
> If the Abbé's lecture did not interest me as much as it interested Joyce, still, it interested me a good deal, and that largely because of its original method of presentation. It took the form of a little play, based on the Gospels. Around the lecturer was a group of girls, who addressed him as "Rabbi Jesus." The words spoken — one of the parables, I think — were, I gathered, in Aramaic, and what was shown was that the word was shaped by the gesture. Joyce was full of the subject.[26]

The date of the lectures comes almost a decade after the publication of *Ulysses*. The specific reference to language as gesture in the "Circe" episode[27] is evidence that Joyce was familiar with the theory before the lectures were given: it is mentioned in *Stephen Hero*. It is perhaps most plausible to consider that, at whatever date, Joyce found the theory congenial because of his own sense of language as conveying meaning in ways other than by denotation. Jousse's theory may have answered to Joyce's practice (and Joyce was never interested in applying other ideas, from Aquinas down, if they did not correspond to his own prior practice). While the Abbé saw lurking behind all spoken language the shadow of original gesture, Joyce saw behind the written word the shadow of expressive form. The schoolboy at Belvedere who was careful to separate the adjective and noun by the end of the line so that they themselves enacted a cliff-hanging showed himself from the outset, long before the Abbé, to be a writer who was aware of language describing and communicating in symbolic formal ways. Early on he recognized that the order of words, or their grouping in the sentence line, conveys meaning, and that their syntactical form can convey a sense more complete than that recognized by Lindley Murray. As Stephen claims in his "theory," language itself renders visible nuance and emotion. Carefully crafted in original patterns, language enacts a meaning and presents what it means in a visual form. With the rules and order of syntax used and misused as its structure, language is an expressive as well as appropriate form.

What can be made of this expressive form, what after all it expresses, and in what way the order of Joyce's unique syntax is appropriate are all questions raised by every sentence in the novel. A sentence like "while his eyes still read blandly he took off his hat quietly inhaling his hairoil" (71) has more lurking behind its syntax than the comedy of ambiguity — whether Bloom blandly read and quietly took off his hat or blandly took off his hat and quietly inhaled — and that effect, not to be captured by statistics, is worthy of consideration.

Notes

1. James Joyce, *Ulysses* (New York, 1961), p. 644. All subsequent references in this study are to this edition and will be cited in the text.

2. *Letters*, ed. Stuart Gilbert and Richard Ellmann, 1:167.

3. Erwin R. Steinberg, "Characteristic Sentence Patterns in 'Proteus' and 'Lestrygonians,' " in Fritz Senn, ed., *New Light on Joyce from the Dublin Symposium*, p. 81.

4. A. Walton Litz, *The Art of James Joyce; James Joyce Quarterly* 12 (1974–75), nos. 1–2, "Textual Studies Issue"; and especially Michael Groden, *"Ulysses" in Progress*.

5. Steinberg, "Characteristic Sentence Patterns"; Liisa Dahl, *Linguistic Features of the Stream-of-Consciousness Techniques of James Joyce, Virginia Woolf and Eugene O'Neill.*

6. Reprinted in Herbert Gorman, *James Joyce*, p. 152.

7. *The Making of "Ulysses,"* p. 20.

8. Several works specifically focusing on Joyce's language have reached similar conclusions, although they do not pursue the consequences and meaning of Joyce's unique style. Liisa Dahl, in a summary article "The Linguistic Presentation of the Interior Monologue in Joyce's *Ulysses*," *James Joyce Quarterly* 7 (1970), observes succinctly, p. 119: "It seems evident that Joyce did not break too many rules at a time. If he chose strange vocabulary or new words his syntax was to a certain extent conventional." Robert Di Pietro, "A Transformational Note on a Few Types of Joycean Sentences," *Style* 3 (1969): 156–67: "Our premise is that most, if not all, sentences in Joyce's *Ulysses* lie within the grammatical confines of English and that his style consists, in no small part, of manipulations in the underlying tree structure."

9. Anthony Burgess, *Joysprick*, p. 76, describes the semantics of this sentence as calling for " 'laved,' not washed, in this ceremony-of-innocence." He claims further that *"pale naked body* would not do" but does not say why. It would not do because Joyce's syntax, as it is here contended, is built up of such necessary lexical scrambling.

10. Two recent studies of Joyce's language have other views. Marilyn French, in *The Book as World*, suggests that the plurality of the separate styles of each chapter combines into a unified authorial view. Hugh Kenner, *Joyce's Voices*, claims that language, primarily through tone and diction, has an objective and independent ontology.

11. Litz, *The Art of James Joyce*, p. 35: "Principles which governed his work in 1920 and 1921 did not differ greatly from those he followed in writing *Finnegans Wake*." These principles are largely thematic and technical, however; a glance at David Hayman's *First Draft Version of Finnegans Wake* (Austin: Univ. of Texas Press, 1963), shows how close the original *Finnegans Wake* was to lexical comprehension. Strother B. Purdy, in an ambitious

article, "Mind Your Genderous: Toward a Wake Grammar," in Senn, *New Light on Joyce*, claims that even in *Finnegans Wake* the syntax "is the same as that of conventional English" (p. 47). Purdy states that a grammar of the *Wake* could be drawn within the general boundaries of transformational grammar.

12. For the issue of norms and deviations, see Levin, "Internal and External Deviations in Poetry," *Word* 21 (1965): 225–37.

13. "Aus dem Nachlass der Achtzigerjahre," *Werke in drei Bänden*, ed. Karl Schlecta (Munich: Hanser Verlag, n.d.), 3:86.

14. *My Brother's Keeper*, p. 108.

15. See Litz, *Art of James Joyce*, p. 39: "Joyce needed as many formal orders as possible to encompass and control his work."

16. Published in Richard Ellmann, *James Joyce*, p. 207.

17. Quoted in Ellmann, *James Joyce*, p. 129, p. 124.

18. Kevin Sullivan, *Joyce Among the Jesuits*, p. 76.

19. *Ibid.*, p. 76.

20. *Critical Writings*, ed. Ellsworth Mason and Richard Ellmann, p. 27.

21. *Letters*, 2:86.

22. *James Joyce*, p. 410.

23. *Letters*, 3:146.

24. See chap. 2 [of my *The Art of Joyce's Syntax in "Ulysses"*] for an incidental use of Saussure in *Ulysses*.

25. See David Hayman, "Language Of / As Gesture" in *"Ulysses," cinquante ans après*, ed. L. Bonnerot, pp. 209–21; also Stephen Heath, "Ambiviolences," pp. 22–42, 64–77. Ellmann, *James Joyce*, p. 647, places the dates of the lectures in 1931.

26. Padraic and Mary Colum, *Our Friend James Joyce*, p. 131.

27. Stephen: "So that gesture, not music, not odours, would be a universal language, the gift of tongues rendering visible not the lay sense but the first entelechy, the structural rhythm" (p. 432).

Part Two

Anatomies of "Nausicaa"

Most books devoted exclusively to *Ulysses* follow the strategy established by Stuart Gilbert of allotting a single chapter for each of the eighteen chapters of Joyce's book, those highly individuated "inner organs" of the convoluted text. Isolating one of those chapters for a chronological tracking of critical attitudes toward it over half a century provides an anatomical survey not only of Joyce's creation but also of the attitudes in *Ulysses* criticism over the decades. The choice of "Nausicaa" is only partially determined by its pivotal placement in the progression of chapters and its tightly framed bipartite cohesiveness: its notoriety is a factor as well, since it was the point at which the Society for the Suppression of Vice in America finally threw down the gauntlet and *Ulysses* was suppressed. It would be difficult to write a dull treatise on "Nausicaa."

That Stuart Gilbert and Frank Budgen were privileged insiders when they published their respective studies in 1930 and 1934 makes their views weighty with authority and also suspect as vested interest, either straight from the horse's mouth or replicas of the Trojan horse. Gilbert assumes the guise of the scientific scholar, while Budgen drops all guises to argue his case as Joyce's friend: between them they present an "official" viewpoint of sorts, but from their own individual positions. Gilbert's "Nausicaa" is Homerically determined, and it would be easy to assert that of all the chapters in *Ulysses* it is the one in which Joyce is able to reap the most rewarding results in Applied Homerics. Budgen, himself a painter, focuses on Joyce's indication that painting is the Art of the chapter, and he paints a painterly version of Joyce's literary accomplishment. Both critics carry their authority lightly, and we now read their pioneer studies as the commentaries of a halcyon stage of *Ulysses* criticism, unbelabored and almost effortless, neither in awe of the masterpiece nor suspicious of its traps and trickery. Certain characteristics that later annotators fretted over and tried to nail down with finality they took as apparent: the provenance of the dog Garryowen, for example (how does the dog actually pass from Giltrap's "ownership" to the Citizen's "possession"?). Gilbert's "study" assumed that few of his contemporary readers could own a copy of the text, fewer still legally, and he quotes extensively, staying close to Joyce's text with the legal *Odyssey* close at hand, producing a tightly knit analysis. Budgen works on a looser weave, suggestively and comparatively, as he folds in parallels from other chapters as well. Both readily accept the stylistic innovations and alterations with little concern, and both are particularly attentive to the morals and mores of 1904, the position of Gerty's sexuality and Bloom's eroticism as relative to the age, more as social than psychological aberration. Budgen in fact is overly elaborative on the subject, of special interest apparently to himself and presumably to Joyce as well—I presume.

A generation separates Harry Blamires from Gilbert and Budgen, both literally and figuratively, and much has transpired in the interim to change the nature of *Ulysses* commentary. The book is now available in both England and America, and Blamires's marginal notations give pages in both additions. The assumed readership of such commentary has changed from an intelligentsia determined to acquire a copy and attain a mastery of it to an academic audience, teachers making the text available to students. With just an introductory nod to Homer, Blamires moves on to a sequential synopsis of the plot line, tracking the action through the thoughts of Gerty and Bloom. For Blamires the complex style does nothing to inform the reading, so that we may wonder how he knows that Gerty is actually beautiful, as he claims. His venture is to determine what the chapter contains, rather than how to read it, and he parallels the pieces of information with each other, and with pieces from the other chapters. He is exact in locating the cause of Gerty's lameness in her thoughts regarding an accident on Dalkey Hill, yet pays little attention to how significant this flaw is for Gerty herself, how much it determines her entire personality. What emerges from the Blamiresean perspective on "Nausicaa" is the overwhelming importance of the Benediction taking place off-stage, the significance of Gerty as the Blessed Virgin far outweighing the significance of her repressed and repossessed sexuality. Budgen's lusty engagement with the Nausicaan situation has no parallel in Blamires's interaction with it: the latter eventually acknowledges that Bloom's clothes are "wet from his emission," but had paid no attention to any such emission at the time it took place.

If Blamires is unrelenting in applying Joyce's Roman Catholicism to *Ulysses*, Stanley Sultan immediately provides an almost comic counter-touch with a reference to the Old Testament: the beauty of "Nausicaa" may be in the eye of the beholder, with Aesop providing the elephant. Sultan focuses on that emission from the very beginning, echoing Budgen on the "rite of Onan," but is not nearly as sanguine in accepting the "compromise" in Bloom's masturbation, regarding the sin as a "turning away from Molly and his unborn son," labeling it "the path to destruction," and "not merely a pathetic and sordid act but a representation . . . of Bloom's self-defeat and self-destruction." For Sultan the Bloom of "Nausi-

caa" is "depressed, resigned, and spiritually broken," quite unlike the
Bloom viewed by Budgen. Nor is Gerty the beauty accepted by Blamires;
Sultan is categorical in stating that she "is not beautiful," but a "pathetically obnoxious girl" and "a mildly libidinous girl," a prey to "vanity,"
"spitefulness and jealousy." What determines Sultan's judgments are the
designs of stylistic presentation in "Nausicaa," which "suits a point of view
very close to and sympathetic with Gerty," but is in actuality "the author's
vehicle for delineating Gerty's character and the significance of her
principal action." The close correspondence of the religious exaltation with
the action of "Nausicaa" that Blamires takes as giving spiritual value to the
chapter Sultan dismisses in his claim that "Joyce is attacking the popular
cult of the Virgin."

Another generation — although hardly a literal one — separates
Blamires and Sultan from Senn, French, and Peake, primarily because the
focus in *Ulysses* studies has shifted to a professional community of Joyceans
in communication with each other. The volume from which Fritz Senn's
"Nausicaa" is extracted was in itself characteristic of the communal effort:
eighteen critics undertook to analyze a chapter of *Ulysses* each from their
individual perspectives, and Senn had ample magnitude in which to
expand and develop his views of "Nausicaa." What he creates is a
palimpsest of elements of the chapter and elements from Joyce biography,
and from other Joyce publications and letters, conscious that "the whole of
Ulysses can be viewed within naturalistic, psychological, symbolic, Homeric, and numerous other contexts."

Despite the volatile nature of the material in "Nausicaa" the judgments in the 1970s veered toward equanimity: Senn in particular is
suspicious of the critic who looks, "with Cyclopean assurance, on the two
lovers, treating them . . . with benign condescension or downright contempt." He echoes Gilbert and Budgen in his view of "the imperfect world
of Dublin, 1904," finding the Bloom of this chapter no more "depressed or
guiltridden than we know him to have been previously," and maintains as
balanced a verdict on Gerty: "Some of the epithets in the Litany can be
related to Gerty, and not only in scathing irony, but, like everything else,
with perspectival modification." Charles Peake is even more benign, seeing
her as "an image not simply of a silly girl who has read too many
novelettes but of an impoverished, handicapped, disappointed and frustrated existence." Marilyn French, however, holds a harsher judgment of
the chapter as "essentially antilife, because it disguises and denies reality."

The style of the chapter continues to attract attention and characterization. Senn in particular calls attention to the "elevation of its language,"
which he considers "exalted," but also notices the relation of the stylistics
to the nature of the narrative: "the forced deportment of Gerty's style has
been felt as essentially lame all along, and correspondingly the limping
procession of Bloom's thoughts emerges as basically more dignified." Peake
elaborates even further on the function of style in "Nausicaa," which

"serves to represent the essence of her consciousness and the fluctuations of her moods" — "through the style we experience the quality of her experience."

Early in the 1980s Paul van Caspel in his dissertation on the middle twelve chapters of *Ulysses* set himself up as an Oversight Committee of one to monitor the critics and translators of Joyce's book, and in 1986 he published a revised version that covers all of it. His chapter on "Nausicaa" synthesizes many of the critical approaches and outlines that of his own. In some ways van Caspel solidifies the basic attitudes of the current decade (on style, for example, he notes that the one used in the Gerty exposition "is colored by the character's very essence," as Senn and Peake had observed). The "Nausicaa" chapter has not been a serious pitfall for mature readers of *Ulysses*, and van Caspel finds few "bloomers" to correct. Yet there are questions still open that a reading of these eight opinions on what happens in "Nausicaa" (and why) should disclose. Is there any agreement on Gerty's age? Van Caspel is categoric that she is twenty-one, but how do other commentators read the conflicting signals on that "fact"? And which of the three girls on the beach is actually the one that Bloom speculates is close to "her monthlies"? Senn has a candidate different from the one most of his predecessors nominate. And surely the most tempting speculation in "Nausicaa" revolves around the unfinished statement Bloom writes in the sand, and as we read these eight essays (and many more as well), we realize how impossible it is for any of us *not* to complete the open statement. Much of what transpires in *Ulysses* tempts the reader into participating in the writing process, a creative response that is very much a factor in the critical demeanor of the recent years, and "Nausicaa" in particular lends itself to such participation.

"Nausicaa"

"The summer evening had begun to fold the world in its mysterious embrace. Far away in the west the sun was setting and the last glow of all too fleeting day lingered lovingly on sea and strand, on the proud promontory of dear old Howth guarding as ever the waters of the bay, on the weed-grown rocks along Sandymount shore and, last but not least, on the quiet church whence there streamed forth at times upon the stillness the voice of prayer to her who is in her pure radiance a beacon ever to the stormtossed heart of man, Mary, star of the sea."

Here, after the volcanic rages of the Cyclops' den and a miraculous escape from seismic catastrophe, rest comes at last to the stormtossed heart of Mr Bloom. By this way Stephen Dedalus passed on his morning walk along the foreshore; it was here that he noticed the two midwives, with their bag, coming down the shelving shore; "flabbily their splayed feet sinking in the silted sand." The scene of this episode is Sandymount shore, and perhaps over these very rocks lay Stephen's shadow ("Why not endless till the farthest star?"), manshape ineluctable, captor of Proteus, as he scribbled on his improvised "tablets" *mouth to her mouth's kiss*, and mused: "Touch me. Soft eyes. Soft soft soft hand. I am lonely here. O touch me soon, now. What is that word known to all men? I am quiet here alone. Sad too. Touch, touch me." Seeds of vague desire strewn in the bright air of morning, their emanations linger yet, pervading the sunset dreams of tired Mr Bloom and Miss Gertrude MacDowell, lonely virgin of the rocks. Mr Bloom, too, has sentimental memories of dear old Howth. "Hidden under wild ferns on Howth. . . . Pillowed on my coat she had her hair, earwigs in the heather scrub, my hand under her nape, you'll toss me all. O wonder![1]

In such an ambiance of sentiment Gerty MacDowell, "gazing far away into the distance," dreams of loves forgotten, love to be. In such a night as this Nausicaa heard in dream Athena's summons to the Phaeacian

*From *James Joyce's "Ulysses": a Study* (London: Faber & Faber, 1930), 273–86. Copyright 1930, 1952 by Stuart Gilbert. © renewed 1958 by Arthur Stuart Gilbert. Reprinted by permission of Alfred A. Knopf, Inc.

149

beach, where a certain godlike wanderer was sleeping, snug in fallen leaves like a seed of fire within black embers. Gerty's girl friends, Cissy Caffrey and Edy Boardman, seated beside her on the rock, jealous creatures of grosser clay, strike, it must be admitted, a jarring note. And Tommy and Jacky Caffrey, the curly-headed twins, for all their tender years, are no better than they should be. They have built a round tower — a little *omphalos* of their own — on the Cape Mortella model, and theirs is the spirit of Corsican brotherhood.

> Boys will be boys and our two twins were no exception to this golden rule. The apple of discord was a certain castle of sand which Master Jacky had built and Master Tommy would have it right go wrong that it was to be architecturally improved by a frontdoor like the Martello tower had. But if Master Tommy was headstrong Master Jacky was selfwilled too and, true to the maxim that every little Irishman's house is his castle, he fell upon his hated rival and to such purpose that the wouldbe assailant came to grief and (alas to relate!) the coveted castle too.

Baby Boardman in his pushcar, though too young to fight, manages to make a nuisance of himself in his own small way.

> "Say papa, baby. Say pa pa pa pa pa pa pa."
> And baby did his level best to say it for he was very intelligent for eleven months everyone said and big for his age and the picture of health, a perfect little bunch of love, and he would certainly turn out to be something great they said.
> "Haja ja ja haja."
> Cissy wiped his little mouth with the dribbling bib and wanted him to sit up properly and say pa pa pa but when she undid the strap she cried out, holy saint Denis, that he was possing wet and to double the half blanket the other way under him. Of course his infant majesty was most obstreperous at such toilet formalities and he let everyone know it.
> "Habaa baaahabaaa baaaa."
> And two great big lovely tears coursing down his cheeks. It was all no use soothering him with no, nono, baby, no and telling him about the geegee and where was the puffpuff but Ciss, always readywitted, gave him in his mouth the teat of the suckingbottle and the young heathen was quickly appeased.

It is a relief to turn to Gerty, "as fair a specimen of winsome Irish girlhood as one could wish to see."

> The waxen pallor of her face was almost spiritual in its ivory-like purity though her rosebud mouth was a genuine Cupid's bow, Greekly perfect. Her hands were of finely veined alabaster with tapering fingers and as white as lemon juice and queen of ointments could make them though it was not true that she used to wear kid gloves in bed or take a milk footbath either. Bertha Supple told that once to Edy Boardman, a deliberate lie, when she was black out at daggers drawn with Gerty (the

girl chums had of course their little tiffs from time to time like the rest of mortals) and she told her not to let on whatever she did that it was her that told her or she'd never speak to her again. No. Honour where honour is due. There was an innate refinement, a languid queenly *hauteur* about Gerty which was unmistakably evidenced in her delicate hands and high-arched instep. Had kind fate but willed her to be born a gentlewoman of high degree in her own right and had she only received the benefit of a good education Gerty MacDowell might easily have held her own beside any lady in the land and have seen herself exquisitely gowned with jewels on her brow and patrician suitors at her feet vying with one another to pay their devoirs to her. Mayhap it was this, the love that might have been, that lent to her softlyfeatured face at whiles a look, tense with suppressed meaning, that imparted a strange yearning tendency to the beautiful eyes, a charm few could resist.

Yet her love affair with young Reggy Wylie, a boy of her own age, seemed likely to end, like Nausicaa's, by a *nolle prosequi*.

He was undeniably handsome with an exquisite nose and he was what he looked, every inch a gentleman, the shape of his head too at the back without his cap on that she would know anywhere something off the common and the way he turned the bicycle at the lamp with his hands off the bars and also the nice perfume of those good cigarettes and besides they were both of a size and that was why Edy Boardman thought she was so frightfully clever because he didn't go and ride up and down in front of her bit of a garden.

Her ideal is changing; he who would win her love must be

a manly man with a strong quiet face who had not found his ideal, perhaps his hair slightly flecked with grey, and who would understand, take her in his sheltering arms, strain her to him in all the strength of his deep passionate nature and comfort her with a long kiss. It would be like heaven. For such a one she yearns this balmy summer eve. With all the heart of her she longs to be his only, his affianced bride for riches for poor, in sickness in health, till death us two part, from this to this day forward.

She will make a tender, loving little wifie; "they would have a beautifully appointed drawingroom with pictures and engravings and the photograph of grandpapa Giltrap's lovely dog Garryowen that almost talked." (Garryowen will be recognized as the "old towser," loaned by grandpapa as boon companion to a "blood and ouns champion.")

Tommy and the baby meanwhile are quarrelling about a ball which Tommy claims for his.

O, he was a man already was little Tommy Caffrey since he was out of pinnies. Edy told him no, no and to be off now with him and she told Cissy Caffrey not to give in to him.

"You're not my sister," naughty Tommy said. "It's my ball."

But Cissy Caffrey told baby Boardman to look up, look up high at her finger and she snatched the ball quickly and threw it along the sand and Tommy after it in full career, having won the day.

"Anything for a quiet life," laughed Ciss.

And she tickled tiny tot's two cheeks to make him forget and played here's the lord mayor, here's his two horses, here's his gingerbread carriage and here he walks in, chinchopper, chinchopper, chinchopper chin. But Edy got cross as two sticks about him getting his own way like that from everyone always petting him.

"I'd like to give him something," she said, "so I would, where I won't say."

"On the beetoteetom," laughed Cissy merrily.

Gerty MacDowell bent down her head and crimsoned at the idea of Cissy saying an unladylike thing like that out loud she'd be ashamed of her life to say, flushing a deep rosy red, and Edy Boardman said she was sure the gentleman opposite heard what she said. But not a pin cared Ciss.

Presently Master Jacky kicks the ball as hard as ever he can towards the seaweedy rocks. A gentleman in black sitting there intercepts the ball and throws it up toward Cissy, but it rolls back down the slope and stops right under Gerty's skirt. Cissy tells her to kick it away and Gerty gives a kick, but misses. The other girls laugh.

"If you fail try again," Edy Boardman said.

Gerty smiled assent and bit her lip. A delicate pink crept into her pretty cheek but she was determined to let them see so she just lifted her skirt a little but just enough and took good aim and gave the ball a jolly good kick. . . . Pure jealousy of course it was nothing else to draw attention on account of the gentleman opposite looking. She felt the warm flush, a danger signal always with Gerty MacDowell, surging and flaming into her cheeks. Till then they had only exchanged glances of the most casual but now under the brim of her new hat she ventured a look at him and the face that met her gaze there in the twilight wan and sadly drawn, seemed to her the saddest that she had ever seen.

Observing the lonely gentleman, she reads the story of a haunting sorrow written on his face.

He was looking up so intently, so still, and he saw her kick the ball and perhaps he could see the bright steel buckles of her shoes if she swung them like that thoughtfully with the toes down. She was glad that something told her to put on the transparent stockings thinking Reggy Wylie might be out but that was far away. Here was that of which she had so often dreamed. It was he who mattered and there was joy on her face because she wanted him because she felt instinctively that he was like no-one else. The very heart of the girlwoman went out to him, her dreamhusband, because she knew on the instant it was him. If he had suffered, more sinned against than sinning, or even, even, if he had been himself a sinner, a wicked man, she cared not. Even if he was a protestant or methodist she could convert him easily if he truly loved her.

Meanwhile the dusk has fallen and Gerty's companions are thinking of going home. But Gerty is in no hurry to move; the gentleman's eyes are fixed on her, "literally worshipping at her shrine." The Mirus Bazaar fireworks begin and the others run down the strand so as to see over the houses and the church. Gerty is left to her lovedreams and the rapt regard of Mr Bloom — for it is he, the sombre gentleman with the haunting sorrow. She "senses" the mute appeal of his adoring eye; inapprehensible, she clutches to her compassion on the aching void of the Bloomish heart.

> Perhaps it was an old flame he was in mourning for from the days beyond recall.[2] She thought she understood. She would try to understand him because men were so different. The old love was waiting, waiting with little white hands stretched out, with blue appealing eyes. Heart of mine! She would follow her dream of love, the dictates of her heart told her he was her all in all, the only man in all the world for her for love was the master guide. Nothing else mattered. Come what might she would be wild, untrammelled, free.

Gerty swings her buckled shoe, transparent stockings, faster and yet faster. She leans back, far, further, too far back, while Mr Bloom follows her movements with the enraptured eyes of love-at-first-sight. And, since apostrophe befits this tender, old-world theme, let us pause, gentle reader, to acclaim the "flappers" of Bloomsday, happy indeed, *sua si bona norint*, before the evil days befell of abridged skirts, when man no longer delights in any girl's legs. The consolations of a rainy day or rugged beach have gone the way of all flesh and left the exhibitionist no better off than a commoner. Leopold Bloom is *aux anges*.

> And then a rocket sprang and bang shot blind blank and O! then the Roman candle burst and it was like a sigh of O! and everyone cried O! O! in raptures and it gushed out of it a stream of rain gold hair threads and they shed and ah! they were all greeny dewy stars falling with golden, O so lovely! O so soft, sweet, soft!

But now Cissy Caffrey vulgarly whistles to call Gerty, who knows that her golden hour is over. But first she makes a gesture of benediction, token that Love's Sweet Evensong is ended.

> *Though the heart be weary,*
> *Sad the day and long,*
> *Still there comes at twilight*
> *Love's Old Sweet Song.*

> Gerty had an idea, one of love's little ruses. She slipped her hand into her kerchief pocket and took out the wadding and waved in reply of course without letting him and then slipped it back. Wonder if he's too far to. She rose. . . . She drew herself up to her full height. Their souls met in a last lingering glance and the eyes that reached her heart, full of a strange shining, hung enraptured on her sweet flowerlike face. She smiled

at him wanly, a sweet forgiving smile, a smile that verged on tears, and then they parted.

She walked with a certain quiet dignity characteristic of her but with care and very slowly because, because Gerty MacDowell was . . .

Tight boots? No. She's lame! O!

Now Mr Bloom sits alone, darkling, in a mood of calm reaction, of afterthoughts on love and woman's ways, embodied in a long silent monologue. But each phase is rounded by a thought of Marion, his wife, for he is faithful in his mild infidelity.

Wait. Hm. Hm. Yes. That's her perfume. Why she waved her hand. I leave you this to think of me when I'm far away on the pillow. What is it? Heliotrope? No. Hyacinth? Hm. Roses, I think. She'd like scent of that kind. Sweet and cheap: soon sour. Why Molly likes opoponax. Suits her with a little jessamine mixed. Her high notes and her low notes. At the dance night she met him, dance of the hours. Heat brought it out. She was wearing her black and it had the perfume of the time before. Good conductor, is it? Or bad? Light too. Suppose there's some connection. For instance if you go into a cellar when it's dark. Mysterious thing too. Why did I smell it only now? Took its time in coming like herself, slow but sure. Suppose it's ever so many millions of tiny grains blown across. Yes, it is. Because those spice islands, Cinghalese this morning, smell them leagues off. Tell you what it is. It's like a fine veil or web they have all over the skin, fine like what do you call it gossamer and they're always spinning it out of them, fine as anything, rainbow colours without knowing it. Clings to everything she takes off. Vamp of her stockings. Warm shoe. Stays. Drawers: little kick, taking them off. Byby till next time. Also the cat likes to sniff in her shift on the bed. Know her smell in a thousand. Bathwater too. Reminds me of strawberries and cream.

The sultry day has reached its sleepy close. Bats are bawking through the velvet sky. "Short snooze now if I had. . . . Just close my eyes a moment. Won't sleep though. Half dream. It never comes the same."

"A bat flew. Here. There. Here. Far in the grey a bell chimed. Mr Bloom with open mouth, his left boot sanded sideways, leaned, breathed. Just for a few."

As Mr Bloom half dreams, his inner voice murmurs an epilogue of the day's memories and encounters, a jumble of words, disjointed yet associative — metempsychosis, Martha's letter, Raoul, and the "heaving embonpoint" of *The Sweets of Sin*, dark, "Spanish" Marion and her earliest lover, returned sailors "smelling the tailend of ports," melonfields of Agendath Netaim. . . . "we two naughty Grace darling she him half past the bed met him pike hoses frillies for Raoul to perfume you wife black hair heave under embon *senorita* young eyes Mulvey plump years dreams return tail end Agendath swoony lovey showed me her next year in drawers return next in her next her next."

It is interesting to compare this summer night's dream of Mr Bloom with another night-piece, those famous last lines of the *Anna Livia Plurabelle* section of *Finnegans Wake*, where two garrulous old washerwomen, metamorphosed into a tree and a stone, are fixed in an ageless dream, beside the dark waters of the Anna Liffey

> Can't hear with the waters of. The chittering waters of. Flittering bats, fieldmice bawk talk. Ho! Are you not gone ahome? What Thom Malone?[3] Can't hear with bawk of bats, all thim liffeying waters of. Ho, talk save us! My foos won't moos. I feel as old as yonder elm. A tale told of Shaun or Shem? All Livia's daughtersons. Dark hawks hear us. Night! Night! My ho head halls. I feel as heavy as yonder stone. Tell me of John or Shaun? Who were Shem and Shaun the living sons or daughters of? Night now! Tell me, tell me, tell me, elm! Night, night! Tellmetale of stem or stone. Beside the rivering waters of, hitherandthithering waters of. Night!

The Phaeacians were a seafaring race and their wealth came to them in ships. The name of Nausithoos, founder of their city, as well as that of the princess Nausicaa, marks their nautical turn of mind. On the Phaeacian strand there was "a goodly temple of Poseidon, furnished with heavy stones deep bedded in the earth." The *Nausicaa* episode of *Ulysses* opens with the mention of a similar shrine. "The Abbey of Howth is situated on a delightful spot overhanging the ocean. Tradition states that its foundation was laid in 1235, on the removal of the prebendal church from Ireland's Eye. It was dedicated to the Blessed Virgin, and hence styled St. Mary's. Over the western door is a ruined belfry, and at the opposite end a triplet window."[4] One of the bells, removed from the Abbey to Howth Castle, bears the inscription: SANCTA: MARIA: ORA: PRO: NOBIS: AD: FILIUM.

The Symbol of this episode is *Virgin* and one of its "colours" is *blue*, and it is fitting that the romance-without-words of Gerty MacDowell and Mr Bloom should develop under the patronage of Mary, Star of the Sea, moist realm no longer Neptune's. For Star has vanquished Trident, our Lady of the Sacred Heart the Shaker of the Earth. Even in Corfu, Nausicaa's isle, the Poseideion has crumbled to dust and on its site there stands a shrine dedicated to Saint Nicholas, patron of seafaring men.

One of the many virtues of a seamanly folk is the cult of cleanliness. The necessity of keeping a ship in applepie order and an immunity from the hydrophobia which afflicts many inland races are factors making for personal immaculateness and frequent laundering; seablue and spotless white are the sailor's — and virgin's — colours. Thus Nausicaa begs Alcinous:

> Father, dear, couldst thou not lend me a high waggon with strong wheels, that I may take the goodly raiment to the river to wash, so much as I have lying soiled? Yea and it is seemly that thou thyself when among the princes in council should have fresh raiment to wear. Also, there are five dear sons of thine in the halls, two married, but three are lusty bachelors, and these are always eager for new-washen garments

wherein to go to the dances, for all these things I have taken thought. When they had washed and cleansed all the stains, they spread all out in order along the shore of the deep, even where the sea, in beating on the coast, washed the pebbles clean.

"The cleanliness of the Phaeacians," M. Bérard observes, "was the wonder of the Achaeans, as that of the Dutch was the admiration of the eighteenth century and that of the English is admirable to contemporaries. Once on shore, seafaring men are eager for white shirts, patent-leather shoes, a change of linen, a new rig-out in which to go to dances. Inland folk are not so particular. I picture the Achaeans as similar to the Albanians, gloriously dirty, decorated with gold, embroidery and grease-stains, redolent of stale oil and goats' butter — as the traveller encounters them at the Corfu jetties or embarking on European boats, whose cleanness appals them. They are clad in felt or woollen fabrics which last a lifetime. The Phaeacians wear white linen, well-laundered, starched, ironed, frilled, which calls for frequent washing."

Gerty is a true Phaeacian.

> As for undies they were Gerty's chief care and who that knows the fluttering hopes and fears of sweet seventeen (though Gerty would never see seventeen again) can find it in his heart to blame her? She had four dinky sets, with awfully pretty stitchery, three garments and nighties extra, and each set slotted with different coloured ribbons, rose-pink, pale blue, mauve and peagreen, and she aired them herself and blued them when they came home from the wash and ironed them and she had a brickbat to keep the iron on because she wouldn't trust those washerwomen as far as she'd see them scorching the things.

As an Irish girl Gerty can claim to be of blood royal, and the wonders of the palace of Alcinous are faintly reproduced by the "artistic standard designs" of Catesby's cork lino (in which her father deals), "fit for a palace, gives tiptop wear and always bright and cheery in the home." Gerty loves lovely things. She has a beautiful almanack picture of halycon days (she found out in Walker's pronouncing dictionary about halcyon days what they meant), a young gentleman offering a bunch of flowers to his ladylove. The latter was "in a soft clinging white in a studied attitude," and the gentleman looked a thorough aristocrat. "She often looked at them dreamily . . . and felt her own arms that were white and soft like hers with the sleeves back." Nausicaa λεωυκώλενος, of the white arms.

The famous game of ball which Nausicaa plays with her young companions has an obvious counterpart in the game which led to Mr Bloom's observation of Gerty and his interception of the ball amid the lusty cries of the players. "So then the princess threw the ball at one of her company; she missed the girl, and cast the ball into a deep eddying current, whereat they all raised a piercing cry. Then the goodly Odysseus awoke and sat up, pondering in his heart and spirit." "Yes, it was her he was looking at and there was meaning in his look. His eyes burned into her . . ."

A rising tide of sentiment and emotion lifts the narrative to the highwatermark of intensity when the rocket bursts in a shower of gold hair and the hour of adieu has struck for both. The soar of the rocket and its fall symbolize the technic of this episode: *tumescence-detumescence*, a quiet opening, a long crescendo of turgid, rhapsodic prose towards a climax, a pyrotechnic explosion, a dying fall, silence. The last firework fades out in a single white spark, *stella maris*, against the blue. "A lost long candle wandered up the sky . . . and broke, drooping, and shed a cluster of violet but one white stars."

Like Gerty, Nausicaa had a maidenly hope regarding the godlike stranger; "would that such an one might be called my husband, dwelling here; and that it might please him here to abide." Gerty hoped for "a nice snug and cosy little homely house, every morning they would both have brekky, simple but perfectly served, for their own two selves. . . ." Nausicaa enjoyed the brief triumph of leading her *trouvaille* to the paternal palace and hearing him tell the tale of his adventures in manly hexameters before he sailed away to his Penelope, whereas poor Gerty had to return alone to her linolean "palace," leaving the hero lonely on the shore.

A sentimental pair, Gerty and Nausicaa, over-ready to fall for the fascination of any "dark stranger." Yet they typify an ineradicable instinct of girlhood. Even in the "Palaces" *dernier cri* of the Riviera, where the blue flower is no longer sported, you will observe that, despite the cavils of outraged nordics, the dark stranger has but to rise to conquer. Gerty's luscious prose—for, though her tale is told in the third person, I see in Gerty the true narrator of the first part of this episode (as Samuel Butler saw in Nausicaa the "authoress of the Odyssey")— is a potpourri of everlastings from the garden of *jeunes filles en fleurs*.

Nausicaa's father, King Alcinous, was a hospitable man who kept a good cellar. The barman Pontonous "mixed the gladdening wine" (Homer's "mixed" has, surely, a very modern tinkle!) and it was not till they had "drunken to their hearts' content" that Alcinous "made harangue." His speech was brief, and briefer still his guest's reply, and, forthwith, there was another drinking to their hearts' content—they were convivial folk, those Phaeacians. Gerty's father too, true scion of the Nausithous stock "exceeded," much to Gerty's distress. "Had her father only avoided the clutches of the demon drink, by taking the pledge or the drink habit cured in Pearson's Weekly, she might now be rolling in her carriage second to none." Her soul-communion with Mr Bloom is accompanied by an anthem of men's voices and the sound of the organ pealing out from the simple fane beside the waves, where a men's temperance retreat, conducted by the Rev John Hughes S.J., is in progress. With no less zeal, we may be sure, did good queen Arete (the master-spirit in the royal household) sermonize the king for his too frequent calls on the services of Pontonous. Through Gerty's musings, across the vibrant intensity of Mr Bloom's gaze, there runs a crosscurrent of sacred song, a waft of fragrant incense and fragrant names; "spiritual vessel, pray for us, vessel of singular devotion, pray for us, mystical rose. . . ." Thus, too, the hearts of the Phaeacians were uplifted and Odysseus was moved even to tears by the lay of divine Demodocus, to whom the gods gave minstrelsy as to none else to make men glad in what way soever his spirit stirred him to sing.

Far out at sea the anchored lightship twinkled, winked at somnolent Mr Bloom. "Life those chaps must have out there. Penance for their sins." Not otherwise did Poseidon penalize the Phaeacians who conveyed Odysseus to Ithaca, for the too notorious swiftness of their ships,[5] a challenge to his might. For the gods love not those who would persistently exceed the proper rhythm of progress — as the modern world is discovering to its cost.

> Now Poseidon went on his way to Scheria, where the Phaeacians dwell. There he abode awhile: and lo! the seafaring ship drew very near, being lightly sped; and nigh her came the shaker of the earth, and he smote her into a stone, and rooted her far down below with the downstroke of his hand.
> Then one to another they spake winged words, the Phaeacians of the long oars, mariners renowned. And thus they would speak, looking each man to his neighbour:
> "Ah me! who is this that hath bound our swift ship on the deep as she drave homewards? Even now she was clear in sight."
> Even so they would speak; but they knew not how these things were ordained.

Mr Bloom's *"penance for their sins"* may be a dim recall of past experience, of "how these things were ordained": an ancient dream fluttering bat-like from the gate of horn. Again, looking out to sea, he evokes a picture[6] of the perils of them that go down to the sea in ships: an old fresco in Akâsa retouched by a modern hand.

> The anchor's weighed. Off he sails with a scapular or a medal on him for luck. Well? And the tephilim no what's this they call it poor papa's father had on his door to touch. That brought us out of the land of Egypt and into the house of bondage. Something in all those superstitions because when you go out never know what dangers. Hanging on to a plank or astride of a beam for grim life, lifebelt round him, gulping salt water, and that's the last of his nibs till the sharks catch hold of him. Do fish ever get seasick?
> Then you have a beautiful calm without a cloud, smooth sea, placid, crew and cargo in smithereens, Davy Jones' locker. Moon looking down. Not my fault, old cockalorum.

> But the daughter of Cadmus marked him, Ino of the fair ankles . . . and sat upon the well-bound raft and spake: "Hapless one, wherefore was Poseidon, shaker of the earth, so wondrous wroth with

thee? . . . Take this veil divine and wind it about thy breast; then there
is no fear that thou suffer aught or perish. But when thou hast laid hold
of the main land with thy hands, loose it off from thee and cast it into
the wine-dark deep." . . . As when a great tempestuous wind tosseth a
heap of parched husks and scattereth them this way and that, even so
did the wave scatter the long beams of the raft. But Odysseus bestrode a
single plank as one rideth on a courser, and fell prone in the sea. . . . But
Athene, daughter of Zeus, turned to new thoughts. She bound up the
courses of the other winds and charged them all to cease and be still; but
she roused the swift North and brake the waves before him. . . . So for
two nights and two days he was wandering in the swell of the sea, and
much his heart boded of death. But when at last the fair-tressed dawn
brought the full light of the third day, thereafter the breeze fell and lo!
there was a breathless calm, and with a quick glance ahead he saw the
land very near.

Notes

1. Page 167.
2. "The dear, dead days beyond recall." *Love's Old Sweet Song.*
3. Their voices grow blurred and indistinct as they call to each other across the turmoil of
"hitherandthithering waters."
4. Black's *Guide to Ireland.*
5. Leur spécialité, leur gloire, c'est d'avoir dompté l'Adriatique et, par un service de
messageries extra-rapides, supprimé ce grand abîe de mer." *Les Phéniciens et l'Odyssée*, Tome,
I, page 584.
6. The "art of this episode is *painting;* Mr Bloom's monologue here is a sequence of
mental pictures, rarely meditative. Gerty, too, visualizes her memories and aspirations.

["Nausikaa"]   Frank Budgen*

Unlike *The Cyclops* episode, in which politics dominated and,
appropriately, no woman appeared, *Nausikaa* leaves the government of
the city to whom it may concern and deals with the way of a man with a
maid, more particularly the way of a middle-ageing married man with a
maid. The social problem set by this relation of man and woman of
different ages is raised by implication. The mystery of women's clothing
and the lures of exhibitionism arise for consideration. The crime of Onan
is suggested and the question arises whether in our present social organisa-
tion the statute of limitations might not apply. Aesthetically considered
Nausikaa is more purely sensibility than any other episode in *Ulysses*.
Sense organs, the eye and the nose, are the presiding organs of the human

*From *James Joyce and the Making of "Ulysses"* (New York: Harrison Smith and Robert
Haas, 1934), 207–20. Reprinted by permission of the publisher.

body: principally, however, the eye, for this is the painters' episode. The scene is on the seashore, the action begins at about eight o'clock, the light is a rich and magical twilight.

Joyce is as little critical of the materials set before him by society as is the landscape painter of the materials set before him by nature and man, but his work is, nevertheless, because of its candour and accuracy, a social document as the painting of seventeenth century Dutch painters and of, say, Canaletto, is a social document. *Nausikaa* shows us (we knew it all along, of course) that those social forces which, at a recent date, endowed the world with the institutions of private property and monogamic marriage have not yet taught the wayward eye of man not to rove. The chemistry of his body and the imagination of his mind are older and newer than his laws and conventions. The eye of Mr. Bloom roves freely throughout the day and his desires are provoked by many women, yet, on the whole, the institution of marriage is triumphantly vindicated in his person. To his wife, who since a little past four o'clock that afternoon, has been studying her concert programme with the aid of her organiser, Blazes Boylan, his memories, desires and hopes constantly return. Leopold's wife is something more to him than his sexual complement. She is his destiny, like the weight of his body, the shape of his nose, his family, race and fortunes.

It has been a fine but, for Bloom, rather tiring day. He is dressed in black and is wearing a bowler hat, not an ideal garb for hot weather. He has walked a lot on the hot stones of Dublin streets, is very nervy about affairs at home, has recently been engaged in an exhausting argument, and now with a headache is down on the seashore for a breath of fresh air. We are to suppose that there is a gap of time between his hurried exit from Barney Kiernan's licensed premises and his appearance on Sandymount shore, which time has been occupied with a visit in the company of Martin Cunningham to the Dignam family at their home in Sandymount. This visit to the widow and orphans was no pleasure to Bloom and he does not pretend that it was. Three girls see him as he comes to rest on a rock not far from them. The girls are Cissy Caffrey, Edy Boardman and Gerty MacDowell, and they are there with baby Boardman and Tommy and Jacky Caffrey, twins, to have a "cosy chat beside the sparkling waves and discuss matters feminine." Of the three girls Gerty MacDowell is the star. She is described in the familiar novelette style of the period, and we must remember that *Poppy's Paper* and *Florrie's Paper*, with their yarns about typists and factory hands who get off with the young governor in his sports Bentley, had not yet, in 1904, supplanted the *Bow Bells* and *Heartsease* novelettes, where the young governess makes the crowded ballroom floor gasp with her beauty, dressed in a simple white frock and wearing a single white rose. Carefully listening we can hear undertones of Gerty's own Sandymount outlook and dialect in the rich prose of the *Heartsease* library.

"The waxen pallor of her face was almost spiritual in its ivorylike purity though her rosebud mouth was a genuine Cupid's bow, Greekly perfect. Her hands were of finely veined alabaster with tapering fingers and as white as lemon juice and queen of ointments could make them though it was not true that she used to wear kid gloves in bed or take a milk footbath either. . . . Why have women such eyes of witchery? Gerty's were of the bluest Irish blue, set off by lustrous lashes and dark expressive brows. . . . But Gerty's crowning glory was her wealth of wonderful hair. It was dark brown with a natural wave in it. She had cut it that very morning on account of the new moon and it nestled about her pretty head in a profusion of luxuriant clusters and pared her nails too. . . . Gerty was dressed simply but with the instinctive taste of a votary of Dame Fashion for she felt that there was just a might that he might be out. A neat blouse of electric blue, self-tinted by dolly dyes (because it was expected in the *Lady's Pictorial* that electric blue would be worn), with a smart vee opening down to the division and kerchief pocket (in which she always kept a piece of cottonwool scented with her favourite perfume because the handkerchief spoiled the sit) and a navy three-quarter skirt cut to the stride showed off her slim graceful figure to perfection. She wore a coquettish little love of a hat of wideleaved nigger straw contrast trimmed with an underbrim of egg-blue chenille and at the side a butterfly bow to tone. . . ."

Gerty is granddaughter to Mr. Giltrap, whose wolfhound, Garryowen, supplies local colour to the Citizen on his propagandist pub-crawls. The heart of the virgin leaps to the tinkle of the bicycle bell of the boy down the street (and Gerty MacDowell loves Reggie Wylie, the boy with the bicycle bell) but it yearns for the handsome, unknown stranger of its dreams. And the heart of the handsome, dark stranger (known to us, unknown to Gerty, for it is Bloom) responds with desire for her youth, as nothing more fervently desires youth than the heart of middle-ageing man, conscious that its beats are numbered. The desires of both are favoured by the warmth and half darkness of the June evening.

Bloom's watch stopped at half-past four, significant hour, but when Cissy Caffrey asks him the time he knows it is after eight because the sun has set. From afar they hear the litany of Our Lady of Loreto, "Refuge of sinners. Comfortress of the afflicted," being sung in the church, Star of the Sea. The devotion in progress is the men's temperance retreat, rosary, sermon and benediction of the Most Blessed Sacrament. Gerty pictures to herself the scene in the church, "the stained glass windows lighted up, the candles, flowers and the blue banners of the Blessed Virgin's sodality." This is an aspect of Catholic Christian worship that seemed to Joyce peculiarly appropriate in an episode the main theme of which is sex appeal. In a letter to me from Trieste he wrote: "*Nausikaa* is written in a namby-pamby jammy marmalady drawersy (alto là!) style with effects of incense, mariolatry, masturbation, stewed cockles, painter's palette, chitchat, circumlocution, etc. etc." We may take it that Stephen is expressing Joyce's own mature view when, in expounding his Hamlet theory, he says: "Fatherhood, in the sense of conscious begetting, is unknown to man. It is a mystical estate, an apostolic succession, from only begetter to only begotten. On that mystery and not on the Madonna which the cunning Italian intellect flung to the mob of Europe the Church is founded and founded irremovably because founded, like the world, macro- and micro-cosm, upon the void." It goes almost without saying that Gerty agrees thoroughly with the immediate social object of the mission because: "Had her father only avoided the clutches of the demon drink, by taking the pledge or those powders the drink habit cured in *Pearson's Weekly*, she might now be rolling in her carriage, second to none. Over and over had she told herself that as she mused by the dying embers in a brown study without the lamp because she hated two lights or oftentimes gazing out of the window dreamily by the hour at the rain falling on the rusty bucket, thinking. But that vile decoction which has ruined so many hearths and homes had cast its shadow over her childhood days. . . ." And now Gerty has got the vote and unless she takes to porter or cocktails herself we shall see.

The dusk deepens and a bat flies through the air around them "with a tiny lost cry." At the Mirus bazaar in aid of funds for Mercer's Hospital a firework display begins, "And they all ran down the strand to see over the houses and the church, helter-skelter, Edy with the push-car with baby Boardman in it and Cissy holding Tommy and Jacky by the hand so they wouldn't fall running." The two girls call to Gerty to follow them, but Gerty prefers to remain where she is, sitting on a rock. She can see just as well from that point and she is glad they are going for it leaves her alone in the gathering darkness with the dark, handsome stranger, who, from his position, leaning against a nearby rock, is devouring her with his eyes. They are letting off Roman candles and Gerty leans back as far as possible to see the display, one uplifted knee clasped with both hands. One strange thing about the light of after sundown is that all white things look mysteriously and dominatingly white in a landscape in which half tones have begun to merge into a predominating dark:

> And she saw a long Roman candle going up over the trees up, up, and, in the tense hush, they were all breathless with excitement as it went higher and higher and she had to lean back more and more to look up after it, high, high, almost out of sight, and her face was suffused with a divine, an entrancing blush from straining back and he could see her other things, too, nainsook knickers, the fabric that caresses the skin, better than those other pettiwidth, the green, four and eleven. . . .

The female form divine, undraped, is a sight for gods, artists, philosophers, physicians and suchlike. It is a majestic object, sometimes awe-inspiring, sometimes pitiful and, but rarely, and to some few, erotically provoking. It is made more alluring and approachable when its majestic beauties and stark realities are appropriately veiled. It is easy to believe the nudists when they claim that nudist colonies are haunts of austere purity. Erudite French writers have maintained that the garments so attractive to Bloom were of Greek origin — that the Greeks had a word for them — that after centuries of eclipse they came back again in the seventeenth century, that during the eighteenth century they again went out of sight and mind, only to reach the point of highest culture at about the time of Zola and Mr. Bloom. Modesty, it is said, was the cause of this development, modest forethought for possible falls from horses and, later on, from bicycles. Then it was also a precaution against masculine invasiveness. Climate also played a part and, in generations when a belief in microbes was prevalent, hygiene. But none of these solid historical reasons seems to explain satisfactorily how colour, form and fabric combined to provide the female sex with such a remarkable instrument of coquetterie.

Change in the concealings and revealings of coquettish allurements seems, as in all other matters, to be the only constant thing about it. That the female form must be veiled is on all sides, excepting nudist colonies, admitted, but not always with the same chiffon, for the imagination of man is lazy and that of the dress designer and tailor active. He is served with a constant novelty of provocation, if he demands it or not. The question whether the tempo of these changes of fashion is conditioned by the tempo of social transformation as a whole is one that the historian of costume must answer (Chapter: Figleaf to Mulberry leaf and beyond). But, so headlong has been the rate of change in the last quarter of a century that if Gerty MacDowell's undies so attractive to Bloom, were displayed (à titre de documentation historique) in a Regent Street shop window they would provoke, but only to laughter. And the loudest and longest laugh would be that of Gerty MacDowell herself, passing the window with her streamlined, grown up daughter. Could Dan Leno now say, "Red or White, Madam?" without mystifying nine-tenths of his audience? The easiest film laugh available is got by showing a bedroom of that epoch, when the great white Queen Victoria ruled these islands, with a lady in it, draped in the voluminous undergarments of the period. The next easiest laugh is got by showing a ten years pre-war motor car. For all its pruderies of speech and manner the period of Bloom's youth and manhood was erotic to a tropical degree. Let anyone behold the ladies' underwear in artificial silk in all colours but the right one exhibited nowadays in shop windows everywhere and admit that they are woefully unerotic. They are a visible sign that the tide is now setting in the direction of candour, co-education and companionate marriages with surgically clean, scientific instruction in erotic and contraceptive mysteries, classic treatises on which will, no doubt, soon be borne home with the latest vitamin cookery book as school prizes. But when the life force, if that most depressing divinity happens to be in fashion at the time, finds that tabulated knowledge, the good pal girl and the fifty-fifty boy lead only to tweeds for everybody and general indifference, then social and sexual taboos, ignorance, inhibitions, white undies, black stockings, and furtiveness, will come in again with all their tensions, as in the days of Gerty MacDowell.

What is the usual result of mutual erotic attraction between the middle-aged, married man and the young virgin? There is a gap of time and experience, not to mention social convenience, between the *grisonnant* and the *grisette* not easily bridged except by some variation, more or less involved, of the expeditious practice of Bloom. The consideration of expediency dominates. One gathers that children in the days of Judah were a form of social riches and that Judah's son objected to increasing his brother's store, just as he might have refused to bear a hand with the ploughing and sowing in his brother's field. Onan was condemned not for a contraceptual practice as such, but for a lack of tribal solidarity, of brotherly love. His excessive individualism was punished. It is as if he had hoarded or wasted national property in time of war or famine. The only thought in Bloom's subsequent monologue that at all bears on this aspect of the question is: "Glad to get away from other chap's wife. Eating off his cold plate." But this is a purely aesthetic or hygienic motive and has nothing to do with social and religious considerations.

Bloom is a married man, a father, and is twenty years the senior of Gerty, the maid. A solution to the problem of their mutual attraction that leaves nobody a penny the worse off cannot be considered entirely unsuccessful. Had Bloom spoken to Gerty, immediate disillusionment might have followed. What seemed so attractive at ten yards might, at arm's length, have left indifferent, in which case mutual embarrassment would have put an end to the matter. But if at the first "Good evening" the attraction had increased, and an affair had started, Gerty would have written letters and started a rivalry with his wife just as, to Bloom's annoyance, Martha Clifford has begun to do. Bloom himself reflects: "Suppose I spoke to her. What about? Bad plan however if you don't know how to end the conversation. Ask them a question and they ask you another." And again: "Might have made a worse fool of myself. . . . Instead of talking about nothing."

It is easy for a rich man, who has energy as well as money to burn, to keep separate establishments for a variety of loves. But Bloom is a poor man. He has work to do and a family to keep. He is, besides, a prudent man and, although open to a variety of sexual excitations, is not a passionate man in the sense that he could ever allow the integrity of his life to be endangered by any one object. Whatever the charms of other women he accepts them as adjuncts to, not as rivals of, his wife. And Marion's fixed empire over his mind is not shaken by his knowledge that she is possessed by other men. In fact, thinking of Boylan's visit to Marion, he even calmly considers whether her lover ought not to pay for the privilege of her love: "Suppose he gave her money. Why not? All a prejudice. She's worth ten, fifteen, more a pound. What? I think so. All that for nothing." After the fall of the greeny, dewy stars of the Roman candle, and Bloom's expense of spirit, Gerty rises and follows her two friends away from the seashore, waving to them as she does so the piece of scented cotton wool she carried in her kerchief pocket. It is one of "love's little ruses." The signal is for them but the sweet scent is for her dark, stranger lover. Then the style of the episode changes from the marmalady circumlocutions of the novelette to the hacked phrases of Bloom's thoughts.

Nausikaa is the one pictorial episode in *Ulysses*. It is pre-eminently the episode of sensibility in both the emotional and physical sense. Sight is the sense most in evidence, but nose, ear and touch reinforce the true organ of vision. A picture of the seashore is built up in the novelettish narrative of the seductive Gerty, and that picture becomes rarer and denser in the tightly woven texture of Bloom's unspoken thoughts. It must be regarded as something of a wonder that the seen thing should play the great part it does play in the writing of a man whose sight was never strong. But the many things in *Ulysses* vividly seen are generally closeups. They are vehemently drawn, sometimes photographed as with a stereoscopic camera, but not painted. Space, air and a diminishing force of sight towards the periphery of the field of vision are lacking. If there is a parallel in the art of painting for Joyce's swift, instantaneous shots of life it is in the art of Matisse, or, when Joyce's vision is graphic rather than pictorial, the art of the draughtsman, Rodin, watching, ready pencil in hand, the model doing whatever it pleased in his studio. For example:

> An elderly man shot up near the spur of rock a blowing red face. He scrambled up by the stones, water glistening on his pate and on its garland of grey hair, water rilling over his chest and paunch and spilling jets out of his black sagging loincloth.

> Broken hoops on the shore, at the land a maze of dark, cunning nets; farther away chalkscrawled back doors and on the higher beach a drying line with two crucified shirts.

> Kind air defined the coigns of houses in Kildare Street. No birds. Frail from the housetops two plumes of smoke ascended, pluming, and in a flaw of softness softly were blown.

> Do you see the tide flowing quickly in on all sides, sheeting the lows of sands quickly, shellcocoacoloured?

The same for the human mannerism, a gesture caught quickly with the model on the move:

> Haines detached from his underlip some fibres of tobacco before he spoke.

He took off his silk hat and, blowing out impatiently his bushy moustache, welshcombed his hair with raking fingers.

He removed his large Henry Clay decisively and his large fierce eyes scowled intelligently over all their faces.

His hands moulded ample curves of air. He shut his eyes tight in delight, his body shrinking, and blew a sweet chirp from his lips.

It may be because these things form part of the momentary life of the person or persons present that they seem to be instantaneously photographed or drawn with the object on the move. They are not presented as something outside, but as something inside, the acting personage. Some conversations ring so true that they might have been caught up from actual life by a sound-recording instrument. The mystery here is, how Joyce, through twenty years of exile, could preserve with such freshness the tones and mannerisms of his fellow citizens. Take, for example, the conversation — incredulous expostulation and confident affirmation — between Joe Hynes and Alf Bergan on the subject of Dignam appearing in the street with Willie Murray after his funeral. This is the same vividness and directness that drew upon Rodin the charge of lifting from nature by means of a plaster cast. And then there are Joyce's imitations with vowel and consonant of natural and mechanical sounds — those of the sea flowing over weed and rocks, those of the machines in the *Telegraph* office, those of the fireworks heard from Sandymount Beach.

Nausikaa is essentially pictorial, not because of any pictorial descriptions (there are very few), but because we are always made to feel conscious of the ambient of air around Bloom, Gerty and her friends. The surroundings of the persons, the beach, the town, the sky with clouds and fireworks, the sea and its crawling surf, Howth Head rising up out of the sea, everything, moving or stationary, affirms the idea of space. All the colour is enveloped in air. Here, too, is realised a landscape, foreshadowing, in conception though not in material, those mysterious dream glimpses of landscape in *Work in Progress*, where the earth comes to life and shares consciousness with its creatures. It occurs in a space of no thoughts while Bloom is still standing on the seashore.

A lost long candle wandered up the sky from Mirus bazaar in search of funds for Mercer's hospital and broke, drooping, and shed a cluster of violet but one white stars. They floated, fell: they faded. The shepherd's hour: the hour of holding: hour of tryst. From house to house, giving his ever-welcome double knock, went the nine o'clock postman, the glowworm's lamp at his belt gleaming here and there through the laurel hedges. And among the five young trees a hoisted lintstock lit the lamp at Leahy's terrace. . . . Twittering the bat flew here, flew there. Far out over the sands the coming surf crept, grey. Howth settled for slumber tired of long days, of yumyum rhododendrons (he was old) and felt gladly the night breeze lift, ruffle his fell of ferns. He lay but opened a red eye unsleeping, deep and slowly breathing, slumberous but awake. And far on Kish bank the anchored lightship twinkled, winked at Mr Bloom.

Sound aids the illusion of space, the hiss and splutter of fireworks, the voices of the girls and children and of the worshippers in the Star of the Sea Church. Smell, too: for Gerty MacDowell's farewell to Bloom is waved with scented wadding across the space that divides them. And movement, in the shape of the receding figures of Gerty, her friends, the twins and the bassinette, of the hither and thither fluttering bat, of the clouds and the on-creeping surf, intensifies the pictorial lyricism. It is a Whistler theme, painted with the greater elegance and liveliness of a Fragonard. It is a stern tale of Swift swiftly told by Sterne. Joyce always held that these two writers ought to change names.

Some of Bloom's thoughts may disconcert, but they will ring true enough for all who have not too well learned the art of forgetting. They are the thoughts of a man who chooses his deeds carefully from among them. Bloom's mood, when he is left alone, is one of attention, dispassionate observation, and finally, as he walks slowly citywards, of trance-like relaxation. Standing still for a moment he closes his eyes and his thought becomes a kaleidoscope of remembered sensations. Then he pulls himself together and goes on. It is too late to go to the performance of *Leah* as he had intended. He will call instead at the lying-in hospital for news of Mina Purefoy. The cuckoo clock in the study of Father Conroy and Canon O'Hanlon sings nine as he re-enters the streets of Dublin.

The Strand (Bloom)   Stanley Sultan*

It is during the half dozen pages at the precise center of this chapter that a girl about twenty years old (the granddaughter of the owner of Garryowen, and so, if she really existed, distantly related to Joyce) first swings one leg back and forth in time with the music emanating from a church service, then gradually reveals more and more of her thighs to a dark stranger, who she regards as romantic and suffering, and who responds to the stimulation by masturbating. The attitudes and conduct of Gerty MacDowell and Bloom at that point constitute the thematic center of the chapter as well as the middle of the action.

The significance of Bloom's act is clear in terms of what has been shown about him. The ultimate expression of his attempted "lotus-eating" in the fifth chapter was his plan to masturbate in his bath (83). The act he contemplated is, as mere passivity of the endeavor to ignore his situation

*From *The Argument of "Ulysses"* (Columbus: Ohio State University Press, 1964), 263–77. Reprinted by permission of the publisher. All rights reserved.

by skirt-chasing and letter-writing is not, a precise symbol of total betrayal of his aspirations as both husband and father. He did not fulfil that intention, however, as he reveals in the present chapter (362). And although the subject came up again at the Ormond Hotel, when Miss Douce caressed the beer-pull, Bloom's gratitude for what he regarded as a proffer to him did not prevent him from leaving the Ormond and thereby rejecting it along with the other "siren songs" in the chapter.

In the present chapter, despite his recent examples of resolution and "heroism," Bloom himself (although under provocation) commits the consummate act of negation. It has a moral as well as a symbolic significance. In a quasi-Biblical recapitulation of the day's experiences in the seventeenth chapter, the encounter with Gerty is referred to as "rite of Onan" (713):

> And Onan knew that the seed should not be his; and . . . he spilled it on the ground. . . .
> And the thing which he did displeased the Lord: wherefore he slew him also. (Genesis 38:9–10)

The Code of Jewish Law (*Shulḥan Aruch*) says: "It is forbidden to cause in vain the effusion of semen, and this crime is severer than any of the violations mentioned in the Torah."[1] And when the admonition of the Lord through the prophet Malachi is recalled, Bloom's "spilling" of his seed in the great sin of Onan is seen to be also that turning away from Molly and his unborn son which is the path to destruction.

The masturbation at the center of the chapter is not merely a pathetic and sordid act but a representation, on every level of meaning, of Bloom's self-defeat and self-destruction. Following it and Gerty's immediate departure, the author presents, in a union of Bloom's natural physio-psychological reaction to his act and the significance that act has for the novel, a long passage of inner monologue in which Bloom is far more pathetic than when he feels frustrated, ashamed, and helpless; for he is depressed, resigned, and spiritually broken.

His thoughts follow a now familiar pattern: they revert again and again from the immediate subject, in this case the girl whose name he never learns, to Molly and her affair with Boylan. At one point he decides that Boylan should give Molly money for her favors because she is "worth" it, and then has an even more masochistic train of thought:

> Funny my watch stopped at half past four. Dust. . . .
> Was that just when he, she?
> O, he did. Into her. She did. Done.
> Ah! (363)

Although sordid, the reversion to the incident with Gerty that directly follows these manifestations of pandering and masochism intensifies the pathos: "Mr Bloom with careful hand recomposed his wet shirt. O

Lord, that little limping devil. Begins to feel cold and clammy. After effect not pleasant. Still you have to get rid of it someway."

Again and again the pattern is repeated. Bloom thinks of Gerty, her two companions, Martha Clifford, the neighbor's maid, the woman he saw accompanying A. E., Nurse Callan, the novice in the Tranquilla convent, the "girl in Meath street," the "high class whore in Jammets," Mrs. Breen, Mrs. Duggan, the aristocratic woman he'd seen in the fifth chapter, and Mrs. Dignam, from whose house he has just come. The catalogue is long, but Molly eclipses the other women right up to his somnolent last thoughts in the chapter, which begin as a tribute to Gerty: "O sweety all your little girlwhite up I saw dirty bracegirdle made me do love sticky we two naughty Grace darling she him half past the bed met him pike hoses frillies for Raoul to perfume your wife black hair heave under embon *senorita* young eyes Mulvey plump years dreams return tail end Agendath swoony lovey showed me her next year in drawers return next in her next her next" (375). Combined with thoughts of Molly's tryst with Boylan is another version of Bloom's revery of her return to him: "years dreams return" and the Zionist (return) motif, "Agendath," are augmented by "next year," a fragment of a Passover Seder catechism expressing the exile's hope of return. Thus the pronoun in "next in her next her next" with which Bloom's long inner monologue ends refers not to Gerty but to Molly.

The irony of Bloom's undiminished ardor for Molly lies in the conclusions at which he arrives before this final paragraph. In the paragraph just preceding, in fact, he decides that he will not accompany Boylan and Molly to her concert at Belfast and categorically assents to being supplanted. Prior to this, he thinks of the hill of Howth and the consummation of their love there, on which he dwelt so fully in the eighth chapter. Only now he concludes, not with a reflection on how far he has fallen ("Me. And me now"), but with the thought that he is foolish to persist in his unrequited love for Molly, that Boylan "gets the plums and I the plumstones" (370). Yet, persist he does. And he does not hesitate to blame himself for having recourse to masturbation because he lacks the simple courage to make love to his wife (367).

The author shows Bloom's love for Molly to be a fundamental theme of the chapter with the help of "Love's Old Sweet Song." By this point in the novel, the association between the song and the tryst of Molly and Boylan has been exploited twice (in the fifth chapter and the eleventh). Now the song is no longer simply alluded to by its title; phrases from it are woven into the narrative. The time of the action is "twilight," and at four separate points that term is used to indicate the time. There is repeated mention of the bats, "flickering shadows," and their coming and going occupies Bloom's thoughts at two points. Finally, Gerty makes the association almost explicit by observing of Bloom: "Perhaps it was an old flame he was in mourning for from the days beyond recall" (358). Although in the most immediate sense Bloom is paralleling the "rehearsal" of it by Molly and Boylan in his own ignominious way ("Still to us at twilight comes Love's old song"), the song is even more significant of his awareness that they have passed the vital point of their "rehearsal" and, as the end of the chapter so sardonically and insistently states, made him "*Cuckoo. Cuckoo. Cuckoo.*" This awareness combines with the depression that follows his masturbation to bring him to his despondency of spirit.

The song is most significant, however, of his persisting love for Molly. Gerty points out that he is mourning for "an old flame," a "flame" of days that he now feels are definitely dead and beyond recall. As the song itself states, Love's "old sweet song" is the song Love sang to the lovers' hearts. Now one of those lovers is deaf to it and to the other lover: "Tho' the heart be weary, sad the day and long,/Still . . . at twilight . . . comes Love's old sweet song." The second of the song's two "verses" describes Bloom's devotion:

> Even today we hear Love's song of yore,
> Deep in our hearts it dwells for ever-more.
> Footsteps may falter, weary grow the way,
> Still we can hear it at the close of day.
> So till the end, when life's dim shadows fall,
> Love will be found the sweetest song of all.

The impressive fact about Joyce's use of the song in the present chapter is that at the same time that its lines and his treatment of it represent Bloom's love for Molly and consequent suffering, the associations it brings to the chapter invoke the two specific causes of Bloom's extreme despondency — the lovemaking of Molly and Boylan and his own pseudo-lovemaking.

The first part of the chapter, from its beginning to the point where Gerty leaves the scene and the novel, is very different in both style and subject from Bloom's inner monologue. Characterized by critics as "dime-novel" or "penny novelette," and plainly a parody of pretentious sentimental fiction, its style suits a point of view very close to and sympathetic with Gerty.

The style is not merely suitable however; it is the author's vehicle for delineating Gerty's character and the significance of her principal action. In the first place, she is a pathetically obnoxious girl. The technique employed to show this is precisely that employed in portraying Father Conmee and the anonymous narrator of Barney Kiernan's: ironic touches in her speech or thoughts and in the language of the sympathetic narrator. Thus, her artificial coyness is revealed simply in the way she is introduced; she is mentioned by one of her companions and the narrator asks, "But who was Gerty?" The narrator then speaks of her "winsomeness," but the specific description contains details like: "Her figure was slight and graceful, inclining even to fragility but those iron jelloids she had been taking of late had done her a world of good much better than the Widow Welch's female pills and she was much better of those discharges she used to get and that tired feeling" (342). And criticism can be little more overt than that contained in the description of Gerty's eyes: "Why have women such eyes of witchery? . . . It was Madame Vera Verity, directress of the Woman Beautiful page of the Princess novelette, who had first advised her to try eyebrowleine which gave that haunting expression to the eyes . . . and she had never regretted it" (342–43). Her vanity, hinted at here, is revealed again and again. She cried before a mirror "nicely," in moderation; and "You are lovely, Gerty, it said." She has "a languid queenly *hauteur*," and feels that one of her "innate refinement" was wronged for not being born a noblewoman. She uses ointments, cosmetic preparations, and treatments of every kind for every part of her body.

More objectionable than her vanity are Gerty's spitefulness and jealousy. Her companions twit her about having lost the interest of a neighborhood boy, and her thoughts about them are painstakingly vindictive (343, 344). She accuses Cissy Caffrey of vying with her for Bloom's attention, although Cissy's attitude toward Bloom is clear: "— Wait, said Cissy. I'll ask my uncle Peter over there, what's the time by his conundrum."

In contrast to Cissy during that incident, Gerty "could see him take his hand out of his pocket" as the other girl approaches, and observes that he changes from a "passionate nature," "fascinated by a loveliness that made him gaze," to a "distinguishedlooking," grave gentleman, and that his voice has "a cultured ring."

Not only interested in Bloom, Gerty is clearly fully aware of what she is about with him from the moment she lifts her skirt in order to kick the ball to the twins (350). She is a mildly libidinous girl, as Joyce suggests early in the chapter with smiling irony: "As for the undies they were Gerty's chief care and who that knows *the fluttering hopes and fears* [italics mine] of sweet seventeen (though Gerty would never see seventeen again) can find it in his heart to blame her?" (344). And as Bloom correctly infers, she is approaching her menstrual period. Because of a combination of nature and circumstances, she undertakes her inversion of Nausicaa's modest confrontation of Odysseus' nakedness. She finds satisfaction in the fact that he is looking at her legs and not those of her companions. She puts on her hat in order to be able to observe him from beneath the brim: "And swung her buckled shoe faster for her breath caught as she caught the expression in his eyes. . . . Her woman's instinct told her that she had raised the devil in him . . ." (354). She sees him remove his hand from his pocket when Cissy Caffrey approaches and return his hand to his pocket. And, as soon as the others leave, she accelerates her performance:

She looked at him a moment, meeting his glance, and a light broke in upon her. Whitehot passion was in that face. . . . At last they were left alone . . . and she knew he could be trusted to the death, steadfast, a sterling man, a man of inflexible honour to his fingertips [!]. His hands and face were working and a tremor went over her. She leaned back far to look up where the fireworks were . . . and there was no-one to see only him and her when, she revealed all her graceful beautifully shaped legs like that . . . and she seemed to hear . . . his hoarse breathing . . . because Bertha Supple told her once in dead secret and made her swear she'd never about the gentleman lodger . . . that had pictures cut out of papers of those skirtdancers and highkickers and she said he used to do something not very nice that you could imagine sometimes in the bed. (359)

Finally she limps off to join the others, and Bloom recomposes his wet shirt. She is exactly like "those skirtdancers and highkickers" for whom she has contempt, and her hero, her ideal lover, is exactly like the lodger.

Gerty is fully aware of what she is doing and what Bloom is doing, yet her awareness is of a strange order. She succeeds in filtering from it every element of reality she finds unpalatable, in deluding herself about herself and the world about her. Thus, when she mentions the "highkickers" and the man masturbating in the bed, she also says: "But this was altogether different from a thing like that because there was all the difference because she could almost feel him draw her face to his and the first quick hot touch of his handsome lips. Besides there was absolution so long as you didn't do the other thing before being married . . ." (359). There is no difference, and Bloom has done nothing to cause her to think he would so much as speak to her. She is able to make such assertions to herself because she is a sentimentalist, because as the very style of the narrative, which does not paraphrase Gerty's thought but renders its essential characteristic, indicates, she sentimentalizes reality, distorts it into a form she prefers. After kicking the ball, and before deciding to swing her legs for Bloom, that is, begin her exhibition, she observes: "Yes, it was her he was looking at and there was meaning in his look. His eyes burned into her as though they would search her through and through, read her very soul. Wonderful eyes they were, superbly expressive, but could you trust them?" (351). Following this transparent combination of romanticizing about Bloom and worrying about her reputation, she begins to swing her legs (to show him "the bright steel buckles of her shoes") and decides: "Here was that of which she had so often dreamed. It was he who mattered. . . . The very heart of the girl-woman went out to him, her dreamhusband. . . . If he had suffered, more sinned against than sinning, or even, even, if he had been himself a sinner, a wicked man, she cared not" (351–2). Having identified her ideal lover, betrothed herself to him, and even decided to accept his wickedness, she needs to take only one more step, in time with the development of her exhibition, to the conclusion:

> If she saw that magic lure in his eyes there would be no holding
> back for her. . . . She would make the great sacrifice. . . . There was the
> allimportant question and she was dying to know was he a married man
> or a widower who had lost his wife. . . . But even if — what then? Would
> it make a very great difference? From everything in the least indelicate
> her finebred nature instinctively recoiled. They would be just good
> friends like a big brother and sister without all that other. . . . (358)

The ridiculousness of Gerty's solution to the problem of an adulterous
triangle (which would be so much less "indelicate" than what she is doing)
is dwarfed by the ridiculousness of her fabricating a problem in the first
place.

The whole combination of Gerty's actions, her misrepresentation of
them, and Bloom's simple relationship to Gerty is manifested in the climax
of the scene:

> She was trembling in every limb from being bent so far back he
> had a full view high up above her knee where no-one ever . . . and she
> wasn't ashamed and he wasn't either . . . and he kept on looking,
> looking. She would fain have come to him chokingly, held out her snowy
> slender arms to him to come, to feel his lips laid on her white brow. . . .
> And then a rocket sprang and bang shot blind and O! then the Roman
> candle burst and it was like a sigh of O! . . . (360)

Gerty has succeeded, by a continual process of sentimentalizing, in
turning black into white. Almost nothing she believes is true. She is not
beautiful, she is not refined, her companions are not jealous of her, the
neighborhood boy does not love her, Bloom does not love her, she is not
experiencing a romantic courtship, and she is not pure and virtuous
(although she probably is physically a virgin); she is a libidinous girl whose
persistent sentimentalizing keeps her from the proscribed normal sexual
activity and yet causes her to act scarcely less immorally. Growing older,
deluding herself about her own charms, the attitude men have toward her,
and the things she does, Gerty seems to have in store for her the emptiness
and sterility indicated for Bloom by his masturbation.

The attention given to a vain, petty, and self-deluding girl would
hardly be justified were Gerty herself the sole subject of Joyce's parody. He
is not breaking a crippled insect on a wheel, however. "Love's Old Sweet
Song" is one of the two principal allusive elements in the chapter; the
other is the style of Gerty's section. In that style Joyce is parodying not just
a general kind of writing but a specific model; and he did his best to
identify it when he had Gerty think that "soon the lamplighter would be
going his rounds . . . like she read in that book *The Lamplighter* by Miss
Cummins, author of *Mabel Vaughan* and other tales" (357). Turning to
The Lamplighter of Maria S. Cummins, first published in 1854, one finds
the exact prototype of the style and the charming little character it
represents:

It was a stormy evening. Gerty was standing at the window, watching for True's return from his lamplighting. She was neatly and comfortably dressed, her hair smooth, her face and hands clean. She was now quite well, — better than for years before her sickness. Care and kindness had done wonders for her, and though still a pale and rather slender-looking child, with eyes and mouth disproportionately large to her other features, the painful look of suffering she had been wont to wear had given place to a happy though rather grave expression.

Miss Cummins' verbal gifts are suited to her subject and the view of life manifested in the novel. Her style is turgid, coy, pretentious, with at times an almost obscene lack of taste. Joyce's parody is satiric, of course, but it is more a crystallization of the faults of the original than an exaggeration of them.

The faithfulness of Joyce's parody of *The Lamplighter* is important because of the importance of that novel, the first work of a highly successful American writer. A reprint published forty-eight years after the original publication is prefaced by the following information:

Here is an American story for young people which has been in constant demand for almost half a century. At the time of its publication, in 1854, it enjoyed an immediate popularity second only to *Uncle Tom's Cabin* and *The Scarlet Letter*. . . . Edition followed edition, in this country and in England . . . and how many "Lamplighters" have been issued in the unauthorized and mutilated forms in which the book has too often appeared can be only a matter of conjecture.[2]

The extreme popularity of *The Lamplighter* is a fact of social history. A very large number of people had sufficiently poor taste and poor judgment to embrace both its prose and its treatment of reality. By showing the insidious quality of sentimentalism in a parody of that book rather than in a general parody of the style of its genre, Joyce has made more pointed his statement about those people. Gerty MacDowell is the ultimate popular development of Flaubert's Emma Bovary, the product of the degeneration of romantic idealism into sentimental wish-fulfilment and self-delusion. She is the representative of all those who, like her, read and enjoyed *The Lamplighter*. And this audience, large enough in itself, is representative of the mass of people blighted by self-deluding sentimentality. It is to make this criticism, familiar in his work, that Joyce parodies *The Lamplighter* and concerns himself with Gerty.

The criticism is levelled not only at individuals, but at their principal institution as well. The chapter has three subjects, not two, which are recapitulated at the end to stress that fact. In the order presented there they are Bloom, Gerty, and, between them, the Star of the Sea Church.

Simultaneously with Gerty's exhibition, the "Lamplighter" narrative presents phases in an evening service at the church. The service is the conclusion of a day-long "men's temperance retreat." At the point in the chapter where the parody ends, all mention of the church service ends.

This is a significant association of the two, but there are more significant ones.

The patron saint of the church is the Virgin Mary, and most of the service appears to consist of prayers to the Virgin for deliverance from bibulousness: "They were there gathered together without distinction of social class (and a most edifying spectacle it was to see) in that simple fane beside the waves, after the storms of this weary world . . . beseeching her to intercede for them, the old familiar words, holy Mary holy virgin of virgins" (347–48). The satiric tone of this first description indicates the subject of Joyce's indictment. Most of the other passages about the church service reiterate the theme of supplication of the Virgin:

> And still, the voices sang in supplication to the Virgin most powerful, Virgin most merciful. (348)

> And care-worn hearts were there and toilers for their daily bread and many who had erred and wandered, their eyes wet with contrition but for all that bright with hope for the reverend father Hughes had told them . . . the most pious Virgin's intercessory power. . . . (350)

> Refuge of sinners. Comfortress of the afflicted. *Ora pro nobis.* Well has it been said that whosoever prays to her with faith and constancy can never be lost or cast away. . . . (352)

> Queen of angels, queen of patriarchs, queen of prophets, of all saints, they prayed, queen of the most holy rosary. . . . (353)

Joyce is attacking the popular cult of the Virgin. He sees it as that seeking after indulgence of weakness, after feminine, which is to say amoral, intercession with the masculine Godhead, which most of its critics say is behind the development into the second object of worship in the Roman Catholic faith of a figure mentioned three times in the Gospels. The charge levelled is sentimentalism. The supplication of the Virgin is most insistently associated with Gerty by the repeated blending in one passage, in the same cloying narrative, of the church service and the action involving Gerty (who is a "daughter of Mary"). And Joyce's indictment points not only at the Church but also at the people, who required the cult and nurtured it, and who, as the passages suggest, delude themselves just as Gerty does about the significance of their actions. They have been willing to believe that however they sin, they "can never be lost"; thus, Gerty is certain that "there was absolution so long as you didn't do the other." Stephen speaks in the librarian's office of "the madonna which the cunning Italian intellect flung to the mob of Europe" (205).

During the morning, Stephen paraphrases an epigram from Chapter XXIV of Meredith's *The Ordeal of Richard Feverel* for the message of his telegram to Mulligan and Haines. Mulligan reads the telegram in the librarian's office "joyfully" (197), although he is really annoyed (418): " —

The sentimentalist is he who would enjoy without incurring the immense debtorship for a thing done. Signed: Dedalus." Stephen's use of the moral apothegm is, like Meredith's, witty, for he is expressing his refusal to meet Mulligan and Haines and pay for their drinking. The serious application of it is made by Joyce in the present chapter. Those who pray to the Virgin for indulgence for petty weakness, like Gerty who romanticizes herself, her actions, and their objects, seek to enjoy the fruits of their frailty without incurring the immense debtorship of moral responsibility for their every act. Joyce has, in the "Lamplighter" part of the present chapter, castigated a fundamental fault of his fellow men.

What the sentimentalism Joyce sees as so pervasive in society has to do with Bloom is not difficult to determine. The first clue is that Bloom's part of the narrative is in his characteristic idiom, not in the sentimental style. The distinction is stressed at the point of transition:

> She walked with a certain quiet dignity characteristic of her but with care and very slowly because, because Gerty MacDowell was . . . Tight boots? No. She's lame. O! (361)

In contrast to the periphrasis, the attempted avoidance of the unpleasant fact, is Bloom's direct statement. It is followed by a frank analysis of what has transpired, one that sees clearly Gerty's motivations ("Thought something was wrong by the cut of her jib. Jilted beauty," "Near her monthlies I expect, makes them feel ticklish"), her ruses ("Will she? Watch! Watch! See! Looked around," "Wait. Hm. Hm. Yes. That's her perfume. Why she waved her hands"), and her character ("Hot little devil," "Go home to nicey bread and milky and say night prayers with the kiddies"). Far more important, Bloom correctly judges the situation and his role in it ("Anyhow I got the best of that," "Suppose I spoke to her. What about?," "you have to get rid of it someway," "Did me good all the same"); it is principally in this respect that he is contrasted with the sentimentalists. He knows that he has failed Molly in "getting rid of it" in meaningless eroticism. He decides that Molly is lost to him, and correctly blames himself for lacking the courage to attempt to win her back by making love to her. He acknowledges that he has incurred the immense debtorship for the thing done. In eschewing sentimentalism, Bloom is in direct contrast to the two other principal elements in the chapter and is superior to them.

It is to Bloom's credit that he is ashamed to return home (373); but his surrender in thought and act to his predicament affirms that despite his apotheosis he is no less the old Bloom, that the revelation at Barney Kiernan's was an elaboration of his character and not the uncovering of a disguise.

His surrender is accompanied by undiminished devotion to Molly and suffering over the loss of her, and by a clear sense of his culpableness in having lost her. For these reasons, it may be premature. He remembers, for the first time in the novel, a dream of the night before which corresponds closely to one twice recalled by Stephen — first in the morning at the very same place, on the beach, and then, in a context suggesting that Bloom would rescue him from his plight, at the end of the ninth chapter.

In an almost exact duplication of phrases in Stephen's first remembrance of his dream ("In. Come. Red carpet spread"), Bloom articulates the memory of his own: "Come in. All is prepared. I dreamt. What?" (364). He remembers it again just before the end of the chapter, this time recalling Molly's appearance in it: "Dreamt last night? Wait. Something confused. She had red slippers on. Turkish. Wore the breeches. Suppose she does. Would I like her in pyjamas?" (374). The fact that Bloom remembers a dream involving himself and Molly which is plainly analogous to Stephen's dream predicting deliverance suggests, at any rate, that Bloom's love for Molly and his willingness to face reality may enable him to escape the fate to which he sees himself condemned, that his potential power of deliverance of himself and the young gentile has not been dissipated by the behavior of his lower self.

Notes

1. *Shulhan Aruch*, chap. cli. Quoted from the Goldin translation (New York, 1929), IV, 17.

2. Maria S. Cummins, *The Lamplighter* (Boston, 1902), p. iii. The passage from the novel is on p. 26 in this edition.

"Nausicaa"   Harry Blamires*

In the *Odyssey* Nausicaa, daughter of Alcinous, king of Phaeacia, comes to the beach, accompanied by her maids, to wash her linen. The girls play ball, laughing and shrieking, and wake up Ulysses who is lying there, worn-out, storm-tossed, naked, cast up by the waves. The girls are frightened and embarrassed, but Nausicaa takes charge, cleans Ulysses and clothes him, then leads him home.

This episode offers respite to the "storm-tossed heart of man"; respite to Bloom after his violent departure from Barney Kiernan's; respite to the reader from the inflated and disorderly stylistic excesses of that interlude. Here Joyce adopts a sentimental, woman's magazinish style which, viewed as literary burlesque, is devastating. Yet the farcical, satirical strain does

*From *The Bloomsday Book* (London: Methuen, 1966), 139–51. Reprinted by permission of Methuen & Co.

not wholly determine the temper of the passage; for the vulgar idiom of the novelette, when exploited to articulate a young, uneducated girl's thoughts and dreams, becomes peculiarly touching by virtue of its sheer aptness to her adolescent self-dramatization. Joyce's linguistic virtuosity and psychological sensitivity together present the two-eyed reader with a feast of blended satire and pathos.

Gerty MacDowell (Nausicaa), Cissy Caffrey, and Edy Boardman are sitting on the rocks on Sandymount shore, where Stephen Dedalus walked and mused this morning. They are looking after Cissy's two brothers, Tommy and Jacky, twins of four years old, and little Baby Boardman. In the background is Howth Hill (for Leopold and Molly Bloom the place of youthful love realized) and the parish church appropriately dedicated to Our Lady as Star of the Sea. Gradually, in this episode, an important parallel is unmistakably established between Gerty MacDowell and the Virgin Mary. Each of them is "in her pure radiance a beacon ever to the storm-tossed heart of man."

Tommy and Jacky dabble in the sand: Cissy plays with baby, eleven months old, trying to get him to talk. Tommy and Jacky begin to quarrel over their sand-castle: Cissy has to reprove Jacky and to comfort Tommy.

Gerty MacDowell, meanwhile, sits lost in thought. She is beautiful, slight in build, graceful, pale in complexion. The description of her, voiced in the sentimental idiom of her own thinking and dreaming, is as much a piece of self-revelation as of objective picturing. (The use of words and phrases like "graceful," "almost spiritual in its ivory-like purity," "veined alabaster," "queenly," and "glory" reinforces the implicit correspondence with the Virgin Mary.) The reader moves in Gerty's mind, richly aware of its absurdities, its naïvetés, and its pathos, piquantly stirred simultaneously to laughter at her and sympathy for her. Her eyes, beautiful and yearning, have a seductive power that owes something to the advice on make-up given in the Woman Beautiful page of the Princess novelette. Her dark-brown hair waves naturally. Her ready blush adds to her loveliness. It is due to Edy Boardman's playful remark to little Tommy. "I know who is Tommy's sweetheart, Gerty is Tommy's sweetheart."

Or *is* it wholly playful? Gerty sees more to it. We hear of Reggy Wylie, whose father is now keeping him in of the evenings to study. (We heard of his brother in the bicycle race on p. 304, 237.) Reggy, it seems, has ridden his bicycle much past Gerty's window, but now has ceased. To Edy this marks the end of Gerty's romance. To Gerty it is a mere phase, a "lovers' quarrel." Tenuous as the foundations seem, the relationship with Reg has been built up in Gerty's mind to the stature of a romantic attachment.

Gerty's dress is described as seen by Gerty herself, in all its neatness, grace, and good taste, with some emphasis on the points where she has the edge on Edy Boardman. Her greatest pride is her "four dinky sets" of undies; and today she is wearing the blue set "for luck." Blue, "her own colour," is of course the Virgin Mary's colour. There are many, many "blues" in this episode.

A romantically dramatized vein of doubting sorrow runs through Gerty's rich dreams of a fashionable marriage to Mr. Reggy Wylie. Doubt and dream alike take their origin from a hurried peck on the end of her nose which Reggy (still at the short-trousered stage) snatched at a party long ago. A new dream of an older, more commanding suitor, more worthy of her girlish self-giving, supersedes.

Then Gerty pictures herself as wife, drenching her husband's days in the hominess of good cooking, warm fire, well-furnished drawing-room, and (less obviously attractive to the reader) "photograph of grandpapa Giltrap's lovely dog Garryowen" on the wall. Against this background moves the tall, broad-shouldered, home-loving husband, complete with sweeping moustache and glistening teeth.

Edy completes the supervision of Tommy's evacuation. Cissy retrieves the boys' ball from baby, whom she jigs and cuddles, laughing and chattering; for Cissy is the gay extrovert, frank and unself-conscious, who shames Gerty's sensitivities by speaking of baby's "beetoteetom" loudly enough for "the gentleman opposite" to hear. This is only the second mention of Bloom, the Ulysses cast up on the shore.

In the background we hear the singing and the organ from the church, where the Reverend John Hughes, S.J., is conducting a men's temperance retreat. (The symbolical significance of this will emerge later.) The sounds touch Gerty sadly, for her father's addiction to the bottle has cast a shadow over her home. As the retreatants have a sentimentalized simplicity of heart and equality before Our Lady; so the MacDowell home sounds for a moment like the stock drunkard's household of the Victorian temperance novel. It has seen violence and a man's hand lifted shamefully against a woman.

But that is not all. The paragraph which begins with a liturgical echo about the "Virgin most merciful" tells us that, in spite of his faults, Gerty loves her father still — for his songs (N.B. "Tell me, *Mary*, how to woo thee") and for the happy family parties together. (Thus the correspondence between Gerty and Our Lady is gradually pressed home.) And Mrs. MacDowell has lately been able to impress on Father the dangers of drink by reference to the sudden demise of Mr. Dignam.

Gerty is the home's "ministering angel," looking tenderly after her mother when ill, turning the gas off at the main every night, tacking up a sentimental picture in the lavatory, "Halcyon Days."

The two boys still play with the ball. Jacky kicks it hard toward the rocks. Bloom intercepts it, then throws it back to them, and it comes to rest at Gerty's feet. She kicks it, misses, blushes, then catches sight of Bloom's face, "the saddest she had ever seen."

The sugary, mellifluous prose flows on; and it catches the verbal echoes of Benediction ("spiritual vessel . . . honourable vessel . . . vessel of singular devotion") through the open window of the church. The twins play merrily. Cissy has lots of laughs and hugs and baby-talk for Baby, and capably attends to his needs at both ends.

Gerty, tired of the squalling baby, indulges an emotional surrender to the influence of sea and sunset, distant music and the perfume of incense, and above all to the searching eyes of Bloom fixed upon her. The dark eyes, the pale intellectual face, the hint of foreign-ness, and the mourning clothes, convey the appeal of mystery and sorrow. She is aware of her own transparent stockings and kicking legs. He becomes the focus of pent-up longings and unrealized girlhood dreams; the suffering dream-husband in need of a woman's comfort; the powerful male seeking a womanly woman to crush to himself in his arms.

The phrases of Benediction flow on, pressing the correspondence between Gerty and the Virgin Mary, for Gerty has just now, in her own words, imagined herself as a "refuge of sinners" and "comfortress of the afflicted." Gerty's mood of emotional self-indulgence carries her mind smoothly from the dark-eyed dream-husband to the saintly figure of Fr. Conroy at the altar, to his white hands in the confessional, and his kind, quiet words after hearing her over-scrupulous confession. (Fr. Conroy's comforting words explicitly draw a parallel between Gerty and Our Lady.) Here, as throughout, Gerty holds off at a distance references to her own sexuality, self-consciously taking refuge in euphemism and evasion. All this indicates her alert sexual sensitivity.

The twins quarrel again and go rushing down to the sea. Cissy pursues them; and it is through Gerty's mind that we see Cissy's tomboy-ish, headlong chase that rashly risks so much in the way of exposure before Bloom. Catching the twins, Cissy is ladylike enough not to clip them with Bloom watching. But Gerty well knows that Bloom is *not* watching Cissy; he is watching her own shapely legs. (At this point the meaning of the correspondence between Gerty and Our Lady becomes clearer. The priests in the church are "looking up at the Blessed Sacrament." Bloom on the shore is looking up at Gerty's legs. We are involved in a double act of adoration.) Cissy, unkempt, drags the children back. Gerty takes off her hat and settles her nut-brown hair, rejoicingly conscious of Bloom's admiration. She puts her hat back so that she can watch him from under the brim, then swings her legs enticingly, blushingly aware of the appetite she has roused.

Edy becomes aware of the silent duologue between Bloom and Gerty. Cissy goes over to ask him the time and Bloom's look of longing is transformed into one of grave self-control. But his watch has stopped, significantly at the hour of Boylan's encounter with Molly (see p. 482, 370).

The *Tantum ergo* and the censing of the Blessed Sacrament proceed in the church behind them, and one of the candles threatens to set fire to the flowers. Gerty swings her leg more, as the censer swings in the church.

Bloom's hands go back into his pockets, and the flow of instinctive understanding between the two of them rises farther. Gerty is conscious of an approaching period and of dark eyes fixed in her worship. It would seem plain that just as the temperance men in the church are given up to adoration of Our Lady and the Blessed Sacrament, so Bloom (an abstainer from actual marital coition as the temperance retreatants are abstainers from actual wine) is given up to adoration of a virgin's womb, a "vessel" now holding the blood soon to be spilt. Benediction is a service which stops short of real "communion." The Virgin is hymned; the sacrament is exposed; but no one partakes. Even so adoring Bloom's only fulfilment is to be a fruitless emission, and Gerty's mounting excitement and increasing exposure are to culminate in the frustration of menstruation.

Edy and Cissy prepare to go. Edy teases Gerty about her lost sweetheart, and the mood of tormented abandonment returns, bringing the sting of tears to her eyes. But she covers her pain in banter and straightway a new mood is upon her, that of the proud, injured woman shrivelling a male trifler with her scorn. Drama upon drama. Gerty reads defeat and rage and jealousy of superiority in the fallen face of Edy. Cissy and Edy, busy with the youngsters, complete the preparations to go.

Hackneyed images of gathering twilight, evening bells, ivied belfry, and the like introduce another surge of emotionalism in Gerty. Her mood is stimulated by all that is most cheaply sentimental in memories of books, souvenirs, personal treasures, journalistic poetry, and the like. (Note the "child of Mary badge.") The passion rises, touched pathetically by a veiled first reference to her one shortcoming — the lameness due to an accident on Dalkey Hill; it rises in a cliché-drenched rapture of girlish devotion that idealizes Bloom into the tragic male in need of woman's aid, and herself into the pure woman who gives all but that which honour forbids her to give.

In the church the Blessed Sacrament is restored to the tabernacle. Over the trees beside the church coloured fireworks from the Mirus bazaar shoot into the sky. Cissy and Edy and their charges run off to watch them. Gerty stays, held by a sense of Bloom's stirred passion, glad to be left alone to answer it. And answer it she does, leaning so far backward, in order to watch the fireworks, that her legs and thighs and knickers are on display. In a few moments of imaginary consummation she is glad and fulfilled in giving herself visually, feeling no shame; for she draws a clear line between the pure fervour of this heartfelt encounter and the exhibitionism of the stage. At the crisis she yearns to have a "little strangled cry" wrung from her in his arms, and a Roman candle (like the candle on the altar in the church) bursts in gushes of green and gold.

She bends forward quickly, a mood of pathetic shy reproach seizing her in her post-crisis moments. From reproach the mood changes to forgiveness, and then to the knowledge of a secret shared between herself and the stranger. Cissy calls her. Gerty takes the perfume-soaked wadding from her handbag and waves in reply, thus sending an olfactory greeting on the wind to Bloom (as the smell of incense was wafted from the altar to the worshippers). She sends a half smile too; then stands and moves away, walking slowly, for the first time revealing her lameness. (The exact nature of the lameness is not explained. Must we assume that Gerty's heel was bruised that day on Dalkey Hill? p. 474, *364*.)

The lameness shocks Bloom: he is glad Gerty didn't spoil his experience of her by revealing it earlier. He rightly guesses that pale Gerty is "near her monthlies" and muses on women's oddities and moodinesses at such times. We gather that Bloom's self-indulgence as a voyeur has given him a crisis and an emission which compensates for what he missed when the tram blocked his view of the lady mounting her cab this morning (p. 90, *74*), a frustration already recalled once (p. 203, *160*), and to be magnified later in the *Circe* episode (p. 567, *435*). He muses on the readiness of women to give these pleasures so freely, on their excitement in dressing themselves up for the purpose of being undressed, on the charm of changing fashions, then on the changeless dress of the east—Mary and Martha (Marion and Martha?), unchanged and unchangeable.

Bloom has summed up the relationship between Gerty and her companions, and dwells upon women's superficial friendliness with one another that covers bitter envies and jealousies.

His mind runs over aspects of the encounter, touching on the oddities of women when approaching their monthlies, wondering what Gerty thought of him, appreciating how she took off her hat to show him her hair, then remembering how he once sold some of Molly's combings for ten shillings when they were "on the rocks in Holles Street." Which leads to the veiled question—does Boylan pay Molly? "Why not? . . . She's worth ten, fifteen, more a pound," says Bloom the businessman. Mentally he sees Boylan's letter to "Mrs Marion" again and then is soon diverted to the question whether he correctly addressed his own love-letter to Martha. He thinks it "funny" that his watch stopped at half past four and feels that it must have been the very moment when Boylan and Molly committed adultery. "O he did. Into her. She did. Done."

He adjusts his shirt, wet from his emission. He thinks how, after this singular achievement, Gerty goes home to the evening activities of innocent girlhood; dwells on men's need of women idealized by dress, lights, music, and assumed purity; wonders whether he might have started a conversation when Cissy came to ask the time; then recalls an occasion when he nearly put his foot in it by mistaking Mrs. Clinch at night for a prostitute. So to memories of the girl he took in Meath Street, making her say dirty words; and of how a single girl will pretend to be shocked when taken by a married man, though "that's what they enjoy. Taking a man from another woman." As for Leopold, he is "glad to get away from other chap's wife." Nevertheless, he pictures himself embarking on an affair and surveys the seductive techniques of women and of men.

Meanwhile he sees Gerty in the distance with the others, watching the fireworks; dwells on Cissy's whistle, her mouth, her over-affectionate attention to the little boy. Gerty didn't look back at him when she was going; but Bloom knows that she knows what has happened. Women have a sharp instinctive awareness and self-awareness. Unlike men, you "never see them sit on a bench marked *Wet Paint*." They notice people; they know when they are themselves noticed. So to further reflections on the minor instinctive seductive devices of the female. At the end of it Gerty, with her shapely limbs, comes out of it better than the frump with the rumpled stockings he saw earlier with A. E. (p. 210, *165*).

A rocket bursts. The children and the girls reappear in the distance and there is a moment of telepathic acknowledgement between Gerty and Bloom. Bloom is grateful for what she has given him. Boylan's song about the seaside girls is indeed right; they make your head "swirl." There has been an unspoken dialogue between them, and at least he has heard her name, "Gerty."

Now he muses on the brevity of a young girl's flowering and on how quickly women must settle down to the female rôle of washing children, potting babies, laying out corpses, giving birth. He remembers that he must call at the hospital and inquire after Mrs. Purefoy (link with the next episode); wonders if Nurse Callan is still there, recalls that the marriage-able girls like her turn into the Mrs. Breens and the Mrs. Dignams, coping with drunkenness and the like. Perhaps the women are in part to blame. But not Molly. Bloom compares her Moorish beauty and her "opulent curves" with the fading wives of other Dubliners. So to the incongruities that the destiny of marriage produces.

Bloom's thoughts return to his stopped watch. He wonders whether some kind of magnetism caused it to stop at the moment of Molly's encounter with Boylan. So to the magnetism "back of everything" and especially that which draws the sexes together, as he and Gerty were drawn, as Molly and Boylan have been drawn.

He smells the perfume wafted his way from Gerty's cotton-wool. Thoughts move to Molly's scent, to the night she first danced with Boylan, her black dance dress, the mysterious nature of perfume, especially the odour given off by women and clinging to their clothes. From the sniffs with which dogs recognize each other thought moves back again to the ubiquitous subject (in this episode) of women's menstruation; then to the question whether men themselves give off comparably meaningful odours for women. He experiments, inserting his nose into his own waistcoat, and is rewarded by the scent of the soap in his pocket. And so back to the forgotten lotion, Hynes's unpaid three-shillings debt, and the fate of debtors.

A "nobleman" passes by for a second time. Bloom thinks he is enjoying an after-dinner constitutional. (By the way, we learn now that Bloom was aware this morning how the newsboys mockingly aped his walk behind him, p. 165, *129*.) The man is a "mystery man," like "that fellow today at the graveside in the brown macintosh" (p. 138, *109*).

On Howth promontory the bailey lights go on. The lights and the fading day turn Bloom's mind to fear of the dark, night travel, stars, clouds, and Ireland, the land of the setting sun. The dew is falling. Bloom remembers the unwisdom of sitting on damp stone; then begins to envy the rock Gerty sat on; notes his growing fondness for young girls; how they open like flowers in romantic situations; and so back again to Molly — in Matt Dillon's garden, where he kissed her shoulder (on a yet much-to-be-recalled occasion). That was June too. And now the month has come round again and he has adored another, the lame Gerty.

He sees the quiet Howth Hill. "Where we" — thus briefly he recalls the day of romantic union with Molly there (already recalled on p. 224, *176*). Feels "a fool perhaps" in that now Boylan enjoys what it is his right to enjoy. "He gets the plums and I the plum-stones." (Once more Bloom's thoughts touch Stephen's. See Stephen's "Parable of the Plums," pp. 183–9, *145–9*, and also p. 802, *685*.) Gerty has left him feeling tired, drained of manhood. The mind switches back to Molly, who kissed him on Howth Hill when he still had youth, and Molly had too. He might revisit Howth Hill — but no; returning doesn't work. He needs the new. So to Martha and the clandestine correspondence carried on c/o P.O., Dolphin's Barn, and then immediately back to Molly and the party at Dolphin's Barn in 1887 when they played charades, acting the words "Rip van Winkle" in three episodes — tear in overcoat for "rip," breadvan for "van," and periwinkles for "winkle". "Then I did Rip van Winkle coming back." He will do so again, for this charade marked the memorable party with prophecy. The tear in the overcoat forecast the tear in Stephen's coat after the climax in night-town (p. 791, *677*). As for breadvan, the connexion between Bloom, Jesus, and the Bread of Life is strengthened here. (See p. 192, *153*, and commentary on p. 802, *685*.) Bloom's performance as Rip van Winkle forecasts the theme of the wanderer's return which occurs repeatedly in episode 16.

A bat flies around. Bloom ponders where he lives. Thus thought moves to the church belfry, to the bell, to what he calls the "mass" (it was Benediction, of course), the liturgy, the priest at his evening meal, till the bat catches his eye again and he studies its appearance, then dwells on the way colours depend on the light: so to the lights on Howth. Again the mind moves quickly: from bats to insects, to birds, to the way they follow ships, to the dismal lot of sailors, "storm-tossed" and separated from their wives, to the protective tokens they carry, to death by drowning, to the moonlit calm which ironically follows storm.

A last stray Roman candle shoots up from the bazaar. It is the hour of tryst, of the evening postal delivery, of lamplighting, of the late *Evening Telegraph* with its racing news of the Gold Cup. Howth Hill settles for slumber. On Kish bank the lightship twinkles.

Bloom muses ever more drowsily — on life at sea, on a pleasure cruise in the *Erin's King*, an occasion of much seasickness and of fear in the eyes of the women. But Milly enjoyed it, too young to fear death — at the age rather of fearing to be lost. He recalls how once they frightened her by hiding from her — and so wonders about the relationship between child's play and seriousness, between mock battle and real war. (The ideal-real dichotomy is again a theme implicit throughout this episode, for Bloom's purely visual relationship with Gerty parallels his purely verbal relationship with Martha. The disintegration represented in Bloom's partial relationships with Molly, Martha, and Gerty seems to reflect a Joycean judgement on modern life.) Memories of Milly's childhood predominate here — her hand in his, her hand at his waistcoat buttons, her little paps, her puberty and the effect of it on her mother, bringing back her own girlhood. So we return mentally with Bloom again to Molly and what she has told him of her Gibraltar days.

Thoughts become sketchier as sleepiness grows. Looking back on his day's activities so far, Bloom sees the row at Barney Kiernan's in a detached, balanced light. The beer-swillers "ought to go home and laugh at themselves." Thus Bloom recommends the two-eyed self-critical attitude which Cyclopean mentalities can never achieve. He even manages to consider the argument from their angle. "Not so bad then. Perhaps not to hurt he meant." The citizen's cry, "Three cheers for Israel" (p. 444, *342*), becomes in Bloom's mind three cheers for the citizen's extremely ugly sister-in-law, and we are back with the theme of the unattractive wife that keeps recurring in this episode. Thought moves, via Dignam, to widowhood, widowerhood, plain women, Denis Breen and his U.P. postcard, the quirks of Fate by which "he" (Breen), not Bloom, is the husband of Mrs. Breen, and, as ever, thought returns then to Molly — to last night's dream of her in Turkish trousers (which has a connexion with Stephen's dream, p. 58, *47*), and to the intention to get the Keyes ad fixed up and to buy Molly petticoats with the proceeds.

Idly he turns over a piece of paper on the strand. Then he picks up a bit of stick, thinks of writing a message in the sand for Gerty, and gets as far as "I. AM. A." leaving the reader's curiosity aroused. He effaces the letters with his foot and flings the stick away, reflecting on the transience of all things, but grateful for Gerty. By an odd coincidence the stick falls into silted sand and sticks upright. There seems to be one more hint of the Cross in this symbol. Correspondingly there appears to be an anticipatory joke, "I AM A . . . stick in the mud" (See p. 571, *440*, "Poldy, you are a poor old stick in the mud," and p. 724, *627*.) Subsequent half-formed thoughts ("And she can do the other. Did too. And Belfast. I won't go. Race there, race back to Ennis") reveal the old preoccupation with Molly's coming tour and the opportunities for adultery with Boylan which it will provide. Bloom's apprehension gives place to acceptance, even forgiveness ("Let him" . . . "No harm in him"), which reinforces the view that

Bloom's writing in the sand carries overtones of Christ's act when He was asked to condemn the woman taken in adultery. ("I. AM. A." suggests the divine "I AM" and "I am Alpha.")

Meantime the desire to snooze has become conscious, amid thoughts and half thoughts of Molly, Gerty, Martha, undies, and the lines from *Sweets of Sin* about Raoul, the frillies, and the "heaving embonpoint," and so on.

The cuckoo clock coos the hour in the priest's house near by. Gerty MacDowell is near enough to hear it. Bloom is now asleep: but the bird, giving its threefold message thrice, presses home the fact that Bloom has been cuckolded once more. Like the ninefold chime of the Angelus, it marks an annunciation. Like the cockcrow in the *Sirens* episode (p. 367, 284), like the cockcrow in the gospels, it announces a betrayal.

"Nausicaa"

Fritz Senn*

The last scene of the preceding chapter transfigured Leopold Bloom and projected him skyward at a specified and ballistically advantageous angle. The ascendant curve is continued into the first part of "Nausicaa," which gratifyingly exalts Bloom, at least as viewed from the favourable angle of one observer, from a particularly one-eyed, romanticized perspective. The observer, Gerty MacDowell, herself intently watched by Bloom, is in turn portrayed at her spectacular best, with fulsome touches and lavish colours. In addition, both she and Bloom are emotionally and physiologically exalted. "Nausicaa" is a chapter of culminations, of aspirations and high expectations, of sky-gazing and firework-gazing, of ecstatic flights and raised limbs.

The sustained flight, in "Nausicaa" as in "Cyclops," owes much to the elevation of its language. Its heights are rhetorical. Stripped of its metaphorical props, the flight becomes no more than fleeing. The escape from the citizen's rage transforms itself into a mysterious embrace, with Bloom, lingering lovingly in a soft world slowly losing its harsh contours, seeking refuge and comfort for his afflictions in illusory fulfillment.

Like all ballistic curves, those described in "Nausicaa" contain a rise, a climax, a descent, and an abrupt return to the ground. The movement is paralleled in such details as the rockets of the bazaar fireworks, a ball thrown and kicked, a stick flung away, and a bat flying to and fro. Within the human body, the movement corresponds to the surge of blood which

*From *James Joyce's "Ulysses": Critical Essays*, ed. Clive Hart and David Hayman (Berkeley: University of California Press, 1974), 277–311. Reprinted by permission of the publisher.

animates Gerty's cheeks with quaint blushes or a "telltale flush" (349.16), implicitly contributing to the underlying genital tumescence.

"BRANDED AS THE LOWEST OF THE LOW" (354.25)

The protagonists' rise to unprecedented heights is counterpointed, conspicuously enough, by a converse movement of which the reader, who inevitably depreciates the various altitudes according to his own scale, is very much aware and to which Gerty MacDowell herself carefully closes her eyes. The parabola of the flight is a parable of frustration and loneliness. In the setting of all-embracing love, Bloom resorts to the most isolated form of sexual gratification, an event made more poignant by his realization that a more vital and more mutually fulfilling embrace has recently been staged at home. Gerty too has been thwarted, by the loss of the attentions of her boy, who has, of late, been distracted by an entirely different kind of "exhibition" (349.31, 352.7); and she is out to gain attention elsewhere. The way in which the two work off their disappointments would have found little sympathy in any culture that produces these frustrations, and none at all in the Ireland of 1904. Masturbation is a sin in the Catholic context, and its essential sterility made it an offence in the Judaic code. We can translate the term into more contemporary condemnatory terms, such as "self-deception" and "escapism."

In Gerty's and Bloom's brief coming together, there is no coition (they do not go together, *co-ire*); both merely linger in relative proximity, within visual range, and then continue on their lonely ways, Gerty on hers, moreover, with a limp. There is no consummation, no physical touch (only, we are told, "consummate tact," and even that is used to "pass . . . off" something unpleasant; 363.24), no verbal contact. Fewer words are spoken in "Nausicaa" than in the other chapters (except the basically silent "Proteus" and "Penelope"). Two monologues, one indirect, one direct, the one before, the other after, are its suitable expression. The cheap satisfaction is brought out in a style of cheap fiction, lacking vitality, incapable of communication.

"Nausicaa" then is a profitable chapter for the critic who may rise to the occasion and comment, with Cyclopean assurance, on the multiple inadequacies displayed by the two lovers, treating them, according to his inclination, with benign condescension or downright contempt. "Nausicaa" yields ample illustration for the marriage counsellor, the preacher, or the moral guide. The moralistic attitude first manifested itself in public through the activities of the Society for the Prevention of Vice, which instituted legal proceedings in 1920, thus stopping the book's first flight in serial publication and bringing it abruptly down to court. Sentences similar to that pronounced in the Court of Special Sessions in New York, in 1921, have been reiterated since, with some relevant fashionable modifications: nowadays the author is generally enlisted on the right side; he is in fact represented as implicitly adding his voice to those expressing righteous disapprobation of his characters.

"LOOK AT IT OTHER WAY ROUND" (380.28)

There is no intrinsic necessity to restrict one's views to censorious glances from superior vantage points. These may even blind us to some of the chapter's scintillating delights. One of the potential moral effects of *Ulysses* is that it can condition us, more than any previous novel, to suspend or, at any rate, postpone the moralizing tendency that consists in dispensing blame and credit, in favour of a series of constant readjustments and a fluctuating awareness of the complexity of motivation. "Nausicaa" at least enables us, besides the pleasures of judicial evaluation, to experience sympathy and to arrive at the kind of intricate understanding that makes the attitude of forgiveness (cf. 358.17) just as pointless as its opposite.

In the imperfect world of Dublin, 1904, the imperfect solution that the two characters allow themselves to be driven to, passively reactive rather than passionately active, does have some advantages. There is relief from various tensions, relief from the conflicts of aggression and prejudice, as in Barney Kiernan's, and relief also from the depressing squalor of the Dignams' household. Bloom's foreignness, usually a cause of trouble, stands him in good stead in "Nausicaa," heightened as it is by some spurious effects. There is compensation for recent setbacks. Bloom knows one has to be "Thankful for small mercies" (368.21). For the moment he feels young again. At the end of the day, the encounter is listed positively as having been accompanied by "pleasant reflection" (722), and there have been few enough such moments. Substitute satisfactions are better than no satisfactions at all, and Bloom, for one, appreciates the benefits to be derived from the momentary shutting off of unpleasant aspects of reality: "Glad I didn't know it when she was on show" (368.4).

Throughout, *Ulysses* interfuses reality with illusion, and in some parts the validity of the distinction is even challenged (it seems to have disappeared entirely in *Finnegans Wake*). "Nausicaa" varies the theme in its own manner, ringing the changes on the mind's inventiveness in superimposing satisfactions of which reality is acutely devoid. Illusion, partly "optical illusion" (376.26), is one way of "smoothing over life's tiny troubles" (347.25). Without some tempering from the imagination, reality might well become unbearable. Belief in "intercessory power" (356.32) or in the curative and beautifying power of advertised goods performs such tempering functions, and so does art. To afford illusory gratifications is one of the legitimate functions of fiction, of highbrow literature no less than of Gerty's favourite reading matter.

Some techniques for putting up with bothersome situations and creating compensatory patterns are compulsorily learned in our child-hood: "Tommy Caffrey could never be got to take his castor oil unless it was Cissy Caffrey that held his nose and promised him the scatty heel of the loaf of brown bread with golden syrup on" (346.36). That sets the tone for "Nausicaa," similarly coated with syrupy "sweetness" (360.23). When baby Boardman is deprived of his ball, his frustration is dealt with by two other mechanisms prominent in the chapter, titillation and the conjuring up of fictitious scenes from a life far higher than one's own, rendered in stylized form: "And she tickled tiny tot's two cheeks to make him forget and played here's the lord mayor, here's his two horses, here's his gingerbread carriage and here he walks in, chinchopper, chinchopper, chinchopper chin" (353.12).

Such escape mechanisms, basically aimed at diverting attention from disagreeable aspects of reality, also have some positive value. Bloom at least meets a being who, by virtue of whatever distorting projections, seems to accept him and to desire him. Something approaching love does, after all, take place, and a kind of rapport is established: "Still it was a kind of language between us" (372.35). The lack of communication in *Ulysses* is perhaps less surprising than the occasional occurrence of *some* imperfect communication. Gerty, injured and slighted, presents herself to her best advantage for one short span, at the proper distance, with just the right degree of illumination to increase her glamour (which is what the advice she gets from the fashion page amounts to). Even after the release of tension and after the effects of the stage setting have worn off, Bloom is capable of sympathizing with her. "Poor girl" is one of his first thoughts. Nor does he appear to be any more depressed or guilt-ridden than we know him to have been previously.

The pathetic climax of the two chance lovers resembles Bloom's confrontation with the citizen, an earlier blend of conviction, tumescent courage, irritation, and pulpit sentimentality, where Bloom is sublimely exalted as well as ridiculously abased — and there it would be equally hard to place him, or the events, conclusively on any evaluative scale.

After Bloom's precipitate proclamation of the gospel of love, he does in fact embark on a tour of love in its varieties. The visit to the Dignams is an act of charity; romantic love culminates in "Nausicaa" (which is steeped in colours of loveliness, including even the "lovely" dog Gar-ryowen); the depths of sexuality are charted in "Circe"; paternal love comes into its own from "Oxen of the Sun" to "Ithaca." At the same time these pursuits are also patently motivated by an unwillingness to face domestic realities. As against any normative ideals, Bloom's performances fall short. Still, in his encounter with Gerty he comes within visible distance of his own definition of love as "the opposite of hatred." The abortive message that Bloom writes into the sand and effaces immediately, "I . . . AM. A." (381), happens to contain, besides himself, the Latin root *ama-*, love, no doubt outside his own consciousness and yet somehow "done half by design" (382.2), indicative more of a wish, unfulfilled like the rest of them, than an achievement. In one respect Bloom attains the Christian aim of forgiving his most recent persecutor, the citizen: "Look at it other way round. Not so bad then. Perhaps not to hurt he meant" (380.28).

"MATTERS FEMININE" (346.15)

With the "Nausicaa" chapter we enter, for the first time, a predominantly female world. So far Stephen and Bloom have moved in a masculine environment. No single woman was present in "Cyclops," except for glimpses of wretched Mrs Breen as the servant of her master (who, through the postcard "U.P.: up," is treated to his own rise and fall). Now we are immersed in the soft cadences of feminine fiction, with three girls in the foreground dominating a triad of young males, reducing Bloom to the role of a spectator. Gerty's is the first feminine mind that is unfolded before us at any length. Before that the reader was favoured with a few parenthetical flashes of the minds of the seductive barmaids in "Sirens," who also provide flirtatious distractions for careworn Dubliners. Miss Douce even performs an exhibitionistic set piece for two ogling males.

An earlier mild prefiguration of Gerty MacDowell is the Miss Dunne of "Wandering Rocks." Her brief succession of thoughts include "mystery," "love," and envious comments on the pictorial exhibitionism of a star of the Dublin stage, named Marie (Kendall), "holding up her bit of a skirt." She considers the fascinated stare of men and a "concertina skirt" for herself (229.28). Like Gerty, she has a secret in her drawer (cf. 442.18), she hopes (as Gerty "wishes") "to goodness" (229.30, 357.18, 361.1), and she uses the tumescent word "swells." Her employer, Blazes Boylan, generally better off than Bloom, is at the same moment viewing the charms of another blushing girl, while anticipating the more palpable charms of Molly.

The oblique characterization of Gerty MacDowell is the first extended delineation of a female psyche. From now on, the book moves through several female phases. The Virgin, Joyce's "symbol" for "Nausicaa," is succeeded by the Mother and the Whore in the next two chapters — three archetypal manifestations of the Feminine. In "Penelope," Molly's fullness encompasses them all. On a smaller scale, the three girls in "Nausicaa" play all these roles, being virginal but having maternal responsibilities in "Nausicaa," and scortatory duties in "Circe."

"THE GATHERING TWILIGHT" (363.30)

The immersion in this female world coincides with the oncoming of night. Gerty appears in twilight; at the end of the chapter darkness has descended. Bloom estimates the time by such signs as the waning of the light and the appearance of the mailboat. The sun set in Dublin at 8.27 p.m. on 16 June 1904 (as indicated in *Thom's Directory*), and lighting up time for cyclists (376.16) was fixed at 9 hours 17 minutes, as the *Evening Telegraph*, sold in the streets at Sandymount a little before that time, told its readers.[1]

In most mythological representations, and in the grammatical gender of Indo-European languages, the night is female. The darker half of *Ulysses* is ushered in by Gerty and closed by Molly's ruminations in her bedroom; at the end of the faint incipient lustre of approaching dawn, and the remembered swelling memory of a scene steeped in the sunlight of Gibraltar and of Howth, herald a new turning toward the sun. Immediately after "Nausicaa," in the first word of the next chapter, "Deshil,"[2] there is another metaphorical turning toward sun and son.

The second, larger part of *Ulysses* extends between opposite poles of womanhood: young, immature Gerty, lame and incomplete (she is only accorded half a chapter), and ripe, fullblown Molly. Bloomsnight is structured symmetrically, enclosed at each end by female outpourings, fluid, subjective, with orgasmic climaxes. These are accompanied by male counterparts, arranged concentrically—Bloom's sober reflective attempt at a reasoned view in "Nausicaa" is set off against the rationalized pseudoscientific and objective inventory of "Ithaca," both down-to-earth, disillusioned stocktakings. Both chapters end, similarly, with Bloom's falling asleep and with a transition into dream language, a dissolution of narrative as masculine control gives way to uninterrupted, associative strings of words and memories (382, 737). In the *Odyssey* too, the isle of the Phaeacians is closest to Ithaca and the last stop on the return journey.

Tucked between enveloping folds of femininity, the meeting, interacting, parting of Bloom and Stephen are circumveloped by a darkness that both does and does not comprehend them. They are thus "wombed in sin darkness" (38.10). The image of an enfolding womb within which the most significant action takes pace is more than a convenient analogy. Regression into uterine security is at the core of infantile notions of illusory escape, as in "Nausicaa"; the same local anatomical habitation is necessary for the more positive interpretations concentrating on birth and rebirth or for Stephen's concept of a creative womb of the imagination. A womb is included in the word "wombfruit" at the beginning of the "Oxen of the Sun" chapter (383.4), whose organ is the womb. The last page of "Ithaca," which is symmetrically opposite and in which Bloom disappears, contains a corresponding image: "the manchild in the womb" (737.13).

There is an uterine quality to the darkness of the night of 16–17 June, enfolded in a female texture, and stretching from the metaphorical all-including embrace that sets the scene in "Nausicaa" (with an early glance at dear old Howth) all the way to the remembered real, carnal embrace on Howth Head.

"A STORY BEHIND IT" (355.25)

Gerty MacDowell is the latest avatar of the temptress in Joyce's fiction. Her first incarnation is as Polly Mooney in "The Boarding House," who exposes herself to a male viewer, at night, against a backdrop of candles. She first emerges in a scene full of social pretence and cliché, e.g., "the *artistes* would oblige" at one of the "reunions." She is both naively innocent and cunningly knowing; her song mentions "sham." She is explicitly referred to as "a little perverse madonna" (D, 62–63). Her grammar, like Gerty's, is imperfect, but what, says Mr Doran – and it could have been said by Gerty or one of her authoresses – "would grammar matter if he really loved her?" (D, 66). Polly and Gerty know how to cry in front of a mirror (D, 68; 351.17). And Polly "knew she was being watched" (D, 63). Her seduction, however, has graver consequences. Mr Doran considers vainly and irrationally escape by flight through the roof but is brought down to reality by the confederate forces of familial and social gravity, and by Cyclopean threats. Bloom, at any rate, is more prudent than Polly's victim, who by the time of *Ulysses* has further declined to a wretched state. A handshake briefly unites the two in "Cyclops," with the I-narrator putting them in the same category: "Shake hands, brother. You're a rogue and I'm another" (313.33).

A *Portrait* presents its own gallery of temptresses, leading up to the vision in Chapter 4 and the villanelle of Chapter 5. The girl who meets Stephen's gaze on the strand connects to otherwise separate strands of sensual eroticism and mariolatric images of purity. The similarity between this twilight scene and the portrait of Gerty MacDowell in *Ulysses* has often been remarked upon. The stage setting in both contains the beach, the dusk, the sea, weedgrown rocks, the display of thighs, pictorial representation, and elevated vocabulary. The mind is turned to higher things. The universe and the world are freely brought to bear on the situation, Stephen relating to "the heavenly bodies, . . . the earth, . . . some new world" (*AP*, 172), while Gerty can be just as liberal with the evocation of "worlds" (351.14, 357.41, etc.). There is neither physical contact nor any spoken word to break the spell. It takes the next section – Chapter 5 of A *Portrait*, part 2 of "Nausicaa" – to re-establish more realistic proportions.

"SAME STYLE OF BEAUTY" (380.31)

To realize just how much the "Nausicaa" chapter metamorphoses elements of Stephen's ecstasy on the beach in A *Portrait*, it is worth collating a few images and phrases. Almost every item, for example, of the catalogue that describes the impression made on Stephen by the bird-girl has been re-used. Both girls are alone, gazing into the distant sea, aware of being watched, and in both cases there is mention of waist, bosom, hair, face, softness, drawers, skirts, slenderness, touch, shame, etc. Some specific transpositions are amusing. The "magic" changing the girl into the likeness of a seabird is at work in "Nausicaa" too, in the "magic lure" (364.22) in Gerty's eyes. The seabird may have become a "canary bird" (359.5), but Bloom himself thinks of "seabirds" (380.11). The girl's legs are "delicate"; delicacy is one of Gerty's strong points, extending to her hands (348.32), her flush (349.16 — flushes are part of the scenery in the *Portrait* too, p. 172), and the "pink" creeping into her pretty cheek (356.10). Since "from everything in the least indelicate her finebred nature instinctively recoiled" (364.32), she would be peeved to know that Bloom callously awards the palm of delicacy to her rival: "That squinty one is delicate" (368.6). The ivory of the bird-girl's thighs is part of Gerty's make-up: "ivorylike purity" (348.19). The term "slateblue" contains Gerty's favourite colour, but Bloom uses "on the slate" (375.36) in quite another context. The "ring-dove" (362.34) associated with Gerty's defiant voice may be compared to the "dove-like" bosom of Stephen's vision, or to her skirts, which are "dove-tailed." The "worship" of Stephen's eyes has its counterpart in Bloom's "dark eyes . . . literally worshipping at her shrine" (361.41). The "faint flame" that trembled on the cheek of the girl in *A Portrait* is re-lit as a "warm flush . . . surging and flaming into her [Gerty's] cheeks" (356.17). Even the precious word "fashioned," which is used for the trail of seaweed in the earlier scene, seems to have been transferred from the literary tradition to the marketplace — to the ambit of "Dame Fashion," one of Gerty's patron saints, whose call she follows as a "votary" (350.8), just as Stephen devoted himself to Art.

A more detailed list of such transferences would include the cry uttered by both Stephen and Gerty at their respective raptures, a trembling of limbs, a phrase like "the palest rose" (*AP*, 172), which becomes "waxen pallor" in conjunction with "rosebud mouth" (348.19). Gerty's climax could be called, as Stephen's in fact is, "an outburst of profane joy" (*AP*, 171). Etymologically, "profane" means "outside the temple" (Lat. *fanum* = fane), which is exactly where the action on Sandymount strand takes place, literally near "that simple fane beside the waves" (354.6).

It is, above all, one of Stephen's choicest terms, "radiant" (see *AP*, 169 and "radiance," *passim*, in the aesthetic theory) which, together with another thematic word of *A Portrait*, is now applied to Gerty MacDowell's showy appearance: "a radiant little vision" (360.22). The "pure radiance" of the Virgin (346.8) is one of many links.

The two visions are made up of the same touches, sometimes with a marked drop in tone and connotation. The purple tinge, noticeable in *A Portrait*, but not easily appreciated with critical nicety, has now been applied much more strongly. One's impressions of the earlier scene will now be readjusted; in the comic exaggerations of "Nausicaa" some traits in *A Portrait* are seen in a different light. The two episodes reflect on each other. In a sense, "Nausicaa" continues the familiar technique of *A*

Portrait, the repetition of an earlier event in a rearrangement, with a change of tone and a new slant (often amounting to a disillusionment) brought about, very often, by a reshuffling of the same verbal material with some additional twists of phraseology. The reading experience is characterized by shifts of perspective (one of the structural devices of *Ulysses*), which should also make us wary of singling out any one of the stages in the process of cognition, however convincing, as the decisive one.

"WITH CAREFUL HAND RECOMPOSED" (370.9)

We know that Joyce, while working on *Ulysses*, met a live incarnation of whoever had inspired the event that had been turned into the vocational epiphany on the beach in Chapter 4 of *A Portrait*. Late in 1918, in Zürich, Joyce saw and addressed a girl, Martha (or Marthe) Fleischmann, bearing a name which itself contained an alluring tangle of Ulyssean motifs, and embarked upon a liaison which was mainly an affair of looks and letters (at least until its climax, a final rendezvous of, presumably, more daring enterprise, shrouded — for us — in appropriate obscurity, but illuminated — for the participants — by candles specially and ritualistically provided; fittingly, the episode has been reported by a painter, Joyce's friend Frank Budgen, in whose studio the meeting took place).[3]

Whether acting on impulse on imitating Bloom's epistolary precedent, Joyce sent his Martha some letters and one postcard (this, addressed from "Odysseus" to "Nausicaa," is now lost;[4] as it happens, Gerty received one "silly postcard," 362.39) — documents of a *Schwärmerei* which prove that the Swiss seductress reinforced some of the attractions that were to be attributed to Gerty MacDowell. The affair, with a strong element of "studied attitude" (355.26) on Joyce's part, no doubt also contained its serious involvement. The letters allow us some rare glimpses into that mysterious process of distillation which turns living experience into distanced art. The situation already has about it an air of a laboratory experiment arranged with a view to literary exploitation. In real life Joyce could adopt fictional roles by comparing himself outright with Dante or Shakespeare, while playing a provincial Romeo or Tristan.

Again it is fascinating to watch Joyce using, to express private feelings for the kinetic purpose of evoking an emotional response, the same turns of phrase (though in French and German) and the same images that served him, not too much later, for the hilarious parodies of "Nausicaa." He did not of course use the letters (which were out of his hands and whose preservation is accidental) as he might use the actual text of previously published works. All we can say with certainty is that concepts and analogies that were in his mind in 1918 to 1919, and which were used for practical purposes, recur in the chapter that was drafted a few months later.[5] The artist is in full control of his material, which seems to be more than we can claim of the lover and correspondent.

In the first letter, of December 1918,[6] Joyce gives voice to his frustration at not seeing Martha, whose name he does not yet know. His first visual impressions include her big hat, similar to the one that Gerty takes off with striking effect, and, in more detail, "la mollesse des traits réguliers et la douceur des yeux." The charm of Gerty's eyes is general all over "Nausicaa," and her "sweetness" is tied to her whole vision (360.23), but the softness of her face is explicitly noted: "her softlyfeatured face" (348.40). Joyce goes on to remark how he thought Martha was a jewess, an illusion, but an endeavour to make life conform to fictional patterns. In the fictional refashioning, the inversion of racial roles corresponds to the shifting of the sentimentality to the female partner. In his letter, Joyce then adduces the symbolism that is central for much of his writing, and in particular for "Nausicaa" and "Oxen of the Sun": "Jesus Christ a pris son corps humain: dans le ventre d'une femme juive." Molly, at least will be turned into a half-jewess.

Joyce confesses to giving in to "une espèce de fascination." Bloom is "fascinated by a loveliness that made him gaze" (361.15). The letter also conjures up the evening scene, "un soir brumeux." Martha has given a sign (". . . vous m'avez fait un signe"), and so does Gerty on page 367. Joyce hints at Byronic repercussions in his life: ". . . je suis un pauvre chercheur dans ce monde, . . . j'ai vécu et péché créé. . . ." The same instances of a dissolute but creative life figure in Stephen's visionary repertoire (AP, 172), and, accordingly, Gerty projects that Bloom "had erred and sinned and wandered" (367.15).

In this long first letter, with its odd confessional urge, Joyce slightly rejuvenates himself to establish a parallel with the great writers. He uses the imagery of an entry into the night: "C'est l'âge que Dante a eu quand il est entré dans la nuit de son être." A few lines later Joyce even refers to the infantile retreat into the darkness of the womb, so basic to the nocturnal chapters in Ulysses: ". . . je m'en irai, un jour, n'ayant rien compris, dans l'obscurité qui nous a enfantés tous." Joyce is paraphrasing Stephen's "darkness shining in brightness which brightness could not comprehend" (28.16), as well as "wombed in sin darkness . . . made not begotten" (38.10) — subtleties that must necessarily have been lost on a somewhat puzzled Martha Fleischmann whose preferred reading is reported to have been sentimental novels. Joyce calls Martha "gracious" and "rêveuse," and both gracefulness and dreaminess are among Gerty's attributes.

In another letter (9 December 1918) Joyce compares Martha's suffering, brought on by illness, to his own: "moi, j'ai souffert aussi." Gerty wonders if Bloom too "had suffered" (358.9). In the last extant letter Joyce switches over to languishing phrases in German. He describes Martha's face: ". . . Dein Gesicht, aber so blass, so müde und so traurig!" This air of sadness suits Gerty's complexion too: her "sad downcast eyes" (349.20), for example, and in another passage: ". . . that tired feeling. The waxen pallor of her face . . ." (348.19). In a last imaginative flight Joyce soars to Gertyan heights of imagery and emotion, kitsching that note of romantic rapture to sweet perfection, though (in *this* case no doubt unwittingly) marring the effect by a grammatical lapse: "Durch die Nacht der Bitterkeit meiner Seele fielen die Küsse Deiner Lippen über meinen Herz — weich wie Rosenblätter, sanft wie Tau." We don't know where Joyce's tongue was when he wrote those cadences. After the enchantment was over, at any rate, the dewy softness acquired a different quality. In "Nausicaa" the rapturous burst, "O so soft, sweet, soft," is followed by "all melted away dewily" (367.4–5). And the dew that covers Sandymount strand is more matter of fact: "Dew falling. Bad for you, dear, to sit on that stone. Brings on white fluxions" (376.29).

The litany of the Blessed Virgin is the source for Joyce's parting address to Martha Fleischmann: "O rosa mistica, ora pro me!" Translated into the novel, it becomes ". . . pray for us, mystical rose" (356.27), and again "*Ora pro nobis*" (358.22).

These letters show that Joyce did not have to look very far for the psychological material he was to deal with, his own *personae* proved a rich quarry. The attitudes of the pining adorer contributed more to the "Nausicaa" chapter than the adored girl herself. Joyce's introspective acumen and capacity to see himself from a distance must have been remarkable. An element of spite, consequence of almost inevitable frustration, may have been at play too in the malicious reversal of roles: the sentimentality and doubtful taste and the languishing are projected on to the girl. Bloom (roughly of the age of Joyce when "Nausicaa' was being written in 1919 to 1920) appears detached and down to earth. It remains one of the mysteries of literary creation how the internal set-up that could produce such dewy epistolary prose could be transmuted, by processes of displacement and transference, into the comic portraits of Gerty MacDowell and Mr Leopold Bloom.

"MUST HAVE THE STAGE SETTING" (370.14)

It is appropriate that Gerty's portrait is made up of strokes found elsewhere in life and fiction (Joyce's and others'). Make-up is her medium. Gerty's plumes are borrowed ones, so much so that some readers deny her any individual character. She is composed of traits assembled in a technique of collage and montage, in keeping with the chapter's art, painting.

However, Gerty MacDowell is not wholly dependent on her models. The coda of the "Wandering Rocks" chapter introduces her in a revelatory vignette which condenses her component traits and limitations, excepting only the posing and the artificial embellishment: "Passing by Roger Greene's office and Dollard's big red printing house Gerty MacDowell, carrying the Catesby's cork lino letters for her father who was laid up, knew by the style it was the lord and lady lieutenant but she couldn't see what Her Excellency had on because the tram and Spring's big yellow furniture van had to stop in front of her on account of its being the lord lieutenant" (252.39). Joyce exposes Gerty's preoccupation with appearance, dress, and position and her attempt to take a vicarious part in Her Excellency's excellency. The sentence has a tenseness about it which we shall notice again in "Nausicaa." Its rhythm, combining a supple pace with a halting awkwardness, suggests Gerty's limp, while the imagery includes three strong primary colours. The little episode is a frustrated vision into which reality crudely interferes. The style exemplifies in a lower key the tone that characterizes Gerty. We learn, indeed, that it is possible to know "by the style."

"Wandering Rocks" emphasizes location in space, and Gerty's meticulously specified location indirectly reveals one of her roles, even if this is frustratingly out of the uninformed reader's range of vision. Some special knowledge of Dublin is required, in keeping with the labyrinthine technique:[7] between Roger Greene's office (referred to in "Nausicaa" as the site of a slightly voyeuristic scene — 372.3), at no. 11 Wellington quay, and Dollard's big red[8] printing house, at nos. 2, 3, 4, and 5 Wellington quay, she must have passed, at nos. 8 and 9, the firm of Ceppi, Peter and Sons, picture frame and looking glass factory, and statuary manufacturers, as they are officially listed.[9] They might well furnish some of the stage property for "Nausicaa": pictures, looking glass, and statuary. Bloom, who follows in Gerty's footsteps a few minutes later, notices that Messrs Ceppi deal in statuary: ". . . by Ceppi's virgins, bright of their oils" (260.37).[10] On her first appearance Gerty is thus tacitly juxtaposed with the Virgin Mary displayed in a shop window, done in bright oils. The bright colours will return in "Nausicaa," where, in her new position on the rocks of Sandymount, she is set off against the Virgin Mary, whose Litany is part of the background.

"ACCIDENTALLY ON PURPOSE" (359.33)

It so happens that the sentence that first announces Gerty contains just two verbs in its main clause, "knew" and "couldn't see." This may give a perverse twist to the first words of the Virgin Mary when confronted with the Angel of the Lord and his announcement. She said: "How shall this be, *seeing* I *know* not a man?" (Luke, 1:34).[11] The only other words uttered by the Virgin are quoted verbatim in "Nausicaa," at 358.42.

Coincidence may play into Joyce's sacerdotal hands, but it is no coincidence that the operative words "see" and "know," with their negations, are prominent in "Nausicaa," often in close conjunction. For example, ". . . Gerty could see by her looking as black as thunder . . . and they both knew that she was something aloof, . . . and there was somebody else too that knew it and saw it . . ." (363.1–6); "so she said she could see from where she was . . . and she knew he could be trusted . . . there was no one to see only him . . . because she knew about the passion of men like that . . ." (365.25, 30, 36, 39), etc. The chapter is, in one sense, a variation on the subject of seeing (with numerous synonyms) and knowing. In the biblical sense there is no knowledge in the encounter. Cognition and vision blend and are both interdependent and complementary. Both Bloom and Gerty see things without knowing and know about what they cannot see. The reader in turn knows more than he sees. Even a limitation of one's perception ("See her as she is spoil all," 370.14) or of one's knowledge ("Glad I didn't know . . . ," 368.4) may at times prove to be an advantage.

Earlier in the day, on the same beach, Stephen contemplated the relation between knowledge and the ineluctable modality of the visible: "thought through my eyes" (37.2), and went on to conduct an experiment by closing his eyes. Indirectly the closing of the eyes also introduces the visually oriented "Nausicaa" chapter, at least etymologically. The initial "mysterious" embrace (346.2) suggests mystery, originally a form of gaining knowledge without the senses. The word derives from Greek *myo*, to close (said of the eyes). Bloom links the word "mystery" with perception in darkness: ". . . into a cellar where it's dark. Mysterious thing too" (374.35). Cognition through vision is connected with Aristotelian "diaphane" in "Proteus," the sensual leering in "Nausicaa" with transparent stockings.

The precedent of the Virgin's own words does not necessarily justify the prevalence of seeing and knowing in Gerty's chapter. Even so it is worth noticing that the phrases singled out as examples of the bad grammar of Polly Mooney, the perverse little madonna and forerunner of Gerty, are "*I seen*" and "*If I had've known*" (*D*, 66). In *Ulysses* she is known for "exposing her person" (303.6) and to be "open to all comers," which suggests an irreverent equivalent for a "refuge of sinners" (358.22).

"SINGULAR DEVOTION" (356.26)

Gerty MacDowell's apposition with the Virgin Mary is transparent enough. In the nearby Star of the Sea church, the Litany of the Blessed Virgin is recited, blending with the main narrative. Stuart Gilbert pointed out that the Abbey of Howth, suggested by the references to Howth Head (especially at the beginning, 346.4), was dedicated to the Blessed Virgin.[12] Sandymount itself is situated in the parish of St. Mary. Some of the Virgin's appellations have been assimilated to the description of Gerty's exterior. Her face is noted for its "ivorylike purity" (348.19), her heart is worth its "weight in gold" (355.12) — gold and ivory had already acquired liturgical overtones in *A Portrait*. The Virgin is undefiled, Gerty's soul "unsullied" (367.11). Physically Gerty remains virginally untouched, while some of Mary's spiritual attributes are also translated into physical terms: she is "full of grace," her figure and face being "graceful" (348.14, 365.36). Joyce conceives of her as wearing "immaculate" stockings: "there wasn't a brack on them" (360.10); "brack" is Gaelic for speck or stain.

Some of the epithets in the Litany can be related to Gerty, and not only in scathing irony, but, like everything else, with perspectival modification. Stylistically, of course, the immutable appellations of the Virgin are not far removed from the stereotypes of cliché. Gerty is, for the time being, "most powerful," and as we are told expressly at 367.13, she is "merciful" (354.27). For practical and not entirely irrelevant purposes, she proves a refuge for one sinner and a "comfortress" for at least one of the "afflicted" (358.22), a momentary "haven of refuge" (358.25) for Bloom who has "erred and sinned and wandered" (367.15). If judged by the same Catholic view, of course, the refuge he finds is in sin itself. But he finds relief and forgiveness and pardon, like the faithful at the retreat (Bloom's tarrying is another form of retreat). He belongs to the "toilers for their daily bread," with "careworn hearts" (356.27, 28). As a "child of Mary" (364.7) Gerty would be pledged to imitate the example of the Virgin as best she could in daily life. Weighed in the balance of orthodoxy, her actual conduct would not rate very high, but in Bloom's valuation it may do. Evaluation is a tricky matter, liable to error and modification: "Remember about the mistake in the valuation" (377.39).

The Annunciation is explicitly referred to by way of the remembered words of the priest in the confession box. He seems to apply the Virgin's words of submission, "be it done unto me according to Thy Word," rather obliquely to the idea of obeying "the voice of nature" (358.42, 38), himself establishing a somewhat mundane parallel. Gerty's thoughts immediately turn to the priest and his home, which features "a canary bird" (359.5). Buck Mulligan, joking joiner of the holy and the ribald, has prepared us for the Holy Family, whose *"father's a bird"* (19.4); Léo Taxil's dialogue about *"le pigeon"* (41.15) has similarly prepared us for another bird in "Nausicaa," for this bird, revealed as a cuckoo.[13] The cuckoo's nine-fold cry reverberates blasphemously up toward the Holy Ghost as well as downward to Bloom's domestic situation. At the end of the chapter the clock speaks with a columbine tongue, it "cooed" (382.26). Gerty's own words, as she says that she can throw her "cap at who I like" (being thus blessed among women), ring out "more musical than the cooing of the ringdove" (362.33).

In the vision of A Portrait, "a wild angel had appeared" (AP, 172); in "Nausicaa" a bird, a bat, and a dark stranger appear, while there is inversion in the phrase "Dark devilish appearance" (369.17). Bloom, when he considers writing a "message" (381.30), comes linguistically close to being an angel (*angelos* = messenger). His message reveals him to be lonely and disappointed, though his confession remains unfinished: "I . . . AM. A." Whether we substitute ". . . a cuckold," ". . . a naughty boy," "alone," or whatever, we bear in mind his earthly *fichue position*, in marked contrast to the more divine overtones contained in the "A." It suggests an incomplete half of the Christ of the Revelation (who is A *and* O, beginning and end). There is a faint adumbration of a Jehovean I AM THAT I AM; or, through another tangential extrapolation, we may be reminded of how, when told about the woman taken in adultery, Jesus "stooped down, and with his finger wrote on the ground, as though he heard them not" (John, 8:6). Bloom, who "stooped" and "gently vexed the thick sand" (381.18, 28), is often motivated by not wanting to hear about a woman taken in adultery.

Such potential divine flutters may be left in limbo or accepted in addition to the direct references to the Annunciation. At whichever elevation we prefer to place the essence of the sterile encounter between Bloom (pitiful human being set off against godlike potentialities) and Gerty, the following chapter contains the real birth of a real son, discussion of the "utterance of the Word" (422.42), and countless theological allusions. As the Annunciation promises, the "fruit of thy womb" (Luke 1:42) will be blessed and come to life, in the thrice repeated "wombfruit" at the beginning of "Oxen of the Sun."

"SUPPOSE THERE'S SOME CONNECTION" (374.33)

Joyce creates, and invites us to treat his chapters almost as individuals, with distinct idiosyncrasies and with affinities for each other. "Nausicaa" has some special bonds. It is certainly paired off against the preceding chapter, "Cyclops," after whose noisy brawling and brute force it appears soothing and quiet. Both are climactic chapters, dealing with sentiment and passion. The men in "Cyclops" are concerned with politics, chauvinism, war, rebellion, execution, punishment, fighting (finding a female counterpart, too, in the three girls' malicious bickerings; the twins in "Nausicaa" are already engaged in strife about the power and possession of castle and ball). The girls in "Nausicaa" dream of love and marriage. Bloom's involvement is significant, he inclines to making love (in "Nausicaa" his participation is voluntary and deliberate) rather than to making war (the entanglement in Barney Kiernan's comes about mainly by accident and imprudence).

In either case views are dimmed by prejudice, combined with hatred or with romantic notions. Stereotypes have replaced judgment and discrimination, attitudes to life fall into ready-made categories. The protagonists see what they have been conditioned to find and remain blind to the rest. Eyes are important, their use in "Nausicaa" ranging all the way from candid glances to blindness: "Thinks I'm a tree, so blind" (377.30). Identities are mistaken. In fact, Gerty's mind is almost incapable of recognizing an identity. There is a pre-existing classification to which phenomena have to conform, and she, herself, seems predetermined: ". . . she was more a Giltrap than a MacDowell" (348.13). Bloom cannot be appreciated for what he is, becoming a dark, handsome foreigner with all the trappings of the mysterious stranger of popular fiction. For Gerty, he consists of projections. Even noses are categorized in advance: ". . . but she could not see whether he had an aquiline nose or a slightly *retroussé* from where he was sitting" (357.37). The citizen's categories were different, but similarly fixed.

There are many oblique views. Edy Boardman, who has a squint, can be acutely and unpleasantly perceptive. Spite, in fact, usually makes the observer more sharp-sighted, and even Gerty grows one-sidedly keen-eyed when it comes to criticizing her rivals, even if she never attains the terseness of the Narrator in "Cyclops."

Soon after Bloom's entry, the conversation in Barney Kiernan's pub veers round to "ruling passion" and erection (304), which are suitably associated with death and execution. Bloom sets himself up as an expert and is parodied as a "scientist" (one who knows). In both chapters Bloom is exalted and humiliated. In his defiant outburst he is seen as "an almanac picture" (333.3), anticipating the one that Gerty keeps in an intimate place: "the grocer's christmas almanac the picture of halcyon days . . . " (355.21). His act is presented as a rise ("Old lardyface standing up . . . ") and a fall ("then he collapses all of a sudden"), followed by detumescent imagery: ". . . as limp as a wet rag" (333.4–8). The subsequent persiflage of the propagation of universal love thematically features our heroine: "Gerty MacDowell loves the boy that has the bicycle" (333.28). The whole of "Nausicaa" could be taken as an extension of this parodic sketch.

The style of Gerty's part could easily have found a place as one of the Cyclopean parodies.[14] The opening caress of the summer evening, which had begun "to fold the world in its mysterious embrace" (346.2), is lifted from such a parody, the Execution scene: "The hero folded her willowy form in a loving embrace" (309.33),[15] a sentence proclaiming the literary execution of Gerty MacDowell, to which loving care is devoted in "Nausicaa."

Bloom's exit from the Cyclops' den is followed by the one explicit naming of the Blessed Virgin in the citizen's benediction: "The blessing of God and Mary and Patrick on you" (333.41). In accordance with the theme of violence, the Virgin Mary is perverted, in the imperialist's creed, into an instrument of brutal force and suppression: "born of the fighting navy" (329.25). In clear contrast, the Virgin offers her friendly protection to all who need it (356.33), while "the fighting navy . . . keeps our foes at bay" (328.36). Gerty, of course, is connected with the navy through her clothes, wearing a "navy threequarter skirt" (350.14). In Joyce's view, even the I-narrator's favourite expletive is etymologically derived from the Virgin ("by our Lady"),[16] so that "bloody" conveniently takes care both of the sanguinary aspect and the blasphemy, the I-narrator of "Cyclops" reversing the manner of the implied narrator of "Nausicaa," choosing a register that is too low and vulgar as against one that is too elevated.

In "Cyclops," Throwaway is announced as the winner of the race, and the outsider Bloom suffers innocently for a causal connexion for which he is not responsible. His hasty flight is clothed in the glory of Elijah's ascension, "clothed upon," "raiment" and "fair as the moon" (345) all pointing forward to the next chapter, which celebrates the coming of this Elijah as a throwing away of seed on Sandymount strand, an onanistic waste of the potential needed for the continuation of the race.

Both chapters have a bi-polar structure, in "Cyclops," as an alternating sequence of rudely clashing passages (fit expression of political strife and conflict), in "Nausicaa," in evident antithetical symmetry. Even the motif of the change of name and address is continued into "Nausicaa": "Might be a false name however like my and the address Dolphin's barn a blind" (372.36).

"BECAUSE IT'S ARRANGED" (374.6)

Both Cyclopean war and Nausicaan love were among the chords struck in the "Sirens" chapter, notably in the song *Love and War*, the stanzas of which are confused by Dollard and mused upon by Bloom (270.5, 8, 31). "The Croppy Boy" prepares us for rebellion and execution, the aria from *Martha* for Gerty's lure. The opening words of the latter set off a corresponding "endearing flow" (273.34), and the culminating "*Come!*" with its soaring imagery and orgiastic tension (275–276), anticipates events and emotions in "Nausicaa," which is after all a visual restaging of temptations manifested as aural charms in "Sirens."

Bloom's voyeuristic inclination was first exposed in the "Lotuseaters" chapter, with its varied possibilities of escape from reality. One vicarious satisfaction is the adoration of Martha Clifford, who corresponds with a Bloom she does not know and who likes a name he doesn't have. Like Gerty, she goes in for thinking (77.40), is interested in perfume, has difficulties with her vocabulary,[17] and inadvertently blows up a disturbing word into a "world" (77.37), equalling the hyperbolic generosity with which Gerty, of whom everyone "thought the world" (355.17),[18] verbally handles whole worlds of experience. Bloom lumps the two girls together on page 368, and Joyce's affair with Martha Fleischmann provides a cluster of extraneous links.

The chemist's assorted "ointments," "alabaster lilypots," and "lotions" toward the end of "Lotuseaters" (84), all recurring in "Nausicaa," might furnish the cosmetic ingredients for Gerty's makeup. Her florid expressions, the "embroidered floral design" of her present (359.2) and of the chapter's style are a kind of "language of flowers," like the one Bloom makes up after reading Martha's letter (78). Almost two pages (374–375) may be seen as a recall of events and motifs introduced in "Lotuseaters." Bloom even remembers that he has forgotten the lotion. It is Gerty, moreover, who with a Wildean touch literally approximates to the

Lotophagoi: "often she wondered why you couldn't eat something poetical like violets or roses" (352.20). The "organ" of "Lotuseaters," the genitals, becomes covertly central to "Nausicaa," Bloom's limpness being foreshadowed in the limp and languid floating flower with which the earlier chapter closes.

The "Proteus" chapter shares its setting, near Leahy's terrace, with "Nausicaa." Stephen, too, changes from one pose to another, but with him it is an intentional arrangement, while Gerty is determined by attitudes that she does not recognize *as* attitudes. Stephen's imitations are volitional, skilful re-creations, recalls of pretences and disguises. His thoughts are evoked in their vivid wayward fluctuations, with unique freshness and originality, at least in their startling combinations. The collage of his thoughts is conscious. Gerty, ineluctably visible, specializes in thinking too. She is "lost in thought" or, soon afterwards, "wrapt in thought" (354.27): this is precise; thinking for her is a becoming pose, to be used like drapery. As against the immediate contents of Stephen's thinking in "Proteus," for Gerty "thinking" is often an intransitive verb (see 354.18, etc.), an attitude familiar from so many paintings. She too tries her hand at "reading" non-verbal phenomena: "the story of a haunting sorrow was written on his face" (357.39), but this is hardly to be equated with trying to read the signatures of all things (Bloom comes closer to it in "All these rocks with lines and scars and letters," 381.34). She would not dream of bringing anything or anyone "beyond the veil" (48.36). No protean flux is caught in the sequence of essentially static pictures that constitute the first part of "Nausicaa."

"THERE FOR A CERTAIN PURPOSE" (355.29)

"Nausicaa" also looks forward to the next chapter. Its close, with the three times threefold call of "Cuckoo," leads directly into the evocation of Helios, with its three paragraphs of three sentences each. Nine is, of course, a significant number for the chapter of Birth. Holles street is associated by Bloom with the once-attentive nurse Callan (373.12; 385.27), who, along with Gerty, figures in the brief list of women attracted to Bloom on 16 June (722.28). The crime inveighed against in "Oxen of the Sun" has been committed in "Nausicaa." Bloom becomes, in Joyce's comments, what he has just wasted — sperm.[19] At the other end of the sterility-fertility axis, the "A" which Bloom attributed to himself in his writing in the sand, reappears as "Alpha, a ruby and triangled sign upon the forehead of Taurus" (414.40).

Of all the pastiches of the "Oxen of the Sun" chapter, the Dickensian paragraph on pages 420–421 comes closest to the style of Gerty's meditations. It abounds in emotional adjectives ("brave woman," "loving eyes," "her pretty head," etc.). Gerty's adolescent sentimentalities are carried over into motherhood. The mother, like Gerty, "reclines," but with "motherlight in her eyes." The mysterious embrace, when domesticized, is transformed into "lawful embraces." Gerty has set the tone for "a nice snug and cosy little homely house" (352.31), complete with tall husband and brekky and all the rest, the details being lovingly filled in by the eulogy of father Purefoy. Through his association with Catesby's cork lino, Gerty's father suggests the comforts of the ideal home ("always bright and cheery in the home," 355.9), while his drinking and gout reveal the actuality.

"THAT'S WHERE MOLLY CAN KNOCK SPOTS OFF THEM" (373.22)

Gerty and Molly Bloom, Nausicaa and Penelope, have some traits in common, and Molly is ubiquitous in Bloom's half of the chapter. Superstition, ignorance, and faulty grammar are common to both of them, as is a splendid inconsistency. Both begin their menstrual cycle. They set great store by their appearance and their clothes; they thrive on admiration; their thoughts circle around men. Bloom is able to assess this last aspect shrewdly, and his condensation "he, he and he" (371.9) summarizes one salient aspect both of Gerty's gush and of the gyrations of Molly's monologue. The scale is always reduced in the younger girl, who can muster fewer males than Molly. Her slim graceful figure and somewhat anaemic nature contrast with Molly's amplitude. Gerty looks away into the distance, or up at the sky, while Molly is earthy, even tellurian, stained, and, on the whole, horizontal. Gerty is only half reclined. Molly's coarseness expresses itself with gusto, even though there is a prudish streak in her too, but Gerty's finebred nature instinctively recoils from everything in the least indelicate.

For all that, their thinking and their language are often very similar. Compare Gerty's ". . . those cyclists showing off what they hadn't got" (358.15) with Molly's ". . . she didnt make much secret of what she hadnt" (750.22). They can be equally catty about members of their own sex and would feel contempt for each other. In many ways the style of "Penelope" is prefigured in "Nausicaa," many of the sentences of which string together without pause or punctuation,[20] and with the same lack of subordination: ". . . but those iron jelloids she had been taking of late had done her a world of good much better than the Widow Welch's female pills and she was much better of those discharges she used to get and that tired feeling" (348.15–18). This could be translated, with few changes, into the rhetoric of the last chapter. Gerty's diction (assuming that this would be her own) is characterized by one of the cardinal words of "Penelope," "because,"[21] which she uses abundantly and usually without any causal function: "But this was altogether different from a thing like that because there was all the difference because she could almost feel him draw her face to his and the first quick hot touch of his handsome lips" (366.4).

Molly, though attached to her own form of sentimentality, would not, however, be caught in Gerty's artificialities, having generally a good sense of what is spurious about others. She makes fun of euphemisms, prefers "a few simple words" to phrases from "the ladies letterwriter" (758), and Bloom remembers that she "twigged at once" that the man Bloom thought goodlooking "had a false arm" (372.1). She has a sharp eye for pretence, circumlocution, and evasive euphemisms. Her "Lord couldnt he say bottom right out and have done with it" (741.6) contrasts with the ripple of thrilled queasiness which even a diluted "beetoteetom" causes in Gerty (353.20).

"PERFECT PROPORTIONS" (350.32)

At a first glance the chapter (it is one of glances) appears bipartite, with distinctly contrasting, complementary halves. Gerty's outlook is characterized by self-inflated infatuations beyond critical questioning, by hyperbole, self-deception, and a basically timid selectivity. There is an upward tendency in the first half, with altitudes as diverse as the promontory of Howth, a castle built of sand, amatory and social aspirations and pretensions, glances at the flying fireworks, at the Blessed Sacrament raised in the benediction service, at a view high up offered by Gerty. The imagery is lofty, and an accumulation of heights such as "queenly *hauteur*, . . . higharched instep, . . . a gentlewoman of high degree, . . . how to be tall increase your height" are to be found in the space of a few lines (348.31–349.9). Language is correspondingly exalted, as though it too had to be kept from touching base ground.

In Bloom's section, eyes, with language, are kept nearer the ground, over which Bloom bends, and on which he writes. He is very aware of the rocks they are sitting on as part of his present reality: "Bad for you, dear, to sit on that stone. Brings on white fluxions" (376.30). His monologue is interspersed with the customary objectifying qualifiers, "but," "all the same," "on the other hand," "look at it other way round." Where Gerty is unthinkingly posing, he does a lot of his usual "supposing." His mind is, of course, revealed to us after the orgasmic release, when he is again in control of his emotions. The effect is a sobering down, a reduction of things to their everyday dimension.

The boundless generalities of Gerty's wishful reveries become concrete trifles. The "infinite store of mercy," noted in Gerty's eyes (367.13), becomes more manageable in Bloom's gratitude for "small mercies" (368.21). The chapter is structured by such contrasts, as when the sweet and homely cosiness of connubial life imagined in the first section is set against Bloom's *précis*: ". . . till they settle down to potwalloping and papa's pants will soon fit Willy and fuller's earth for the baby when they hold him out to do ah ah" (373.4). The earthiness is unmistakable, and it is the "setting *down*" that is typical of the second half of "Nausicaa." It is

exemplified in the baby's "ah ah," so different from the high-pitched "O!s"
that go before (367.1) or from the evasive terms that are used for similar
bodily processes of Baby Boardman. Again, we may compare the various
perfections that adorn Gerty—showing off "her slim graceful figure to
perfection" (350.16), her "perfect proportions" (350.32), her rosebud
mouth, "Greekly perfect" (348.21),—with Bloom's aside that a "defect is
ten times worse in a woman" (368.3). The first half presents a rich palette
of colours, especially blue but with liberal daubs of scarlet, crimson, rose,
coralpink, etc., against which the second half appears grey, and Bloom
"off colour" (372.29).

"A KIND OF LANGUAGE BETWEEN US" (372.35)

Despite numerous contrasts of that kind, the chapter is not the simple
dichotomized structure it appears to be at first blush (it is a chapter of
blushes too). Not all the colours are reserved for the first half, but those
toward the end of the chapter are less visualized, more abstractly thought
about (376.23). Not all the ups are scattered over the first half. Bloom too
looks up at rockets, at the stars and the moon, if with a weary mind.
Conversely, Gerty's section has its downs, the "fallen women" (364.34) and
the "fine tumble" she wishes on Cissy Caffrey (359.34) (significantly to
dethrone her from the elevation of "her high crooked French heels"). Most
poignantly, her own accident occurred "coming *down* Dalkey hill"
(364.21—not, of course, Gerty's italics). The general pattern, then, is
mirrored as a succession of smaller movements within either section, so
that each part potentially contains the whole.

The two halves are also intricately dovetailed, separated by a definite
break and yet joined by a gliding transition. When Gerty's gush gives way
to dewy melting, there follows a quiet paragraph which temporarily
blends Bloom and Gerty. Both seem painted by the same painter's brush,
and he "coloured like a girl" (367.8). Even Bloom's physical position
becomes identical with hers: "He was leaning back against the rock
behind. Leopold Bloom (for it is he) . . ." (367.8). His identity is revealed
for the first time (in a novelistic fashion reminiscent of 348.8), and he is
judged by the morality appropriate to this kind of literature. But there is a
drop in tone, and one sentence—"At it again?"—reached down to Bloom's
half. The accustomed pitch is immediately resumed and Bloom is stylistically approximated to Gerty: "A fair unsullied soul had called to him and,
wretch that he was, how had he answered?"

The opposite occurs in the next long paragraph, describing Gerty's
farewell greeting, in which she briefly touches the ground of typically
Bloomesque prose: "Wonder if he's too far to" (367.27), one bit of direct
inner monologue, with the typical trailing off. But she at once rises again,
literally and stylistically: "She rose. . . . She drew herself up to her full

height . . . ," and prepares her exit. Her actual movements bring her in touch with the earth, and her walk is expressed in the plainest possible language, without artificial embellishment: "Slowly without looking back she went down the uneven strand. . . ." Only when she sublimates the awkwardness of her gait into a stylized pose is there a last, short-lived ascent: "She walked with a certain quiet dignity characteristic of her . . . ," but by now the line of vision is clearly directed at her feet and Bloom's sudden realization plunks the narrative down with a final jolt: "Tight boots? No. She's lame! O!" Even the "O" conveys a fall. From now on the language jogs along in relatively short, halting steps.

The transition has been prepared for in another interlacing counter-movement. In spite of appearances, the forced deportment of Gerty's style has been felt as essentially lame all along, and correspondingly the limping procession of Bloom's thoughts emerges as basically more dignified.

"IT WAS ALL THINGS COMBINED" (372.31)

Nor is Bloom's half all of a piece. Though it would have to be read aloud with a level voice, it has its ups and downs. Even the narrative is lifted from Bloom's perspective at some points, notably when a "lost long candle [wandering] up the sky" (379.6) raises the point of view and brings about a sweeping motion of the camera for a survey ranging from the streets of Sandymount across the bay to Howth Head, re-personified, as in the opening shot (346.4). The style, too, is raised and broadened, reverting to the novelette manner, with pretty pictures and a touch of Thomas Moore's glow-worm, until the lighthouse of Kish far away, winking at Mr Bloom, brings the perspective, along with the tone of the tale, back to Bloom's level. For one paragraph the narrative has risen above Bloom's head, in a "tryst" (379.10) that is also stylistic.

The first postorgasmic rocket, at 372.22, also widens the perspective to take in the party of girls and children in the distance, resulting in a quickening of Bloom's pulse and a little climactic flutter "Will she? Watch! Watch! See!" imitative of the central outburst of the chapter and, in its wording and rhythm, echoing the morning scene outside the Grosvenor hotel (74.27).

With Bloom's dozing off at the end, the style shifts again, to become unpunctuated associative alogical dream language (382.13). Afterwards the narrative splits up into three parallel strands, separated by the voice of the cuckoo clock, a temporal divider for an action going on in three different places. A short Bloom passage is followed by an evenly descriptive bit relating to the priest's house, before a last jerk brings the tone back to Gerty's more homely vein and a style that virtually closes the embrace indicated in the opening lines of the chapter.

"HER HIGH NOTES AND HER LOW NOTES" (374.30)

"Nausicaa" is technically complex, numerous discordant ruptures disturbing the basic division into two main parts. Not even the style of Gerty's half is as monotonous or uniform as critics have assumed. Like "Cyclops" and "Oxen of the Sun," "Nausicaa" is a compendium of moods and styles, though the spectrum is narrower. Apart from flat descriptive passages, baby talk, a sermon, a recipe, and other variants, there is Gerty's own palette, of which it may be useful to distinguish such sub-categories as:

"Luxuriant clusters" (349.15)

— the sweetly romantic passages that we usually consider the trade mark of the first half of "Nausicaa." "Mayhap it was this, the love that might have been, that lent to her softlyfeatured face at whiles a look, tense with suppressed meaning, that imparted a strange yearning tendency to the beautiful eyes, a charm few could resist" (348.39). Their features are precious, elevated diction, pretentious and threadbare metaphors, ample adornment. Few nouns lack decorative epithets: "There was an innate refinement, a languid queenly *hauteur*, . . . her delicate hands and higharched instep . . ." (348.30). Such lines cannot simply be read aloud, they have to be declaimed.

"Endearing ways" (346.22)

— a more homely sentimental vein, with less variety in its imagery, but full of feeling: ". . . he would give his dear little wifey a good hearty hug and gaze for a moment deep down into her eyes" (352.34).

"Sumptuous confection" (351.24)

— the fashion page of the women's magazine: "She wore a coquettish little love of a hat . . ." (350.16).

"Madame Vera Verity" (349.4)

— the column of practical advice: "Then there was blushing scientifically cured" (349.8).

"Persuasive power" (346.39)

— advertisement slogans: "the fabric that caresses the skin" (366.27).

"Little tiffs" (348.27)

— more straightforward girlish thoughts that often move at a brisk pace with a touch of vicious directness: ". . . irritable little gnat she was" (360.37).

"Unmentionables" (347.24)

— at times Gerty's voice drops to evasive vagueness when an unpalatable or unladylike subject is bypassed in the flattest way, with phrases like "when there for a certain purpose," "that thing must be coming," "without all that other," "the other thing," "a thing like that."

Such styles and tones and other variants that we might mention could be arranged in a kind of hierarchy. The most conspicuous effusions of (what Gerty would consider) poetical (and we condescendingly classify as) *kitsch* occur as high points in the narrative rather than as a continual performance. It is difficult to remain in the upper register throughout.

"KEEP THAT THING UP FOR HOURS" (374.22)

Stylistically, and psychologically, there is a strenuous attempt to sustain that high tone together with repeated failures "to keep it up" (those words are also implied by Bloom's recall of the song about Mary who "lost the pin of her drawers," 368.38, thematically in tune). The different stylistic elevations are juxtaposed in free and surprising discords, with comic drops and new flights. The tone keeps changing within a limited range so that the chapter is one of those characterized by the marvellously attuned wrong note. The ups and downs can be seen as sequences of tumescence and detumescence, pathos and bathos, or inflations and deflations (Bloom remembers blown-up phrases from "Aeolus," "moonlight silver effulgence" — 370.17; "Nausicaa," like "Aeolus," depends on airy distensions; Gerty's figure is composed of rhetorical ones).

Some of the shifts in the exposition illustrate this (significantly, "Nausicaa" is the only chapter that has an exposition). The opening description of the *dramatis personae*, not ostensibly lofty, still aims at a stately pace and is clearly literary: "The three girl friends were seated on the rocks, enjoying the evening air which was fresh but not too chilly" (346.11). Somewhere around the middle the tone flops; "seated" does not quite match the conversational "but not too chilly"; the implied situational contexts jar, if only slightly (another change from the clashing strong contrasts in "Cyclops"). Some readjustments will occur later in the reading, when the epithet "girl friends" will be undercut by the give and talk of girlish gall and by Edy Boardman's speaking "none too amiably" (347.41). Even if an identical phrase is repeated, such as "on the rocks," it can assume a baser meaning: "when we were on the rocks in Holles street," Bloom remembers (369.39). This sense can retrospectively obtain in the opening scene too. Gerty's life is on the rocks.

While the strained-after grace of the sentence quoted above is not, perhaps, decisively marred, there is nevertheless a chill. A bit of fresh air, real air, has interfered with the air of refinement. All through the chapter, natural or common things, like "stones and bits of wood," or else parts of the physical (not figurative) body (". . . but it was only the end of her nose," 351.31) have a way of breaking the spell.

After "chilly," the effort to elevate the diction is evident in redundancy: "Many a time and oft were they wont. . . ." A tiny drop follows, "to come there," and a gentle rise, "to that favourite nook," and another descent into a more homely strain, "to have a cosy chat," then a spurring of the poetic impulse: "beside the sparkling waves. . . ." But after this sparkle we are in for a trivialized tumble — ". . . to discuss matters feminine." And so the chapter stumbles forward and tension mounts, the stylistic heights grow dizzier, and the ecstatic flights correspondingly longer. Toward the centre the sentences swell and punctuation decreases (every comma or period is, after all, a stop to fetch breath and a brief touching of the ground), until we reach the magnificent sweep of the climax and are ready for the final descent and the last drop.

"JUST CHANGES WHEN YOU'RE ON THE TRACK" (368.39)

The stylistic metamorphoses, some rapid, others gliding, need not be interpreted as merely vertical shifts. The language could be recorded on a sort of oscillogram, but it would not be simple to articulate the discernment of modes of language which we believe we can grasp intuitively. The flexibility of the style, with its odd traverses and sudden bounds, contrasts pointedly with Gerty MacDowell's inflexible fixedness and her unconscious and tacit acceptance of the several poses of which the styles are the outward and visible form. The constant re-focussing obliges the reader to sharpen his sense of the disparities (some inherently comical) and the perpetual clashes between illusory disguises and chilly reality. Each new attitude is apt to invalidate the previous one. But even within one given stylistic level, the metaphors often jostle each other incongruously: "that vile decoction which has ruined so many hearths and homes had cast its shadow over her childhood days . . ." (354.18). And Gerty is able to move unconcernedly from the "scorn immeasurable" that emanates from her eyes, to "one look of measured scorn," on the same page (362.17, 41; the more liberal, unmeasured quantity, by the way, is reserved for the female rival).

Scenic changes implicit in the stylistic and metaphorical potential of this chapter's language will be taken literally in "Circe," where they are grotesquely staged. Stylistic guises adapted to the current themes are, of course, the distinctive mark of *Ulysses*; in the later chapters the method is intensified by formal intricacy, and the adaptability of the style, corresponding to the mercurial assumption of expedient roles, may perhaps be understood as a reflection of Odyssean tactics. Odysseus is known for his versatility: he cunningly suits his language, form of address, and guise to the immediate purpose and has on occasion recourse to impersonation (at times divine agencies help along with a touch of transfiguration). When he appears to Nausicaa from the bushes, he is in fact quickly considering alternative approaches to win her over and decides on sweet words and the pretence that she is a goddess, queen, or bride.[22] (Gerty's presumptions are similar.)

To change one's voice according to the situation is common to Odysseus and to *Ulysses*, whose true hero is language. The language of the book is *polytropos*: ingenious, resourceful, resilient, of many turns — wiles or tropes.[23]

At the same time, the style chosen for Gerty's parts (and within the framework of her own ambitions), the cliché and the shopsoiled charms of stereotyped fiction or commercial slickness, is manifestly unable to characterize anything outside itself. It reflects only its own vacuity, it hardly illuminates or communicates, its glitter is narcissistic, its essence is self-gratification.

"ALL PUT ON BEFORE THIRD PERSON" (374.13)

Montage helps Joyce to convey both the interior landscape of Gerty's mind and her environment. The question is whether the various items fit together. To the reader's delight, they do not. Gerty's fashions and styles do not do what articles of clothing should do — they do not "match" (which is one of the thematic words: "with caps to match," 346.22; "to match that chenille," 350.19; "blue to match," 366.15; "As God made them He matched them," 373.32). Thematic references to fashion are highly appropriate. Fashion is a matter of putting something on, of a careful array of different elements to create a type, its success depending on taste and discernment. It is also changeable. Fashion and cosmetics serve to touch up the appearance, and Gerty's appearance is put together from many little touches. We are privileged to experience her charms along with the means by which she will achieve them: "Her hands were of finely veined alabaster with tapering fingers and as white[24] as lemon juice and queen of ointments could make them" (348.21).

We are also treated to a close-up of Gerty's mind and, simultaneously, are made aware of the forces that helped to shape it. The first half of the chapter is a novelette conveying the de-formation of Gerty MacDowell: what she is and what made her what she is. The kind of writing here parodied would lead to that kind of thinking, which, in turn, if it could articulate itself, would produce that kind of culture. In one way, Gerty is indistinguishable from the forces that determine her. That through such a mélange of set pieces and trash, she does emerge as a person in her own right, however limited, is a triumph of indirect characterization.

"PIQUANT TILT" (353.27)

Part of the humour of the paradoxically slanted episode may result from reading certain phrases as though they belonged to a context different from the apparent one. Each verbal unit seems to belong to a number of situational frameworks, just as the whole of *Ulysses* can be viewed within naturalistic, psychological, symbolic, Homeric, and numerous other contexts. Some of the turns language takes are inversely appropriate. Gerty is introduced as "in very truth as fair a specimen of winsome Irish girlhood as one could wish to see" (348.10). She is precisely such a *specimen*, by definition something selected as typical of its class, by etymology something to look at, something in fact that one might be content to see, as Bloom is, wishing for little other contact. There *is* "suppressed meaning" in her look (348.41), she has "raised the devil" in Bloom (360.30). The "studied attitude" of the lady in the almanac picture (355.26) epiphanizes Gerty's own posing and describes a scenic principle of the "Nausicaa" chapter. Not only does Gerty wrap herself "in thought," she is really "lost in thought" (348.10). It seems appropriate to offer "A penny for [her] thoughts" (360.40).

By expressing unmitigated disdain for the cliché, for *kitsch*, and for a victim like Gerty MacDowell (or Bloom's inept endeavours), we also, of course, are adopting a Gertyan pose, pretending to remain perpetually above their inefficacious lure. But the lure affects us too, on and off. Romantic *kitsch* in "Nausicaa" (or in "Sirens") also serves to embody the motif of seductiveness, to which most readers are not wholly immune. There is a fascination about that glamour too, an appeal that we hesitate to acknowledge. In fact, clichés could not have become popular but for some inherent charm, however cheap. The *Portrait* expressed this lure in all its elusive complexity. That Joyce (like the best of us) was attracted to *kitsch*, in music, in painting, and in literature is fairly obvious but less relevant than the skill with which he knew how to work on our susceptibilities, seducing us and at the same time allowing us to laugh about the tricks that are being used. Our laughter sometimes becomes a bit ostentatious and the clichés in which *we* give voice to distaste for the literary cliché testify to the intricacies of structure and tone, and, finally, to the complexity of response that is closely tied up with human motivation — difficult to trace and even more elusive of evaluation.

The axis along which we might measure our own attraction or repulsion is only one among the many subtly graduated scales that make up the network of multiple foci that is *Ulysses*. There is a protean quality about "Nausicaa" too. Its simple outlines and the even-textured appearance are deceptive. The surface alone reveals itself as jagged as the uneven strand, "stones and bits of wood . . . and slippy seaweed" (367.37) — full of ups and downs. For *this* relief, too, much thanks.

Notes

1. *Evening Telegraph*, Thursday, 16 June 1904, p. 2, column 4.

2. P. W. Joyce, in *A Social History of Ancient Ireland*, Dublin, 1920, has a chapter on "Turning 'Deisol,' or Sunwise" (vol. I, p. 301). The word *deisol* or, in modern spelling, *deiseal, deisil*, is pronounced "deshil."

3. Ellmann, p. 462; Frank Budgen, *Myselves When Young*, London, 1970, pp. 189–194.

4. Heinrich Straumann, in *Letters*, II, pp. 430–431.

5. A. Walton Litz, *The Art of James Joyce*, London, 1961, writes that "*Nausicaa*, begun in Zürich in the autumn of 1919, was finished in Trieste early in 1920" (p. 144).

6. *Letters*, II, pp. 431–432. These and other parallels between Joyce's letters to Martha Fleischmann and phrases in "Nausicaa" were pointed out in my review of Richard Ellmann's edition of the *Letters* in *Neue Zürcher Zeitung* (Zürich), 26 February 1967. Other biographical sources are to be found in the unpublished letters to Nora of 1909.

7. "Symbolic Juxtaposition" in *JJQ*, V, 3 (Spring 1968), 276–278.

8. The same words mean erection to Molly: that "big red brute of a thing" (742.3).

9. For example in *Thom's Official Directory* for the year 1905, Alex. Thom & Co., Dublin, 1905, p. 1667.

10. Bloom is carrying the *Sweets of Sin*, to complete the missing traits in Gerty's presentation: seduction and cliché language. There is another inversion of roles here: it is Gerty who appears occupied with solid, down-to-earth matter, Catesby's cork lino, meant for the ordinary home, while Bloom is after illusory wish-fulfillment through the written word.

11. The Douay version does not use "seeing," but another favourite word of Gerty's: "*because* I know not man." See p. 301.

12. Gilbert, p. 281.

13. Also heralded by Buck Mulligan, at 212.35; it is Mulligan too who has introduced masturbation as a major theme connected with literature.

14. One passage from such a parody, indiscriminately scattering loveliness over the scenery, anticipates the style of the first part of "Nausicaa": "Lovely maidens sit in close proximity to the roots of the lovely trees singing the most lovely songs while they play with all kinds of lovely objects . . ." (294.7).

15. Even the willow returns in "Nausicaa": "Weeping willow" (377.32).

16. Joyce writes about the use of "bloody" to Grant Richards: ". . . it is strange that he should object more strongly to a profane use of the Virgin than to a profane use of the name of God" (5 May 1906, *Letters*, II, 134). Stuart Gilbert, perhaps prompted by Joyce, refers to it as "Our Lady's adjective" (p. 255).

17. Both mistake singular forms for plural ones: "my patience are exhausted" (78.8); "the perfume of those incense" (357.25).

18. ". . . those iron jelloids . . . had done her a world of good" (348.15); "she would give worlds to be in the privacy of her own familiar chamber" (351.14 — it might be simpler just to leave and go to her chamber); "She would have given worlds to know what it was" (357.40); "Dearer than the whole world would she be to him" (364.25); "the only man in all the world for her" (365.4). Joyce is also parodying his own macrocosmic aspirations in writing *Ulysses*.

19. "Bloom is the spermatozoon, the hospital the womb . . ." (*Letters*, I, 140).

20. Note that the sentence which introduces Gerty on pp. 252–253 has little punctuation in its first part and none in its second.

21. Penelope's four cardinal points being the female breasts, arse, womb and cunt, expressed by the words *because, bottom, . . . woman, yes*" (*Letters*, I, 170).

22. *Odyssey*, VI, 141–185.

23. Fritz Senn, "Book of Many Turns," *JJQ*, X, 1 (Fall 1972), 29–46.

24. The whiteness of Gerty's hands, and the "snowy slender arms" (366.37) may also owe something to Homer's Nausicaa: "*Nausikaa leukolenos*" (*Odyssey*, VI, 101), "Nausikaa of the white arms," Butcher and Lang translate it (p. 95). A number of Gerty's traits can be traced back to Homer.

The World: "Nausikaa"   Marilyn French[*]

From a world entirely male in its occupants and concerns, we move in Nausikaa to one exclusively female. Barney Kiernan's contains a world that is not only male but crudely so, pervaded by the worst stereotypes of maleness: violent language, bravado, aggressive attitudes toward everything, interest only in aggressive activities, in short, what has come to be called *machismo*. There is no compassion or love in such a world; sex is not love but crime (adultery) or an aggressive, self-proving act ("organise her," "corned beef"). Even moderate statements, like those of Nolan and Cunningham, get drowned in the storm of hostility. The two expressions of gentler feeling—Doran's and Bloom's—are seen as ridiculous and somewhat shameful aberrations from proper masculinity. The world shown in Cyclops is essentially antilife.

Nausikaa presents the feminine complement to that environment. It contains a world in which every action and emotion is coated in a frilly, concealing cloak of seeming gentleness, gentility, and love. It is pervaded by the worst stereotypes of femaleness: euphemistic language, coyness, romantically idealizing attitudes toward everything, and interest only in self-image. It too is essentially antilife, because it disguises and denies reality. While it is possible to say that Cyclops perverts reality and Nausikaa idealizes it, both constrict: one can be choked to death as well by a lace scarf as by a pair of brutal hands.

There is no question of Joyce's accuracy: the world of Gerty Mac-Dowell is as true and recognizable as that of Barney Kiernan's pub. Things have not changed much in the fifty years since *Ulysses* was completed. Both scenes reflect still living ideals. Many people, if forced to articulate their standards for male and female behavior, would uphold the modes of behavior and points of view that are examined—and satirized—in Cyclops and Nausikaa. In fact, both scenes slander actual men and women:

*From *The Book as World: James Joyce's "Ulysses"* (Cambridge: Harvard University Press, 1976), 156–68. Reprinted by permission of the Charlotte Sheedy Literary Agency, Inc.

"That's not life for men and women" (333) could as truthfully be said of the first half of Nausikaa as of Cyclops. It is Bloom, "the most inadequate Messiah imaginable," as Kenner calls him, who challenges and defies both these constricting and falsifying ideals.[1]

The subject of Nausikaa is love, sexuality, but primarily female sexuality and the concerns clustered around it: clothes, children, house-wifery, marriage, spinsterhood. Bloom and Gerty think about the same topics, but in very different ways. The narrator is detached from and above all three centers: Gerty, the church service, and Bloom. The style in which Gerty is presented is parodic, satirizing commercial language, particularly in advertisements aimed at women and in "women's" novels and magazines.

The technique in the first part of Nausikaa parodies by imitation, that is, the prose imitates faithfully, reproduces accurately, the style of what used to be called "women's" literature. The comedy and ludicrousness arise from the Rabelaisian technique of accumulation. So many details are heaped on details that the whole becomes ludicrous. Gerty's consideration of "eyebrowleine" (349), for instance, is not a parody but direct imitation of the language of the advertisement of cosmetics. The exaggeration, repetition, and incongruity that characterize Joyce's parodies in Cyclops do not exist here. The parody occurs as a result of the simple accumulation of details. By accumulating many such items and by slanting his presentation of them to emphasize the goal of concealment and disguise that is implicit in such advertisements, Joyce satirizes not only the commercial language but the assumptions and attitudes that underlie it. Again the technique has a multiple effect: it builds a kind of language into a way of life, exposes it, and in the process explodes it.

Gerty is pitiful because the attitudes she holds are those her society has told her are good: she tries to be the "sterling good daughter," the "ministering angel" (355) she believes she ought to be. It is difficult to decipher, through the concealing style, what sort of person Gerty "actu-ally" is: she is a Maria, a Conmee, shrouding certain areas of reality from her own awareness. Among these hidden gulfs are her own anger and impatience, her sexual desires, and her envy of other girls not impaired as she is.

Concealment is the essential quality of the technique in the first part of the chapter. The style works to conceal, and it points to concealment as the basic moral stance of the literature and ways of thinking it satirizes. During her musings, Gerty considers the subjects of physical violence, alcoholism, defecation, menstruation, and masturbation by both men and women, but the language in which she approaches these subjects makes close reading necessary if one is to realize what she is thinking about. Analogous to Joyce's use of language to disguise or transform violence in Cyclops is his use of it here to conceal the force of profound areas of experience on Gerty's consciousness, and consequently on ours. The significance of Gerty's experience of life is snarled and hidden in a knot of petticoat strings.

Her feelings toward her father—surely a profound area of our experience of life—never emerge from the shroud of clichés and devoirs in which they are wrapped:

> Had her father only avoided the clutches of the demon drink, by taking the pledge or those powders the drink habit cured in Pearson's Weekly, she might now be rolling in her carriage. (354)

> Nay, she had even witnessed in the home circle deeds of violence caused by intemperance and had seen her own father, a prey to the fumes of intoxication, forget himself completely for if there was one thing of all things that Gerty knew it was the man who lifts his hand to a woman save in the way of kindness deserves to be branded as the lowest of the low. (354)

> Poor father! With all his faults she loved him still when he sang . . . and they had stewed cockles and lettuce . . . for supper. (354)

Dignam's death is held up as a cautionary example: "her mother said to him to let that be a warning to him for the rest of his days and he couldn't even go to the funeral on account of the gout" (355). All of this sounds suspiciously like a less than peaceful domestic life. It suggests that Gerty might have some rather strong feelings about her father. But she is so busy saying what she ought to say and feeling what she ought to feel that she is able to conceal from herself truths that might be unpleasant.

The outhouse is "that place where she never forgot every fortnight the chlorate of lime" and to which she repairs "for a certain purpose." She never thinks of it by name, and disguises it by hanging in it "the grocer's christmas almanac the picture of halcyon days." Her ways of thinking about the outhouse bring into larger perspective Joyce's reason for including in such detail the scene of Bloom in the outhouse in Calypso. That scene, matter-of-factly described even to the extent of Bloom wiping himself with part of the prize story (which is funny in its own right and a wry comment on the story, as Beaufoy indignantly points out in Circe), symbolizes Bloom's mental acceptance of body and bodily functions. Gerty manages not to have to think directly about defecation even when she is performing it: she sits looking "dreamily . . . and felt her own arms that were white and soft just like hers with the sleeves back and thought about those times" (355).

For Gerty, menstruation is "that" or "that thing":

> He told her that time when she told him about that in confession crimsoning up to the roots of her hair for fear he could see, not to be troubled because that was only the voice of nature and we were all subject to nature's laws, he said, in this life and that that was no sin

because that came from the nature of woman instituted by God, he said,
and that Our Blessed Lady herself said to the archangel Gabriel be it
done unto me according to Thy Word. (358)

She felt a kind of sensation rushing all over her and she knew by the feel
of her scalp and that irritation against her stays that that thing must be
coming on because the last time too was when she clipped her hair on
account of the moon. (361)

Beyond the self-deception involved in her thoughts about blushing and her
mistaking sexual excitement for premenstrual sensation, beyond the fear,
ignorance, guilt, and superstition implicit in these thoughts, lies the
appalling fact that Gerty must *confess* the onset of menstruation, that no
one else has ever discussed it with her. That she cannot think of it by name
is characteristic of her way of dealing with reality.

Although she is a virgin and ignorant of sex, she knows perfectly well
what Bloom is about. There are frequent references to his hands in his
pockets; it is one realistic detail that she sees, selects:

His hands and face were working and a tremor went over her . . . there
was no one to see only him and her [the word "no-one" occurs frequently
in this section, on pp. 365, 366, and in a different context, 363]. (365)

She seemed to hear the panting of his heart, his hoarse breathing,
because she knew about the passion of men like that, hot-blooded,
because Bertha Supple told her once in dead secret and made her swear
she'd never about the gentleman lodger that was staying with them out
of the Congested Districts Board that had pictures cut out of papers of
those skirtdancers and highkickers and she said he used to do something
not very nice that you could imagine sometimes in the bed. (365–366)

But if one were in fact as ignorant about sex as Gerty pretends to be, how
could one imagine masturbation at all? Gerty knows what happens in the
sexual act and has masturbated herself: "Besides there was absolution so
long as you didn't do the other thing before being married and there ought
to be women priests that would understand without your telling out and
Cissy Caffrey too sometimes had that dreamy kind of dreamy look in her
eyes so that she too, my dear, and Winny Rippingham so mad about
actor's photographs and besides it was on account of that other thing
coming on the way it did" (366). Some place in her head, Gerty has firm
ideas of the meanings of "that," "that thing," "the other thing," and
something even more amorphous.

In the same way that these subjects are obscured and their nature
concealed, large blocks of experience are sugared over and romanticized.
Joyce underlines the unreality of Gerty's notions by having Bloom muse on
the same subjects. Contrast the two on the nature of marriage and
housewifery:

She would care for him with creature comforts too for Gerty was womanly wise and knew that a mere man liked that feeling of hominess. Her griddlecakes done to a golden-brown hue and queen Ann's pudding of delightful creaminess had won golden opinions from all because she had a lucky hand also for lighting a fire . . . and they would have a beautifully appointed drawingroom with pictures and engravings and the photograph of grandpapa Giltrap's lovely dog Garryowen that almost talked, it was so human, and chintz covers for the chairs and that silver toastrack in Clery's summer jumble sales like they have in rich houses. . . . They would go on the continent for their honeymoon . . . and then, when they settled down in a nice snug and cosy little homely house, every morning they would both have brekky, simple but perfectly served, for their own two selves and before he went out to business he would give his dear little wifey a good hearty hug and gaze for a moment deep down into her eyes. (352)

Sad however because it lasts only a few years till they settle down to potwalloping and papa's pants will soon fit Willy and fullers' earth for the baby when they hold him out to do ah ah. No soft job. Saves them. Keeps them out of harm's way. Nature. Washing child, washing corpse. Dignam. Children's hands always round them. Cocoanut skulls, monkeys, not even closed at first, sour milk in their swaddles and tainted curds . . . Worst of all at night. . . . Husband rolling in drunk, stink of pub off him like a polecat. Have that in your nose in the dark, whiff of stale boose. Then ask in the morning: was I drunk last night? Bad policy however to fault the husband. Chickens come home to roost. They stick by one another like glue. Maybe the woman's fault also. (373)

Gerty's main interest after herself, however, is romance, romance as a scented, sweatless, rickless version of sex. She gazes at Bloom, romanticizing:

Till then they had only exchanged glances of the most casual but now under the brim of her new hat she ventured a look at him and the face that met her gaze there in the twilight, wan and strangely drawn, seemed to her the saddest she had ever seen. (356)

Here was that of which she had so often dreamed. It was he who mattered and there was joy on her face because she wanted him because she felt instinctively that he was like no-one else. (358)

Joyce allows no subject to pass without irony, and here, despite her deceitful ways of thinking and seeing, Gerty is seeing a true thing that no one else in *Ulysses* sees: Bloom *is* sad. And her musings on his foreignness are a parallel to Molly's answer when Bloom asks her why she chose him: "Because you were so foreign from the others" (380). If one seeks for the "whole" truth, one must include even a Gerty MacDowell. Gerty's picture of Bloom nevertheless provides an amusing contrast to his own self-image:

No prince charming is her beau ideal to lay a rare and wondrous love at her feet but rather a manly man with a strong quiet face who had not found his ideal, perhaps his hair slightly flecked with grey. (351)

She could see at once by his dark eyes and his pale intellectual face that he was a foreigner, the image of the photo she had of Martin Harvey, the matinée idol . . . but she could not see whether he had an aquiline nose or a slightly *retroussé* from where he was sitting. (357)

Saw something in me. Wonder what. Sooner have me as I am than some poet chap with bearsgrease, plastery hair lovelock over his dexter optic. . . . Ought to attend to my appearance my age. Didn't let her see me in profile. Still, you never know. Pretty girls and ugly men marrying. Beauty and the beast. Besides I can't be so if Molly. (369)

Gerty's musings on sex are funniest of all (italics mine):

If she saw that magic lure in his eyes there would be no holding back for her. Love laughs at locksmiths. She would make the great sacrifice. *Her every effort would be to share his thoughts.* Dearer than the whole world would she be to him and gild his days with happiness. . . . But even if — what then? Would it make a very great difference? From everything in the least indelicate her finebred nature instinctively recoiled. She loathed that sort of person, the fallen women off the accommodation walk beside the Dodder . . . *degrading the sex and being taken up to the police station.* No, no: not that. They would be just good friends like a big brother and sister without all that other *in spite of the conventions of Society with a big ess.* . . . Heart of mine! She would follow her dream of love, the dictates of her heart that told her he was her all in all, the only man in all the world for her for love was the master guide. Nothing else mattered. Come what might she would be wild, untrammelled, free. (364–365)

Free, wild, defiant toward the conventions of society, she will fight her way through to be just good friends. Again, however, Gerty is putting her finger on a bit of truth: such a friendship does defy the conventions of some segments of society.

Gerty really believes masturbation to be preferable to intercourse: "besides there was absolution so long as you didn't do the other thing before being married." Such an attitude is probably inevitable in a society that regards sex as sinful. In earlier chapters, the theme of onanism is tied to solipsism; here it is tied to narcissism. The root of both is likely the same: sexual guilt. For Gerty's sense of values about sex is not a result of her narcissism; both her narcissism and her sexual values are symptoms of the constricted world in which she breathes. Vain, stupid, dishonest, and mean though she is, that she is also poignant and pathetic is a result of our sense of her as a victim, like Dilly, of the thin, unnourishing air she lives in. The most crucial and indicative of Gerty's thoughts is her brief allusion to her lameness: "The years were slipping by for her, one by one, and but for that one shortcoming she knew she need fear no competition and that was an accident coming down Dalkey hill and she always tried to conceal it" (364). But what kind of mind would imagine such a thing possible? How can one conceal a limp? Gerty's handling of a real misfortune reveals an ingrained habit of concealment and exposes the underlying attitudes of the society that has taught her what she is supposed to be, for Gerty has not mind enough to penetrate that pale.

Henry James once discussed realism in fiction by using the metaphor of a balloon that rises with imagination but must always be somehow anchored to earth.[2] Bloom's prose hits us like the fresh air we encounter as our very tenuously anchored balloon descends safely to earth. Yet the subjects he thinks about are the same as those Gerty considers.

It is not possible to distinguish whether the subject of this episode is sexuality or women, because the two are completely bound up. The focus is on women, but in all areas — clothing, body, relationships with other women, women as children, virgins, nuns, married, mothers, widows — women are seen in their sexual aspect. Even Lizzie Twigg, who was actually a poet of sorts, is glanced at only with regard to her attractiveness to men. I suspect that for Joyce women had identity only as sexual beings, that is, they were defined exclusively by the sexual roles they occupied. Certainly that is the approach in this chapter and also in the rest of the novel.

Throughout this episode, Bloom riffles through a host of theories and old wives' tales about women's sexuality, menstruation, virginity, but even when his information is false or shaky, he looks directly at his subject. Gerty's thoughts about clothing are amusingly different from Bloom's, yet they are based on the same premise — of which Gerty is unconscious — that its use is for illusion in sexual attraction. Bloom's thoughts about women's relationships with each other are verified by Gerty's feelings about her friends and her perception of their feelings about her. She is probably accurate in her estimate of their feelings; Bloom thinks "the others inclined to give her an odd dig" (369). Bloom wonders about her motivation in flirting with him in a humorous contrast to her "literary" romanticization and shows himself to be almost uniquely without vanity: "She must have been thinking of someone else all the time. What harm?" (371).

Beneath all his thoughts lies Bloom's sense of sexuality as ordained in nature, as an inevitable, undeniable, and natural, if troublesome, part of every experience. The crux of his section is the passage on magnetism:

> Very strange about my watch. Wristwatches are always going wrong. Wonder is there any magnetic influence between the person because that was about the time he. Yes, I suppose at once. . . . I remember looking in Pill lane. Also that now is magnetism. Back of everything magnetism. Earth for instance pulling this and being pulled. That causes movement. And time? Well that's the time the movement takes.

Then if one thing stopped the whole ghesabo would stop bit by bit.
Because it's arranged. Magnetic needle tells you what's going on in the
sun, the stars. Little piece of steel iron. When you hold out the fork.
Come. Come. Tip. Woman and man that is. Fork and steel. Molly, he.
Dress up and look and suggest and let you see and see more and defy you
if you're a man to see that and, like a sneeze coming, legs, look, look and
if you have any guts in you. Tip. Have to let fly. (373–374)

He sees both sexes as pulled by this force: "Yours for the asking. Because
they want it themselves. Their natural craving. Shoals of them every
evening poured out of offices" (368).

Bloom's sense of sexual magnetism is connected with his thoughts
about Molly and Boylan, which is the one subject he can not specify in
words. The thought of the two of them together is still very painful for
him:

Was that just when he, she?
    O, he did. Into her. She did. Done.
    Ah! (370)

Although Bloom sees sexual attraction and its fulfillment as natural and
inevitable, he suffers the whole range of emotions responsive to Molly's
infidelity. He is angry with Molly, as in the passage from Sirens: "Leave
her: get tired. Suffer then. Snivel. Big Spanishy eyes goggling at nothing.
Her wavyavyeavyheavyeavyevyevy hair un comb:'d" (277). He feels resignation when he remembers with anguish his love-making with Molly
sixteen years before and considers its irretrievability: "My youth. Never
again. Only once it comes. Or hers" (377), and ponders searching for a
renewal of passion in a new love: "No. Returning not the same. . . . The
new I want" (377). But he decides that a new love is not possible: "Nothing
new under the sun. . . . So it returns. Think you're escaping and run into
yourself. Longest way round is the shortest way home. And just when he
and she. Circus horse walking in a ring" (377).

Bloom understands the meaning of his relinquishment: "All quiet on
Howth now. The distant hills seem. Where we. The rhododendrons. I am
a fool perhaps. He gets the plums and I the plumstones" (377). But finally,
although still vacillating, he renounces possessiveness: "Liverpool boat
long gone. Not even the smoke. And she can do the other. Did too. And
Belfast. I won't go. Race there, race back to Ennis. Let him" (382). The
end of his half-dream implies a hope to return to full intercourse. The
context merges Molly, Martha, and Gerty—"next in her next her next"
(382)—but the passage is extremely ambiguous.

Bloom's section of the chapter shows us again his great decency, not
only in thoughts about sexuality but in his thoughts about people, even the
citizen: "that bawler in Barney Kiernan's. Got my own back there.
Drunken ranters. What I said about his God made him wince. Mistake to
hit back. Or? No. Ought to go home and laugh at themselves. Always

want to be swilling in company. Afraid to be alone like a child of two. Suppose he hit me. Look at it other way round. Not so bad then. Perhaps not to hurt he meant" (380). Bloom extends the same charity to Molly, remembering an occasion when she was cruel to Milly: "What do they love? Another themselves? But the morning she chased her with the umbrella. Perhaps so as not to hurt. I felt her pulse. Ticking" (379–380). His decency appears in his quiet acceptance of a humiliating event of the morning: "Walk after him now make him awkward like those newsboys me today" (375–376), and in the acceptance that lies beneath his comic misrecollection: "That brought us out of the land of Egypt and into the house of bondage" (378).

Bloom's decency and honesty provide a norm, a standard, in a chapter on sexuality that points to the hypocrisy, craven deceit, and artificiality in society's approach to, or rather retreat from, the subject. Fritz Senn offers some humane and judicious conclusions about the chapter: "In the imperfect world of Dublin, 1904, the imperfect solution that the two characters allow themselves to be driven to, passively reactive rather than passionately active, does have some advantages. . . . Bloom knows one has to be 'Thankful for small mercies'. . . . Substitute satisfactions are better than no satisfactions at all. . . . Something approaching love does, after all, take place, and a kind of rapport is established. . . . The lack of communication in *Ulysses* is perhaps less surprising than the occasional occurrence of *some* imperfect communication."[3]

Still, it is an outrageous and highly comic idea to have the very character who provides the standard, who upholds a saner view of sexuality, perform so flagrant a violation of sexual mores as to masturbate in public. Bloom is never permitted to become an ideal figure: the closer he approaches moral perfection in any given episode, the harder he is pulled down to the level of the messy, smelly, ridiculously human. Joyce is adamant in his refusal to offer the reader the ideal: he insists we see and know, as far as possible, the real.

The narrator stands above the whole chapter. There are portions of Bloom's section that take place outside his consciousness, although they are here, as in Sirens, woven into his monologue. The paragraph beginning "A monkey puzzle" (372) starts outside Bloom's consciousness; the paragraph beginning "A long lost candle" (379) is written entirely outside of Bloom's consciousness, as is the conclusion of the chapter, from "A bat flew" (382). The comment "Cuckoo" is the narrator's. Although Gerty can and does imagine what is going on in the church, we are told about events inside the church that she could not possibly be aware of, such as the accident of the candle flame about to reach the flowers. Some of the satire in the episode is accomplished by the juxtaposition of events within the church with events occurring outside it. At other times, one of Gerty's thoughts is juxtaposed with a contrary thought or act, a technique used for comedy in Molly's soliloquy also. The largest juxtaposition of the chapter is that between Gerty and Bloom. The same is true of the satire: some of it is aimed at Gerty, and by extension at a way of thinking and feeling; some mocks Bloom for his sensuality and sentiment: "Howth settled for slumber tired of long days, of yumyum rhododendrons (he was old) and felt gladly the night breeze lift, ruffle his fell of ferns. . . . Far on Kish bank the anchored lightship twinkled, winked at Mr Bloom" (379). During Gerty's section the satire also glances at both figures: she knew he was "a man of inflexible honour to his fingertips" (365). The satire that arises from the juxtaposition of the church service with the events on the beach is also a double-headed arrow, mocking some notions of Catholicism along with the characters. The service is a benediction, a ritual in which, according to Kenner, the sacrament, like Gerty, "is exhibited but not eaten."[4] The counterpoint parallels the worship of the Virgin and Bloom's "worship" of Gerty: "His dark eyes fixed themselves on her again drinking in her every contour, literally worshipping at her shrine" (361). Gerty is and remains a virgin; the shrine Bloom worships is her genitals. The analogy is funny, but it also points seriously to religion as the root of Dublin's sexual sickness. The canon hands the thurible back to Father Conroy and kneels down "looking up at the Blessed Sacrament" (360) at the same time, the narrator informs us, that Bloom is looking fixedly at Gerty. The problem of the candle—"Canon O'Hanlon . . . told Father Conroy that one of the candles was just going to set fire to the flowers and Father Conroy got up and settled it all right" (361)—occurs just as Bloom is returning his hands to his pockets and inflaming Gerty with that "sensation rushing all over her." The canon has the "Blessed Sacrament in his hands" (363), and Bloom has *his* chalice in his. As Gerty decides she will not be sexual but will remain like brother and sister in her "dream of love," Canon O'Hanlon "put the Blessed Sacrament back into the tabernacle and . . . then he locked the tabernacle door" (365).

There is a circle of ironies here: the idealization of sex in the benediction of the Virgin is related to but also contrasted with Gerty's sentimentalization of sex; the idealization of sex in the benediction of the Virgin parallels and contrasts with Bloom's sexual idealization of Gerty while he is masturbating; and Gerty's romantic sentimentality parallels and contrasts with Bloom's realistic sensuality during the masturbation. Gerty's sentimental and romantic notions are an ironic comment on the bleak life she lives and her actual inadequacy, her moral and physical lameness. Bloom, ambivalently circling, as always, provides contrasts within his own monologue; and his public masturbation—his form of worship—during a service celebrating the Virgin (what better way to celebrate virginity?) has its own sensational irony.

We are presented with three basic standing places: the position of the church on sex, the position of Irish womanhood on sex (a similar view on the sexuality of Irish womanhood is presented in the Swiftian satire in Oxen of the Sun), and the position of Bloom. Because of Bloom's decency and honesty and his approach to sex as natural and human (if a problem), we find ourselves standing with him rather than with either of the others. We also therefore find ourselves defending or at least countenancing his outrageous act. We are voyaging across the abyss of incertitude in the fragile bark of human decency with a fellow passenger who is:

Cuckoo
Cuckoo
Cuckoo. (382)

Notes

1. Kenner, *Dublin's Joyce*, pp. 255–256.
2. Henry James, *The Art of the Novel* (New York and London, 1934), pp. 33–34.
3. Senn, "Nausicaa," in *James Joyce's "Ulysses,"* pp, 279–81.
4. Kenner, *Dublin's Joyce*, p. 258.

Ulysses: Techniques and Styles: "Nausicaa"

C. H. Peake*

The unnamed narrator's interior monologue resembles a protracted barroom anecdote because such a manner best reflects the nature of his self-awareness: he feels himself and others to be permanently involved in an endless gossipy tale. Gerty MacDowell's consciousness, on the other hand, is like a flattering mirror before which she performs, just as she performs before a real mirror: "she knew how to cry nicely before the mirror. You are lovely, Gerty, it said." Although the style borrows freely from novelettes of the time, it is not critical parody—Joyce is not out to ridicule the patently ridiculous—nor even pastiche. It is rather a purée of clichés, extracted and condensed not only from the stories in girls' papers, but from their beauty pages, cookery tips, fashion notes, advice ᵗ the lovelorn, correspondence columns and advertisements, to which are added clichés, equally sickly, from religious tracts, temperance propaganda, popular superstitions and all the current affectations of popular culture and respectability. Through this oversweetened mess, the dry facts of Gerty's real situation occasionally emerge, and the vulgarities of her undoctored self erupt. Her monologue is not a repetitious or laborious exercise. There are continuous fluctuations of style from high-flown romanticism to coarse spitefulness, from pious pretense to naive exhibi-

*From *James Joyce: The Citizen and the Artist* (Stanford: Stanford University Press, 1977), 243-49. Reprinted by permission of the publisher. © 1977.

tionism, from airy vagueness to drab particulars. Joyce himself found it impossible to describe the style fully: *"Nausikaa* is written in a namby-pamby jammy marmalady drawersy (alto là!) style with effects of incense, mariolatry, masturbation, stewed cockles, painter's palette, chit chat, circumlocution, etc., etc."[1] There is a constant tendency to sink from the fantasy levels of consciousness towards the mundane and vulgar, so that Gerty repeatedly has to snatch up her thoughts again, and this erratic movement is reflected in a style far removed from the comparative inflexibility of parody. Illusion is repeatedly interrupted by the common-place facts of Gerty's life and resentments. The dream of being "pro-nounced beautiful by all" stumbles a little on the memory of real comments about her resemblance to one or other side of her family; the image of a graceful figure breaks up into the less elevated particulars of iron jelloids, pills, discharges and the advertisers' catchphrase, "that tired feeling." The stock phrases of loveliness from advertisements for creams, powders and lipsticks raise the tone again until it is lowered by the names of specific preparations, and shattered by Gerty's anger at Bertha Supple's "deliberate lie." The attempt to modulate into the "little tiffs" of "girl chums" doesn't succeed, but Gerty dismisses this unfortunate, catty episode by creating the dream of her own "innate refinement," leading upwards to the view of herself as a natural aristocrat, presented in such appropriate terms as *"hauteur"* and "devoirs." Deprived by fate of her true position in society, she quickly transmutes the loss into a love-deprivation and so brings in the note of melancholy passion. Through mention of Gerty's "eyes of witchery," the train of association leads to eyebrows, and thence to the synthetic world of "eyebrowleine" and remedies for blushing, shortness and small noses. Gerty cannot resist a sly dig at Mrs. Dignam's button nose, before returning to her dream of her own beauty, of her crowning glory, and a momentary slip into superstitions about haircutting and nailparing is quickly recovered by consciousness of her own shy and rosy flush at Edy's remark about Gerty's being Tommy Caffrey's sweet-heart.

The style is as various as Gerty's moods, and the manner in which her experience of what lies around her is presented changes abruptly and radically. The Caffrey twins, first seen as "darling little fellows with bright merry faces and endearing ways about them," later become "exasperating little brats," and their sister, Cissy, undergoes more complex transforma-tions. At first she is seen as a girl of merry sweetness: "A truerhearted lass never drew the breath of life, always with a laugh in her gipsylike eyes and a frolicsome word on her cherryripe red lips, a girl lovable in the extreme," (U 330/450). When Cissy makes an unladylike remark about smacking Tommy "on the beetoteetom," Gerty is able to reconcile herself to this by the image of "Madcap Ciss with her golliwog curls." However, when Cissy's tomboy behaviour threatens Gerty's dream about the gentleman on the beach, resentment presents Cissy in quite a different light, mounting through sarcastic comments on Cissy's skimpy hair, "long gandery strides" and tomboy behaviour to scorn for this "forward piece" who is trying to show off by exposing "her skinny shanks up as far as possible." The coarsening of the language and the reference to the vulgar joke about "up as far as possible" indicates how far Gerty's anger is carrying her. At this point the reader does not know that the bitterness towards Cissy's running and tight skirt and "her high crooked French heels" is because Gerty is lame and cannot compete in that sort of display. She can pull herself out of a mood of cattiness only by assuming feelings of haughty superiority — represented in the monologue by such terms as "*Tableau!*" and "exposé" — and then by associating herself with the overheard prayer to the Virgin. The ease with which her religious sentimentality can coexist with her erotic dreams is comically expressed by her foot-swinging, moving to the rhythm of the hymn, but designed to reveal titillating glimpses of her legs in their transparent stockings. The religiosity provides a disguise for her desire to compete with the brazen revelations of Cissy. Even the interweavings of the elements in the style of the monologue expose aspects of Gerty's mind of which she herself is not fully aware.

The function of the style is not to ridicule the silly daydreams of a young girl; Gerty is ridiculous but she is also pitiable, and the image of her circumstances and nature is too complex to permit of a simple response. The style, like that of the earlier monologues, serves to represent the essence of her consciousness and the fluctuations of her moods; what we are told about Gerty is, for the most part, exaggerated, misleading, garbled or quite untrue, yet, through the style, we experience the quality of her experience. Gerty's escapism represents a temptation to which Bloom is vulnerable, as Nausicaa was a temptation to Ulysses to abandon the long struggle homeward. Her daydreams are a flight from her homelife with a drunken and violent father and from her lameness; Bloom too has family and personal disabilities. The "tumescence" of the "technic," culminating in her self-induced orgasm and his masturbation, is figured equally in the action and the style of her monologue.

For Gerty, the self-deception and the auto-eroticism are enough; tomorrow or another day she will attach similar fantasies to Reggy Wylie or Father Conroy or some other stranger. The danger is that it will also be enough for Bloom. For a moment, he is caught up in the false romanticism of the style:

> He was leaning back against the rock behind. Leopold Bloom (for it is he) stands silent, with bowed head before those young guileless eyes. What a brute he had been! At it again? A fair unsullied soul had called to him and, wretch that he was, how had he answered? An utter cad he had been. He of. all men! But there was an infinite store of mercy in those eyes, for him too a word of pardon even though he had erred and sinned and wandered. (U 350/478)

Perception of Gerty's lameness jerks him back to reality, and the return to the characteristic style of his earlier monologues signifies that a "detumescence" of his imagination is accompanying his physical detumescence.

The sudden shift back to the earlier kind of monologue is the most important feature of the style of the latter part of the chapter, representing as it does a release from the strains and pressures that have been building up in Bloom: "Did me good all the same. Off colour after Kiernan's, Dignam's. For this relief much thanks." (U 355/485). The silent relationship with Gerty has the double effect of tiring him physically ("Exhausted that female has me. Not so young now") and restoring him psychologically ("Goodbye, dear. Thanks. Made me feel so young.") He can now face up to what has happened between Boylan and Molly and see it as something over and done with: "O, he did. Into her. She did. Done": though it may happen again on the Belfast tour, he can't be bothered about it. Molly is again a source of pride to him rather than humiliation and distress: she can "knock spots off" other men's wives, and now, if he wonders why she chose him, he recalls her answer, "Because you were so foreign from the others." Gerty has strengthened him, not only by providing the stimulus for his masturbations, but by choosing him now as Molly chose him in the past. He cannot be as contemptible as some of his recent encounters have suggested: "Saw something in me. Wonder what." One cannot distinguish the style of the monologue from its content. Both are relaxing, quiescing: the paragraphs draw out longer and more leisurely than before, because Bloom is less troubled by turbulent emotions. The scene, too, grows sleepy as the light fails and Bloom prepares to have a short snooze:

> Twittering the bat flew here, flew there. Far out over the sands the coming surf crept, grey. Howth settled for slumber tired of long days, of yumyum rhododendrons (he was old) and felt gladly the night breeze lift, ruffle his fell of ferns. He lay but opened a red eye unsleeping, deep and slowly breathing, slumberous but awake. (U 362/494-5)

Howth has become a projected image of Bloom's own sleepiness. The "yumyum rhododendrons," a mocking reference to the courtship of Molly, the memory of which had so excited Bloom in Davy Byrne's, no longer disturb him. Like Howth, Bloom intends to rest—not sleeping but "slumberous." After the tensions of his day and the unexpected relief supplied by Gerty, Bloom dozes off, and the style represents the dissipation of his consciousness, with words and phrases echoed from earlier phases of his interior monologue:

> O sweety all your little girlwhite up I saw dirty bracegirdle made me do love sticky we two naughty Grace darling she him half past the bed met him pike hoses frillies for Raoul to perfume your wife black hair heave under embon *señorita* young eyes Mulvey plump years dreams return tail end Agendath swoony lovey showed me her next year in drawers return next in her next her next. (U 365/498)

The fusion of Bloom's memory of Gerty's display with his awareness of what has happened in his bed that afternoon is clear and effective enough but Joyce traces the movements of Bloom's dozing mind more closely to suggest the resumption of its odyssey after this temporary distraction. At first, feelings of gratitude ("O sweet little, you don't know how nice you looked"), the memory of his excitement ("Darling, I saw your. I saw all"), the vision of Gerty's white underclothes are all confused with his notion that women's lingerie is designed to tempt men ("I'm all clean come and dirty me") and that Gerty's performance was somewhat stagy, like the fascination exerted by such actresses as Mrs Bracegirdle. This leads, via the image of their mutual excitation and subsequent stickiness to the phrase from Martha's letter (which he had remembered just before), "naughty darling," the name "Grace" being intruded as a result of his passing thought of the Victorian heroine, Grace Darling. Martha's letter had borne the address "P.O. Dolphin's Barn," and this had led his mind to his early courtship of Molly; thus "naughty darling," though borrowed from Martha, leads at once to "she him," Molly and Boylan, to their meeting that afternoon at half-past four (the time at which his watch had stopped), and to the bed in which the adultery took place. In that bed, that morning, Molly had asked him to explain "met him pike hoses" (the word, "metempsychosis," has occurred to him, in another connection just before): "met him" is a euphemism for what has taken place between Molly and Boylan, while "hoses" leads, through the memory of the Mutoscope pictures of "A dream of welfilled hose," to the "frillies" worn by the heroine of *Sweets of Sin* for her lover, "for Raoul." In "Sirens" Bloom had imagined Molly awaiting Boylan, "perfumed for him," and that now blends with Gerty's farewell wave of a piece of perfumed wadding to leave behind a scented memory, and with Martha's enquiry about his wife's perfume. He remembers Molly's first meeting with Boylan, when she was "wearing her black and it had the perfume of the time before," and his earlier thoughts of the sources of female odour, in particular the hair, "strong in rut." All of these thoughts of Molly and Boylan, of Raoul and the heroine of *Sweets of Sin*, and of perfume shift easily to the picture of a woman's "heaving embonpoint" (Molly's, the novel heroine's, and Miss Douce's—already shortened to "her heaving embon") lying under a lover, and thence to Molly as she must have been at the time of her first affair with Mulvey, a young "señorita" with her fine "Spanishy eyes" and her breasts already "developed"—the word "plump" seems to link this with an earlier image of Molly when she was just beginning to plump out her elephantgrey dress. He has remembered, too, his own first wooing of his wife, in an earlier June, and the passage of time has brought to his mind the succession of years, "The year returns." Mixed with this motion of the returning year is a later thought that a dream "never comes the same," and the succession of "years dreams return" is also associated with the charades at Dolphin's Barn, when he was courting Molly, and he played the part of

Rip Van Winkle. "Return" is an aspect of his earlier thoughts of sailors, "smelling the tail end of ports," while "tail end" is linked to another kind of return, the smutty picture of a husband returning to find his wife with her lover — on which Joe Hynes had commented, "Get a queer old tailend of corned beef off of that one, what?" But the word "end" suggests by its sound "Agendath," the name of the plantation company, a symbol of the return of the Jews to Palestine. These various returns now become confused as Bloom's consciousness fades: the sexual image recalls the image of orgasm suggested to his mind when he first read *Sweets of Sin* ("Whites of eyes swooning up"), and his own sensation while watching Gerty "on show"; but the Agendath memory brings in a phrase from the Passover ritual, "Next year in Jerusalem," the dream of return. (He has just recalled, or misrecalled, the *Exodus* praise of God who "brought us out of the land of Egypt and into the house of bondage.") Does "drawers" refer to Gerty's underclothes or to Molly's: "Drawers: little kick, taking them off. By by till next time"? The combination of "drawers" and "next" may suggest that it is the reference to Molly's underclothes which is in his mind, but Bloom is now close to sleep; Molly and Gerty are blending in his dim consciousness as are the notions of returning home, of the possibility of returning to see Gerty again, and of the Jewish return to Palestine. Similarly there is no knowing whether "next" refers to next year in Jerusalem, the next time he sees Gerty or the next of Molly's infidelities. Everything is fusing as Bloom dozes off. The paragraph thus presents a kaleidoscopic image of a mind slowly fading into sleep, joining together remembered words and phrases (as in the closing paragraphs of "The Dead") moving along a train of associations, sometimes verbal, sometimes phonetic, sometimes emotional, sometimes of linked thoughts and experiences. It shows how, in Bloom's mind, despite the certainty of Molly's adultery and despite his own sexual satisfaction through masturbation, the image of his wife slowly absorbs the images of Gerty and of Martha; the dominant thought in his darkening consciousness is that of return — a return essentially to Molly, for she is his Ithaca and the Promised Land to which he hears the summons of recall.

As the cuckoo-clock in the priest's house sounds nine o'clock, everything inconclusively fades away. Bloom, openmouthed, leaning sideways thinks "just for a few"; the priests are at their supper "and talking about"; Gerty notices that the gentleman "that was sitting on the rocks looking was." The nine times repeated cry of "Cuckoo" seems to publish Bloom's situation: earlier, in the library, Mulligan has quoted "Cuckoo! Cuckoo! O word of fear!": and later, in the brothel, the clock again signals Bloom's place in the register of Dublin cuckolds. But if the cuckooing was simply to announce Bloom's cuckoldry, one would have to say that the clock was four and a half hours slow, and that the stale joke was a feeble conclusion to the chapter. In fact, it offers a brief image of the attitudes of the two central figures of the chapter. Gerty's persistent romanticism transforms the cuckoo into "a little canarybird bird," while Bloom, now able to accept the situation which has troubled him all day, shows his resigned unconcern ("Let him") by falling asleep while his cuckoldry is being proclaimed.

But Gerty is more than an agent by whom Bloom is enabled to achieve physical and emotional "detumescence"; for that purpose, the whole chapter could have been restricted to Bloom's point of view. She also incarnates a temptation to which Bloom is vulnerable. The vague doctrine of "love," with which he countered the old Citizen's racial and religious prejudices, could, in its own sentimental and religiose way, be just as blinding and paralysing as bloodyminded chauvinism. In "Cyclops", Gerty has been used as an image of this tendency in Bloom; the paragraph, ridiculing Bloom's affirmation of love, includes the sentence, "Gerty MacDowell loves the boy on the bicycle." To realize, focus and pass judgement on this kind of escapism, it has to be shown at work in the consciousness of one of its victims; but to use a convention of interior monologue, akin to that used for Bloom and Stephen, would be uneconomical and inappropriate. Gerty is a subordinate figure: to capture her essence, a convention is needed which, without ignoring the girl's specific qualities or the fluctuations of her mood, will characterize and assess the retreat from reality which she represents. The conglomerate of clichés establishes and implicitly comments on the escapist fantasy; the variations among the phrases belonging to schoolgirl slang, bitchy gossip, and romantic, patriotic, moral and religiose sentimentality create Gerty's individuality within the general image. It is an image not simply of a silly girl who has read too many novelettes but of an impoverished, handicapped, disappointed and frustrated existence, consoling itself with the illusions offered by the Dublin environment and the prevailing attitudes to love, friendship, family, country and religion.

Notes

1. *Letters* I, 135. I find incomprehensible Father W. T. Noon's opinion that "there is nothing satirical about the opening paragraph of this chapter. Here is the sort of praise of Our Lady that might be found in St. Bernard" (*Noon*, 100). On the contrary, here are "effects of incense, mariolatry."

"Nausicaa"

Paul van Caspel *

In "Nausicaa," in Senn's words, "we enter, for the first time, a predominantly female world" (1974:281). This is reflected in the style of the first half of the episode, comprising some twenty pages devoted to Gerty MacDowell, twenty-one years old and a virgin, presumably. In these pages the reader witnesses what Burgess calls a "total takeover of woman's magazine style" (1973b:94). They are, as French puts it, "pervaded by the worst stereotypes of femaleness" (1976:157); in short, they are a perfect imitation of what has come to be called *Trivialliteratur* (popular literature). We should avoid, however, speaking too condescendingly about this type of writing. Granted that Joyce was somehow fascinated by this feminine type of prose, there is no need to condemn the novelette style bluntly, without any qualifications whatever, as a form of "bad writing" (Adams, 1966:152). Moreover, we should not wax moralistic over readers of such "sub-literature" (Goldman 1966:94); they are seeking a road of escape, a flight from the oppressive reality of their environment, but that may be true with regard to other forms of literature as well. As Senn puts it: "To afford illusory gratifications is one of the legitimate functions of fiction, of higher literature no less than of Gerty's favourite reading matter" (1974:280).

Particularly persistent has proved the term *cheap*, whatever that may mean. It seems to come to mind readily whenever critics try to define the type of writing upon which the style of Gerty's thoughts has been modeled. It is generally agreed, in other words, that Gerty's reading matter must have been a kind of "pulp fiction" (Henke, 1978:153) or may have been found in the "cheap women's magazines of the day" (Hodgart, 1978:108). Her appreciative thoughts about "Madame Vera Verity, directress of the Woman Beautiful page of the Princess Novelette" (13.109–10/ 349.04–5), who seems to have given her valuable advice on make-up problems, show that the term *novelette* may have more than one meaning. It may stand for "cheap short novel," but this *Princess Novelette* (Homer's Nausicaa was a princess, after all) must have been one of those Victorian or Edwardian women's magazines so popular at the time. From advertisements of the period we know that such magazines were published weekly at what seems to have been the standard rate of one penny. It is hard to say whether this would have been considered inexpensive by ordinary people in 1904. A shopgirl such as Eveline, in the story of that name in *Dubliners*, who earned, as Gifford reminds us (1974:58), seven shillings a week, might have thought twice before spending a penny on what was, after all, a luxury. However, such girls might have been badly in need of just this

*From *Bloomers on the Liffey: Eisegetical Readings of Joyce's "Ulysses"* (Baltimore: John Hopkins University Press, 1986), 193–200. Reprinted by permission of the publisher.

kind of fiction in order to survive, mentally and emotionally, in their drab surroundings.

As we have seen, there is complete agreement among critics as to the *sources* of the style Joyce applied in the first part of the episode. There is considerably less agreement with regard to the *technique* used in elaborating the basic material, especially as to the question whether the style should be called "parody" or "pastiche."

French holds that the technique in the first part "parodies by imitation," but she has to concede that the style is markedly different from that of the parodies in "Cyclops" with their extremely high degree of exaggeration. "That parody occurs as a result of the simple accumulation of details" (1976:157), she says, which is more or less what Solmecke means to say when he maintains that Joyce forces the trivial prototype to parody itself (1969:148). According to Peake (1977:243), the style is neither parody nor pastiche, but having digested the lengthy exposition of what it is in *his* view, the reader may feel inclined to ask: If this is not pastiche, whatever *is*? Anyway, it fits Burgess's definition of pastiche: "an imitation of an existing artistic style, so close and skilful as to be indistinguishable from the original" (1973b:93). This "borrowed style," Burgess says elsewhere, is "cliché-ridden and euphemistic rather than inflated," and its language is "apt for a plebeian virgin, brought up on religion and niceness, who is eager to engage life" (1973b:102ff). The language may be Gerty's but the first half of the episode is nonetheless third-person narrative. The point is that this narrative is imbued with just those clichés and colloquialisms that Gerty herself might have used had she been articulate enough to use them. "Nausicaa" is one of those episodes in which, according to Henke, "we become increasingly aware of a narrative voice independent of the characters — a fictional persona whose role in the novel approximates that of the traditional omniscient author" (1978:114). It was Edmund Wilson who at an early stage (1931) remarked that in the later episodes of the novel the reader would find himself wondering "at the introduction of voices which seem to belong neither to the characters nor to the author" (1974:57). The reader, however, would do well not to start wondering or worrying too much about fictional personae or mysterious voices independent of the characters. What matters to the reader is that the resulting style is one with the easy flow of free indirect speech, without the author's pretending (as in interior monologue) to reproduce the character's intimate thoughts and feelings and that, on the contrary, the reader gets the definite feeling that this style is colored by the character's very essence, the author remaining invisible, or, as Burgess words it: "The idiom has entered Gerty's very soul and is the medium of all her musings: we stand midway between an interior monologue and a *genre* narrative" (1973b:103).

This notion of "voices" has been taken up again by Kenner. Discussing the opening sentence of "The Dead," a story in *Dubliners* ("Lily, the caretaker's daughter, was literally run off her feet"), he shows that this idiom reflects what Lily herself would say ("I'm literally run off my feet"), concluding: "So that first sentence was written, as it were, from Lily's point of view, and though it looks like 'objective' narration it is tinged with her idiom. It is Lily, not the austere author, whose habit it is to say 'literally' when 'figuratively' is meant, and the author is less recounting the front-hall doings than paraphrasing a recounting of hers" (1978:16). What happens here, long before *Ulysses*, is that we find, as Kenner says, "the normally neutral narrative vocabulary pervaded by a little cloud of idioms which a character might use if he were managing the narrative" (1978:17). Hence, Kenner adds, the manifold styles of *Ulysses*, and having asked, rhetorically: "What is the first half of 'Nausicaa,' for instance, but Gerty MacDowell's very self and voice, caught up into the narrative machinery?" he formulates the underlying principle as: "*the narrative idiom need not be the narrator's*" (1978:18).

This principle may indeed be perceived to be active in such unobtrusive phrases as "It would be like heaven" (13.214/352.01), which is Gertyese for "It would be heaven," and in this episode Kenner might even have found an instance similar to the line he quotes from *Dubliners*. In the scene where Gerty sits eying Bloom (she "could see without looking that he never took his eyes off of her" [13.495–96/360.02–3]) the narrative has: "His dark eyes fixed themselves on her again, drinking in her every contour, *literally* worshipping at her shrine" (13.563–64/361.41–42, italics mine). Here we note the same illiterate, illogical use of the term *literally* where *figuratively* or just *as it were* would be expected, and even "her every contour" sounds dubious, as if Gerty might not have been too sure of the exact meaning of the noun.

In these passages, the reader knows some definite characters (Lily, Gerty), who may be blamed, so to speak, for the somewhat anomalous use of this term, but such is not always the case. In an anonymous account such as the interpolation in "Cyclops" in which the Citizen's throwing of the biscuit tin is described as a devastating earthquake hitting the center of Dublin (12.1858–96/344.03–345.06), the idiom is just part of the narrator's, in this case the reporter's, own vocabulary. But when the reporter writes that the courthouse, totally demolished, "is literally a mass of ruins" (12.1867–68/344.14), his "literally" does *not* mean "figuratively"; it has practically no meaning at all, it only lends some emphasis to the statement.

Curiously enough, similar cases may be found in modern usage. A White House social secretary, reminiscing about the day Charles, Prince of Wales, called on President Reagan, told a reporter from the *New York Times* (29 October 1982) that there had been some confusion because nobody seemed to know for sure at which entrance the visitor was expected. "By this time," she is quoted as telling the reporter, "*it was literally two minutes before the Prince's arrival. I ran down to the*

Diplomatic Reception Room entrance. The rug was rolled up, two men were mopping the floor and *the Prince's car was literally coming up the driveway*" (italics mine).

Several critics have remarked on the counterpoint effect Joyce achieves in this scene, establishing a parallel between the worship of the Virgin going on in the nearby church and Bloom's "worship" of virginal Gerty on the beach. In her detailed analysis of this passage, French, not without a certain aplomb, says that "Gerty is and remains a virgin; the shrine Bloom worships is her genitals" (1976:167); however, what Bloom is, not *worshipping*, but *worshipping at*, is Gerty's drawers. For him, they are the shrine that holds the blessed sacrament, and it is their sight that arouses and excites him enough to make him masturbate secretly. In "Circe," the apparition of Bloom's grandfather mentions this predilection of his. Lynch, Stephen's companion, had lifted up a side of the slip of one of the prostitutes, and the apparition, addressing Bloom, comments in a matter-of-fact way: "Inadvertently her backview revealed the fact that she is not wearing those rather intimate garments of which you are a particular devotee" (15.2314–16/511.32). From Molly's soliloquy, moreover, we learn that she is fully aware of the fascination drawers hold for her husband: "of course hes mad on the subject of drawers thats plain to be seen" (18.289/746.08–9), and again: "drawers drawers the whole blessed time" (18.305/746.27). At the end, when Gerty has left the beach and Bloom is dozing off, his confused thoughts still circle round her underwear: "O sweety all your little girlwhite up I saw . . . made me do love sticky . . . swoony lovey showed me her next year in drawers . . . her next" (13.1279–85/382.13–19).

The moment Gerty gets up to leave and then limps away "with care and very slowly" Bloom realizes that she is lame; the shock he experiences marks the return to his characteristic brand of interior monologue, which the reader must have become familiar with by now (13.771ff/367.41ff). Still, there are a few passages in the remaining pages of the episode by which critics have been puzzled or, in at least one case, confused. Such passages are found in the final pages, where Bloom deeply feels how tired he is and where the snatches of his interior monologue tend to become shorter and shorter. Looking over toward the Howth Hill peninsula, he remembers the day, sixteen years ago, when he lay there with Molly among the rhododendrons: "She kissed me. Never again. My youth. Only once it comes. Or hers. Take the train there tomorrow. No. Returning not the same. Like kids your second visit to a house" (13.1102–4/377.11–14). In his interpretation of this passage, Maddox seems to relate the phrase "Or hers" to Bloom's daughter, Milly, for he explains that Bloom "totally shies away from the possibility of a return to the happy days, or even *the possibility of taking the train to see his daughter*" (1978:83, italics mine). In fact, Milly does not come in at all. The entire scene, of which these are the opening sentences, is about Molly in the first place. The memory of their youthful lovemaking, a recurrent motif in the book up to its final lines, represents a unique and simply unforgettable experience in Bloom's life. He reflects, with regret but also with a certain amount of resignation, that neither his nor Molly's youth will ever come again. His next thought is that he (perhaps even both of them?) might go and revisit the place where they were happy once. It is a journey Molly remembers, too; it is one of those numerous memories that crop up in her soliloquy: "that was an exceptional man that common workman that left us alone in the carriage that day going to Howth" (18.369–71/748.20–22). It does not take Bloom long, however, to realize the futility of such an attempt at retrieving what is, essentially, irretrievable. Tired, resigned, Bloom now feels it is no use trying to recover the past. What he wants is something new, such as this pitiable romance with Martha Clifford. He is reminded of the letter he had been writing in the Ormond, and the address he wrote on the envelope, "c/o P.O. Dolphin's Barn Lane" (11.898–99/280.16–17), and the pointed question Martha had asked him in *her* letter about his not being happy in his home (5.246/77.38–39). This complex, the address and the question, is not a topic he cares to pursue in his present mood, so his thoughts switch to the days when he *was* happy, and he recalls the games they used to play with other young people, before their marriage, "in Luke Doyle's house" (13.1106/377.16), the association being reinforced by the coincidence of the addresses, as the Doyles' residence was situated in the same neighborhood, Dolphin's Barn. As Bloom himself realizes, his efforts at escaping (Martha, Gerty) have not been very effective; he always comes back to Molly somehow: "So it returns. Think you're escaping and run into yourself. Longest way round is the shortest way home" (13.1109–11/377.20–22).

Bloom's abortive attempt at leaving a message for Gerty—he picks up a bit of a stick and starts writing in the sand but does not get any further than "I AM A"—has had critics guessing and speculating for years, but none of them has discovered the failing noun (assuming, that is, that "A" is to be read as the indefinite article). Bloom does not finish his message, trumping up all kinds of excuses: people may walk on it; the incoming tide will wash it away; there is no room anymore in that particular spot—in short, he gives up ("No room. Let it go") and effaces the letters slowly with his boot. There is one excuse, however, that stands out as being of a different order altogether; it is followed immediately by a few phrases (more or less scrambled) that Bloom remembers from Martha's letter: "Besides they don't know. What is the meaning of that other world. I called you naughty boy because I do not like" (13.1262–63/381.35–37). what Martha wrote, actually, typing "world" instead of "word," was: "I called you naughty boy because I do not like that other world. Please tell me what is the real meaning of that word?" (5.244–46/77.36–38). The reader never learns what the word was that Martha neither liked nor understood; in his reply, written in the Ormond dining room, Bloom does not explain, as far as we can make out. This is very regrettable, because it might have provided a clue as to the message Bloom was going to write in the sand. He may well have intended to print here the same word he had used in an earlier letter to Martha, in the context of which it may have referred to himself also, because Martha wants to substitute another phrase for it, "naughty boy." Then, however, Bloom checks himself, reflecting: "Besides they don't know." Now who are "they"? In Bloom's stream of consciousness "they" usually are *women* in general; we find the pronoun with this connotation ten times within the space of about one page (13.790–830/368.22–369.25). So, the experience with Martha has led him to suppose that if she failed to grasp the meaning of "that word" (voyeur? masochist?), other women were not likely to understand such words either. That is, most probably, why he lets it go.

Having flung away the stick, Bloom sits down on the beach, presumably leaning back against one of the rocks. Before he dozes off, his thoughts revolve around Molly's upcoming concert tour to Belfast (he himself has to go to Ennis for the anniversary of his father's death), on which tour she will be accompanied by Boylan: "Short snooze now if I had. Must be near nine. Liverpool boat long gone. Not even the smoke. And she can do the other. Did too. And Belfast. I won't go. Race there, race back to Ennis. Let him. Just close my eyes a moment. Won't sleep, though. Half dream. It never comes the same. Bat again. No harm in him. Just a few" (13.1274–78/382.07–12). Most readers, no doubt, will infer from this passage that Bloom has more or less come to accept Molly's affair with Boylan. In Maddox's words, "nowhere else in the book does Bloom's mood of acceptance pass over so completely into a shrug of surrender" (1978:77). Yet there is disagreement as to the exact meaning of some of the snatches from Bloom's interior monologue. Blamires, switching from summary and commentary to interpretation, says that "Bloom's apprehension gives place to acceptance, even forgiveness ('Let him' . . . 'No harm in him'), which reinforces the view that Bloom's writing in the sand carries overtones of Christ's act when He was asked to condemn the woman taken in adultery" (1966:150–51). The inexperienced reader, for whom the text must be difficult enough as it is, should not be overly concerned about any hypothetical overtones (after all, Bloom, unlike Christ, is concerned with the adultery committed by his *own* wife). Aside from that, such a reader might easily be influenced unfairly by Blamires's careless way of quoting. By lumping together the two phrases, "Let him" and "No harm in him," which do not occupy adjoining places in the text, Blamires leads readers to believe that the pronoun "him" refers to Boylan both times. Actually, it might be argued that Bloom's thought "No harm in him" refers to the bat that keeps flitting about above his head. He had noticed the animal before (hence "Bat again"), and the shape his thoughts take (note the pronouns!) shows that he conceives of it as a male being:

Ba. What is that flying about? Swallow? Bat probably. Thinks I'm
a tree, so blind. . . . There he goes. Funny little beggar. Wonder where
he lives. Belfry up there. Very likely. Hanging by his heels in the odour
of sanctity. Bell scared him out, I suppose. . . . Ba. Again. Wonder why
they come out at night like mice. . . . What frightens them, light or
noise? Better sit still. . . . Like a little man in a cloak he is with tiny
hands. (13.1117–31/377.29–378.04)

Bloom may have been just a little bit scared of the bat ("Better sit still"),
but, in the last conscious or semiconscious moments before he drops off to
sleep, his common sense — or simply his drowsiness — takes over: He closes
his eyes, reassuring himself that the bat will not do him any harm. As
Kenner puts it, "he dismisses the bat ('no harm in him') as casually as he
has just dismissed Boylan" (1955:204).

Bloom may have resigned himself to the fact that Boylan will most
probably share Molly's bed on the concert tour to Belfast ("Let him"), but,
if there is forgiveness on his part, it will be Molly he is willing to forgive,
and surely not the man he considers, as we know from his thoughts in the
funeral carriage, to be the "Worst man in Dublin" (6.202/92.25).

"Nausicaa" is, as Maddox phrases it, "a stopping place in the book, a
place for summing up" (1978:76), but the same passage in which we find
Bloom looking back on the tiring day he has had also provides an explicit
link between this episode and the next, "Oxen of the Sun." Sitting on the
beach in the dusk, Bloom reflects that it is too late now to go to a theater to
see either *Leah* or *Lily of Killarney*. He briefly considers going home, but
decides not to, because the idea that Molly might still be up does not
appeal to him. He remembers Mrs. Breen telling him (a functional
meeting from the point of view of plot: in the hospital, at last, Bloom will
meet Stephen) that Mrs. Purefoy, a mutual acquaintance, is still in the
lying-in hospital on Holles Street, having lain in labor for three days
(8.276ff/158.34ff.). Molly must have paid a visit, on more than one
occasion, to the Purefoys' home, where the children were milling around,
as we learn from her silent soliloquy: "the last time I was there a squad of
them falling over one another and bawling you couldnt hear your ears"
(185.163–65/742.27–29). Later, Bloom's thoughts by some association
return to the subject of "Poor Mrs Purefoy," conjuring up the image of the
latter's husband, and, remembering that the couple has a baby practically
every year, he reflects: "Hardy annuals he presents her with" (8.362–63/
161.11). In her comment on the maternity scene, Henke has spoiled the
effect of Bloom's witticism; without indicating the source of the quotation, which, moreover, turns out to be a misquote, she says: "Theodore
Purefoy, by presenting Mina with 'hearty [sic] annuals,' has reduced her to
perpetual broodmare" (1978:176). Thus, the allusion to Bloom's witty
thought in an earlier episode has gone overboard.

Before looking back, briefly, on the long day he has had, Bloom decides to pay a call to the clinic to inquire after Mrs. Purefoy:

> Better not stick here all night like a limpet. This weather makes you dull. Must be getting on for nine by the light. Go home. Too late for *Leah. Lily of Killarney* [Joyce's italics]. No. Might still be up. Call to the hospital to see. Hope she's over. *Long day I've had. Martha, the bath, funeral, house of Keyes, museum with those goddesses, Dedalus' song. Then that bawler in Barney Kiernan's. Got my own back there. . . . what I said about his God made him wince. . . . But Dignam's put the boots on it. Houses of mourning so depressing . . .*   (13.1211–26/ 380.18–36, italics mine)

In a discussion of patterns in *Ulysses*, Senn (1982a) lists the final lines of this passage as the first of what he calls the three "major synoptic abridgments," occurring in "Nausicaa," "Circe," and "Ithaca," respectively. We recognize these lines for what they are—a very brief summary, a psychologically determined selection of the day's events so far. Out of the nine preceding episodes ("Calypso" through "Cyclops") Bloom touches only on six: "Lotus Eaters" (Martha, the bath), "Hades" (funeral), "Aeolus" (house of Keyes), "Scylla and Charybdis" (museum with those goddesses), "Sirens" (Dedalus's song), and "Cyclops" ("Then that bawler . . ."), a list notable for events remembered by the reader but left out from Bloom's recall (e.g., the breakfast scene), as well as for events recollected by Bloom but not recorded explicitly in the novel (e.g., Bloom's visit to the Dignam family).

Part Three

Future Indicative

Predicting the future of *Ulysses* studies depends on an accurate reading of the greater bulk of recent criticism, that which is indicative of the future within the present. Where the future begins can be problematic, but a conference marking the fiftieth anniversary of the publication of *Ulysses* consisted of various attempts to chart the direction. Of particular interest in this regard was Robert Scholes's "Structuralist Perspective." Scholes places Joyce (and *Ulysses*) in a global context, as do many of the newer Joyce critics, in effect rescuing him from the exclusive hold of literary critics and relating him and his achievement within a larger framework of ideas. For Scholes the "extended" Joyce can be found in the later chapters of *Ulysses* (and, by extension, in *Finnegans Wake*), the resistance to which he conflates with the resistance to structuralist theory. Joyce anticipated the "structuralist revolution" in these chapters by developing his characters so that they are no longer "bounded by their own skins," and actions that no longer "take place at one location in space-time," offering a unique explanation of the Homeric function different from those of the literalists or the skeptics, operating as a system of checks and balances on runaway randomness. He interprets the chaos at the end of "Oxen of the Sun" as *structural*, "because it is a linguistic transformation of the anti-structural randomization of an afterbirth: a melange of entropic noises. It is what structure prevents *Ulysses* from becoming." Six years later Dorrit Cohn examines the "Penelope" chapter as an independent text, an "Autonomous Monologue," insisting that there is a structure to the chapter that does not allow it to be entered into at any random point. A common sense of theoretical thinking characterizes the approaches of Robert Scholes and Dorrit Cohn in the 1970s, anticipating the fuller thrust of the 1980s.

What characterizes the 1980s is the "intrusion" of non-Joyceans, more welcome to some than to others, into a field institutionalized by professional Joyceans. The former include philosophers, psychologists, linguists, and political scientists, into whose fields Joyce has "intruded." In effect we are returning to those "halcyon" days: neither Jung nor Gilbert nor Budgen was a literary critic. Cohn approaches *Ulysses* as a narratological theorist for whom Joyce's text is one among many; therefore her perspectives are multiple. Her close examination of "Penelope" notes the "absolute correspondence between time and text," as well as the "absence of a manipulating narrator" (of which that one chapter may be an extreme example, but perhaps diagnostic of the structure of the entire narrative). Like Scholes she locates "an over-all structure" creating a "classic unity" that is "matched and mirrored by its linguistic texture"; her breaking down of the syntax of Molly's sentences anticipates the work of Roy Gottfried, whose book was in the early printing stages when Cohn's was published. Nor is she unaware of Molly's feminine consciousness and its feminist potential — a major critical point in the 1980s — as she discerns that in the "cryptic privacy" of Molly's thoughts (into which are implanted "just enough signposts to guard against total incomprehensibility") exist linguistic pockets of the female "we" and the masculine "they," undercut by Molly's occasional irritation with some of the "they."

Of all the new approaches to *Ulysses* the most problematic has been that of Marxian (or neo-Marxian) criticism: throughout the 1980s the International James Joyce Symposia have featured panel discussions on Marxist analyses of Joyce, and the subject has proven a potent one. But few texts have suffered from a single source of attack as has *Ulysses* during the 1930s, so that redefining Marxist literary theory is as difficult as finding those elements of Joyce's text that respond to any Marxian approach. Jeremy Hawthorn's 1982 essay, "*Ulysses*, Modernism, and Marxist Criticism," is largely devoted to unsettling the tenacity of 1930s antagonism and clearing the battlefield of old and rusty weapons. A fresh look at *Ulysses* might offer new possibilities. "For all that Joyce's vision in the novel is partial and selective," Hawthorn notes, "(which is hardly avoidable), one could counter-claim that few novels show their characters less as free, autonomous beings or more tied to their society and its history." Hawthorn retains the basic Marxian touchstones as he talks in terms of "affirmation" and "humanism," and a "real grasp of its historic situation," concluding that *Ulysses* "affirms certain human values in their social and historical specificity with such force that we cannot afford to dismiss it or them." The turning point for Hawthorn, ironically, is found in Soviet psycholinguistics of the 1930s, and what he anticipates is a greater confluence of Marxian analysis with linguistics and psychology, a new amalgam of Marx and Freud.

In their different ways Brook Thomas and Karen Lawrence are representative of the multifaceted critical approaches of the early part of this decade, approaches only partially identifiable with a theoretical ideology and highly inventive within their critical constructs. Thomas develops and redevelops the possibilities (and limitations) of reader-response theory in relation to *Ulysses*, emphasizing Joyce himself as a reader and rewriter (the 1970s was "The Age of the Notebooks," so that the product of Joyce's reading could be reapplied to a text that was endangered by being fixed as computer-definitive). Thomas is conscious of the "protean nature" of the forms of *Ulysses*, and suspicious of any defined norms. Lawrence, in her chapter on the early portions of *Ulysses*, undercuts the existence of narrative norms *beyond* the first six chapters, having uncovered those norms in the "dominant narrative voice" of the Telemachiad, which she reads very distinctly as a "novel." The establishment of a "confidence in the adequacy of the novel form" proves short-lived for Lawrence, as the work moves inextricably away from plot to a "fiction in which plot becomes synonymous with digression." In parallel order Thomas, in his concentration on the later chapters (the basic field of play for much contemporary, nontraditional investigation), considers the process of Joyce's rereading as determining the movement away from the "initial style" of the opening chapters, as well as away from the innovation of "interior monologue" (the former a crutch for many of the less daring readers of *Ulysses*, the latter the heights of experimentation for them). Lawrence concurs on the overemphasis "placed on the stream-of-consciousness technique" so that critics "have tended to underestimate the importance of the narrative norm."

A common denominator for Thomas and Lawrence is the important position of language in the Joyce narrational scheme, an aspect of *Ulysses* that has become the centerpiece of almost all new assaults upon its "difficulties." Thomas concentrates on the "play of language" to the extent of watching Joyce outstrip Stephen's acceptance of "the words he has inherited," so that he can "allow language continually to repeat itself with a difference." Lawrence anchors her linguistic concerns less in this Joycean play than in the relationship between language and narrative stance in *Ulysses*, asserting that even in the opening chapter one can discern the "beginning of an interest in language apart from character, language that calls attention to its own clichéd nature without providing the vehicle for the ironic exposure of a character." Criticism has moved dramatically away from the assumption that *Ulysses* can be viewed essentially as a narrative determined — at least until "Penelope" — by either Bloom's or Stephen's field of experience and observation. For Lawrence there is still some variation of this assumption in her view that "It is Bloom's rather than Stephen's sensibility that dominates the *kind* of book *Ulysses* will become," while Thomas reserves the right to read the book from back to front as well as in the conventional sequence, rewriting as he rereads.

As the 1980s come to a close what seems indicative of future trends is both a greater diversity in *Ulysses* commentary, bringing in various other disciplines of learning, and an attempt at a new synthesis of divergent approaches. Patrick McGee's chapter on "Gesture" (a topic that has fascinated various scholars for many years) represents such a synthesis along poststructuralist lines, combining psychoanalytic and linguistic, as well as sociopolitical and feminist, contributions to a patterned analysis. Like Lawrence's "The Narrative Norm," McGee's "Gesture: The Letter of the Word" is the opening chapter of his book, one of the most recent published on *Ulysses* (1988), and also tracks those important early chapters for the basic elements that establish the "norms" of Stephen's and Bloom's fields of operation. An important tendency in contemporary *Ulysses* investigation is the dual emphasis on the extensive complexities of the last half of the book (McGee has no qualms about calling it a "novel," a reconsideration of its genre that is currently making some headway), as well as attention to the formative chapters as containing complexities of their own that have hitherto been dismissed as excessive nitpicking. The "initial style," as we have already seen in Brook Thomas, is no longer merely accepted as a traditional narrative device, but mined for its intimations of later complexities. Furthermore, "interior monologue" has lost its privileged status as the most important stylistic innovation in the narrative, especially as a psychological indicator for Stephen and Bloom. Instead, the complexities of their minds are read as defying any such easy access, and parallel importantly the complexities of the "halcyon" world exposed in Joyce's Dublin and the concomitant complexities in the styles developed to carry the narrative. From the "structuralist perspective" of Robert Scholes to the poststructural perspectives of Patrick McGee a line of new investigation is being achieved.

Ulysses: A Structuralist Perspective

Robert Scholes*

"We are still learning to be Joyce's contemporaries." So run the opening words of that extraordinary achievement in biography, Richard Ellmann's *James Joyce.* I take it that a conference on "*Ulysses*: From the Perspective of Fifty Years" is asking for a progress report on our attempt to become contemporaneous with Joyce. What have we learned in fifty years that enables us to see *Ulysses* more clearly than it could have been seen by those who were contemporary with it in mere chronology? And by this question is implied some progress not only in that narrow domain called "Joyce studies," to which some of us present here may claim a partial title, but in the larger world of humane learning as a whole.

My response to this question is a fairly simple thesis. I believe that the most important thing we have learned in the past fifty years is a way of thinking called "structuralism," which is based on linguistics and cybernetics, and has profoundly altered our ontology and our epistemology. Or rather it *should have* altered our fundamental concepts of being and mind, but it has met with a very understandable resistance — especially in literary studies. We men of letters have been reluctant to give up a view of the human situation that has seemed correct since Copernicus, and which we hold responsible for all individual achievement since the Renaissance. As a part of my thesis, I will maintain that the reluctance of many critics to accept the later Joyce (and by this I mean the last chapters of *Ulysses* as well as *Finnegans Wake*) is an aspect of this larger reluctance to accept the structuralist revolution. In a very real sense, some of us do not *want* to become Joyce's contemporaries, and we find the collapse of individuated characterization in the later Joyce as threatening as the loss of our own identities in some dystopian nightmare of the future. In this perspective the closing words of the first mini-version of *A Portrait*, which once seemed merely the posturings of a confused young idealist, appear much more concrete and consequential:

> Perhaps his state would pension off old tyranny — a mercy no longer hopelessly remote — in virtue of that mature civilization to which (let it

*From the *James Joyce Quarterly* 10 (Fall 1972):161–71. Reprinted by permission of the *James Joyce Quarterly*.

allow) it had in some way contributed. Already the messages of citizens were flashed along the wires of the world, already the generous idea had emerged from a thirty years' war in Germany and was directing the councils of the Latins. To those multitudes, not as yet in the wombs of humanity but surely engenderable there, he would give the word: Man and woman, out of you comes the nation that is to come, the lightning of your masses in travail; the competitive order is employed against itself, the aristocracies are supplanted; and amid the general paralysis of an insane society, the confederate will issues in action.[1]

This passage could be dissected at length, for it is a strange and wonderful combination of Marx, Nietzsche, and D'Annunzio. Certainly that brand of National Socialism which came to be called Nazism might seem to have been rooted in this kind of thought. But it should be clearly noted that the worst crimes of Nazism had to do with its nationalistic character (nationalism leading naturally to racism, genocide, and even ecocide) rather than with its socialism. Joyce's "nation that is to come" is not a nation state but a kind of global village: individuals cybernetically related through "the wires of the world." As I say, it is tempting to dwell on this passage and explore its implications, but more pertinent matters lie ahead. Let it serve notice here that what I am going to call the revolutionary aspects of the later Joyce are not revolutionary merely from my own perspective, as a critic writing in 1972. Over seventy years ago, Joyce saw himself as one who "would give the word" to those not as yet in the wombs of humanity. Though we have been learning to read him, he may speak more clearly and more powerfully to our children. And the word he brings, in his final work, is the good news of a structuralist revolution.

Of course, both of these terms are so abused currently that it takes some temerity to introduce them in a serious discussion such as this one. If it is possible to have a "bell bottom revolution," or a "hot pants revolution," and so on, what mild shift in the breezes of fashion cannot be proclaimed revolutionary? "Structuralism," too, has suffered from linguistic inflation, acquiring meanings not only in the sciences but, as Jean Piaget has ruefully noted, "at cocktail parties." Both of these terms are disturbingly modish, and I can only partially take the curse off them by trying to give the phrase "structuralist revolution" a clearly delimited meaning for the rest of this discussion. Once that is accomplished, we may turn more directly to *Ulysses*.

First of all, let it be clear that by revolution I mean a turning-over of our ways of thinking. Of course, such turnings-over have political implications. The medieval world view and the feudal political system stood and fell together. But revolution in the sense of a single action confined to the political sphere is not what I am thinking about here. I mean revolution in the larger sense—as we might say that the American revolution and the French revolution were instances of some larger meta-revolution called "liberalism" or "democracy" or some such thing. The revolution I am calling structuralist begins, then, with a turning-over of our ways of thinking. This turning-over is summed up neatly and vigorously in a recent collection of essays by Gregory Bateson called *Steps to an Ecology of Mind*:

> In the period of the Industrial Revolution, perhaps the most important disaster was the enormous increase of scientific arrogance. We had discovered how to make trains and other machines. . . . Occidental man saw himself as an autocrat with complete power over a universe which was made of physics and chemistry. And the biological phenomena were in the end to be controlled like processes in a test tube. Evolution was the history of how organisms learned more tricks for controlling the environment; and man had better tricks than any other creature.
>
> But that arrogant scientific philosophy is now obsolete, and in its place there is the discovery that man is only a part of larger systems and that the part can never control the whole.[2]

In short, this revolution has put something like God back in the universe—but not a God made in man's image, bursting with individualism and subject to temper tantrums when His will is thwarted. But a God who truly "is not mocked" because It *is* the plan of the universe, the master system which sets the pattern for all others. This God cannot intercede for His chosen favorites and suspend the natural law. Nor can He promise comforts in some afterworld for pain endured here. Here is where It is. God is immanent. It offers us only the opportunity to learn Its ways and take pleasure in conforming to them. For certainly there is only frustration in trying to thwart them. If in some ways this resembles the theology of Dante, then so be it. It would be a strange comment on the ecology of ideas if Catholicism could persist for two millennia without a grain of truth in its theology. It is not Catholic theology which has made the Church obsolescent, but Catholic fundamentalism. Freed from the letter, the spirit of Catholic theology is quite capable of accommodating all the truths of science. But lest I sound too much like an Apologist for the Church I left some twenty years ago, let me hasten back to Joyce.

The point of this particularly "commodious vicus of recirculation" is that Dublin's Dante could work himself into a structuralist position more easily by taking medieval theology as a point of departure than could someone handicapped by conversion to a more "reasonable" world view. Thus, I submit that Joyce, taking a few ideas well learned from Catholic theology, and adding notions from Vico and others, worked himself into an intellectual position which has much in common with that of Lévi-Strauss, or Piaget, or Bateson. Let us listen to Bateson again, with Joyce's later work specifically in mind:

> Ecology currently has two faces to it: the face which is called bioenergetics—the economics of energy and materials within a coral

reef, a redwood forest, or a city—and, second, an economics of information, of entropy, negentropy, etc. These two do not fit together very well precisely because the units are differently bounded in the two sorts of ecology. In bioenergetics it is natural and appropriate to think of units bounded at the cell membrane, or at the skin; or of units composed of conspecific individuals. These boundaries are then the frontiers at which measurements can be made to determine the additive-subtractive budget of energy for a given unit. In contrast, informational or entropic ecology deals with the budgeting of pathways and probability. The resulting budgets are fractionating (not subtractive). The boundaries must enclose, not cut, the relevant pathways.

Moreover, the very meaning of "survival" becomes different when we stop talking of something bounded by the skin and start to think of the survival of the system of ideas in the circuit. The contents of the skin are randomized at death and the pathways within the skin are randomized. But the ideas, under further transformation, may go on out in the world in books or works of art. Socrates as a bioenergetic individual is dead. But much of him still lives as a component in the ecology of ideas.[3]

It is clear to me that Joyce is one of the few writers of his time, perhaps the only one, who arrived at a concept of fiction which is cybernetic rather than bioenergetic. As his career developed, he accepted less and less willingly the notion of characters bounded by their own skins, and of actions which take place at one location in space-time, and then are lost forever. Unlike Lawrence, for instance, who reacted against "the old stable ego of the character" simply by giving us characters with unstable egos, Joyce attacked the ego itself, beginning with his own. But not initially. The cybernetic serenity of his later work was long coming and hard won. For he had a good deal of ego to disperse. Nothing could be sharper than the division between self and others as we find it in his early Epiphanies, with their focus upon the verbal or gestural "vulgarity" of others and the "memorable" phases of his own mental life. This same bioenergetic separation persists through *Stephen Hero, Dubliners*, and *A Portrait*. Though there are hints of it in this latter work, it is only in *Ulysses* that we really find the ego breaking down. I think it is reasonable to say that Stephen Dedalus is Joyce's bioenergetic self-portrait, while Leopold Bloom is his cybernetic self-portrait.

Since Ellmann's biography of Joyce, we have complacently referred to Bloom as well as Stephen as "autobiographical"—but surely we need to distinguish between these two kinds of autobiography. And it is not enough to say that Stephen is a young Joyce and Bloom is a mature Joyce. For Stephen "is" Joyce in a different way from the way Bloom "is" Joyce. Stephen is Joyce in his skin, with all the significant features that would make him recognizable. And with no features that Joyce himself did not possess. Insofar as Joyce could create a "true" self-portrait, Stephen is that portrait (somewhat retouched from book to book). But Bloom contains large elements of Joyce's neural circuitry without being recognizable as Joyce; and at some important levels of experience he is a "truer" representation of Joyce than Stephen. But that cellular integrity which marks Stephen as Joyce himself and not any other person is lacking in Bloom. He is a Joyce interpenetrated with others: with the far-wandering Odysseus and with a pathetic Dubliner that the Joyce family actually knew. (And with other figures from life and art as well.) This characterization of the peripathetic Bloom is remarkable not because it shows Joyce creating a great character who is un-autobiographical, but because it shows us an autobiographical characterization without egocentricity.

If Flaubert truly thought of Emma Bovary on occasions as himself ("*C'est moi!*"), he must have donned her skin with a naturalistic *frisson*, prompted by his sense of how different it was from his own. But for Joyce in *Ulysses* there is no hint of such *nostalgie de la boue*. He lived *là-bas*, and thus his works lack the delight in slumming which is often one aspect of naturalism. And by *Finnegans Wake* he had come to accept the Homais in himself as Flaubert never could. It might also be well to recall at this point how in the *Wake* Joyce's ego is not only diffused among the whole range of major figures and minor; it has also spread out to include the "inanimate" rivers, rocks, and trees of Dublin and the world. Which ought to remind us that if Beckett is Joyce's heir, he is a model of filial rebellion. For the nausea and alienation which he has chronicled so articulately are the very antitheses of the acceptance of the ecosystem that animates *Finnegans Wake*.

It should be clear by now that from my perspective on *Ulysses* "fifty years after," it is a transitional work *par excellence*. It is transitional in Joyce's treatment of his own ego and in many other respects as well. This very transitional nature of the book has led one school of critics (call it the Goldberg variation) to see the book as a failed novel, which goes off the novelistic track in the later chapters due to Joyce's self-indulgence in various lingusitic capers. It would be just as reasonable to invert this critique and see the early chapters as a false start of somewhat too traditional flavor, corrected by the brilliant new devices of the last part. These views I reject as equally wrong. *Ulysses* is a transitional work for us as well as for Joyce. In reading it we learn how to read it; our comprehension is exercised and stretched. We are led gradually to a method of narration and to a view of man (the two inseparable) different from those found in previous fiction. This method and this view I am calling structuralist, asserting that Joyce's later work can not only be seen more clearly from a structuralist perspective but that it is structuralist in its outlook and methodology.

In testing this thesis against the mass of *Ulysses* in such short space, much will have to be taken for granted. But I will try to look at certain representative aspects of *Ulysses* in the light of a few structuralist notions derived from Saussurian linguistics and the genetic epistemology of Jean

Piaget, beginning with Piaget's definition of structure: "In short, the notion of structure is comprised of three key ideas: the idea of wholeness, the idea of transformation, and the idea of self-regulation."[4] This triad leads to a more satisfying esthetic than the one Joyce called "applied Aquinas," and in fact it is more applicable to Joyce's later work. But before applying it we must elaborate on it a little bit. By *wholeness* Piaget indicates elements arranged according to laws of combination rather than merely lumped together as an aggregate. Such wholeness is a quality of all recognizable literary works. It is, in fact, one way we recognize them. They have the wholeness of all linguistic utterances and the more intense wholeness of discourse specifically literary. Since this is a characteristic of all fiction, it need not be especially remarked in *Ulysses*. By *transformation* Piaget means the ability of parts of a structure to be interchanged or modified according to certain rules, and he specifically cites transformational linguistics as an illustration of such processes. In *Ulysses* the metempsychotic way in which Bloom and Odysseus are related is one notable principle of transformation, and there are other transformational aspects of the book to which we will return. By *self-regulation* Piaget refers to the "interplay of anticipation and correction (feedback)" in cybernetic systems and to "the rhythmic mechanisms such as pervade biology and human life at every level." Self-regulating structures are both "self-maintaining" and "closed." I would like to suggest that in *Ulysses* the Homeric parallels function as a kind of feed-back loop, operating to correct imbalance and brake any tendency of the work to run away in the direction of merely random recitations from Bloom's day. And there are many other such loops. Each chapter, in fact, is designed to run down when certain schematic systems are complete and when a certain temporal segment of the Dublin day has been covered. Whereupon the next Homeric parallel is activated to provide a diachronic scheme for the following chapter.

This system can be illustrated by a brief consideration of the much maligned "Oxen of the Sun" chapter. It exhibits all of the structural properties I have been discussing, and can thus serve to illustrate their working in some detail. This chapter is basically a simple narrative segment of the day: Stephen and Bloom happen to come to the same place, a lying-in hospital where Mrs. Purefoy is engaged in a long and difficult accouchement. After young Mortimer Edward is born, Stephen and some medical students, accompanied or followed by Bloom, go off to a pub for some superfluous drinking. This base narrative is transformed according to a complex set of rules. Rule 1: the events must be narrated by a sequence of voices that illustrate the chronological movement of English prose from the Middle Ages to contemporary times. Rule 2: each voice must narrate an appropriate segment of the events taking place. That is, a Pepysian voice must deal with Pepysian details and a Carlylean voice with a Carlylean celebration. Which assumes Rule 3: the voices must be pastiches or parodies of clearly recognizable stylists or stylistic schools.

The purpose of these rules is not merely to show off Joyce's skill as a parodist and pasticher, which is considerable, but to enrich our experience of the characters presented and events narrated. And it is their interaction which gives shape to events that in themselves are only minimally shapely. In this chapter Joyce operates with roughly six sets of narrative materials, to be arranged according to these rules. He has Bloom's present words and deeds, plus his thoughts of the past, and the same two sets of present and past for Stephen. He also has the simultaneous actions of the medical students, Haines, and so on, along with a sixth item, the birth itself. The selection of what comes when, in the necessarily linear sequence of prose narrative, is thus the result of a complex interaction among these rules and sets of possibilities. (The Homeric parallel, in this chapter, offered the initial idea, but had less influence on structure than in some other chapters.) In this chapter, the selection of the moment of birth, for instance, is saved from arbitrariness by the appropriateness of the voices of Dickens and Carlyle to celebrate the new arrival. And if *they* are to celebrate him, young Mortimer must appear in the middle of the nineteenth century, the ear of phyloprogenitiveness. Similarly, the drunken conversation that closes the chapter functions in a structural way because it is a linguistic transformation of the anti-structural randomization of an afterbirth: a melange of entropic noise. It is what structure prevents *Ulysses* from becoming, though for those who cannot perceive the structure it is precisely what the book seems to be.

This kind of structure, of course, is a function of Joyce's massive unwillingness to get on with it and tell a simple linear tale. And thereby hangs a good deal of critical hostility. In discussing this aspect of *Ulysses* some terminology from linguistics will be helpful. Saussurian structuralism is founded on a distinction between synchronic and diachronic views of language. From this initial position a further distinction between the syntagmatic and paradigmatic aspects of any particular utterance has been derived. In a given sentence, for example, the meaning of a single word is determined partly by its position in the sentence and its relation to the other words and grammatical units of that sentence. This is the word's syntagmatic aspect, often conceptualized as a horizontal axis along which the sentence is spread out in its necessary order. The meaning of a single word in a sentence is also determined by its relation to some groups of words *not* in the actual sentence but present in a paradigmatic (or "vertical") relationship to the actual word. A word is thus defined partly by all the words which might have filled its place but have been displaced by it. These displaced words may be conceived as belonging to several paradigmatic sets: other words with the same grammatical function, other words with related meanings (synonyms and antonyms), other words with similar sound patterns — these are three obvious paradigmatic sets. Our actual selection of a word in a sentence involves something like a rapid scanning of paradigmatic possibilities until we find one that will play the appropriate role in the syntax we are constructing. In structuralist literary theory, it is customary to see narrative literature as a transformation by enlargement of our basic sentence structure. Characters are nouns; their situations or attributes are adjectives; and their actions are verbs. And fiction is defined by its emphasis of the syntagmatic or linear (horizontal) dimension of linguistic possibilities, whereas poetry is less concerned with syntagmatic progression and more inclined to play with paradigmatic possibilities.

Joyce, in *Ulysses*, is often very reluctant to speed along the syntagmatic trail like an Agatha Christie. Often, it is as if he cannot bear to part with many of the paradigmatic possibilities that have occurred to him. He will stop and climb up the paradigmatic chain on all sorts of occasions, such as the various lists in "Cyclops" (I shall resist the temptation to pause and make a meta-list at this point), in which displaced possibilities are allowed to sport themselves and form syntagmatic chains of their own. These lists *do become* syntagmatic in themselves, and they further relate to other lists and other parts of the whole narrative in a syntagmatic way. A book as long as *Ulysses* which was really paradigmatic in its emphasis would be virtually impossible to read — as *Ulysses* is for those who do not see its structure. But even the lists in *Ulysses* if examined closely will prove to have both an internal syntagmatic dimension and an external one.

The lists in "Cyclops" for instance, tend to follow some basic comic laws which depend on syntagmatic expectation. For instance, they may establish an innocent pattern, apparently a simple process of repetition, and then violate it while appearing to continue in the same manner — as in this sequence from the opening of the list of ladies attending the "wedding of the grand high chief ranger of the Irish National Foresters with Miss Fir Conifer of Pine Valley. Lady Sylvester Elmshade, Mrs Barbara Lovebirch . . ." and so on (*U* 327). We quickly pick up the basic principle of these names — or we think we do. There is to be an appropriateness between the first and last names of these arboreal damsels which makes it amusing to consider them. Such names further down the list as "Miss Timidity Aspenall" or "Miss Grace Poplar" are constructed by animating an attribute of the tree names in the last name and deriving a first name from this attribute. Poplars are graceful and aspens may easily be thought of as timid. (And by extension, Miss rather than Mrs. is appropriate for them too.) In this list, the opening "Fir Conifer" and "Sylvester Elmshade" establish this pattern without being as clever as some of the later combinations — thus allowing for some syntagmatic progression. But this pattern is enriched by some others, which add a different kind of comedy to the list and complicate its syntagmatic relationships. That third name,

"Barbara Lovebirch" introduces into this green world the whole motif of sado-masochistic perversion which will culminate in the "Circe" chapter. The name "Lovebirch" not only includes the masochistic idea but refers to the author of the pornographic novel *Fair Tyrants* (James Lovebirch), which Bloom has inspected in "Wandering Rocks" and rejected ("Had it? Yes.") as not so much in Molly's line as *Sweets of Sin*. And of course in "Circe" Mrs. Yelverton Barry accuses Bloom of making "improper overtures" to her under the *nom de plume* of James Lovebirch. Among the list of innocent trees the barbaric lovebirch is comically sinister. And once directed this way the reader may well see sexual connotations lurking beneath every bush. Is "Mrs Kitty Dewey-Mosse" innocent? Thus even what appears to be a purely paradigmatic excursion in *Ulysses* proves to have a system of its own and beyond that to exhibit connections of the syntagmatic sort with other events and episodes.

The process illustrated here in little is related to the larger processes of the book. The "Oxen of the Sun" is written as it is not merely to vary our perspective on Stephen and Bloom, showing aspects of them that could only be shown through the styles employed. The chapter also represents an acknowledgment of all the narrative voices that have been displaced by Joyce in uttering *Ulysses*. The whole chapter is a climb up a particular paradigmatic ladder on the level of style. And it serves not only to throw new light on Bloom and Stephen. It also takes Bloom and Stephen and the whole world of *Ulysses* back through the system of English literature and allows this work of 1922 to intermingle with the past. If Carlyle's voice can celebrate Theodore Purefoy in 1922, then Carlyle's cybernetic self still lives through Joyce's agency. And if the "Oxen of the Sun" chapter serves partly to install Bloom and Stephen among the literature of the past, the "Ithaca" chapter serves a similar purpose with respect to science.

The technological and scientific perspectives of "Ithaca" extend Bloom and Stephen to new dimensions without aggrandizing them. (And without dwarfing them as is sometimes contended.) Space-time does not permit me to trace this process in detail, but I want to close by focussing on what I take to be the final lesson of "Ithaca" and one of the most deeply embedded meanings in the entire book. At the end of this chapter, after a day of anxiety, Bloom rearrives at an equilibrium which is not merely that of a body at rest but that of a self-regulated system operating in harmony with other systems larger than itself. He views his wife's adulterous episode "with more abnegation than jealousy, less envy than equanimity" for a very important reason. Because it is "not more abnormal than all other altered processes of adaptation to altered conditions of existence, resulting in a reciprocal equilibrium between the bodily organism and its attendant circumstances . . ."(*U* 733). Blazes Boylan is Molly's adjustment to Bloom's sexual retreat. As she might say herself, "It's only natural." Bloom is homeostatic man, centripetal, his equilibrium achieved. And Stephen is young, therefore centrifugal, and therefore to be forgiven. In time he too will return, like Shakespeare reading the book of himself, and writing it too. Stephen and Bloom and Molly have other roles to play in *Finnegans Wake*, permutations and combinations hardly dreamed of in 1922. And for this total achievement, we may say of Joyce what Bateson said of Socrates. As a bioenergetic individual he is indeed dead. "But much of him still lives in the ecology of ideas."

Notes

1. "A Portrait of the Artist," in *The Workshop of Daedalus: James Joyce and the Raw Materials for "A Portrait of the Artist as a Young Man,"* ed. Robert Scholes and Richard M. Kain (Evanston: Northwestern University Press, 1965), pp. 67–8.

2. *Steps to an Ecology of Mind* (New York: Ballantine Books, 1972), p. 437.

3. Ibid., p. 461.

4. *Structuralism*, trans. Chaninah Maschler (New York: Basic Books, 1970), p. 5.

The Autonomous Monologue   Dorrit Cohn*

"PENELOPE" AS PARADIGM

Within the limited corpus of autonomous interior monologues the "Penelope" section of *Ulysses* may be regarded as a *locus classicus*, the most famous and the most perfectly executed specimen of its species. Given its position within the broader context of Joyce's novel, however, the question must be raised whether it is at all legitimate to consider "Penelope" as an example of an autonomous fictional form. Would it even be comprehensible to a reader unfamiliar with the preceding sections of the novel? A difficult question to answer empirically, since it would be very nearly impossible to find an experimental subject untainted by at least a hearsay acquaintance with Joyce's work. This much seems certain: Joyce's task of making the "plot" of an interior monologue text comprehensible to the reader despite the strict implicitness of reference demanded by the logic of the form was greatly eased by placing it at the end of his novel rather than at its beginning. The fact, moreover, that we know so much of what Molly knows before we hear her silent voice enhances our enjoyment of it by myriad cross-references to the rest of the novel. Even more important, the fact that we know much that Molly does *not* know (for example, the entire truth about Bloom's erotic experiences on Bloomsday) interjects an element of dramatic irony into our reading experience that would be lost if "Penelope" were read as a separate novella.

*From *Transparent Minds: Narrative Modes for Presenting Consciousness in Fiction* (Princeton, N.J.: Princeton University Press, 1978), 217–32. Reprinted by permission of the publisher.

Nonetheless, more than any of the other chapters of *Ulysses*, and more than ordinary narrative units within other novels, "Penelope" stands apart from its context, as a self-generated, self-supported, and self-enclosed fictional text. Joyce himself stressed its extra-mural status when he commented on the ending of *Ulysses*: "It [the "Ithaca" chapter] is in reality the end as 'Penelope' has no beginning, middle or end."[1] The spherical image he used to describe "Penelope" in a well-known letter to Frank Budgen further underlines its self-enclosure: "It begins and ends with the female *Yes*. It turns like the huge earthball slowly surely and evenly round and round spinning."[2] Joyce's two self-exegetical schemas add yet another element that sets "Penelope" apart: in contrast to the numbered hours that clock all the other episodes, the "Time" marked for the ultimate episode is infinity (∞) in one schema, "Hour none" in the other.[3] But surely the most important sign of "Penelope" 's formal independence is its form itself: the only moment of the novel where a figural voice totally obliterates the authorial narrative voice throughout an entire chapter.[4] No matter how closely the content of Molly's mind may duplicate, supplement, and inform the fictional world of *Ulysses* as a whole, the single-minded and single-voiced form of "Penelope" justifies its consideration as an independent text, a model for that singular narrative genre entirely constituted by a fictional character's thoughts.

One of the most striking structural peculiarities of an autonomous monologue, classically illustrated by "Penelope," is the stricture it imposes on the manipulation of the time dimension. Before we discuss this point, a brief glance at the over-all temporal sequence of Molly's thoughts will dispel a critical commonplace. Critics have tended to take Joyce's mythical image of the spinning earth-ball (in the letter cited above) so literally that they have overstressed the eternal return of the same in "Penelope," while neglecting its sequential unrolling in time.[5] Yet the circularity of Molly's arguments (including the identity of its first and last words) is decisively counteracted by elements that underline its temporal sequence. Prime among these is the fact that her monologue contains a central happening: the inception of her menses (769)[6]; on this account alone it seems to me impossible to maintain that "breaking into ["Penelope"] at any point does not upset the order or sequence."[7] This event is more than incidental; it alerts the direction of Molly's thoughts, clearly dividing them into a before and after: whereas her thoughts of Boylan and others concerning the immediate and distant past dominate before, Boylan almost disappears and all memories diminish after. They are replaced by thoughts of the future, largely in the form of scenarios for seducing Stephen and for re-seducing Bloom. Molly, in other words, enters a "new moon" in the course of her monologue — a decidedly temporal event, no matter how eternal its mythological overtones.[8] It is an event, moreover, that strongly ties Molly to biological time, the time of a biological organism on its way from birth to death. If we can talk of the circular shape of Molly's monologue at all, then only in the modified sense of the coils of a spiral whose direction (upward or downward?) is left ambiguous, but whose linear advance along the coordinate of time is never left in doubt.

This advance, even if we disregard the evolution of Molly's thoughts, is built into the very technique Joyce chose to express them: for a continuous interior monologue is based on an absolute correspondence between time and text, narrated time and time of narration.[9] The single mark for the passage of time here is the sequence of words on the page. Whereas in ordinary narration time is a flexible medium that can be, at will, speeded up (by summary), retarded (by description or digression), advanced (by anticipation), or reversed (by retrospect), an autonomous monologue—in the absence of a manipulating narrator—advances time solely by the articulation of thoughts, and advances it evenly along a one-way path until words come to a halt on the page. Note, however, that this chronographic progress is associated only with the successive moments of verbalization itself, and not with their content: it remains unaffected by the a-chronological montage of events that prevails in a monologist's mind, notoriously in Molly's helter-skelter references to different moments of the past and the future.[10]

This even-paced unrolling of time in an autonomous monologue is analogous to the temporal structure of a dramatic scene (or the uninterrupted rendition of dialogue in a narrative scene). The dramaturgic concept of unity of time, in the strictest neo-classical sense of identifying time of action with time of performance, could be applied here, except that the terms of the identity would have to be modified. For if monologue time flows evenly, there is no telling how fast it flows—unless the monologist explicitly clocks himself. Molly's sense of time being what it is ("I never know the time," 747), the exact length of her insomnia cannot be known.[11] But since it starts sometime after two and ends sometime before daybreak (four o'clock on a June day at Dublin's latitude?) Molly probably thinks faster than most readers read her thoughts, and certainly faster than anyone can recite them. The time of "Penelope" would thus correspond to the common view that thoughts move faster than speech.

The relentless continuity of Molly's text, reinforced as it is by the omission of punctuation, makes its division into eight paragraphs (or "sentences," as Joyce called them) stand out the more distinctly: even these brief interruptions in the print inevitably convey moments of silence, time passing without words. These instant pauses appear like a drawing of mental breath before a new phase of mental discourse; or, to use the analogy with drama again, a curtain quickly drawn closed and reopened between the acts of a play in which absolute unity of time prevails. The very fact that paragraphing calls for an interpretation of this kind in "Penelope" shows that paginal blanks, regardless of their size, tend to carry much more than routine significance in interior monologue texts:

they convey not only passage of time, but interruption of thought. For this reason lapse into sleep is the most convincing ending for a text of this sort, just as waking out of sleep is its most logical beginning. Molly's monologue, of course, ends in this optimal fashion, but its beginning does not coincide with her awakening. Instead, "Penelope" begins in the only alternate way available to an autonomous monologue, namely in medias res, or, better, in mediam mentem, casting the reader without warning into the privacy of a mind talking to itself about its own immediate business: "Yes because he never did a thing like that before as to ask to get his breakfast in bed with a couple of eggs since the City Arms hotel when he used to . . ."(738). This beginning is obviously meant to give the impression of being "no beginning" (" 'Penelope' has no beginning, middle or end"), not even a syntactical beginning. Both "Yes" and "because" (not to mention "he") refer to a clause antecedent to the text's inception, which the reader can only gradually reconstruct from clues that will eventually appear in the text. Not until one reaches the words at the very bottom of the first page ("yes he came somewhere") does it become entirely clear that the thought immediately antecedent to "Yes because" must have concerned Molly's suspicion of her husband's infidelity. But beyond this specific syntactic riddle, this beginning leaves unexplained whose voice speaks, where, when, and how.

The inception of "Penelope" points up the special limitations imposed on a fictional text if it is to create for the reader the illusion that it records a mind involved in self-address. Since it would be implausible for Molly to expound to herself facts she already knows, all exposition (in the usual sense of conveying information about past happenings and present situations) is barred from the text. The facts of Molly's life pass through her consciousness only implicitly, incidentally, by allusive indirection. And all that remains understood in her thoughts can be understood by the reader only by means of a cumulative process of orientation that gradually closes the cognitive gap.

Yet Joyce could not have exposed Molly's inner life without exposition if he had not placed her in a highly pregnant moment, a crisis situation that brings into mental play the key conditions of her life (and of life). Though Molly's may be an ordinary mind, Bloomsday is not — for Molly any more than for Bloom or Stephen — an entirely ordinary day. Its extraordinary events (the afternoon tryst, Bloom's tardy return) are necessary to awaken in her the thoughts that keep her awake, and thus to make what is implicit at least partially explicit. Though she does not tell herself the story of her day, nor the story of her life, both stories transpire through her agitated thoughts, or better, in spite of them.

Doubtless the most artful stratagem Joyce employed, however, is to set Molly's mind into its turbulent motion while setting her body into a state of nearly absolute tranquility. This obviates a major difficulty inherent in the autonomous monologue form: to present through self-address the physical activities the self performs within the time-span of the monologue. Molly, to be sure, does once rise from her bed (769–772), but her gestures during this brief interlude are so obvious and so elemental that they can be gathered without being directly recorded. As Dujardin's *Les Lauriers* and Schnitzler's *Fräulein Else* show, when monologists become much more enterprising they begin to sound much less convincing; forced to describe the actions they perform while they perform them, they tend to sound like gymnastics teachers vocally demonstrating an exercise.

But Joyce not only places the monologizing mind in a body at rest; he also places that body in calm surroundings.[12] The sensations that impinge on Molly's consciousness are few and far between: the whistling trains (754, 762, 763), the chiming bells (772, 781), a lamp (763), a creaking press (771), the sleeping Bloom (771). Only minimally deflected by perceptions of the external world, her monologue is "interior" not only in the technical sense of remaining unvoiced, but also in the more literal sense: it is directed to and by the world within. The perfect adherence to unity of place thus creates the condition for a monologue in which the mind is its own place: self-centered and therefore self-generative to a degree that can hardly be surpassed.

The classic unity (and unities) in the over-all structure of "Penelope" are both matched and mirrored by its linguistic texture. Without intending a complete linguistic-stylistic description of the text,[13] I will focus on three features of its language that spring directly from the autonomous monologue form, and at the same time contrast sharply with the language of retrospective narration: 1) the predominance of exclamatory syntax; 2) the avoidance of narrative and reportive tenses; and 3) the non-referential implicitness of the pronoun system. Note that my approach to Molly's language is different from the approach I took to Bloom's language in the chapter on quoted monologue: there the emphasis was on the contrast between monologue and dialogue, here it is on the contrast between autonomous monologue and narration.

The following excerpt from "Penelope" (769) will serve as the starting-point. I have divided it into thirty numbered segments, each of which corresponds to a "sentence" in the generally accepted sense of a syntactic unit of meaning, or (as one linguist defines it[14]) "a word or set of words followed by a pause and revealing an intelligible purpose":

1. I bet the cat itself is better off than us
2. have we too much blood up in us or what
3. O patience above its pouring out of me like the sea
4. anyhow he didnt make me pregnant as big as he is
5. I dont want to ruin the clean sheets
6. the clean linen I wore brought it on too
7. damn it damn it

8. and they always want to see a stain on the bed to know youre a virgin for them

9. all thats troubling them

10. theyre such fools too

11. you could be a widow and divorced 40 times over

12. a daub of red ink would do or blackberry juice

13. no thats too purply

14. O Jamesy let me up out of this

15. pooh

16. sweets of sin

17. whoever suggested that business for women what between clothes and cooking and children

18. this damned old bed too jingling like the dickens

19. I suppose they could hear us away over the other side of the park till I suggested to put the quilt on the floor with the pillow under my bottom

20. I wonder is it nicer in the day

21. I think it is

22. easy

23. I think Ill cut all this hair off me there scalding me

24. I might look like a young girl

25. wouldnt he get the great suckin the next time he turned up my clothes on me

26. Id give anything to see his face

27. wheres the chamber gone

28. easy

29. Ive a holy horror of its breaking under me after that old commode

30. I wonder was I too heavy sitting on his knee

The most immediately apparent aspect of this language is its agitated, emotional tone. Leaving aside for the moment the several interrogatory sentences (2, 17, 20, 25, 27, 30), almost every sentence would in normal punctuation, deserve — and some would require — a final exclamation mark: most obviously the seven sentences that are, or contain, interjections (3, 7, 14, 15, 16, 22, 28). But since the essence of exclamations is that "they emphasize to the listener some mood, attitude, or desire of the speaker,"[15] almost all the other sentences could be classed as exclamations as well. The passage abounds in emphatically expressive forms: wishes (5, 26), fears (29), disparaging generalizations (9, 10). A highly subjective tone pervades even those sentences that come closest to statements of fact. They are either marked by introductory verbs of conjecture: "I bet" (1), "I suppose" (19), "I think" (21, 23); or by patent overstatement: "divorced 40 times over" (11); or by omission of the copula (18); or by emphatic adverbs and conjunctions: "and" (8), "anyhow" (4), the thrice-uttered "too" (6, 10,

18). No sentence, in short, takes the form of a simple statement; all contain emotive, expressive signals, whether they concern past events or present happenings.

If we remember that interior monologue is, by definition, a discourse addressed to no one, a gratuitous verbal agitation without communicative aim, then this predominance of exclamatory syntax appears perfectly in keeping with the nature of monologue. As the form of discourse that requires no reply, to which there *is* no reply, exclamation is the self-sufficient, self-involved language gesture par excellence.[16] Since interrogation, by contrast, is uttered in the expectation of a reply, and thus dialogic by nature, it at first seems surprising that this passage contains so many questions. But Molly's questions are of a kind fitting easily into a monologic milieu: they are themselves essentially exclamatory. This is most obvious where they are rhetorical, either implying their own answer ("wouldnt he get the great suckin the next time he turned up my clothes on me," 25) or uttered without the expectation of an answer ("whoever suggested that business for women," 17, "have we too much blood up in us or what," 2). The latter type is particularly characteristic for Molly: existential questions abound in her dialogue, questions pleading against the absurd order of the universe, especially its division into pleasure-seeking males and long-suffering females: "whats the idea making us like that with a big hole in the middle of us" (742); "clothes we have to wear whoever invented them" (755); "why cant you kiss a man without going and marrying him first" (740); "where would they all of them be if they hadnt all a mother to look after them" (778); and many more. But also when Molly asks herself genuinely interrogatory questions, she asks them in an exclamatory fashion, usually by introducing them with the phrase, "I wonder": "I wonder is it nicer in the day" (20), "I wonder was I too heavy sitting on his knee" (30). A kind of pathetic anxiety or insecurity comes to the fore in this form of query, especially when the unknown is the impression she made on Boylan (cf. "I wonder was he satisfied with me"; "I wonder is he awake thinking of me or dreaming am I in it," 741). In this sense self-interrogation seems the natural complement to exclamation in the turbulent syntax of language-for-oneself, counterpointing attitudes toward the known with attitudes toward the unknown.

But even as exclamation and interrogation stamp Molly's discourse with subjectivity, these sentence forms also orient it away from a neutral report of the present moment, and away from the narration of past events. Since language-for-oneself is by definition the form of language in which speaker and listener coincide, the technique that imitates it in fiction can remain convincing only if it excludes all factual statements, all explicit report on present and past happenings. The various tenses in Molly's monologue further determine its anti-narrative, anti-reportorial orientation.

I have intentionally chosen my sample passage from the section of Molly's monologue where she begins her most ambitious physical activity of the night — the excursion to the "chamber" — in order to show how Joyce manages to convey Molly's bodily gestures without a single direct statement of the I-am-doing-this-now type. If her activity becomes clear to an attentive reader, it is not because she explicitly reports what she does, but because what she does is implicitly reflected in her thoughts, roughly as follows: "O patience above its pouring out of me . . . I dont want to ruin the clean sheets" (she decided to get a sanitary napkin); "O Jamesy let me up out of this" (she strains to raise her body); "this damned old bed too jingling" (she moves her body out of bed); "I think Ill cut all this hair off me" (she lifts her nightgown); "wheres the chamber gone" (she decides on the interim stop, and reaches for the needed object); "easy Ive a holy horror of its breaking under me" (she lowers herself onto it). Her subsequent performance — "O Lord how noisy" (770), its conclusion — "Id better not make an all night sitting on this affair" (771), the activity with "those napkins" — "I hope theyll have something better for us in the other world . . . thats all right for tonight" (772), and finally the return to bed — "easy piano O I like my bed" (772), are all rendered by exclamatory indirection as well. In sum, we search in vain through "Penelope" for a first-person pronoun coupled with an action verb in present tense — precisely the combination that creates the most jarring effect in less well-executed interior monologues (like *Les Lauriers sont coupés*), because it introduces a reportorial dimension of language into a nonreportorial language situation.

The first-person, present-tense combination in Molly's monologue occurs exclusively with verbs of internal rather than external activity. She supposes, thinks, wishes, hopes, and remembers many times over on every page, so that the punctual present of her inner discourse continuously refers to and feeds on the very activity she literally performs at every moment of her monologue.[17] It is in this present moment of mental activity that all Molly's other verbal tenses and moods are anchored. And she uses them all: past, future, indicative, conditional, and quite prominently the present of generalization. This constant oscillation between memories and projects, the real and the potential, the specific and the general, is one of the most distinctive marks of freely associative monologic language. Our sample passage contains it in motley display, especially toward its end, when we get in rapid succession past (19), present (20–21), future (23), conditional (24–26), and again present (27–29) and past (30). Note how the punctual present of the mental verbs in turn subordinates the past ("I suppose they could hear us"), the generalizing present ("I wonder is it nicer in the day I think it is"), the future ("I think Ill cut all this hair") and the reversion to the past ("I wonder was I too heavy").

There are moments in Molly's monologue when she adheres more extensively to one or another of these tenses and moods. Since she is not much of a planner,[18] her looks into the future verge on the imaginary, whether she uses the conditional or the indicative: thus "supposing he stayed with us" introduces the wish dream of the *ménage à trois* with Stephen (779–780), whereas her dreams of glory as a poet's muse (776) and the alternate scenarios for seducing Bloom (780) are cast in future tense. Her fantasies — "the cracked things come into my head sometimes" (779) — cluster in the last third of "Penelope," whereas memories are denser in the first two-thirds.

In the earlier sections the recalls are so extensive that the past tense actually predominates over the present, with the past sentences at times in straight narrative form, unsubordinated by thinking verbs. Yet even where a consecutive sequence of events takes shape in her mind, the narrative idiom rarely prevails without being interrupted by opinionated comments. The following samples from the courtship scene alternate typically:

> he was shaking like a jelly all over *they want to do everything too quick take all the pleasure out of it* . . . then he wrote me that letter with all those words in it *how could he have the face to any woman after* . . . dont understand you I said and wasnt it natural *so it is of course* . . . then writing a letter every morning sometimes twice a day *I liked the way he made love then* . . . then I wrote the night he kissed my heart at Dolphins barn *I couldnt describe it simply it makes you feel like nothing on earth* . . . (746–747)

I have italicized the sentences that regularly turn a reflective gaze back on each narrative sentence — generalizing, questioning, evaluating; and this discursive language retards, and eventually displaces, the narrative language, as the concern for the present moment again prevails. In this fashion even the moments of Molly's monologue when she comes closest to narrating her life to herself — see also the recall of the Mulvey affair (759–761) and the love-scene on Howth Head (782–783) — never gain sufficient momentum to yield more than briefly suggestive vignettes.

Molly's memories occur to her in thoroughly random order, her mind gliding ceaselessly up and down the thread of time, with the same past tense now referring to the events of the previous afternoon, now reaching back to her nymphet days in Gibraltar, now again lingering on numberless intervening incidents. This a-chronological time montage — as Robert Humphrey calls this technique [19] — provides the data for a fairly detailed Molly biography; but her monologue itself is autobiographical only in spite of itself.

A further, and perhaps the most telling, symptom for the non-narrative and non-communicative nature of Molly's language is the profusion and referential instability of its pronouns.[20] This initially bewildering system puts the reader into a situation akin to that of a person eavesdropping on a conversation in progress between close friends, about people and events unknown to him but so familiar to them that they need not name the people or objects to which they refer. In this sense Molly's pronominal implicitness combines both traits of language-for-oneself discussed earlier in connection with Bloom's monologic idiom: grammatical abbreviation and lexical opaqueness—traits in other respects far less prominent in Molly's than in Bloom's language. But even as Joyce creates this impression of cryptic privacy he plants just enough signposts to guard against total incomprehensibility.

The only pronoun that has an invariant referent in "Penelope" is the first person singular. Since "I" is by definition "the person who is uttering the present instance of discourse containing I,"[21] and since an autonomous monologue is by definition the utterance of a single speaker, this fixity of the first person is endemic to the genre. So, of course, is its frequency. In the sample passage more than half the sentences contain a self-reference, and several contain more than one. This egocentricity is typical of Molly's entire monologue.

All her other pronouns confront the reader with more or less unknown quantities, mostly without immediate antecedent, identifiable only from the broader context. Third-person pronouns—particularly in the masculine gender—display the most obvious referential instability, and may contain significant equivocation as well. Molly presumably always knows the who-is-who of her pronouns, but the reader is sometimes left guessing as to which *he* is on her mind at any moment. The *he* who "didnt make me pregnant as big as he is" (4) is clearly Boylan (who must also be the owner of the knee in 30)—even though his name has not been mentioned for three pages. But the *he* whose face she wants to see "the next time he turned up my clothes" (25–26) could be either Bloom or Boylan. And watch the rapid shuttling of the he-reference (between Bloom and Stephen) in the following passage: "he [Stephen] could do his writing and studies at the table in there for all the scribbling he [Bloom] does at it and if he [Stephen] wants to read in bed in the morning like me as hes [Bloom] making the breakfast for 1 he can make it for 2 . . . " (779).

On the larger scale of her monologue, a slower relay of he-men can be observed as the Bloom-Boylan alternation gives way to the Bloom-Stephen one, an evolution that coincides with the decreasing past and mounting future and conditional tenses. But the "he" of the exact mid-pages of "Penelope" (759–762) is the explicitly introduced "Mulvey was the first," who will return only pronominally to fuse with Bloom at the very end: "and how he kissed me under the Moorish wall and I thought well as well him as another and then I asked him with my eyes to ask again yes and then he asked me would I yes" (783). As Richard Ellmann has remarked, this is the point when "her reference to all the men she has known as 'he' has a sudden relevance";[22] for here the undifferentiated reference at the point of sleep underlines the contingency of the erotic partner. But this ultimate indifference is counterpointed by an overarching constancy,

Bloom being the referent for the first "he" she uses in her monologue, as well as for the last.

In his play with the male pronoun, then, Joyce makes symbolic and amusing use of a realistic feature of speech-for-oneself. Other pronominal games attain their effect more by pointing to Molly's fixed ideas than to her fickle feelings. Their key lies in the discovery not of her past, but of her private logic and its system of notation. The neuter pronoun refers with comic constancy to her favorite unmentionable, most densely on the first pages:

> anyway love its not or hed be off his feed thinking of her so either it was one of those night women if it was down there he was really and the hotel story he made up a pack of lies to hide it planning it . . . or else if its not that its some little bitch or other . . . and then the usual kissing my bottom was to hide it not that I care two straws who he does it with . . . (738–739).

The plural pronouns are equally specific in their generality: they express Molly's sexual polarization of the world. "We," whenever it does not signify the self and a specific partner (as in 19), signifies the genus women, as in "I bet the cat itself is better off than us have we too much blood up in us or what" (1–2).[23] The pronominal enemy of this female kinship group is *they*, the genus men: "they always want to see a stain on the bed . . . all thats troubling them . . . theyre such fools too" (8–10). This meaning attends the third person plural in the clichés Molly coins: "they havent half the character a woman has" (761), "1 woman is not enough for them" (739), "arent they thick never understand what you say (757), "grey matter they have it all in their tail if you ask me" (758), etc. But when Molly's kinship with other women turns to venom, *they* turns into a feminine pronoun: "lot of sparrowfarts . . . talking about politics they know as much about as my backside . . . my bust that they havent . . . make them burst with envy," etc. (762–763). Our passage also shows Molly's feminine perspective on the second person pronoun in the impersonal sense of *one*: "to know youre a virgin for them" (8) or "you could be a widow" (11).[24]

"You" as the pronoun of address, finally, is used very sparingly by Molly, and in this she differs from most other monologists. If we leave aside an occasional rhetorical phrase ("if you ask me," 758; "I tell you," 751), imagined interlocutors are almost entirely absent. I find only three exceptions: one is the "O Jamesy let me up out of this" (14) in our passage — with Molly perhaps calling on her creator-author in a spirit of Romantic irony;[25] "give us room even to let a fart God" (763) is her only address to another higher power; and "O move over your big carcass" (778) her only address to a fellow human being. Molly also occasionally uses the second person for self-address, but only in brief admonishments: "better lower this lamp" (781), "better go easy" (763), "O Lord what a row youre making" (770), "now wouldnt that afflict you" (769). The extended inner debates that feature second- and even third-person self-references in some of her fellow monologists would be out of character with the single-minded monologist who spins her yarn here.

Notes

1. Letter to Harriet Weaver, 7 October, 1921. *Letters of James Joyce* I, ed. Stuart Gilbert (London, 1966), p. 172.

2. *Letters* I, p. 170.

3. See the reproduction of the schemata in the Appendix of Richard Ellmann, *Ulysses on the Liffey* (New York, 1972).

4. This narrative voice, or "arranger" as David Hayman prefers to call it (*James Joyce's "Ulysses,"* eds. Clive Hart and David Hayman [Berkeley, 1974], p. 265) is present even in those earlier chapters that are most nearly given over to other voices: in the "asides" of "Cyclops" (see Hayman's comments, *op. cit.*, pp. 265–271), the stage instructions of "Circe," and, of course, in the intermittent narrative passages that interrupt Bloom's or Stephen's thoughts in such chapters as "Proteus" and "Lotus Eaters."

5. Diane Tolomeo reacts against this oversimplification in "The Final Octagon of *Ulysses* " (*James Joyce Quarterly* 10 [1973], 439–454): "This is not a simple linear movement, and yet it is not entirely as circular as it is often made out to be. It cannot steadfastly be maintained that the chapter ends where it began merely because the initial and final words are identical. Quite an amount of yardage has been gained by the time the eight sentences reach their ending . . ." (p. 449). But even Tolomeo overstresses the circularity of the episode earlier in her article, when she discusses its analogy to the Viconean cycle (pp. 441–442).

6. Page references in the text will be to the "New Edition" (New York: Random House, 1961).

7. Tolomeo, p. 442.

8. See the final chapter of Ellmann, *Ulysses on the Liffey* ("Why Molly Bloom Menstruates") for some of these universal implications (esp. pp. 170–171).

9. The autonomous monologue therefore corresponds to what Genette calls "récit isochrone"—a limit case of time-structure, which he takes to be purely hypothetical (*Figures III* [Paris, 1972], pp. 122–123).

10. Erika Höhnisch draws a distinction in interior-monologue texts between "temps du corps" (the experienced present moment) and "temps de l'esprit" (the past, present, and future within the reflecting consciousness). (*Das gefangene Ich: Studien zum inneren Monolog in modernen französischen Romanen* [Heidelberg, 1967], p. 20 and *passim*). The "temps du corps" is chronologically bound, the "temps de l'esprit" totally unbound.

11. Since we gather from the time scheme of "Ithaca" (and from the schemata) that Bloom joins Molly in bed around 2 A.M., "3 quarters the hour wait 2 oclock" (772) thirty-four pages into "Penelope" must be inaccurate counting on Molly's part (unless Joyce is being inconsistent). Two pages before the end it is "a quarter after what an unearthly hour" (781) which is not much help; but we are also told here that "the nuns ringing the angelus" and "the alarm-clock next door at cockshout" still lie in the future.

12. Several critics, pointing out the contrast between Molly and the two male characters in this respect, have noted the correspondence between form and content: the less the surrounding world changes (and the less the body moves), the more dispensable the narrator becomes. See John Spencer, "A Note on the 'Steady Monologuy of the Interiors,' " *Review of English Literature*, 6 (1965), 32–41, p. 40; and William M. Schutte and Erwin R.

Steinberg, "The Fictional Technique of *Ulysses*" in Thomas F. Staley and Bernard Benstock, eds., *Approaches to "Ulysses"* (Pittsburgh, 1970), p. 173.

13. To my knowledge, no close linguistic analysis of "Penelope" has appeared to date. It would be interesting to apply to it the kind of analysis Irena Kaluza applied to the monologues of *The Sound and the Fury*.

14. Alan Gardiner, *The Theory of Speech and Language* (Oxford, 1951), p. 98.

15. *Op. cit.*, p. 315.

16. In the article "Les Régistres de la parole" (*Journal de Psychologie* [1967], 265–278) Todorov draws a theoretical distinction between monologue and dialogue on the basis of the contrast between exclamation and interrogation: "Just as one can interpret dialogue as an application and extension of interrogative syntax, so one can interpret monologue, on the statement level, as exclamatory syntax" (p. 278). Although, as Todorov himself points out, examples from classical drama contradict his theory (pp. 276–277), he would find it decisively confirmed in the less rhetorical interior monologues of modern fiction.

17. Emile Benvéniste calls a phrase of the "I suppose" type an "indicator of subjectivity" that characterizes the speaker's attitude toward the statement he is making. (*Problems in General Linguistics*, trans. M. E. Meek [Coral Gables, Florida, 1971], p. 229).

18. Except when she briefly thinks about tomorrow's menu (764) or the program and wardrobe for her forthcoming concert tour (763).

19. *Stream of Consciousness in the Modern Novel* (Berkeley, 1954), p. 50.

20. David Hayman has previously noted the "proliferation of pronouns" in "Penelope," and their many ambiguities (*"Ulysses": The Mechanics of Meaning* [Englewood Cliffs, N.J., 1970], p. 100).

21. Benvéniste, p. 218.

22. *Ulysses on the Liffey*, p. 171.

23. See also: "till they have us swollen out like elephants" (742); "theres always something wrong with us" (769), and *passim*.

24. See also: "thats all they want out of you" (742), "you cant fool a lover" (748), "you want to feel your way with a man" (754), "it makes you feel like nothing on earth" (747).

25. Joseph Campbell's interpretation, as reported by Diane Tolomeo ("The Final Octagon," p. 447).

Ulysses, Modernism, and Marxist Criticism

Jeremy Hawthorn*

Very soon after its initial publication *Ulysses* came to perform the unenviable role of whipping–boy for Marxist attacks on modernist literature — a rag to the red bull. Karl Radek singled it out for vituperative attack in a speech given at the 1934 Soviet Writers' Congress in spite of the fact that, unlike *Dubliners*, it had not been translated into Russian, and in spite of the fact that his description of it as a book of 800 pages without stops or commas casts grave doubt upon whether he had actually read it.

*From *James Joyce and Modern Literature*, ed. W. J. McCormack and Alistair Stead (London: Routledge & Kegan Paul, 1982), 112–25. Reprinted by permission of the publisher.

Joyce himself was rather bemused by this treatment: "I don't know why they attack me," he said to Eugene Jolas, "nobody in any of my books is worth more than a thousand pounds."[1] This, ironically, was for his attackers one of the things that was wrong with *Ulysses*; as Radek put it,

> A capitalist magnate cannot be presented by the method which Joyce uses in attempting to present his vile hero, Bloom, not because his private life is less trivial than that of Bloom, but because he is an exponent of great world-wide contradictions, because, when he is battling with some rival trust or hatching plots against the Soviet Union, he must not be spied on in the brothel or the bedroom, but must be portrayed on the great arena of world affairs.[2]

That this was no merely idiosyncratic view can be seen by comparing it to a complaint made by Ralph Fox in his *The Novel and the People* (1937) that the modern novelist shied away from the treatment of men such as "Cecil Rhodes, or Rockefeller, or Krupp."[3]

One of *Ulysses'* earliest Marxist commentators — R. D. Charques, in his *Contemporary Literature and Social Revolution* (1933) — argued that not only did Joyce follow earlier novelists in restricting himself to "the narrowest and most intimate kinds of relationships," but in addition to this he also omitted "the most obvious of the material and impersonal forces of society."[4] For Charques, this meant that Bloom's odyssey was thus "deprived of almost all social meaning as well as stinted of ordinary humanity."[5]

What lay behind such criticisms was the belief that if, as Marx had suggested in a famous comment, social being was not determined by consciousness but determined it,[6] then in order to understand human consciousness the novelist had to examine it in the context of determining social and historical forces. Beyond this there was what David Craig has described as the "*anti-psychological* legacy of Stalinism,"[7] the belief that any concern with subjective or inner states would detract from action to change the world and would result in a rash of unproductive navel-gazing on the part of writers and their readers. Georg Lukács, perhaps the most famous Marxist literary critic and also, perhaps, the most implacably anti-modernist, argued that the job of the artist was to "penetrate the laws governing objective reality and to uncover the deeper, hidden, mediated, not immediately perceptible network of relationships that go to make up society."[8] One presumes that the argument for writing about a capitalist magnate is that here the determining social relationships become visible, so that the artist can simultaneously deal with an individual consciousness and also the hub of a network of determining social relationships.

Thus Radek saw *Ulysses* (as did many other Marxist critics) as a development, in part, of naturalism, in which the artist gave up the task of trying to reveal and understand underlying laws of social development and merely reproduced appearances — even if they were "inner" appearances:

The "new method," by which naturalism is reduced to clinical observation, and romanticism and symbolism to delirious ravings [has as its basic feature] the conviction that there is nothing big in life—no big events, no big people, no big ideas; and the writer can give a picture of life by just taking "any given hero on any given day," and reproducing him with exactitude. A heap of dung, crawling with worms, photographed by a cinema apparatus through a microscope—such is Joyce's work.[9]

Poor Joyce should have given his characters a rise in salary! This alone, however, might not have done the trick. For many Marxists it was not their income, but their social class that counted against them. Nearly every Marxist account of *Ulysses* written in the 1930s commented upon the fact that its characters belonged to the petty-bourgeoisie, the class which, from a Marxist perspective, was most detached from decisive and influential social action, and was thus least able to understand social development. Alick West, in a generally very sympathetic essay on *Ulysses* in his *Crisis and Criticism* (1937), drew attention to the fact that the novel contained no industrial workers, no sign of productive activity, and generally no concern with what Marxists refer to as the relations of production: "The reality of Joyce's social world is not its production and the conflict in that production; it is numberless acts of consuming, spending, enjoying of things that are already there. His selection of the social relations to be described is that of the consumer."[10]

It was the individualism and subjectivism alleged of *Ulysses* for which it was attacked most severely by Marxist critics. Joyce was accused of having abandoned society and history to look at the isolated individual, and of them having abandoned a concern with the individual in his or her social relationships in order to study inner thoughts and sensations. Radek, as usual, summed up the case for the prosecution most forcefully:

> Should we really tell the artist at the present time—the revolutionary artist here or abroad: "Look at your inside"?
> No! We must tell him: "Look—they are making ready for a world war! Look—the fascists are trying to stamp out the remnants of culture and rob the workers of their last rights!" . . . We must turn the artist away from his "inside," turn his eyes to these great facts of reality which threaten to crash down upon our heads.[11]

It was not just the Marxists of the 1930s who felt that Joyce's concern for characters' "insides" in *Ulysses* had led him away from crucial larger matters; writing in 1976 Terry Eagleton argued that in the "alienated worlds of Kafka, Musil, Joyce, Beckett, Camus, man is stripped of his history and has no reality beyond the self; character is dissolved to mental states, objective reality reduced to unintelligible chaos,"[12] and in another comment published the same year he suggested that Joyce's aesthetic ideology marked "a retreat from a history in crisis."[13]

Marxist critics have also had many problems with the formal structure of *Ulysses*. Lukács has argued that the modernist novelist's retreat from plot is a retreat from the social world, as a plot forces the writer to examine character in a social and historical context,[14] and many Marxist critics have felt that in the absence of an order imposed by this "discipline of the real," Joyce has injected a purely formal, artificial literary order into *Ulysses*, an order which makes no real contact with the experiences and inner lives of its characters. Thus a Soviet essay on the novel, published in English in 1938, claimed that "the whole stylistic structure of *Ulysses* is contradictory. Designed to reveal the subconscious, to bring to the surface the primeval element in human psychology, and to establish the supremacy of the irrational, this novel is distinguished by the iron logic of its construction."[15] More recently, Arnold Kettle has argued that at least half the "significances" of *Ulysses* are arbitrary ones, and that the relationship between Bloom and Stephen is a fraud, imposed from above.[16] Terry Eagleton has suggested, in similar vein, that aspects of the novel draw attention to their flagrantly synthetic basis in Homeric myth, and that "the factitiousness of that formal resolution is satirically revealed in the novel's *content* — in the unepiphanic non-event of the meeting of Stephen and Bloom."[17]

The foregoing criticisms of *Ulysses* raise serious objections to the novel. How are they to be answered? I think that one should, first of all, recognise that in extremely difficult and unusual historical circumstances it may be the case that people's attention needs to be directed towards large social and political issues. It may also be the case that a concern for one's own subjective experiences and feelings *can* lead to one's cutting oneself off from social realities. In her 1972 preface to *The Golden Notebook* Doris Lessing complained that when she began writing there was pressure on writers not to be "subjective," a pressure which according to her began in communist movements and is still potent in communist countries.[18] But Doris Lessing's subsequent literary development suggests that those who were responsible for this pressure may not have been entirely wrong; certainly her novels written under this pressure do relate more meaningfully to the social world than those written after Lessing had reacted against it; the fantasy and desocialised mysticism of her recent work makes it seem shallow in comparison with what preceded it. And particularly in the social and political context of the 1930s it is hard to feel that Radek's position can be simply dismissed. After all, he is not saying things all that different from what Auden argued in his poem "Spain" — tomorrow the enlarging of consciousness, but today the struggle (although Radek says less of tomorrow than does Auden).

Auden does however make the point in "Spain" that there is an important relationship between our "inside," as Radek puts it, and the "great facts of reality which threaten to crash down upon our heads":

On that table and scored by rivers,
Our thoughts have bodies; the menacing shapes of our fever

Are precise and alive. For the fears which made us respond
To the medicine ad, and the brochure of winter cruises
Have become invading battalions.[19]

If so, then one cannot help feeling that the investigation of such thoughts
and fears is not utterly irrelevant to the battle against those great facts of
reality with which Radek is concerned. Theodor Adorno has suggested
that the achievements of modernist writing could be measured by en-
quiring whether "historical moments" are given substance within the
works in question, or whether "they are diluted into some sort of
timelessness."[20] As Margaret Schlauch put it, in a temperate and analytical
Marxist essay on *Finnegans Wake* in 1939: "It is not illegitimate to try a
new technique in presenting a new world. It would however be a mistake
to assume that this new inner world had nothing to do with the 'objective
material' one. So palpable an error Joyce does not commit. The proper
criticism would concern itself with the terms of correlation between the
two."[21] Such a correlation can certainly be found in *Ulysses*, as I shall go
on to argue later. For all that Joyce's social vision in the novel is partial and
selective (which is hardly avoidable), one could counter-claim that few
novels show their characters less as free, autonomous beings or more tied
to their society and its history. What a striking contrast there is, for
instance, if we compare *Ulysses* with the plays of Harold Pinter. Pinter has
said on a number of occasions that he was profoundly influenced by the
silent, menacing encounters between Jews and Mosleyites in east London
soon after the last war. But in his plays such silent, menacing encounters
are utterly decontextualised; presented as somehow representative of all
human relationships. This is certainly not true of *Ulysses*. In one sense
Eagleton is right that there is a sort of flight from history in the novel, for
neither the characters nor their creator seem to have any conception of
how change can take place — and this is as much true of personal
relationships as it is true of the situation of Ireland. But paradoxically,
Joyce shows very clearly how this paralysis is born of a particular social
situation. Bloom is, after all, neither Everyman or Noman; his particular-
ity is born of what, in an ugly modish jargon, one could call a given
historical conjuncture, and this is as true of his secret thoughts, fantasies
and dreams as it is of his public behaviour.

One suspects that one of the problems for Georg Lukács was that he
really didn't have any confidence that there were "terms of correlation"
between the inner world and the "objective material" one. At the head of
his essay, "The Intellectual Physiognomy in Characterization," Lukács put
a quotation from Heraclitus: "Awake, men have a common world, but
each sleeper reverts to his own private world." Whatever shortcoming
Marxists may find in Freud's work, his analysis of the dream world makes

such a claim as Heraclitus' extremely tendentious, and had Lukács paid a little more attention to the substance of Bloom's dreams he might have realised this.

It is one of the great ironies of history that in 1934, the same year that Radek was savaging *Ulysses* and calling for attention to be turned away from our "inside," a book was published in the Soviet Union which paid considerable attention to our inside: L. S. Vygotsky's *Thought and Language*. What is more, Vygotsky's account of the development of conceptual thought through the progressive internalisation of language advances hypotheses about the nature of the "language of thought" which offer a fascinating way in to the study of Joyce's presentation of inner cerebration in *Ulysses*. Vygotsky argues for a dialectical relationship between thought and language in which developments in the one facilitate and enable developments in the other. In particular, he suggests that language develops socially for the child, but that language developments are progressively internalised to structure new levels of thought, so that, for example, the acquisition of literacy has implications for the individual's ability to think. In the course of this argument he suggests that a sort of linguistic "half-way-house" is what he terms "egocentric speech"; when the growing child talks to itself not to communicate to others, but to organise its own thoughts. The relevance of this to our immediate subject is that Vygotsky suggests that "The inner speech of the adult represents his 'thinking for himself' rather than social adaptation; i.e. it has the same function that egocentric speech has in the child. It also has the same structural characteristics: Out of context, it would be incomprehensible to others because it omits to 'mention' what is obvious to the 'speaker.' "[22] Vygotsky suggests that the main distinguishing feature of inner speech is its peculiar syntax; compared to external speech it appears disconnected and incomplete, and that, in particular, "it shows a tendency toward an altogether specific form of abbreviation: namely, omitting the subject of a sentence and all words connected with it, while preserving the predicate."[23]

This is certainly one of the general characteristics of Bloom's internal monologues:

> Could buy one of those silk petticoats for Molly, colour of her new garters.
>
> Today. Today. Not think.
>
> Tour the south then. What about English watering places? Brighton, Margate. Piers by moonlight. Her voice floating out. Those lovely seaside girls. Against John Long's a drowsing loafer lounged in heavy thought, gnawing a crusted knuckle. Handy man wants job. Small wages. Will eat anything. (*Ulysses*, p. 180)

If we remember that the predicate of most of Molly's thought is herself and her relationships, then we can recognise the same sort of abbreviation in her inner speech as we see in Bloom's.

Vygotsky makes a number of other points about inner speech which are interesting in the context of an analysis of *Ulysses*. He suggests that in inner speech the personal "sense" of a word will be more important than its public "meaning." He also advances the hypothesis that inner speech is characterised by "agglutination" — the merging of several words into one composite — and another process whereby "the senses of different words flow into one another . . . so that the earlier ones are contained in, and modify, the later ones."[24] This is something that lovers of *Ulysses* hardly need telling! One cannot but regret that in addition to his analyses of passages from the work of Tolstoy and Dostoyevsky, Vygotsky had not been able to look in detail at the depiction of inner speech in *Ulysses*.

Analysis of one's own thought processes suggests that some thought seems to contain almost no verbal element at all, whereas on other occasions our thought seems structured through — and even constituted by — language. It is interesting to note, therefore, that Vygotsky's pupil, A. R. Luria, has suggested a distinction between "taxonomic" and "graphic" cognition; the former, which is the basis of conceptual thought is heavily dependent upon "the shared experience of society conveyed through its linguistic system," whereas the latter is based on the "individual's practical experience," and tends not to be structured through language.[25]

This perhaps helps us to understand the difficulties — or some of them — that Joyce has in *representing* thought in *Ulysses*. When Bloom is carrying out one of his extraordinary calculations — concerning the number of people buried in Dublin, and then the world, every day, for instance — the representation of his thought is relatively easy, as this sort of thought relies very heavily on language and is structured through it anyway. You cannot think, "Must be twenty or thirty funerals every day" purely graphically; this level of conceptualising has to be done through language, and thus can far more easily be represented in written language. But take a passage like the following one: "He stood up. Hello. Were those two buttons of my waistcoat open all the time. Women enjoy it. Annoyed if you don't. Why didn't you tell me before. Never tell you. But we. Excuse, miss, there's a (whh!) just a (whh!) fluff. Or their skirt behind, placket unhooked. Glimpses of the moon. Still like you better untidy" (*Ulysses*, p. 85). The problem Joyce faces here is the representation of thought which mixes both graphic and verbal modes. We do not mentally verbalise our annoyance when we notice that our clothing is disarranged, but when we think about our relations with other people our thoughts generally become far more verbal, as we are having to think about communication which in practice already contains a significant verbal element. Joyce uses a number of techniques to overcome the difficulty here. "Hello," is what one might say in a comparable public situation, discovering something unexpected; it therefore "stands for" the moment of Bloom's surprised discovery. The sentence following is, I have suggested, a verbal representation of that which normally wouldn't be thought in words; here Joyce leaves out the question mark that, grammatically, would be required. This indicates the non-social, self-enclosed nature of the thought to the reader; the reader takes this grammatical abnormality as a sign of the non-verbal nature of the thought.

Molly's stream of consciousness is often seen as the most extreme form of technical innovation on Joyce's part in *Ulysses*, but it is worth noting that as nearly all of her thoughts concern her relationships with other people rather than merely physical sensation, their expression in words presents fewer problems than do some of Bloom's more ephemeral thoughts and sensations. In spite of her physicality and concern with sexuality, Molly consistently conceptualises; she does not just remember events, she comments upon them and tries to put them into some sort of order. We may remember Molly as an "experiencer" rather than a "thinker," but when we go back to her monologue we discover that she never stops interpreting and commenting upon her experiences. This is why we never feel any strain has been caused by representing her thoughts in words; they are generally at that level of conceptualisation which requires words anyway. In addition, of course, many of the events she is thinking about have had a significant verbal element in the first place.

Vygotsky claims that inner speech normally has the form of a monologue, public speech that of the dialogue.[26] I am not sure; my own introspection suggests to me that the more that one thinks about social relationships, the more one's thought processes mimic dialogue. We have all had the experience of going through an unsatisfactory conversation, "replaying it," as it were, so as to determine what it would have been better for us to have said. In addition to such exercises taking place after the event, it seems to me that we often go through elaborate mental exchanges prior to meetings with another person or other people which we know will be difficult. Such rehearsals are not only highly verbal — as verbal as thought can get, in my experience — but they typically take the form of a dialogue. *Ulysses* contains no examples of this sort of mental process, and this, surely, is indicative of a certain absence in the novel. None of the characters in the novel plans for conflict. To put it another way; none of the characters in the novel is engaged in fighting to change his life or society in such a way as necessitates such mental planning. No one goes through the "If he says this then I'll say that" process in his thoughts. To this extent some of the early criticisms of the novel's social selectivity made by Marxist critics are perhaps justified. There is an acceptance of "how things are" on the part of the characters we get to know in *Ulysses* that goes very deep.

The novel does, however, offer what Margaret Schlauch asks for: some indication of the "terms of correlation" between inner and outer worlds; it is certainly quite untrue that Joyce presents us with characters whose "insides" are unrelated to larger external contexts. Leopold Bloom is a classic example of this. There is, I think, clearly a relationship between the objective social fact that Bloom is a Jew living in a society rife with anti-semitism, and the nature of his inner world. Joyce clearly goes to some lengths to stress the hostile environment in which Bloom lives; before he has appeared in the novel two characters—Haines and Deasy—have expressed ludicrous anti-semitic remarks; Deasy on two occasions. When Bloom is then introduced, the first sentence referring to him associates him with what we can call "internality": "Mr Leopold Bloom ate with relish the inner organs of beasts and fowls." Bloom's impulse towards the internal is surely connected to the factor of anti-Jewish prejudice in the society in which he lives. I am reminded very strongly of the illustrations depicting first-generation Jewish immigrants in America in David Efron's book *Gesture, Race and Culture*. Efron's book, first published in 1941, aimed to counter Nazi theories concerning the racial inheritance of gesture. Efron studied Italian and Jewish immigrants to the USA through a number of generations, demonstrating that with each stage of assimilation gestural habits changed, being related not to race but to cultural environment. But in some of the drawings depicting groups of Jewish people in New York who had just escaped from extremely oppressive, anti-semitic societies, are extremely thought-provoking. There is intense energy in the groups, but it is all directed inwards. No threat is directed towards outsiders, no demand made upon them—in marked contrast to the gestural behaviour of first-generation Italian immigrants, whose expansive behaviour immediately involves the onlooker. The picture that sticks in my mind is of a group of Jewish men, bending towards each other, gesturing and pointing at each other with extreme energy, but offering an unruffled, unchallenging exterior to the outside world. All the energy is directed inwards.

Bloom is surely not unlike this, except that all his energies are inside himself rather than between himself and a small number of fellows. On the outside, we are told of Bloom, "he bore no hate" (*Ulysses*, p. 283), and that "I resent violence or intolerance in any shape or form" (*Ulysses*, p. 564). Inside, as his sado-masochistic sexual fantasies show, the energies that are repressed in public behaviour mould and direct his fantasy life. Bloom's behaviour in the brothel acts out those larger conflicts he can only occasionally respond to in public (Cyclops). Even his masturbation—like the masturbation of Alexander Portnoy—represents a turning inwards for solutions to problems which cannot be solved on the social plane. (Philip Roth's definition of "Portnoy's Complaint," at the front of his novel, has interesting points of contact with Bloom's predicament.)

Erich Auerbach, contrasting the original Homeric *Ulysses* with the biblical account of Abraham's journey to sacrifice his son, comments upon the "simultaneous existence of various levels of consciousness and the conflict between them" expressed by the Jewish writers, and contrasts this with the lack of such complexity in Homer.[27] The contrast he makes is curiously reminiscent of that made by Efron between the first-generation

Italian and Jewish immigrants; the former are fleeing from poverty, the latter from persecution. Thus it is in the Jewish writers, like the Jewish immigrants to America, that one finds *internal* complexity, as conflicts which cannot be resolved publicly by a persecuted people are forced inwards to create complex and divided inner states. Very similar points could be made about Stephen, who fears not persecution but engulfment from mothers he still partly belongs to but needs to reject. Thus his dominant mode is that of irony, a mode that grants partial assent to the claim made on him by his biological and religious mothers, but at the same time establishes a private space of his own.

Since the 1930s Marxists have grown more interested in subjectivity as a result of a number of theoretical developments within Marxism. The work of Soviet psycholinguists such as Vygotsky represents one influential strand of work, the increasing concern with questions of ideology represents an even more persuasive theoretical development. If people's beliefs, habits of mind, modes of perceiving the world are important, then study of the manner in which these arise and are perpetuated is also crucial. Marilyn French points out that early on in *Ulysses* we are introduced to the idea that the "real" is knowable only through a particular mode of perception, and that this insight of Joyce's is related to the question of *style*, as "mode of perception dictates mode of expression."[28] She goes on to suggest that in the second half of the novel Joyce increasingly points to the fact that people do not perceive reality except by means of interlinked assumptions and strategies, which is not to say that reality is unimportant. Her claim that Joyce's stream of consciousness technique "reflects a world with no deity" in which "standards are internal"[29] comes rather too close for my liking to the thesis advanced by Colin MacCabe in his *James Joyce and the Revolution of the Word* (1978). MacCabe claims that there is no metalangauge in *Ulysses*, and that thus the book rejects a representational view of language, breaking with the idea of internal thought or external reality outside of language.[30] I do not agree. Surely the truth is that throughout *Ulysses* Joyce actually eschews this sort of relativism; at most points in the book the reader is given a pretty clear idea of what is "actually happening" alongside the perhaps different perceptions of events that the characters have. Nowhere do we have the straightforward lack of a metacommentary that I was amused to note on the title page of MacCabe's book, where the reader is informed in the same statement that the book was printed in Great Britain and printed in Hong Kong.

We know, of course, that it must have been printed in either one place or the other, and Joyce — like any orthodox Catholic or Marxist — never denies the existence of a world existing independent of our consciousness of it. Very often this is the result, in *Ulysses*, of the creation for the reader of the sense of a consistent narrative point of view. In one sense, of course, this seems a wild statement to make, for in few novels does the technical point of view — the standpoint from or through which we perceive events — change so frequently. But most readers of *Ulysses*, surely, react to the particular selection and juxtaposition of characters, events, styles, and so on by building up an idea of the guiding principles behind such selection and juxtaposition. Take, for instance, the following passage:

> But Gerty was adamant. She had no intention of being at their beck and call. If they could run like rossies she could sit so she said she could see from where she was. The eyes that were fastened upon her set her pulses tingling. She looked at him a moment, meeting his glance, and a light broke in upon her. Whitehot passion was in that face, passion silent as the grave, and it had made her his. At last they were left alone without the others to pry and pass remarks and she knew he could be trusted to the death, steadfast, a sterling man, a man of inflexible honour to his fingertips. His hands and face were working and a tremor went over her. (*Ulysses*, p. 363)

Now clearly on one level this represents a comic misperception. Bloom is a dirty old man misperceived by Gerty in terms of the hero of a romantic novel. The reader knows without any confusion "what is happening"; Bloom is looking at Gerty and masturbating, while she, conscious of his attention, is encouraging him indirectly. On another level, however, Joyce indicates quite clearly that in another sense of the word what Gerty feels is "real"; the pulp-novel style used to describe the episode represents Gerty's way of perceiving sexuality, it is the stuff of her thought, not just a means of presenting it. But of course the sort of novel Joyce is drawing upon would never include such an element as public masturbation in response to deliberate self-exposure; to this extent the passage, as it reveals the extent to which Gerty is in thrall to a particular set of assumptions about sexuality, also reveals the inadequacy of those assumptions, that mode of perception, and indicates how in practice more sordid realities can be encompassed within what initially appears to be rather unpromising organising material.

But this, surely, is not all. When we are shown Gerty thinking of Bloom as a man "of inflexible honour to his fingertips," the deliberate reference to fingers on Joyce's part reminds us what Bloom is actually doing with his hands and, in so doing, clearly reveals the presence of an organising intelligence behind the passage. The humour here reveals the humorist, a humorist who — like all good comedians — gets his laughs by building up his audience's knowledge of his assumed values. It is the construction of this "value-centre" that allows Joyce to make the novel such an affirmation of human values.

One of the ways in which this set of positive values is assembled and conveyed to the reader — in fact, the most important way — is through the humour of the novel. So few critics, Marxist or non-Marxist, talk about the fact that *Ulysses* is one of the funniest novels in the English language that it is worth repeating Arnold Kettle's point that it *is* a very funny novel, "including passages as uproarious as anything in modern fiction."[31] The humour in the novel, however, is in no sense peripheral to the work, a sort of icing spread over the cake of learning that constitutes its bulk. Laughter is only possible when we feel the presence of an intelligence holding values we recognise as positive, confronting forces which we are led to see as antagonistic to those values. For all the complexity of *Ulysses*, its humour testifies to the existence of shared values, common perceptions. We can see this in miniature in the way in which humour is extracted from the contrast between Joyce's use of indirect speech and the actual words which we know will have been used.

A similar affirmation takes place on a larger scale within the novel. It is true that *Ulysses* is structured in a way that is in a sense artificial; the structuring is beyond the perception of the characters (not to speak of the average reader), and exists on a different plane from the depicted life of the work. But this can be seen to mirror the order of a society which, also, makes little direct contact with the lived experience of its members, an order at odds with their essential humanity. And as this order is one that is imposed by two foreign masters there seems no reason why Marxists should expect it to be otherwise, or symbolically depicted in a more sympathetic light. In very broad terms the humanism of *Ulysses* is revealed through techniques similar to those employed by Sterne in *Tristram Shandy*: in both novels the richness and diversity of human life is threatened by alien and artificial forms of order, but in both novels life breaks through in triumph. Mrs Shandy forgets everything her philosopher husband tells her, and Uncle Toby's fortifications collapse under the weight of Trim's love-making. Indeed, the following passage could well apply as much to Mrs Shandy as to Molly Bloom:

> What compensated in the false balance of her intelligence for these and such deficiencies of judgment regarding persons, places and things?
>
> The false apparent parallelism of all perpendicular arms of all balances, proved true by construction. The counterbalance of her proficiency of judgment regarding one person, proved true by experience. (*Ulysses*, p. 607)

The humanist thrust of passages such as this, for all their humour, is not to be underestimated. *Ulysses* is a novel with absences, omissions, incompletenesses. But as a recent critic of Lukács's — John Thompson — has pointed out, we do not necessarily have to accept that the burden of giving an audience "a real grasp of its historic situation" has to be borne "by each text singly and anew." As he adds, "effects in themselves much smaller but cumulatively benign" can be welcomed.[32] *Ulysses* certainly does not give us an exhaustive and comprehensive view of the historical situation of Ireland at the start of this century — although it gives more than some have conceded. But it does show us much about the relationship between inner and outer worlds, it gives us fascinating evidence concerning the connexion between mode of perception, style, belief, and reality. And it affirms certain human values in their social and historical specificity with such force that we cannot afford to dismiss it or them.

Notes

1. Richard Ellmann, *James Joyce* (London, 1959), p. 3.

2. Karl Radek, "Contemporary World Literature and the Tasks of Proletarian Art," in *Problems of Soviet Literature*, ed. H. G. Scott (London, 1935), p. 154.

3. Ralph Fox, *The Novel and the People* (London, 1937), p. 94.

4. R. D. Charques, *Contemporary Literature and Social Revolution* (London, no date [?1933]), p. 92.

5. R. D. Charques, p. 92.

6. Karl Marx, Preface to *A Contribution to the Critique of Political Economy* in *Early Writings* (Harmondsworth, 1975), p. 425.

7. David Craig, Introduction, in *Marxists on Literature*, ed. David Craig (Harmondsworth, 1975), p. 21.

8. Georg Lukács, "Realism in the Balance," in *Aesthetics and Politics* (London, 1977), p. 38.

9. Karl Radek, p. 153.

10. Alick West, *Crisis and Criticism* (London, 1937), p. 169.

11. Karl Radek, p. 179.

12. Terry Eagleton, *Marxism and Literary Criticism* (London, 1976), p. 31.

13. Terry Eagleton, *Criticism and Ideology* (London, 1976), p. 157.

14. Georg Lukács, "Marx and the Problem of Ideological Decay," in *Essays on Realism*, ed. Rodney Livingstone (London, 1980), p. 145.

15. R. Miller-Budnitskaya, "James Joyce's *Ulysses*," *Dialectics* (New York), 5 (1938), p. 10.

16. Arnold Kettle, *An Introduction to the English Novel*, 2 vols, (reprinted London, 1962), vol. 2, pp. 157, 156.

17. Terry Eagleton, *Criticism and Ideology*, p. 156.

18. Doris Lessing, Preface, *The Golden Notebook* (2nd ed, Frogmore, St. Albans, 1972), p. 12.

19. W. H. Auden, "Spain," written 1937. See *The English Auden: Poems, Essays and Dramatic Writings 1927–39*, ed. Edward Mendelson (London, 1977).

20. Theodor Adorno, "Reconciliation under Duress," *Aesthetics and Politics*, p. 159.

21. Margaret Schlauch, "The Language of James Joyce," *Science and Society* (New York), Fall 1939, p. 489.

22. L. S. Vygotsky, *Thought and Language*, ed. and trans. Eugenia Hanfmann and Gertrude Vakar (Cambridge, Mass., 1962), p. 18.

23. L. S. Vygotsky, p. 139.

24. L. S. Vygotsky, p. 147.

25. A. R. Luria, *Cognitive Development* (Cambridge, Mass., 1976), p. 52.

26. L. S. Vygotsky, p. 142.

27. Erich Auerbach, *Mimesis*, trans. Willard R. Trask (3rd printing, Princeton, N.J., 1971), p. 13.

28. Marilyn French, *The Book as World: James Joyce's "Ulysses"* (Cambridge, Mass., 1976), p. 10.

29. Marilyn French, p. 65.

30. Colin MacCabe, *James Joyce and the Revolution of the Word* (London, 1978), p. 4.

31. Arnold Kettle, p. 142.

32. John O. Thompson, "Up Aporia Creek," *Screen Education*, 31, Summer 1979, p. 37.

Formal Re-creation: Re-reading and Re-joycing the Re-rightings of *Ulysses*

Brook Thomas*

Perhaps one of the most interesting results of the current fascination with "reader-response" criticism will turn out paradoxically to be an explanation of what for lack of a better term we call the "creativity" of writers such as James Joyce. Of course, normally (another term that requires closer scrutiny) reader-oriented criticism is applied to the role of the reader in literature. Rejecting the textual model which emphasizes the active role of the writer in reproducing it, the advocates of reader-response criticism remind those who need reminding that reading is not merely a passive process. The reader's activity varies from theory to theory, from a reader "adducing" meaning to a reader "producing" meaning, but in almost all cases the reader is seen more and more as an accomplice in the creation of the meaning of a text, a necessary partner who re-creates or, for some, "re-writes" the text.

For me, however, the converse of the argument is just as interesting. If reading is shown to be a form of writing, writing is also shown to be a form of reading. Just as reading is no longer considered merely a passive process, so writing is no longer considered a totally active process. Instead writing itself is shown to involve an act of passivity. As we often tell students of composition, writing is a continued process of revision, and as that master of the craft, Henry James, puts it: "To revise is to see, or to look over, again — which means in the case of a written thing neither more nor less than to re-read it."[1]

This merger of the roles of reader and writer is perhaps no better in evidence than in the case of James Joyce and *Ulysses*. With the widespread availability of Joyce's notesheets and revisions for *Ulysses*, plus Michael Groden's detailed study of Joyce's process of writing the book, we have a privileged opportunity to watch closely how one of the twentieth century's most "creative" users of language wrote his masterpiece.[2] What we find is

*From Genre 13 (Fall 1980): 337-54. Reprinted by permission of the publisher. Copyright © 1980 by the University of Oklahoma.

that what we have come to consider *Ulysses'* creation and transformation of the norms and forms of literature comes as a result of Joyce's "passive" act of reading and re-reading what he has already written, a process which, I will suggest, is made continually possible in our own reading and re-reading of the signatures of all things Joyce has left behind for us to read.

That many readers try to find ways to halt this process of continual re-reading will lead me to reverse an argument that is often levelled against these advocates of reader-response criticism. More traditional critics accuse the advocates of reader-response criticism of distorting the text and/or authorial intention by allowing the reader's subjective response to be imposed on the text. It is my position, however, that those critics who claim to have found the underlying theme, moral message, authorial intention, or indeed form of *Ulysses* are the ones who impose their norms on the text, since the text as Joyce wrote it (and read it) has no inherent norm, a situation that leads to the protean nature of its forms. Even so I want to acknowledge that the norms that these critics use to guide their reading of *Ulysses* cannot really be called "subjective" norms. They rarely originate with any one critic. Instead, they are inherited norms, norms agreed upon by an entire segment of culture, norms which by the strength of convention seem to have an ontological status. But there is no better way to see the limits of these norms than to see their inability to account for all of the different ways that we can read and re-read *Ulysses*. This is not to say that the advocates of reader-response approaches do much better. One needs only to look at the special Structuralist/Reader Response Issue of the *James Joyce Quarterly* to see how little reading of *Ulysses* gets done when critics are intent on fitting the book into a theory of reading.

Joyce, however, was much more interested in words than the theories that words produce, and it is Joyce's creative reading of his own book that is one of the reasons why *Ulysses*, which started as a short story for *Dubliners*, kept expanding until Joyce finally had to stop adding to it to meet the publication deadline on his 40th birthday. As one of those late revisions reminds us, "*It grew bigger and bigger and bigger*" (U 172.36). Joyce, the writer, was such a sensitive reader of his own work that he continually detected new verbal connections and possibilities to be developed in re-writing. In his study Groden lists a number of the most obvious examples, and the interested reader can compare early drafts and final text to find examples of his own.

Most readers, however, are more interested in the effect of these revisions on their reading of the final text. For them some of the most interesting additions may be those which, while fitting into the naturalistic tale, also suggest different ways of reading the words of the text. Readers who are apt to take the book too seriously are reminded by a revision in "Hades" that, "You must laugh sometimes so better do it that way. Gravediggers in *Hamlet*. Shows the profound knowledge of the human heart" (*U* 109.13). Readers who even before the book was published complained about its randomness might well consider that *Ulysses* consists of, "A few well-chosen words" (*U* 140.1). Readers are also invited to enjoy the book's extravagance, as when Joyce adds the comment he made in a letter to Budgen on "Oxen of the Sun" to part of Ned Lambert's response to Dan Dawson's inflated rhetoric: "How's that for high?" (*U* 123.31). Furthermore, many late revisions help steer the reader towards the *Odyssey*, such as when Joyce adds to Mulligan's comment, "Ah, Dedalus, the Greeks": "I must teach you. You must read them in the original" (*U* 5.7). Finally, for readers who may forget the metaphoric nature of language, we have late reminders such as: "metaphorically speaking" (*U* 143.38).

Joyce also wants us to read quite literally, for as Fritz Senn remarks, "Part of the dynamism of Joyce's prose arises from the contrast of figurative to literal meaning, or the ironic unfittingness of a metaphor or a cliché fixed in some no longer congruous roles."[3] Joyce, of course, does not invent either language's figurativeness or its literalness; he merely makes us aware of qualities already contained in language. In fact, as his revisions of "Eumaeus" show, his literal reading of old metaphors is one way in which he breathed new life into what is too often considered that chapter's tired language.

Thus, when we read the following passage in which Bloom considers the possibility that the stories W. B. Murphy spins might after all have a bit of truth in them it might be wise to consider what Murphy has quite literally on his chest, although to do so will involve us in a series of not so literal connections with other parts of the text. "Yet still, though his eyes were thick with sleep and sea air, life was full of a host of things and coincidences of a terrible nature and it was quite within the bounds of possibility that it was not an entire fabrication though at first blush there was not much inherent probability in all the spoof he got off his chest being strictly accurate gospel" (*U* 635.36). What we find is that when Murphy unbuttons his shirt, he reveals "on top of the timehonored symbol of the mariner's hope and rest . . . the figure 16 and a young man's sideface looking frowningly rather" (*U* 631.21). The young man's face turns out to be none other than a portrait of the tattoo artist himself ("Fellow the name of Antonio done that. There he is himself, a Greek" [*U* 631.27]). In other words, this not entire fabrication which our storyteller is trying to get off his chest is a portrait of the artist as a young man, a connection between Joyce and his fictional character which is reinforced later in the chapter when we are explicitly warned not to confuse Antonio with "the dramatic personage of identical name who sprung from the pen of our national poet" (*U* 636.11). Literally, of course, this phrase refers to the character in Shakespeare's *Merchant of Venice*, but it also suggests Ireland's new national poet. Furthermore, we should not be surprised to find that the key phrase in this connection, "all the spoof he got off his chest being strictly accurate gospel," is a late revision. In the manuscript version that we have Joyce ends the sentence with the rather bland "though at first blush there was not much inherent probability about it," with "inherent" a marginal addition. In the typescript he revised this to "though at first blush there was not much inherent probability in all he said being strictly accurate," a change which emphasizes the act of narration and makes possible a further revision which will include the reference to Murphy's tattoo, as well as allowing the addition of "gospel" to reinforce the effect of "host" earlier in the sentence. Host and gospel in turn connect the passage to Stephen's and Bloom's comments on the previous page about those "passages in Holy Writ" which Stephen calls proof of "the existence of a supernatural God" and Bloom considers "genuine forgeries" (another late revision) "put in by the monks most probably." Reference to the monks recalls Old Monks the dayfather in "Aeolus," who as James H. Maddox remarks, "might well serve as a model of Joyce, dayfather of June 16, 1904."[4] To be sure, Bloom's thoughts about the dayfather could apply as easily to Joyce as to Old Monks. "Queer lot of stuff he must have put through his hands in his time: obituary notices, pubs' ads, speeches, divorce suits, found drowned" (U 122.8). It is materials like these that make up "a host of things and coincidences of a terrible nature" which, like Ulysses, constitutes not an entire fabrication but a series of events that actually happened in Dublin.

What my example, which is by no means unusual, should make clear is that Joyce's process of writing, re-reading, and re-writing is potentially an endless one. Having once revised a passage Joyce would re-read his revisions, causing him to discover even more potential verbal connections, causing more re-writing, and so on. Thus, it is easy to see how Ulysses came to be more and more about its own creation.[5] The book becomes reflexive because as Arnold Goldman claims, "By its fifteenth chapter, Ulysses has begun to provide its author enough in the way of material to become self-perpetuating." It also becomes reflexive because Joyce re-read every sentence he wrote in so many different ways that each one required expansion and qualification. Or put another way, the material that the book has amassed is not only character, plot or details of a Dublin setting, but its own language. That language, as part of a language system without beginning or end, allows Joyce continually to create new meanings and formal possibilities for his book. But in one sense, it is not really Joyce who is "creating" these meanings or potential forms. They are meanings and forms already available in a language which exists prior to any one reader or writer of that language. It is Joyce's awareness of this potentiality of language that allows us to talk about the book writing itself and that makes Ulysses the perfect example of Valéry's statement that "a work of art is never finished, but only abandoned." My point is, however, that Ulysses has been abandoned only by Joyce, not by its readers, for each time that a reader reads and re-reads *Ulysses*, he repeats with a difference the process by which Joyce created the book.

But before going on to the reader's role as "writer," I'd like to spend a little more time looking at the writer's role as a reader. In his study, Groden tries to isolate three major stages in the composition of *Ulysses*.

> In the first stage ("Telemachus" — "Scylla and Charybdis") he developed an interior monologue technique to tell his story. In the middle stage ("Wandering Rocks" — "Oxen of the Sun") he experimented with the monologue and then abandoned it for a series of parody styles that act as "translations" of the story. He balanced his growing attraction to stylistic surface with a continuing interest in the human story. Finally, in the last stage ("Circe" — "Penelope") he created several new styles and revised the earlier episodes.[6]

What Groden does not point out, however, is that the changes from stage to stage correspond closely to Joyce's own re-reading of his text in preliminary form. A major departure from his initial technique occurred soon after Joyce must have re-read drafts of the early chapters for publication in the *Little Review*. Similarly, Joyce's final revisions, many reflexive in nature, are prompted by his reading of the book in proof before final publication.

That the re-reading of the earlier chapters leads to experiments with the "initial style" and parodies of it only makes sense. Someone as sensitive as Joyce to narrative possibilities would soon see the limitations of any one technique, including the famous "interior monologue," which was once considered a major deviation from narrative norms but, as I will try to show, is now grasped at by critics seeking to define *Ulysses'* stylistic norm. It is important to remember, however, that not only do the later stages of the book grow out of and depend on the first stage, but that by the time *Ulysses* reaches print the first stage has been revised in light of the later strategies and intentions and, thus, depends on them as well as the other way around. As Groden argues, Joyce's strategies and intentions changed and developed as he wrote and read his book, until he created a final draft that would be "a record of all the stages he passed through and not merely a product of the last one."[7] Joyce's process of writing makes possible a perpetual interaction between all of the book's chapters, styles, and words.

Thus, complaints about Joyce's overly mechanical structure might be reconsidered. Joyce did not simply impose a mechanical structure on the work, since the various structures which he himself discovered grow out of the act of composition. For instance, the famous schema did not appear until late in Joyce's work on the book, indicating that he may not have seen the possibility for many of his elaborate, encyclopedic parallels until after the book amassed more and more words. In fact, as Groden points out, a comparison of the Linati schema with the Stuart Gilbert schema indicates that the schema itself was revised to fit new work on the book. Furthermore, it is typical of Joyce that what Joseph Frank calls the book's spatial structure grows out of the artist's writing process. It is Joyce's continual revisions that give the book the appearance of having a preconceived structure in which all the details fit neatly together. And it is, of course, the book's "spatial" character that allows the reader to participate in a reading *process* with no end, jumping from page to page, reading backwards to forward as well as forward to backwards. As Bloom says of the proofreader in "Aeolus": "Reads it backwards first. Quickly he does it. Must require some practice that" (*U* 122.18).

It is this reading process with no end, started by Joyce and continued by his readers, that more than anything accounts for *Ulysses'* breaking down and stretching of the traditional norms and forms of fiction. To understand why we can turn to that expert on the problem in the visual arts, E. H. Gombrich. After having tried to banish the sort of essentialistic thinking that art historians traditionally rely on to defend the privileged status of the classical form as a norm, Gombrich remarks, however: "We have a right to talk in Aristotelian terms when we discuss what Aristotle called 'final causes,' that is human aims and human instruments. As long as painting is conceived as serving such a human purpose, one has a right to discuss the means in relation to these ends. There are indeed quite objective criteria for their assessment. The idea of an 'economy of means,' even the idea of perfection, makes complete, rational sense in such a context. One can say objectively whether a certain form serves a certain norm."[8]

The point I have tried to make, however, is that the reading process made available by *Ulysses* makes it extremely difficult to talk about final causes. A book that cannot be read, only re-read, can have only provisional norms, not final ones. As the norm which we adopt to fix a certain reading changes, so does the book's form. This is perhaps most easily seen in the way critics have tried to structure the book's eighteen chapters. Joyce himself emphasizes one possibility by dividing the chapters into the Telemachia, the Odyssey, and the Nostos. Richard Ellmann, trying to attempt a grand synthesis, stresses a triadic structure which allows him to perform dialectical stunts. Others divide the book between "Scylla and Charybdis" and "Wandering Rocks," others between "Wandering Rocks" and "Sirens," and so on. The book itself, as Fritz Senn puts it, is Protean, a book of many turns. "*Ulysses* is Homerically polytropical. Voices change, characters are not fixed, language is versatile and polymorphous. The reader is puzzled by new turns. . . . Language, the most polytropic invention of the human mind, fascinated Joyce. Skeat's *Etymological Dictionary*, a catalogue of the historical roles of words, makes us aware of morphological and semantic transformations. Joyce makes us aware, moreover, of the various roles that even the most ordinary and familiar words always play."[9]

The only disagreement that I have with Senn's description of the book is with his reference to language as an invention of the human mind, since, as I have suggested, reading *Ulysses* raises the possibility that the human mind, as we know it, is as much a product of language as vice versa. Indeed, it is exactly when we stop looking at language only as a human instrument, and as something having a life not totally controlled by human aims, that our ability to talk about *Ulysses* in Aristotelian terms loses its authority.

Having raised the possibility of the limited priority of language over the human subject, I cannot avoid evoking the name of Jacques Derrida. In fact, Derrida's notion of the "free play" of language[10] seems particularly appropriate to any discussion of the forms created through the reading of *Ulysses*, for while it is to the credit of reader-response criticism that it reminds us that language does not play without players to read it, it is important to see that the general rules of the game are established by language, not any one player. One could argue that because the words comprising the text of *Ulysses* are a subset of language, which Joyce has chosen and arranged, Joyce has set the rules by which this particular arrangement of words should be read. But Joyce's reading of his own work seems to indicate that for him an important rule to remember is that no subset of language is totally cut off and isolated from the system of which it is a part. The inexhaustible possibilities which *Ulysses* allows its readers result from the inexhaustible possibilities of language itself.

Having now argued that the free play of *Ulysses*' language accounts for the book's continual construction of norms and forms, I have to face the reality of *Ulysses* criticism which abound in attempts to stop this free play. Given the countless attempts to fix the book's language, there is no way in conscience that I can claim that *Ulysses*' language *demands* inexhaustible readings. Quite the opposite. One could almost say that the effect the language has on most readers is to demand that they fit it into certain norms and forms. Yet taken together, all of the interpretations that the Joyce industry has produced undercut this attempt to fix a "reading" on *Ulysses*. Because so many ways of reading the book already exist in print, each reading that offers a new interpretive schema by which the book should be judged points out the arbitrariness of that claim. Nonetheless, it should go without saying that the need to construct form is a necessary aspect of the reading process, even for readers reading in the spirit of free play, since without the construction of form there would be no form to destroy.

What I can claim, then, is that while *Ulysses*' language does not demand free play, it allows it, even encourages it. Furthermore, I can claim that the attempts to stop the "free play" of *Ulysses*' language teach us more about the norms or *Ulysses*' critics, including that norm which demands form, than about the norms and resulting forms of *Ulysses*.

Here I would like to follow the lead of Wolfgang Iser who in the *Act of Reading* makes an effort to distinguish between aesthetic and non-aesthetic experience.[11] Iser, to be sure, is not arguing for a theory of literature which relegates our reading of texts to empty aestheticism. Instead, he argues that aesthetic experience (in the case of literature, reading) inevitably leads to non-aesthetic experience. What he argues against, however, is confusing the values that we bring to a text in order to make it cohere with values within the text itself. I would like to add, however, that it is wise to remember that Iser's two most important terms "Wirkungsstruktur" and "Leerstellen" are metaphors. They do not refer to an objective presence within the text but to the way in which the reader is signaled to read the words of a text. They are rhetorical rather than metaphysical concepts and, as such, are a product of the conventions of language. Ultimately, the distinction between aesthetic and non-aesthetic experience, while a useful construction, may itself be exposed as a necessary rhetorical strategy. Even if we assert the priority of language over the subject (Iser does not), it is hard to imagine language – and that includes literary language – outside of a human context, a context that implies human norms and values.

This is not to say that in reading *Ulysses* we should try to grant our norms and values privileged status. Indeed, as Iser argues, reading a text might cause us to reflect on those values and norms and perhaps see their limitations. His student Eckhard Lobsien, for instance, has written a stimulating book, *Der Alltag des "Ulysses,"* in which he tries to prove that the norms that allow us to produce coherent readings of *Ulysses* act in a capacity similar to the norms which ethnomethodologists claim allow members of a social group to create a world of everyday reality that they take for granted.[12] In Derrida's terms these norms allow us to create structure by "centering" a system of signs. In *Ulysses*, however, a completed, structured world is never taken for granted. Instead, as we have seen, the process of creation itself is a subject for reflection. Everyday reality is not presented as an already existing world, but in a continual process of being constructed. Like Derrida's notion of the center, norms serve a necessary function in the construction of coherent readings of the world and texts – we cannot imagine a structure which lacks a center – but as *Ulysses'* reflexiveness allows us to see, norms and centers have no ontological status.

It is exactly in granting our norms ontological status that we run the risk of stopping the reading process of *Ulysses*. While in day-to-day activities it may be a matter of survival to reject or distort an unsettling event so as not to disturb our coherent vision of the everyday world and get on with the task at hand, with *Ulysses* the task at hand is to read the text. Yet, instead of reading the book's language we are continually trying to fit it into our preconceived norms or rejecting it for not conforming to those norms.

One norm which academic critics frequently impose on *Ulysses* and one that assures that it will remain human centered is the generic label of the novel, that product of Western Europe's "liberal imagination." An advantage (and disadvantage) of fitting a work into a certain genre is that we have guidelines as to how to read it. If someone first reads Swift's "A Modest Proposal" in a class on satire rather than as a pamphlet bought on the streets of eighteenth-century London, certain choices in reading will have been made for him. He knows to look for "irony," a "persona," etc. Similarly, someone reading *Ulysses* as a novel — even if an exceptional one — knows to look for the humanistic revelation of character brought about in dramatically rendered action.

Even at this point *Ulysses* presents problems because readers are uncertain as to which strain of the novel it belongs. Does it belong to the Irish Comic tradition as Vivian Mercier would have it? The Flaubertian tradition as Pound read it? Twentieth-century British fiction as it is most often taught in American universities? Or the tradition of self-conscious fiction as Robert Alter defines it? Nonetheless, once *Ulysses* has been labelled a novel, a great amount of critical effort is spent trying to uncover the plot which is said to be "screened" by the language of the book's second half: an effort which can easily distract us from the primary task of concentrating our efforts on reading the book's language As James Maddox says of "Oxen of the Sun": "It is proper to say, then, that we do not so much *read* this chapter as we *translate* it."[13] This is, of course, exactly the point. If a reader tries to translate the chapter into the familiar forms and norms of the novel, he no longer reads the words before him, but replaces them with another text of his own making.

At this point it would be easy to claim that the reason that *Ulysses* allows so many readings is because readers continue to look for something behind the "screen" of language, but there is nothing behind that "screen" to be found. This approach, however, is too easy. To be sure, there are no "real" historical events which occur to be screened by the book's language, although Joyce's meticulous realism continues to confuse some readers. Nonetheless, a plot does exist, making Blamire's translations of the book into a plot summary in *The Bloomsday Book* and Hart and Knuth's *Topographical Guide* of the action through the Dublin streets useful reading tools. But far from screened by the book's language, the plot depends on it for its existence. The plot remains a product of the book's language *and* our reading conventions which allow us to turn words into characters and events. To see to what extent the plot depends on the words as they are written, we need only compare an early draft of one of the later chapters to the final text to watch the action change as the language changes.

What bothers some critics, however, is that the language of these chapters is doing so much more than advancing the book's action, showing also what language freed from a purely referential function can do. And while even Gombrich will venture that "the achievement of lucid narrative" is a norm that has "a permanent meaning," there is little evidence that lucid narrative is the norm by which we should judge *Ulysses*. Nonetheless, it is easy to see why critics who consider this *the* norm will complain about *Ulysses'* "excess of language" and find some way to avoid reading that language. Indeed, their very complaint is revealing. In *Ulysses* we may well have an "excess of language," words refusing to be fixed by the traditional form of the novel or any other traditional literary form, an excess that, as any "real" translator could tell us, makes any attempt to translate the book's words rather than merely to re-read them impossible.

Ulysses' excess of language (more sympathetic critics call it a richness) also plays havoc with another attempt to impose a set structure on *Ulysses*. A great mass of the criticism produced by the Joyce industry tries to dig beneath *Ulysses'* language to reveal its underlying theme or moral vision. Whether this theme or vision turns out to be the depravity of the modern world, the integrity of the individual, caritas, the classical temper, the relationship between father and son, or incest, the "discovery" of a theme or vision gives the book's language a purpose. It is there to illustrate that theme or vision and when it does not contribute to that purpose, it is excessive. But even if we overlook the fact that more often than not the moral visions that critics posit are ones they had before reading the book and that their themes are ones that happen personally to interest them, we can see that rather than admitting the limitations of their reading most critics prefer to reject those parts of the book which do not contribute to elucidating what they have decided it should be doing. Or, when critics do decide to revise their choice of theme or vision to account for all of the book's language, their new theme or vision becomes so general and banal that it does not help us in our reading of the book at all.

What the attempts to uncover plot, theme, and vision show is that what we have come to call "a reading" of the book is in effect a misnomer. To produce "a reading" is inevitably to limit the possibilities of reading. It turns a process into an object, thus keeping us from reading the book's words with the openness that Joyce did in writing the book.

Joyce, of course, had the advantage that since he was the book's author he did not have to read with an eye towards the author's intention, theme, moral vision, or even implied consciousness. Instead, he could concentrate more than later readers on reading language on its own terms. As a result, I would like to make an important variation on Georges Poulet's description of the experience of reading. Poulet tells us that, "Reading, then, is the act in which the subjective principle which I call *I*, is modified in such a way that I no longer have the right, strictly speaking, to consider it as my *I*. I am on loan to another, and this other thinks, feels, suffers, and acts within me."[14] I would agree that in reading the subject can be modified, but when it is, what it is on loan to is not so much "another" as language itself. In other words, to a large extent reading at its best retains its passive character, but it is not the case that, as Scho-penhauer claimed, "When we read, someone else thinks for us: we merely repeat his mental process."[15] Instead, reading is an activity that can heighten our awareness that it is language that thinks through us. The reader is necessary to activate the language of the text, but not necessarily in total control over it.

Readers, of course, continue to try to control *Ulysses'* language, even if that attempted control manifests itself in an attempt to use it to prove the priority of language over the subject. Indeed, this desire to control *Ulysses'* language, to fit it into "a reading," may be a necessary part of our reading process. Even though producing "a reading" halts the reading process, reading without a purpose is difficult to conceive of. As Gombrich has so convincingly shown, the eye does not see innocently. Similarly, as I have tried to argue, we ultimately cannot read a text outside of a human context. Only by positing norms, themes, or authorial intensions do we seem to have a stable point from which to set the book's language in motion. Reading from one point of view brings certain aspects to the foreground; reading from another brings others to our attention. We learn from reading *Ulysses* both *as* a novel and *as* a precursor to *Finnegans Wake*, both *as* Joyce's *Odyssey* and *as* his *Hamlet*. But because no one way of reading answers all of the questions that the language of *Ulysses* raises, the only answer seems to be to re-read the book again and again. And so long as readers continue to read and re-read *Ulysses*, new forms and patterns will be constructed and deconstructed.

Nonetheless, even critics who stress the uncertainty of our reading experience in *Ulysses* find ways to limit the reading process. One of the most subtle attempts can be found in Marilyn French's *The Book as World*. French is adamant in insisting that *Ulysses* and our reading of it are founded on the void of incertitude. "By building incertitude into the method of the novel, Joyce places the reader in the same dilemma as the characters. . . . He insists that the reader experience relativity while reading about it." But she goes on to contradict her insight by thematizing uncertainty itself. One sentence embodies the contradiction in her method. "Since the theme of the book is the incertitude implicit in the human condition, and since everything in the novel is wound up tightly with this theme, Joyce's point should be clear."[16] Can French be sure of this?

What her notion of the reading process of *Ulysses* makes clear to me is that she has not fully understood the implications of founding a work on the void of incertitude. In her chapter "The Reader and the Journey" she wisely relies on Joyce's own metaphor and claims that the reader is the Ulysses of the title and that his journey through the book is his odyssey. The problem with her notion of the journey is that it is finite. The reader experiences the odyssey of reading the book, only to return to the "rock of Ithaca" where the motion stops. In describing the reader's journey through

Ulysses as one with a beginning, middle, and end, French can posit the book's "initial style" as the book's norm, the middle styles as a deviation from the norm and the end as a return home. As the description of a first reading this is fine, but *Ulysses* is often read from back to front as well as front to back. In re-reading we can easily posit one of the middle chapters as the book's stylistic norm, "Oxen of the Sun," for instance, whose many styles mirror the effect of the entire book. Or we can read the first chapter reflected by the mocking mirrors of "Circe," a reading which emphasizes the role-playing that dominates the chapter and its adverbs which act as stage directions. Because the reader's journey is potentially endless, the book has no established norm. We might remember that when the motion of Shakespeare's odyssey ends, he dies (*U* 213.4).[17]

French's reader can enjoy the luxury of a finite voyage through *Ulysses* because despite arguing for a limited notion of man French posits a super-reader in total control of the language he confronts. Even though the reader is supposed to be facing uncertainty, we are assured: "The reader is the only person who sees it all, who is aware of all elements inside the novel as well as all things outside to which it alludes." The omniscient author has been replaced by the omniscient reader. "The journey taken in *Ulysses* is the book itself, and only the reader traverses it entirely."[18]

French's reader sounds much like what James H. Maddox calls the book's "ideal first time reader,"[19] although to his credit Maddox admits that such a reader probably does not exist. He cannot exist because of the nature of the act of reading. The reader cannot "see it all" because while *Ulysses* may *allow* alternative readings, it does not necessarily *contain* them in the sense that a forest contains trees. *Ulysses* does not contain readings; it contains words. To be sure, by arranging those words in a variety of patterns we produce a reading, but that pattern only comes into existence when someone recognizes its potential through the act of reading much in the way that Joyce recognized the potential of recycling the *Odyssey* through one day in Dublin. In fact, the word pattern — or its counterpart, mosaic — is misleading because of its spatial implications. While Frank is certainly helpful to point out the "spatial" character of a work like *Ulysses*, the term only remains helpful so long as we remember that it is a metaphor. No matter how many details and phrases we store in our memory later to arrange into a pattern, that arrangement is always sequential. Reading remains a temporal activity. Producing one pattern rules out, for that moment, producing another. We can no more perceive all of the alternative readings in our mind at the same time than — to use a visual example that does seem applicable in this particular case — we can simultaneously see both rabbit and duck of the famous gestalt figure. To produce one pattern we have to go through the process of reading (or in re-reading, shorthand version of it). Then to produce another pattern we have to go through another act of reading, creating an endless number of structures.

But by the time I stoop to talking about the general nature of the act of reading, it could be objected that if what I say has validity, it could be applied to all literary texts and does not help us to understand what is particular about *Ulysses*. Indeed, by arguing for the limited priority of language over both writer/reader and reader/writer, I seem to agree with the notion that all texts allow the free play of language that I attribute to *Ulysses*. If we re-read them enough, all texts seem potentially to construct and deconstruct norms and forms. All are, after all, part of a larger system of language. As Stanley Fish puts it, literature is "language around which we have drawn a frame, a frame that indicates a decision to regard with a particular self-consciousness the resources language has always possessed. . . . What characterizes literature then is not formal properties, but an attitude—always within our power to assume—toward properties that belong by a constitutive right to language."[20]

What seems particular about *Ulysses*, therefore, is the way in which it draws attention to the possibilities to be gleaned in re-reading it. And it is here that I would like to hold out in part for the role of the subject. If, as I have argued, Joyce is a reader of language open to language's infinite possibilities, chances are good that he will arrange the words of his text in such a way as to foreground some of those possibilities. Perhaps Shklovsky's term "defamiliarization" would be helpful here, although what is defamiliarized is language itself.[21] For Joyce, that process of defamiliarization, which is recorded in the important late revisions, seems to have come in the act of re-reading. Having externalized language by giving it objective existence in a text he was free to read it with renewed freshness, rather than as product of his own consciousness. A reader reading that text in which the main character's name is declined as a part of speech, temporarily loses a letter due to a misprint, is turned into a variety of anagrams, and merges with that of another character is invited to see that the words of the text he is reading cannot be pinned down.

Yet it seems to be the nature of a text to do exactly that—to pin words down by mumming them in the black ink of print. The fact that the words of *Ulysses* are fixed in a certain order on the printed page seems to constitute the major difference between author Joyce and later readers of the book. It is Joyce, after all, who does the fixing. Or to be more accurate, it is Joyce who supervised their fixing, since many people—typists, typesetters, proofreaders—intervened between Joyce and the printing of his book.

This process of getting the book into print presents the critic intent on reading "Joyce's text" with a number of problems. It is common knowledge that all of the texts of *Ulysses* that we have are replete with errors. Thus, when Fritz Senn makes a brilliant reading of a paragraph in "Telemachus" because he finds Stephen's phrase of "Agenbite of inwit" (*U* 17.3) within a "Mulligan passage," he later finds that "Agenbite of inwit" is most likely a printing error that Joyce overlooked in proofreading.[22] Careful readers are not always careful proofreaders. I for one, however, believe that the particular conclusions that Senn makes about the potential of the first chapter's language remain valid. Perhaps the mistake helped him to see an aspect of language that others had long overlooked. If so, his act of reading would be much like Joyce's, who upon reading the printing error in the *Little Review* at the beginning of "Aeolus" which repeated the sentence "Grossbooted drayman rolled barrels dullthudding out of Prince's store and bumped them up on the brewery float" (*U* 116.23), turned the error to his advantage by repeating the sentence in reverse order, thus creating an example of the rhetorical figure of chiasmus. In fact, there is no way for us to be sure whether Joyce overlooked the printing error of "Agenbite of inwit" or, as unlikely as it seems, upon reading it liked its effect and intentionally left it in. Even the proposed computer assisted text will not be able to decide that for us. The play of language remains.

Nonetheless, no matter how creative a reader other than Joyce is we will not give him the authority that reader Joyce had to change the words of his text. The reader must work with the words as given, a limitation that puts him in a position similar to the one Stephen complains about while talking to the Dean of Studies in *A Portrait*. "The language in which we are speaking is his before it is mine. . . . His language, so familiar and so foreign, will always be for men an acquired speech. I have not made or accepted its words" (*P* 189). Indeed, when Stephen, the artist, appears in *Ulysses* he is still speaking, thinking, and writing in someone else's language. His most notable sayings are cribbed from Wilde and others, his thoughts are full of quotations, and his attempt at a poem echoes one by Douglas Hyde. In this respect the forger of his race's conscience is much like his creator who creates one of the century's most original works by forging together already existing material, for *Ulysses* as we have it results not only from Joyce's re-reading of what he has already written, but also from Joyce's reading of obituary notices, pubs' ads, speeches, divorce suits, and even other works of literature. There is, however, a major difference between Joyce and Stephen. Joyce, unlike Stephen, seems to have learned to accept the words he has inherited, an acceptance that allows him, using the technique of bricolage, to write *Ulysses* by fitting together already existing myths and historical events and already existing words and phrases. Joyce's creation and transformation of literary forms is less a matter of "natural genius"[23] than an ability to allow language continually to repeat itself with a difference—which could well be a rudimentary description of the act of reading, which Joyce has made available to those readers of *Ulysses* willing to repeat (with a difference) the process by which Joyce wrote the book, thereby helping once more to bring into existence that "world without end" (*U* 37.31).

Notes

Parenthetical references *U* and *P* within the text refer respectively to James Joyce, *Ulysses* (New York: Random House, 1934 ed., reset and corrected 1961) and James Joyce, *A Portrait of the Artist as a Young Man* (New York: Viking Press, 1964). I wish here to express my thanks to the von Humboldt Stiftung of the Federal Republic of Germany for supporting the research and writing of this essay.

1. Henry James, *The Art of the Novel* (New York: Scribners, 1934), pp. 338–39). See Walter Benn Michaels, "Writers Reading: James and Eliot," *MLN*, 91 (1976), 827–49, for a valuable discussion of James' theory of reading.

2. Michael Groden, *"Ulysses" in Progress* (Princeton: Princeton University Press, 1977); James Joyce, *Ulysses: The Manuscript and First Printings Compared*, annotated by Clive Driver (New York: Octagon Books, 1975); James Joyce, *Ulysses*, general editor Michael Groden (New York: Garland Press, 1978).

3. Fritz Senn, "Book of Many Turns," *JJQ*, 10 (1972), 42.

4. James H. Maddox, *Joyce's "Ulysses" and the Assault upon Character* (New Brunswick: Rutgers University Press, 1978), p. 95.

5. Groden suggests that the "Done" (*U* 291.13) at the end of "Sirens" announces the end of Joyce's experimentation with the "initial style" (p. 42). He also remarks that, "It is probably not coincidental that, just as Joyce was about to expand *Ulysses* through innumerable revisions, he wrote a scene extending Bloom's dreams to apocalyptic dimensions" (p. 188). I also would like to think that the trial scene in "Circe" owes something to the fact that portions of *Ulysses* published in the *Little Review* were on trial for obscenity at the time Joyce was writing the episode. Similarly, it may not be accidental that Joyce added "Print anything now" (*U* 69.10) to the passage in "Calypso" which Pound had censored because it described Bloom defecating.

6. Groden, p. 4. See note 13 on Groden's use of the term "translations."

7. Groden, p. 203.

8. E. H. Gombrich, "Norm and Form," in *Norm and Form* (London: Phaidon Press, 1966), p. 96.

9. Senn, 41–42.

10. Jacques Derrida, "Structure, Sign, and Play in the Discourse of the Human Sciences," in *The Languages of Criticism and the Sciences of Man*, ed. Macksey and Donato (Baltimore: The Johns Hopkins Press, 1970), pp. 247–65.

11. Wolfgang Iser, *The Act of Reading* (Baltimore: The Johns Hopkins Press, 1978).

12. Eckhard Lobsien, *Der Alltag des "Ulysses"* (Stuttgart: Metzler Verlag, 1978).

13. Maddox, p. 173. That considering the later chapters as "translations" is widespread is indicated by Groden's use of the term in the passage I quote from him above. Groden wisely clarifies his use of "translation" on p. 44.

For an account of Joyce as a not so literal translator of his own work see Jacqueline Risset, "Joyce traduit par Joyce," *Tel Quel*, 55 (Autumn 1973), 47–58.

14. Georges Poulet, "Phenomenology of Reading," *NLH*, 1 (1969), 57.

15. Arthur Schopenhauer, *Schopenhauers Sämtliche Werke in fünf Bänden* (Leipzig: Grossherzog Wilhelm Ernst Ausgabe, 1910), V, 291.

16. Marilyn French, *The Book as World* (Cambridge: Harvard University Press, 1976), pp. 34, 52.

17. I have a similar discussion of French's notion of the reader's journey in "Not a Reading *of*, but the Act of Reading *Ulysses*," *JJQ*, 16 (Fall 1978/Winter 1979), 82–83.

18. French, p. 4.

19. Maddox, p. 207.

20. Stanley Fish, "How Ordinary Is Ordinary Language?," *NLH*, 5 (1973), 52.

21. *Russian Formalist Criticism: Four Essays*, trans. Lee T. Lemon and Marion J. Reis (Lincoln: University of Nebraska Press, 1965), p. 12.

22. Senn, 41. He told me of the possible misprint in conversation after looking at the Garland edition of "Telemachus."

23. It is interesting to look at the sentence that precedes the comment, "Sheer force of natural genius, that" (*U* 646.29). In the text it reads, "However, reverting to the original, there were on the other hand others who had forced their way to the top from the lowest rung by the aid of their bootstraps." If we revert to the original mss., however, "forged" replaces "forced." Whether Joyce wanted "forged" or "forced" in this context is problematic. For my purposes, "forged" works better as a not too subtle reminder that "natural genius" has more to do with creating "genuine forgeries" (*U* 634.25) than originals. Stephen, by the way, has on a pair of borrowed boots. See *Manuscript and First Printings Compared*, p. 601.

The Narrative Norm   Karen Lawrence*

The first three chapters of *Ulysses* pay homage to both the personal tradition Joyce had created in his previous works of fiction and to the traditional novel. In its dominant narrative voice and interest in the character of the artist, the "Telemachiad" resembles *A Portrait* in particular, and even the reader of *Ulysses* who fails to recognize this continuity will experience a sense of security from the presence of this narrative voice. The staples of the novel — third-person narration, dialogue, and dramatization of a scene — also promise narrative security to the reader who begins *Ulysses*: they act as signposts promising him familiar terrain on the subsequent pages. No matter what we may know about the structural apparatus and levels of allegory in the work after reading Joyce's worksheets, letters, and tips to Stuart Gilbert, what we experience when beginning *Ulysses* is a novel that promises a story, a narrator, and a plot. "Stately, plump Buck Mulligan came from the stairhead" (pp. 2–3) is a plausible beginning for any novel. *Ulysses* begins like a narrative with confidence in the adequacy of the novel form.

It is important to underscore the initial narrative promises to the reader made in the novel not only because they will be broken later on but also because they provide an interesting contrast to the change in Joyce's basic conceptions of plot and significance in fiction, a change that must have antedated, at least in part, the beginning of the novel. *Ulysses* offers, in a sense, a "rewriting" of *Dubliners*: it presents another portrait of Dublin designed to reveal the soul of the city and its citizens. But in arriving at the basic conception of *Ulysses* — the condensing of the wander-

*From *The Odyssey of Style in "Ulysses"* (Princeton, N.J.: Princeton University Press, 1983), 38–54. Reprinted by permission of the publisher.

ings of Odysseus to one day in the life of certain Dublin citizens—Joyce
radically altered his conception of what a portrait of Dublin should be.

In the initial conception of *Ulysses*, Joyce departed from the aesthetic
of economy and scrupulous choice that had directed the writing of
Dubliners in favor of an aesthetic of comprehensiveness and minute
representation. This aesthetic is implied in Joyce's statement to Budgen
about his desire to give so complete a picture of Dublin in *Ulysses* that if
the city were to disappear it could be reconstructed from the book.[1]
Although the "story" of *Ulysses* takes place during one day only, this day is
infinitely expansible by being infinitely divisible—the rendering of the
complete "details" of life almost obscure the sense of story. Unlike
Dubliners, which promises to end the narrative as soon as the "soul" of a
character is revealed, *Ulysses* offers no clear principle of completeness.
The frustration critics felt at what they thought of as Joyce's infidelity to
the minimal requirements of a story is reflected in Edmund Wilson's
comment in *Axel's Castle*: "It is almost as if he had elaborated [the story]
so much and worked over it so long that he had forgotten . . . the drama
which he had originally intended to stage."[2]

Ulysses also offers no clear principle of emphasis or proportion. In the
stories of *Dubliners*, the right "trivial" incident in the life of a character
epiphanizes the meaning of life; in *Ulysses*, no one particular incident in a
life is considered to be of supreme importance. Because the characters
carry within them the same problems, desires, and past, no matter when
we see them, no day is essentially different from any other. If *Dubliners*
focuses on a particularly significant day in the lives of its characters,
Ulysses focuses on any day in Dublin's diary, and the day happens to be
June 16, 1904. It is as if an entry in the diary of Dublin, rather than in a
personal diary such as the one that ends *A Portrait*, was blown up in a
great, Brobdingnagian gesture; in the world of *Ulysses*, as in Brobdingnag,
a molehill can indeed become a mountain. The slight rise in the plot that
the theory of epiphany suggests is almost completely eliminated in the
narrative of *Ulysses*. What is important here is not the transition between
a "short story" and the long story of development told in a traditional
novel but the transition from fiction interested in plot to fiction in which
plot becomes synonymous with digression.

The stream-of-consciousness technique in the "Telemachiad" does
alert the reader to some of these changes in overall conception. In using
this technique increasingly until it almost dominates the narrative in
Chapter Three ("Proteus"), Joyce offered his third-person narrator less and
less to do. The retrospective narrative voice of a conventional novel is
replaced almost entirely, so that "plot" changes from a form of narrative
memory to a rendering of "the very process in which meaning is appre-
hended in life."[3]

But in the first three chapters of the novel (even in "Proteus"), the
third-person narrator exists and serves some important narrative func-

tions. The dominant narrative voice in the "Telemachiad" provides the narrative norm for the novel (and continues in subsequent chapters), and it is the voice that, for a long time, was ignored in critical discussions of *Ulysses.* Although some critics have described the quality of this voice,[4] many recent critics have tended to pass over this narrative norm on the way to discussions of narrative distortions that occur primarily in the latter half of the book.[5] But the primary reason for this omission is the importance that decades of critics have placed on the stream-of-consciousness technique in the early chapters: in focusing on the "innovativeness" of this technique, they have tended to underestimate the importance of the narrative norm.

The narrative conventions established in the early chapters of *Ulysses* include the presence of an identifiable and relatively consistent style of narration that persists in the first eleven chapters of the book and the tendency of the narrative to borrow the pace and diction of the characters' language. In other words, the conventions include *both* the continued presence of a particular style *and* the adaptability of style to character. Critics who focus on the stream-of-consciousness emphasize the importance of the character's mind and treat the third-person narration as an adjunct of character.[6] This is only partly correct, since it fails to acknowledge the recognizable, idiosyncratic narrative voice that does exist.

For example, the following sentences, the first from "Telemachus," the second from "Proteus," display the characteristic Joycean qualities seen in *A Portrait* and now heightened in *Ulysses*: "Two shafts of soft daylight fell across the flagged floor from the high barbicans: and at the meeting of their rays a cloud of coalsmoke and fumes of fried grease floated, turning" (p. 11); and "The cry brought him skulking back to his master and a blunt bootless kick sent him unscathed across a spit of sand, crouched in flight" (p. 46). The denotative style in *A Portrait* is evident here, with greater syntactic dislocation and more unusual diction. The extreme concern with the sounds of words — that is, the alliteration ("flagged floor," "blunt bootless," "spit of sand") and what Anthony Burgess has called the "clotted" effect of the double and triple consonants[7] — and the strange placement of the modifying adverb ("fried grease floated, turning") produce a sentence that, as Burgess says, reveals "a distinctive approach to what might be termed literary engineering."[8] This is prose that is competently, indeed masterfully crafted, precisely and poetically written.

Especially in the "Telemachiad," this literate, formal, poetic language is associated with the character of Stephen Dedalus. In the first three chapters, we perceive the world largely through the eyes of an aspiring artist, and, as in *A Portrait*, the linguistic "sympathy" between character and narrative voice blurs the distinctions between them. "Woodshadows floated silently by through the morning peace from the stairhead seaward where he gazed" (p. 9) is a narrative statement that "borrows" Stephen's lyricism. Throughout the chapter, the narration will often present

Stephen's poetic and melancholy perceptions of things in language appropriate to his sensibility.

But despite the close connection between the style and the mind of Stephen in the "Telemachiad," the style exists independently in subsequent chapters, as is evident from the following examples:

> The caretaker hung his thumbs in the loops of his gold watch chain and spoke in a discreet tone to their vacant smiles. ("Hades," p. 107)

> It passed stately up the staircase steered by an umbrella, a solemn beardframed face. ("Aeolus," p. 117)

> The young woman with slow care detached from her light skirt a clinging twig. ("Wandering Rocks," p. 231)

> Miss Douce's brave eyes, unregarded, turned from the crossblind, smitten by sunlight. ("Sirens," p. 268)

In the first eleven chapters of *Ulysses*, this narrative style establishes the empirical world of the novel; it provides stability and continuity. The persistence of this type of narrative sentence provides a sign of the original narrative authority amidst the increasingly bizarre narrative developments of the later chapters, until it disappears in "Cyclops." (It reappears briefly in "Nausicaa," for reasons I will discuss later.) It is a style that orients the reader and offers him a certain security by establishing the sense of the solidity of external reality.

It seems to me that this type of narrative sentence, along with the other staples of the narrative mode of the early chapters—interior monologue, free indirect discourse, and dialogue—functions as the "rock of Ithaca," "the initial style" to which Joyce alluded in a letter to Harriet Weaver in 1919: "I understand that you may begin to regard the various styles of the episodes with dismay and prefer the initial style much as the wanderer did who longed for the rock of Ithaca."[9] This is the nonparodic style that establishes the decorum of the novel. When it disappears later on in the text, we realize that it too was a choice among many possibilities, a mode of presentation. But in its seeming fidelity to the details of both the thoughts and actions of the characters it provides us with a sense of the real world of the novel. With all its precision and fastidiousness, it functions for us as a narrative norm.[10]

However, while the decorum of the novel is established, the presence of another narrative strand in the first chapter slyly questions the assumptions about language upon which the normative style is based. The effect of this narrative strand is subtle, nothing like the radical disruptions of narrative stability in the later chapters. And yet this narrative fluctuation in the first chapter of the book serves as a warning to the reader of the strange narrative distortions to come. The following passage illustrates the intertwining of the narrative strands in the first chapter:

> He [Mulligan] shaved evenly and with care, in silence, seriously.
>   Stephen, an elbow rested on the jagged granite, leaned his palm
> against his brow and gazed at the fraying edge of his shiny black coat-
> sleeve. Pain, that was not yet the pain of love, fretted his heart. (p. 5)

The second sentence is an example of the denotative narrative norm. The past participle "rested," surprising the reader prepared to encounter the present participle "resting," is a characteristic kind of dislocation. The third sentence, "Pain, that was not yet the pain of love, fretted his heart," is a clear example of free indirect discourse. But the first sentence is puzzling — the number of adverbs and adverbial phrases surprises us. There is a naive quality to this writing that separates parts of speech as if they were about to be diagrammed.

In fact, the first chapter of *Ulysses* provides numerous examples of this naive narrative quality. This strand of the narration reveals itself in the repeated use of certain formulaic narrative constructions of which no student of creative writing, however inexperienced, would be proud. The proliferation of the following phrases in the early pages of the novel suggests that something strange is taking place in the narrative: "he said sternly," "he cried briskly," "he said gaily" (p. 3); and "He laid the brush aside and, laughing with delight, cried," "Stephen said quietly," "he said frankly," "Stephen said with energy and growing fear," "he cried thickly" (p. 4). What kind of narrative world is created by these descriptions and what purpose could Joyce have had in using this type of prose in the beginning of the novel?

Joyce called the technique of this chapter "narrative young," and this description, while it probably refers to Stephen to some extent, also applies to the quality of narration: it is appropriate to the self-conscious, naive literary style exemplified above. Unlike the naiveté of the narrator in stories like "Clay" in *Dubliners*, stories in which through free indirect discourse the narrator ostensibly accepts his protagonist's assessment of the world, the naiveté of the narrative in "Telemachus" is literary as well as psychological. We notice an innocence concerning the very act of telling a story, an innocence that is a quality of the narrative itself rather than a property of a particular character.

What we are provided with in the early pages of *Ulysses*, disturbing the basically serious and authoritative narrative voice that creates a world we can believe in, is a different narrative strand that parodies the process of creation. Prose like "he cried thickly" and "he said contentedly" is the unsophisticated prose of fourth-rate fiction; a novel that begins this way parodies its own ability to tell a story. Even in the first chapter of the novel, Joyce begins to turn novelistic convention into novelistic cliché, and it is here that the reader glimpses language beginning to quote itself, its characteristic activity in the latter half of the book. While making use of the conventional tools of the novel, Joyce uses one strand of the narrative to upset the stability created by these conventions and to point to their inadequacy. As the normative style asserts its ability to capture reality in language, this narrative voice advertises its own incompetence. The world in which Buck Mulligan wears a "tolerant smile" and laughs "with delight" or in which Stephen says something "with energy and growing fear" is about as far from Henry James's world of "delicate adjustments" and "exquisite chemistry"[11] as a novelist can get. The sentences of this naive narrative point to the falsification and oversimplification that language wreaks on emotions by organizing them in discrete grammatical parts.

This narrative strand in Chapter One provides the first example of narrative performance and stylistic bravado in *Ulysses*, different from that in later chapters like "Cyclops" and "Ithaca," but stylistic exhibition nonetheless. There is a comic excess of labor in evidence in the narration: the narrator seems to wrestle with the discrete parts of speech available to him only to pin down the most commonplace of descriptions. The subtle nuances captured in sentences of the "initial style" elude the narrator's grasp. The excess of labor here is the antithesis of the coolness of scrupulous meanness in *Dubliners* — the production of meaning seems to be a Herculean task.[12] But there is an air of safety that surrounds the "risks" the narrator seems to take. He is like a clown walking a tightrope only one foot above the ground. What is suppressed here is not so much a narrator as a grin.

It is possible to explain this adverbial mania in "Telemachus" in relation to the characters described. Hugh Kenner, for example, has discussed the presence of these adverbs in regard to the role playing of Stephen and Buck Mulligan.[13] While the thematic connection between the adverbial style and the role playing of the characters makes sense, it limits the significance of the strange verbal tic by giving it so exclusively a character-based explanation. The adverbial style tells us something about the kinds of utterances we find in certain types of narratives, as well as something about the characters in this one. The presence of the naive literary style suggests that the text as well as the character is trying on a costume. In Chapter One, we get a brief glimpse of the kind of narrative mimicry that dominates the later chapters of the book — the mimicry of a type of text rather than a particular character. What I find most interesting about the naive narrative strand in Chapter One is the beginning of an interest in language apart from character, language that calls attention to its own clichéd nature without providing the vehicle for the ironic exposure of a character. Instead of parodying the linguistic idiosyncrasies of a type of character, the narrator dons a stylistic mask of innocence to parody the very enterprise of telling a story. Parody is cut loose from the concerns of character and becomes an aspect of narrative.

Thus, Steinberg and other critics interested in the early chapters of *Ulysses* seem to me to have erred in assuming that if the narrator is not an *unreliable character* in the story (like the lawyer in Melville's "Bartleby, the Scrivener," for example, or the narrator in Ford's *The Good Soldier*), then the narrative can be trusted. Frank Kermode writes in an essay entitled "Novels: Recognition and Deception" that "we have bothered too much about the authority of the narrator and too little about that of the narrative,"[14] and this distinction between the authority of the narrator and the narrative is an extremely important one for the reading of *Ulysses*.

The tone of the opening chapter of *Ulysses*, then, seems to oscillate: in certain parts of the narrative *Ulysses* announces itself as a comedy, but for the most part it is dominated by the rather bitter and serious Stephen Dedalus. The copresence of the naive aspect of the narrative and the well-written, precise narrative norm makes it difficult for the reader to form a clear perception of a unified narrator.

And yet, this one narrative strand found in the first chapter of the novel is quickly overshadowed by the narrative norm and the stream-of-consciousness technique in the rest of the "Telemachiad." The mimicry of a type of text rather than a character will resurface in later chapters — most obviously in "Cyclops" and "Oxen of the Sun." But after Chapter One, this naive parodic style vanishes. Despite Joyce's developing interest in representing the inadequacies of language, despite the warning about the enterprise of novel writing in the first chapter, it is character, not narration, that is the most important subject of the first six chapters of the novel. Simultaneous with Joyce's perceptions of the limitations of both the conventional novel and his own previous fiction was an interest in further developing a method with which to present the workings of consciousness. The "Proteus" chapter is, as critics have suggested, the culmination of the "Telemachiad," not only chronologically, but stylistically as well; here the stream-of-consciousness technique reaches its peak in transcribing an educated, artistic mind. The use of stream-of-consciousness was experimental for Joyce when he wrote the "Telemachiad" — it carried further the "direct" representation of the mind of the artist begun in *A Portrait*. It is the drama of the character's mind, rather than the drama of novel writing, that is still paramount. As S. L. Goldberg has pointed out, the paragraph is still a dramatic unit of consciousness, the "artistic medium of a particular *act* of understanding."[15]

In the next three chapters of *Ulysses*, devoted to Leopold Bloom, this interest in character is still paramount. In these chapters, the reader finds the same texture of narration as in the "Telemachiad": a combination of third-person narration, dialogue, free indirect discourse, and the stream-of-consciousness of the character. The denotative norm of the "Telemachiad" persists in these chapters: "By lorries along Sir John Rogerson's Quay Mr Bloom walked soberly, past Windmill Lane, Leask's the linseed crusher's, the postal telegraph office" (p. 71, "Lotus-Eaters"); "The metal wheels ground the gravel with a sharp grating cry and the pack of blunt boots followed the barrow along a lane of sepulchres" (p. 104, "Hades").

The denotative norm continues to establish our sense of external reality and our sense of a narrative presence by assuring us that despite the introduction of a new character who sees the world differently from Stephen Dedalus, the world is the same. This second triad of chapters continues to build up our sense of what the world of Dublin and the world of the novel are like. The symmetry of this second triad with the "Telemachiad" and the persistence of the same basic rules of narration encourage us to group the first six chapters together as providing the norm of the book.

As in the "Telemachiad," one finds in these chapters a sympathy between narrator and character that again involves the borrowing of linguistic habits. To turn the page from the heraldic image of Stephen Dedalus "rere regardant" and to encounter Leopold Bloom eating "with relish the inner organs of beasts and fowls" is to sense a difference in mood that depends in part on a change in style. The language associated with Bloom (both his stream-of-consciousness and some third-person narration) is more simple syntactically, more colloquial, and more redundant than Stephen's. (See, for example, the prose of the opening of the chapter.)

What is most interesting about the "sympathy" between narrator and character in Bloom's chapters, however, is its occasional comic manipulation. Although the exchange between character and narrator in these chapters follows the rules set in the "Telemachiad," at times this exchange seems to pick up speed. In the following passage from "Hades," for example, Bloom and the narrator carry on a rapid and weird exchange of images:

> The whitesmocked priest came after him tidying his stole with one hand, balancing with the other a little book against his toad's belly. Who'll read the book? I, said the rook.
>   They halted by the bier and the priest began to read out of his book with a fluent croak. (p. 103)

The narrator describes the priest's belly as "his toad's belly"; then it is Bloom presumably who thinks "Who'll read the book? I, said the rook." Again, the third-person narration resumes in what seems like the initial style, except for the presence of the word "croak." Soon after this passage, Bloom looks at the priest and thinks, "Eyes of a toad too," and the word "too" must refer to the "toad's belly" mentioned in the narrator's statement. There is a strange kind of play between narrator and character, almost a parodic form of sympathy between the two. This is a kind of "sympathy" that reduces the distance between the telling of the story and the story itself, a distance that will be manipulated in increasingly bizarre ways as the book progresses. This passage in "Hades" looks forward to the exchanges between narrator and speaker in "Scylla and Charybdis":

> — Yes, Mr Best said youngly, I feel Hamlet quite young. (p. 194)

— Bosh! Stephen said rudely. A man of genius makes no mistakes. His errors are volitional and are the portals of discovery.

Portals of discovery opened to let in the quaker librarian, softcreakfooted, bald, eared and assiduous. (p. 190)

Recently, Hugh Kenner has pointed out another anomaly of the second triad of chapters that emphasizes the artifice of the text. In his article, "The Rhetoric of Silence," Kenner cites several omissions in the text, some of which are highly significant to the plot. Chief among these gaps is a missing scene between Molly and Bloom, in which she tells him when Boylan is coming to Eccles Street ("At four"), and Bloom tells her he will attend the Gaiety Theatre (the cue she needs to assure her Bloom will not be home at four). Based upon Bloom's later recollection of Molly's words ("At four, she said" [p. 260]), and Molly's recollection of Bloom's statement that he would be dining out ("he said Im dining out and going to the Gaiety" [p. 740]), Kenner deduces that the painful scene between the two is omitted or repressed in the narrative. Since we cannot locate this conversation among the exchanges between Molly and Bloom that are recorded, Kenner concludes that they must have occurred offstage, like Molly's adultery or Bloom's visit to the insurance office on behalf of Paddy Dignam's widow.[16] Although this particular gap in the conversation can be recognized only retrospectively, when the missing lines are recollected, this playfulness in the selection of dramatized details puts into question our initial assumption that the narrative is recording all significant action. But, as Kenner says, we can reconstruct the scene in our minds, based on our knowledge of the characters and our sense of the empirical world that Joyce goes to such lengths to depict.[17] As Stephen discovers in "Proteus," the world is "there all the time without you . . . world without end" (p. 37). Narrative selection rather than empirical reality is questioned; the concept of omission presupposes that something in particular is being omitted.

In the second triad of chapters, we move closer to the comic play to come. In fact, I would argue that the mind of Leopold Bloom and the more comic and parodic tone of his chapters predict the direction of the rest of the narrative. It is Bloom's rather than Stephen's sensibility that dominates the *kind* of book *Ulysses* will become. The opening of the book to the subliterary as well as the literary and the movement from statement to cliché are predicted by the movement from Stephen Dedalus to Leopold Bloom. In some ways, the general tone and feeling of the book and some of the narrative strategies of the later chapters are also predicted in the book's first half.

By the end of "Hades," we have been introduced to the two main characters in a thorough way. In the stream-of-consciousness of each character, in each private memory emerges a particular way of making sense of the world and the self. In "reading" the world, the characters rely on different tools of interpretation: Bloom on clichés and bits of popular information, Stephen on abstruse allusion and esoteric philosophy. Both characters, however, are concerned with making sense of their pasts, not by an act of retrospection, as can be found in the novels of James or Proust, but in random associations that surface while they live their lives. "It is the 'stream of consciousness' which serves to clarify or render intelligible both the element of duration in time and the aspect of an enduring self. The technique is designed to give some kind of visible, sensible impression of how it is meaningful and intelligible to think of the self as a continuing unit despite the most perplexing and chaotic manifold of immediate experience."[18] Amidst the sense of the "immediate experience" of life that we get in the first six chapters of *Ulysses* is the faith in character not as a "construct" seen from the outside but, nevertheless, as a "self" that is constant.

Thus, in the early chapters of *Ulysses* the characters carry the main burden of interpreting the world. "Proteus" is the culmination of Stephen's attempt to interpret his surroundings. In fact, his portentous announcement, "Signatures of all things I am here to read," is one of the most explicit declarations of character as interpreter in literature. As Fredric Jameson has said of psychological novels in general (and this applies to the early chapters of *Ulysses*), the character "from within the book, reflecting on the meaning of his experiences, does the actual work of exegesis for us before our own eyes."[19] In subsequent chapters, the reader and the writer participate more strenuously in the hermeneutic process. But in the beginning of the book, the major "burden" of interpretation is placed on the characters.

By providing a norm in its first six chapters that later would be subverted, the novel encompasses its author's changing interests; it can thus be said that the book, as well as Joyce, the author, changes its mind. When he wrote the first six chapters, Joyce did not yet fully realize the direction the second half of the novel would take. But his decision to leave the first chapters substantially intact was made after writing the entire novel. The opening section of the book was left as a kind of testimony to an older order, a norm for the reader at the same time as it is an anachronism in terms of the book as a whole. Consequently, the opening of the novel does not prepare the reader for what follows. A novel usually offers its reader built-in strategies for interpreting the world it presents. The concept of development in most novels insures that the early parts of the work in some way prepare the reader for what is to come (Henry James's *Prefaces* devote considerable space to this idea of preparation). But the first six chapters of *Ulysses* lead the reader to have certain unfulfilled expectations, that is, they make a certain contract that is subverted (for instance, that the normative voice will be sustained throughout the novel, that character will be the major concern). Although Joyce, unlike Kierkegaard, never openly confessed to this kind of "deception,"[20] *Ulysses* begins by deliberately establishing narrative rules that are bent and finally broken later on.

In *Ulysses*, Joyce leaves the "tracks" of his artistic journey. Throughout his career Joyce transformed and developed his materials, but in the process he tended to outgrow a specific form and move on to another. Before writing *Ulysses* he had abandoned poetry for the short story and the short story for the extended narrative record of the growth of the artist's mind in *A Portrait*. Then, as S. L. Goldberg has observed, discovering that the record of the growth of the artist's mind was severely limited by the artist's awareness,[21] he began *Ulysses*. Realizing that Stephen had "a shape that [couldn't] be changed,"[22] he became more interested in Leopold Bloom. And, finally, finding obsolete the idea of a narrative norm that tells a story, with "Aeolus" as a clue and with "Wandering Rocks" and "Sirens" as the new formal beginning, he went beyond the novel to something else. In each case, the changes in form and style reflect the shedding of an artistic belief no longer sufficient to his vision.

Notes

1. Frank Budgen, *James Joyce and the Making of "Ulysses"* (1934; reprint ed., Bloomington: Indiana University Press, 1960), pp. 67–68.

2. Edmund Wilson, *Axel's Castle: A Study in the Imaginative Literature of 1870–1930* (New York: Charles Scribner's Sons, 1959), p. 217.

3. S. L. Goldberg, *The Classical Temper: A Study of James Joyce's "Ulysses"* (London: Chatto and Windus, 1961), p. 92.

4. See David Hayman's *"Ulysses": The Mechanics of Meaning* (Englewood Cliffs, N.J.: Prentice–Hall, Inc., 1970), especially pp. 75–79, and Anthony Burgess's *Joysprick: An Introduction to the Language of James Joyce* (London: André Deutsch, 1973) for two of the earliest and best discussions of this narrative norm. Recently, discussions of the narrative norm have become more common. See, for example, Hugh Kenner's *Joyce's Voices* (Berkeley: University of California Press, 1978), and Marilyn French's *The Book as World: James Joyce's "Ulysses"* (Cambridge, Mass.: Harvard University Press, 1976).

5. See, for example, Wolfgang Iser, *The Implied Reader: Patterns of Communication in Prose Fiction from Bunyan to Beckett* (Baltimore: The Johns Hopkins University Press, 1974), pp. 179–233, and Ben D. Kimpel, "The Voices of *Ulysses*," *Style* 9 (Summer 1975):283–319.

6. See, for example, Erwin R. Steinberg's *The Stream of Consciousness and Beyond in "Ulysses"* (Pittsburgh: University of Pittsburgh Press, 1973) for the most extensive treatment of Joyce's use of the stream-of-consciousness technique.

7. Burgess, *Joysprick*, p. 68.

8. Ibid., p. 74.

9. Letter, 6 August 1919, *Letters of James Joyce*, Vol. 1, ed. Stuart Gilbert (New York: The Viking Press, 1957), p. 129. However, when I refer to the "initial style" henceforth, I mean specifically the prose style of the third-person narration.

10. Hugh Kenner's ingenuity and prolificacy illustrate the possibilities for characterizing the early narrative style of *Ulysses*. In *The Stoic Comedians: Flaubert, Joyce, and Beckett*

(Berkeley: University of California Press, 1962), the following narrative sentence is cited as an example of Joyce's characteristic manipulation of language and his "resolute artistry": "Two shafts of soft daylight fell across the flagged floor from the high barbicans: and at the meeting of their rays a cloud of coalsmoke and fumes of fried grease floated, turning" (pp. 30–31). In *Joyce's Voices*, the same marked precision is said to exemplify the "fussiness of setting and decor" of "Edwardian novelese" (pp. 68–69). Both descriptions are intriguing, the second moving us, as it does, further away from a view of the early style as normative and nonparodic. The style becomes just another example of a particular kind of rhetoric, despite its temporal primacy in the text. Although the sentence does exhibit stylistic idiosyncrasies, I favor Kenner's first description of it as an example of Joyce's characteristic style, more normative at this point than parodic.

11. See James's Preface to *The Tragic Muse*, reprinted in *The Art of the Novel: Critical Prefaces* by Henry James (New York: Charles Scribner's Sons, 1962), p. 87: "To put all that is possible of one's idea into a form and compass that will contain and express it only by delicate adjustments and an exquisite chemistry . . . every artist will remember how often that sort of necessity has carried with it its particular inspiration."

12. This sense of the excess of labor in the writing appears again in subsequent chapters like "Sirens," "Eumaeus," and "Ithaca," even though different styles are used in each case.

13. See Kenner, *Joyce's Voices*, pp. 69–70.

14. Frank Kermode, "Novels: Recognition and Deception," *Critical Inquiry* 1 (Sept. 1974):117. Kermode's comment, made in reference to Ford's *The Good Soldier*, seems to me to apply much more appropriately to *Ulysses*.

15. S. L. Goldberg, *Joyce* (Edinburgh, 1962; reprint ed., New York: Capricorn Books, 1972), p. 90.

16. Hugh Kenner, "The Rhetoric of Silence," *James Joyce Quarterly* 14 (Summer 1977):382–394.

17. Ibid., p. 383.

18. Hans Meyerhoff, *Time in Literature* (Berkeley: University of California Press, 1955), p. 37.

19. Fredric Jameson, "Metacommentary," *PMLA* 86 (Jan. 1971):13.

20. See Søren Kierkegaard, *The Point of View for My Work as an Author: A Report to History and Related Writings*, trans. Walter Lowrie; ed. Benjamin Nelson (New York: Harper & Brothers, 1962). The work announced that for the purpose of arriving at "truth," Kierkegaard had lulled his unsuspecting readers into a sense of narrative security in his aesthetic writings, only to subvert this security later in the religious writings.

21. See Goldberg, *Joyce*, p. 63.

22. Quoted in Budgen, *James Joyce and the Making of "Ulysses,"* p. 105.

Gesture: The Letter of the Word　　　　Patrick McGee*

*So why, pray, sign anything as long as every word, letter, penstroke,
paperspace is a perfect signature of its own?*

　　　　　　　　　　　　　　　　　　　　　　　　— Finnegans Wake

　　As Joyce learned from Vico, in the beginning was the gesture.[1] Even
the first word of *Ulysses* has the force of a gesture: "Stately"— an adjective
of manner, language, person, literary style, rhythm, building, proportions, and so on. The material aesthetic or antiaesthetic underlying Joyce's
literary work receives its ultimate expression in "Circe" when Stephen
Dedalus says that "gesture, not music not odour, would be a universal
language, the gift of tongues rendering visible not the lay sense but the
first entelechy, the structural rhythm."[2] As I will suggest throughout this
reading, in *Ulysses* Joyce goes beyond Stephen's idealistic aesthetic theory
in *A Portrait of the Artist as a Young Man;* while the vocabulary remains
more or less the same, the practice that frames and illustrates it becomes
gradually more radical and forces us retrospectively to regard *A Portrait of
the Artist* itself as a more subversive text than it initially appears to be. The
word "gesture" describes a writing practice that resists definition and
evaluation,that resists the preestablished code it simulates, that resists the
law of value, particularly the law of aesthetic value. This writing as
transgression is the structural rhythm of symbolic exchange that my
reading will attempt to capture in process.

STEPHEN'S MO(U)RNING: "TELEMACHUS" TO "AEOLUS"

> Stately, plump Buck Mulligan came from the stairhead, bearing a bowl
> of lather on which a mirror and a razor lay crossed. A yellow dressing-
> gown, ungirdled, was sustained gently behind him on the mild morning
> air. He held the bowl aloft and intoned:
> — *Introibo ad altare Dei.*
> 　　Halted, he peered down the dark winding stairs and called out
> coarsely:
> — Come up, Kinch! Come up, you fearful jesuit!
> 　　Solemnly he came forward and mounted the round gunrest. He
> faced about and blessed gravely thrice the tower, the surrounding land
> and the awaking mountains. Then, catching sight of Stephen Dedalus,
> he bent towards him and made rapid crosses in the air, gurgling in his
> throat and shaking his head. Stephen Dedalus, displeased and sleepy,
> leaned his arms on the top of the staircase and looked coldly at the
> shaking gurgling face that blessed him, equine in its length, and at the
> light untonsured hair, grained and hued like pale oak. (1.1–16)

*From *Paperspace: Style as Ideology in Joyce's "Ulysses"* (Lincoln: University of Nebraska
Press, 1988), 12–36. © 1988 by the University of Nebraska Press. Reprinted by permission
of the publisher.

As Mulligan demonstrates with his parody of the mass, a gesture is an act that speaks, articulating between one subject and another a relation of power. Stephen looks coldly on the relation expressed by Mulligan's mockery of the act of consecration for the simple reason that he knows who stands in the position of priest and who in the position of server. For the moment, Mulligan carries the mirror and the razor, the gaze of authority and the blade, the cutting edge, of art. Both precursor and high priest, a combination of prophet and pharisee (like Cranly in *A Portrait of the Artist*), he stands before Stephen in the role of the accuser and says, "He kills his mother but he can't wear grey trousers" (1.122). Stephen's answer is only another parody; he recognizes Mulligan's equine head, the head of a Houyhnhmn, a member of the Anglo-Irish élite, whose traditions Stephen knows how to use to effect. Mulligan's mirror, taken from the room of his mother's servant, has a crack in it:

> Laughing again, he brought the mirror away from Stephen's peering eyes.
> — The rage of Caliban at not seeing his face in a mirror, he said. If Wilde were only alive to see you!
> Drawing back and pointing, Stephen said with bitterness:
> — It is a symbol of Irish art. The cracked lookingglass of a servant.
> (1.141–46)

After Mulligan uses Wilde to imply that Stephen's rage is naively romantic, Stephen retorts with another of Wilde's aphorisms; he insists that if art is a mirror, it is always possible that genius is a "cracked lookingglass."[3] From Jonathan Swift to Oscar Wilde the "cracked looking-glass" is the Irish vision within English literature, the symptom of a contradiction that periodically drives the writers of that tradition to the brink of madness and death, whose structural rhythm expresses the historical alienation of the Anglo–Irish or Irish subject from the dominant culture of England. This contradiction is reflected in Mulligan's relation to Haines and, more dramatically, in Stephen's relation to Mulligan. These relations are not symmetrical, however, as there is more than one mirror in "Telemachus." Stephen also sees himself in the old milkwoman who exercises a mythological power over him: "Silk of the kine and poor old woman, names given her in olden times. A wandering crone, lowly form of an immortal serving her conqueror and her gay betrayer, their common cuckquean, a messenger from the secret morning. To serve or to upbraid, whether he could not tell: but scorned to beg her favour" (1.403–7). This woman is the image of Ireland, whom Stephen spoke of in *A Portrait of the Artist* as the "old sow that eats her farrow," though here he cannot decide whether she is for or against him.[4] He only knows that the language Haines speaks to her is a language that neither he nor she can speak: the Irish language.

Mulligan accuses Stephen of killing his mother, but from Stephen's perspective something more complicated has happened. His mother's dying wish, the wish he refused to honor, was that Stephen submit to the symbolic order imprisoning her, to patriarchy, or the law of the father as it is manifested in the church of the fathers. Had Stephen obeyed her, he would have betrayed her, though in not obeying her he still betrays her by depriving her life of its meaning and its justification; he makes her die a double death, both of the letter and of the spirit, by pushing aside the only means both she and he have of resolving the relation between life and death symbolically. In confronting the death of his mother, Stephen now confronts his own double bind in the nightmare of a world without purpose, a self without its ground in the being of another. Stephen's mother, his original mirror, has become a hole in the real. She comes to him both from the outside and from the inside, "her wasted body within its loose grave clothes giving off an odour of wax and rosewood, her breath, bent over him with mute secret words, a faint odour of wetted ashes" (1.270–72). He tries to drive her away with the words "Ghoul! Chewer of Corpses!" (1.278), but her "mute secret words" stay with him, like the names of the old woman, names of the mother.

The riddle of these feminine figures follows Stephen into the classroom, where, unlike Oedipus, who answered the riddle of the Sphinx, he speaks riddles that cannot be answered, at least not by univocal discourse:

> The cock crew,
> The sky was blue:
> The bells in heaven
> Were striking eleven.
> 'Tis time for this poor soul
> To go to heaven.
> (2.102–7)

Stephen disguises "*love's bitter mystery*" (1.240), the mystery of his own love for the mother, in these words. His students, like Joyce's readers, are baffled first by the riddle and then by the answer: "The fox burying his grandmother under a hollybush" (2.115). It would seem that Stephen intends to mystify not only his students but himself; by speaking in riddles, he speaks without saying anything, without committing himself to a message that can be decoded. He rejects the symbolic while remaining inside it and playing the part of the teacher or the one who is supposed to know. Nevertheless, Stephen begins to relax his defenses with Cyril Sargent, who has his own kind of language block. With Stephen, Cyril learns how to solve an algebra problem, not by copying the finished equations that somehow keep hidden the secret of what they know, but by imitating Stephen, by relating to knowledge as performance. Stephen works out a problem in front of Cyril and then has Cyril repeat the performance on a different problem. Cyril copies the data that Stephen gives him; but then, "Waiting always for a word of help his hand moved faithfully the unsteady symbols, a faint hue of shame flickering behind his dull skin" (2.163–65). Stephen also learns something from Cyril, from the shame which recalls his own shame before the mystery of words in *A Portrait of the Artist*; he ponders the meaning of mother love, what Cranly called "the only true thing in life":

> Was that then real? The only true thing in life? His mother's prostrate body the fiery Columbanus in holy zeal bestrode. . . . A poor soul gone to heaven: and on a heath beneath winking stars a fox, red reek of rapine in his fur, with merciless bright eyes scraped in the earth, listened, scraped up the earth, listened, scraped and scraped. (2.143–50)

Stephen identifies with "fiery Columbanus" in more than one sense. On the one hand, because this saint, a sixth-century Irish missionary to continental Europe, embodies the Roman church in its militant, creative aspect, he stands for what Stephen would have been had he invested his desire in the religion of his mother. On the other hand, as Paul van Caspel comments, "It is said that the mother of Columbanus — in an impulse, no doubt, to protect him from the dangers of the world — tried to prevent him from setting out into that world to preach the Gospel: She threw herself on the threshold of their house, whereupon he just stepped across her prostrate body."[5] By attempting to become the Columbanus of art, Stephen violates his mother while fulfilling her dreams for him. He refuses to endorse her symbolic rape in life by the Irish church and patriarchy but finds himself compelled to violate her in death. He is the fox with the "red reek of rapine," driven to listen and scrape, to disturb the peace of the dead and to search for what he cannot live with but cannot live without: the woman under the hollybush.

After mesmerizing his students and himself, Stephen finds he cannot mesmerize the modern Nestor, Mr. Garret Deasy. Standing in front of his employer, Stephen runs his hand over the shells in a cold stone mortar, thinking: "Symbols too of beauty and of power. A lump in my pocket: symbols soiled by greed and misery" (2.226–28); but Stephen has to listen to Mr. Deasy (who collects not only shells and silver spoons but clichés and truisms) as the voice of experience: "You don't know yet what money is. Money is power. When you have lived as long as I have. I know, I know. *If youth but knew*. But what does Shakespeare say? *Put but money in thy purse*" (2.236–40). Mr. Deasy uses the words of Iago to speak for Anglo-Irish and English power; he reminds his Irish subordinate of Ireland's dependency on England with the usual platitudes: "We are a generous people but we must also be just" (2.262–63); and he ironically represents, along with Haines, the rationalist view of history which legitimates the structural violence of the present (the system of economic and cultural inequality) through an appeal to teleological necessity: "All human history moves towards one great goal, the manifestation of God" (2.380–81). For Stephen, the only goals to be reached are those on the children's playfield:

history is a nightmare from which he is trying to awake, and God is merely a "shout in the street" (2.386). This is one way to subvert authority—not to take it seriously; but Stephen has little real impact on Mr. Deasy, who, trivial though his words may be, has some social power to authorize his anti-Semitism and antifeminism and the historical lies on which such prejudices are founded.

In "Proteus," however, Stephen begins to learn where his own power lies in seeking mastery of the visible, the surface of the real:

> Ineluctable modality of the visible: at least that if no more, thought through my eyes. Signatures of all things I am here to read, seaspawn and seawrack, the nearing tide, that rusty boot. Snotgreen, bluesilver, rust: coloured signs. Limits of the diaphane. But he adds: in bodies. Then he was aware of them bodies before of them coloured. How? By knocking his sconce against them, sure. Go easy. Bald he was and a millionaire, *maestro di color che sanno*. Limit of the diaphane in. Why in? Diaphane, adiaphane. If you can put your five fingers through it it is a gate, if not a door. Shut your eyes and see. (3.1–9).

The visible is a Proteus infinitely more elusive than the Greek sea god, and Stephen has to construct a disguise so subtle as to be invisible. This is not only thought through his eyes but thought through his "I," that is, through the classical subject from which his discourse seems to originate, the "living" presence behind the phrase "Signatures of all things I am here to read." Still, Stephen does not perceive the world unmediated, for the living subject is grounded in the dead—those other subjects, those texts, which feed into Stephen's discourse, which read Stephen even as he reads the world: Aristotle, Dante, Shakespeare, Boehme, Berkeley, Lessing, and Blake, to list only the obvious. Stephen does not read passively; he writes in an act that subordinates the speaking subject to its process, its work. Between world and text, between the signatures to be read and the trace of what has been read, lies a process containing both terms of the opposition, a gesture which empowers Stephen as a subject without centering on him: "See now. There all the time without you: and ever shall be, world without end" (3.27–28).[6]

A thread in the "strandentwining cable of all flesh," a post in the transhistorical system of telecommunications ("That is why mystic monks. Will you be as gods? Gaze in your *omphalos*. Hello! Kinch here. Put me on to Edenville. Aleph, alpha: nought, nought, one" [3.38–40]). Stephen as subject discovers himself as eccentric, as divided from the One by the desire that motivates him to seek it. This eccentricity implies a break with the dominant post-Cartesian ideologies that locate the subject in the position of sovereignty over the world and the word and over the origin of the world in the presymbolic, in the body of a woman: "Spouse and helpmate of Adam Kadmon: Heva, naked Eve. She had no navel. Gaze. Belly without blemish, bulging big, a buckler of taut vellum, no whiteheaped corn, orient and immortal, standing from everlasting to everlasting. Womb of sin" (3.41–44).

Eve had no navel. She was not marked by any writing, not touched by any signifying chain; she was outside the authority of any human system of power—never posted, never stamped. Her body was (is) the immortal, unblemished surface on which everything impure, incomplete, mortal—that is, the visible—emerges, the space in which the symbolic appears as the writing of the world. But Eve's body is more than "a buckler of taut vellum"; it is the "whiteheaped corn . . . standing from everlasting to everlasting," that is, standing in eternal erection. As the phallic mother, the repository of masculine fear and fantasy, Eve embodies contradiction in her constriction, like the Virgin Mary, who has to answer some difficult questions: "*Qui vous a mis dans cette fichue position? – C'est le pigeon, Joseph*" (Who got you into this sorry situation?—It's the pigeon, Joseph [3.161–62]). If the mother is compromised, so is the son; and should the mother die before the son (which is what did not happen to Christ), he loses her gaze, the ideal erection, the mirror. Of course, language and culture are supposed to be there to close the gap, to erect the self into the transcendental subject whose signifier (Lacan tells us) is the phallus. But what if culture is called into question? what if the subject directs its *ressentiment* against itself, against the symbolic erection? One result will be sexual ambivalence bordering on violence, as when Stephen recalls standing on "the top of the Howth tram alone crying to the rain: *Naked women! Naked women!* What about that, eh?" (3.133–34). Stephen answers his own question: "What else were they invented for?" (3.135). The counterpart to Stephen's misogyny, however, is the masculine paranoia of this fantasy from his first trip to Paris: "On the night of the seventeenth of February 1904 the prisoner was seen by two witnesses. Other fellow did it: other me. Hat, tie, overcoat, nose. *Lui, c'est moi*" (3.181–83).

Eve without a navel is a symptom of the repressed feminine body, restricted and constricted by the patriarchal code. As a representation, Eve's body, like Mary's immaculate conception, represses the feminine body by devaluing its pleasure and the force of its labor through the identification of the womb with a tomb, with death. In other words, if Stephen is in a double bind, so was his (particular) mother. Given her cultural situation and the social posts available to her, she had a choice between life inside the patriarchal family or outside of it; she had either to assume the symbolic title and position of Mother (which should not be confused with biological motherhood) or risk losing her "good name" on the fringe of society or in the area of the exceptional. Stephen sees the possibility of his mother's alternative existence in the gypsy, the strolling mort who follows her ruffian: "Across the sands of all the world, followed by the sun's flaming sword, to the west, trekking to evening lands. She trudges, schlepps, trains, drags, trascines her load. A tide westering, moondrawn, in her wake" (3.391–93). The gypsy is the woman without a place or the woman whose place is always the place of the other. In this sense, every woman has some of the gypsy in her, including every mother:

> Tides, myriadislanded, within her, blood not mine, *oinopa pon-ton*, a winedark sea. Behold the handmaid of the moon. In sleep the wet sign calls her hour, bids her rise. Bridebed, childbed, bed of death, ghostcandled. *Omnis caro ad te veniet.* He comes, pale vampire, through storm his eyes, his bat sails bloodying the sea, mouth to her mouth's kiss. (3.393–98)

As long as the social symbolic is dominated by patriarchal law, then every woman (inside or outside the law, as long as it implicitly determines her position) is bound to a death principle, a marriage to the pale vampire, which represses the body's desire (its productive force) and replaces it with the myth of maternity, of the pure origin, the virgin mother, who, having once overthrown the archaic authority of death, must forever contain it and thus assume its identity. The "sun's flaming sword" ensures obedience to the law, as does another son, Stephen, when he reaches for pencil and paper in order to write: "His lips lipped and mouthed fleshless lips of air: mouth to her moomb. Oomb, allwombing tomb. His mouth moulded issuing breath, unspeeched: ooeeehah: roar of cataractic planets, globed, blazing, roaring wayawayawayawayaway. Paper" (3.401–4). From the womb issues a formless, speechless breath that he wants to shape into the word of man before it bursts upon the world with apocalyptic force. Whether he knows it or not, he writes the law.

A patriarchal subject who perceives women as sexual objects, Stephen nevertheless has an ambivalent relation to his own objectifying desire. The law Stephen writes both restricts and transforms; the tissue of words covers and reveals. In any case, the near identity of the words *vellum* and *velum* warns against our seizing on a feminine essence within Eve's body, beneath the veil, so to speak, and reminds us that what gets repressed as the feminine body is not an object or an identity but a process and a creative-destructive force that Stephen both desires and fears, since it creates and destroys the fiction of the subject's autonomy. Like Leopold Bloom (as we will see), Stephen would and would not; he tells himself, "You will not be master of others or their slave" (3.295–96); but he contradicts that imperative with the misogynist stance he takes toward women and with the will to mastery evidenced everywhere in his language. For example, he remembers a "virgin at Hodges Figgis' window" (3.426–27) who initially merits his critical attention: "She lives in Leeson park with a grief and kickshaws, a lady of letters"; but an instant later she receives his scorn: "Talk that to someone else, Stevie: a pickmeup" (3.429–30). After this abrupt change comes an even more sudden shift from aggressive to passive desire: "Touch me. Soft eyes. Soft soft soft hand.

I am lonely here. O, touch me soon, now. What is that word known to all men? I am quiet here alone. Sad too. Touch, touch me" (3.434–36).

Stephen wants to be touched by the woman who can tell him the word known to all men. But in this chapter (the art of which is philology), we need to consider carefully the way we read the question "What is that word known to all men?" Is it a matter of information, of Stephen's really learning what other men know? Or is the word "love" in the new *Ulysses* (9.429–30) a satisfactory answer to the question, as Richard Ellmann thinks? Or is this word the logos of theological and phenomenological speculation?[7] These readings are all possible, but it is also possible to read the question differently, to shift the accent from "word" to the copulative "is." In this way, it is no longer a question of finding the word, the signifier, or the symbol that is absent or lost but of mastering the meaning of the word. For the word "word" does not have to refer to a single, particular signifier but to the whole sequence of signifiers that we call a discourse. Thus the original question could be rephrased to read: What is the essential value and meaning of that discourse known to all men? Obviously, one way of defining the discourse known to all men is as the discourse of man, that is, patriarchal discourse; men know it because they are inserted into it and subjected by it. Stephen's question leads to problematic ground. If the patriarchal subject is an effect of discourse, he can never know or master that discourse from the outside; he can never know the objective meaning of his subjective experience without an appeal to *the other*. His word fails to grasp "reality" as its meaning. Ironically, posing the question of meaning, of the absolute significance of patriarchal discourse, subverts the truth of patriarchy. If meaning and reality (or the real) were to coincide, there would be no way of posing the question of the meaning of a discourse, since meaning would be manifest in the pure unity of word and thing. Meaning, however, is always other, always extrinsic to the word. In posing the question of meaning, Stephen posits meaning as difference, the meaning of man's word as its difference from the word it excludes or restricts inside the symbolic. Stephen's question, in other words, consumes itself.

Paradoxically, the word known to all men must be solicited from a woman. Or rather the limit to man's will to knowledge, the edge which bends that will back against itself (like the rhythmic gesture of the tide, the chapter's symbol according to Joyce's schema) is woman's word, her silent word (the "mute secret words" of Stephen's mother). It resembles the crack in the mirror; through it we glimpse the truth about man's word — the truth that man's knowledge, his disinterested knowledge, masks the will to power. At the end of "Proteus," Stephen calls himself "Toothless Kinch, the superman" (3.496). But if he is the superman, the one who speaks the discourse of power, gesturing forth the desire to master the surfaces of the visible, he also parodies that discourse and subverts the will to power that he serves. The superman appears as the toothless servant of the will to power, and the will to power as the servant of death. Through parody and self-irony, Stephen chooses to live: "Yes, evening will find itself in me, without me" (3.490). He accepts his position as a decentered subject and rewrites the opposition between life and death as the impossible and necessary combination, life death.[8] One process, life death becomes "God becomes man becomes fish becomes barnacle goose becomes featherbed mountain" (3.477–79).

In "Proteus," Stephen's "morose delectation" may be a kind of mourning; but it also involves the production of pleasure, a production that continues in "Aeolus" and in "Scylla and Charybdis," as once again Stephen tries to write the law in the language of the outlaw, to subvert power with pleasure.[9] In "Aeolus," where he is literally seduced by rhetoric, Stephen's critical moment comes when he tells the story of the two Dublin vestals who climb Nelson's pillar with their brawn, their panloaf, and their plums. The story seems simple and utterly pointless; its title, *A Pisgah Sight of Palestine* or *The Parable of the Plums*, links it to the speech of John F. Taylor recited by Professor MacHugh, a speech that ends with the image of Moses descending Sinai's peak, *"bearing in his arms the tables of the law, graven in the language of the outlaw"* (7.868–69). Stephen's story differs from Taylor's speech, however: while the latter speaks *of* the language of the outlaw, Stephen attempts to speak *in* that language (since he implicitly recognizes that what was the language of the outlaw when Moses descended the mountain is now the law itself).[10] Like his fox riddle, Stephen's narrative produces a complex effect; instead of provoking immediate laughter, it baffles and frustrates the desire for pleasure that it invites. Professor MacHugh (living up to his title) struggles to fit the story into an acceptable code (which turns out to be the code of obscenity), while Stephen carefully structures his telling in an ironic relation to such a code, in a language indeterminate as to meaning, however simple it may appear to be on the surface. The story is not unreadable, but the reader has to take the same risk as the teller.

How should we read it? More than an obscene joke, it is an allegory of power and desire disguised as an obscene joke; it tells of patriarchal power and of the desire that subverts such power through the production of a pleasure that cannot be assimilated by its code: a pleasure of the female subject, patriarchy's other, when it suddenly forgets itself, its self, its *subject*ion. The two Dublin vestals, "peering up at the statue of the onehandled adulterer" (7.1018–19), get a crick in their necks and "are too tired to look up or down or to speak. They put the bag of plums between them and eat the plums out of it, one after another, wiping off with their handkerchiefs the plumjuice that dribbles out of their mouths and spitting the plumstones slowly out between the railings" (7.1023–27). They turn their backs on the monument to patriarchy, its cultural erection, and eat the fruit symbolic of the original woman's transgression against the father's law; they slake their thirst with the juice and throw the stones away. In doing so, they teach us that symbolism can be subverted or at least displaced by the redirection of desire from the fetishism of the code toward a pleasure that refuses the signifier, that desacralizes the system of values. As opposed to facing and visually acquiring the symbol of patriarchal power, the phallic monument, they prefer to sit in its presence without possessing it, to use it without exchanging it. They refuse to be mirrors, and so their pleasure does not enter into the phallocentric economy. They merely use what is available to them until they exhaust themselves in the enjoyment of it. Their unknown, incommensurable pleasure is what I will call *jouissance*.[11]

Still, this episode contains more than one pleasure, as we see when Stephen ends the story with "a sudden loud young laugh" (7.1028). This recalls the "nervous laughter" that followed the riddle in "Nestor" (2.116) and anticipates the laughter that frees Stephen's "mind from his mind's bondage" in "Scylla and Charybdis" (9.1016). Going beyond the "joy" in Joyce's "Paris Notebook" and the "aesthetic pleasure" in Stephen's theory from *A Portrait of the Artist*, this laughter is not the arrest, the stasis, of the subject before the beauty, the whatness, of a thing; nor is it above desire and loathing. Having neither an exchange value nor a use value, Stephen's laughter has no value, except in the transgressive pleasure of using itself up, in the annihilation of self — the pleasure the subject takes from its effacement in production, from the work of becoming other. In other words, Stephen's laughter rewrites the aesthetic theory of James Joyce.[12]

The scene in "Aeolus" suggests a parallel and a communication between Stephen's situation, his double bind, and what we may think of as Joyce's double bind. This communication insists itself throughout *Ulysses*, though its critical moment comes in "Scylla and Charybdis." Concerning "Aeolus," however, we can say this: if Stephen's parable displaces and reverses a rhetoric of sentiment, the chapter as a whole displaces and reverses the entire rhetorical tradition. The language of the outlaw deconstructs the language of the law through the aesthetic of exile — exile not outside of but within a given position: a displacement of position, a reversal of the code, producing a pleasure beyond the pleasure of recognition, a pleasure no longer antithetical to pain, a joy no longer antithetical to sorrow. But of whose joy and whose pleasure are we speaking? Or rather of whom does Professor MacHugh speak when he addresses this remark to Stephen? "You remind me of Antisthenes, . . . a disciple of Gorgias, the sophist. It is said of him that none could tell if he were bitterer against others or against himself. He was the son of a noble and a bondwoman. And he wrote a book in which he took away the palm of beauty from Argive Helen and handed it to poor Penelope" (7.1035–39).

BLOOM'S LETTERS: "CALYPSO" TO "LESTRYGONIANS"

Leopold Bloom is the Ulysses of the postal era. If his original was a master in the art of giving and receiving the signs of power and class, Bloom is a master in his own class, a master of the writing that circulates from mouth to ear, from hand to hand, on slips of paper, on cards, in newspapers, across telegraph wires and telephone lines, in trucks, in boats, and so on. As a post, a register, a trace in the system of linguistic exchanges, Bloom is a symptom of the modern symbolic.[13] From the beginning, in every situation and position, Bloom either responds or reacts to a letter or letters, either a piece of writing stamped by the postal system or a word, a phrase, a speech (spoken, written, or printed) that bears the mark of its social or symbolic value. For example, near the beginning of "Calypso," Bloom checks on the white slip of paper in the leather band of his hat with the number of his secret post box written on it (4.70–71); a while later he lifts a printed sheet from the pile at the porkbutcher's and reads about "the model farm at Kinnereth on the Lakeshore of Tiberias" (4.154–55); at home he finds two letters and a card on the hall floor, notes the writing of a "bold hand" on the letter to Molly and scans Milly's letter to him (4.243–82); later he looks for Molly's dime novel, *Ruby: The Pride of the Ring*, and explains the meaning of the word "metempsychosis" to her while gazing at a poster from *Photo Bits*, *The Bath of the Nymph*, hanging over the bed (4.331–77); back in the kitchen he reads Milly's letter in full while eating (4.393–414) and then retreats to the jakes with an old number of *Titbits* in which he reads *Matcham's Masterstroke* by Mr. Philip Beaufoy, a writing for which he finds more than one use (4.500–540).

The first act in this drama of the letters puts into play a number of signifiers that will circulate throughout the novel. If we seek a hierarchy of relations among them or a thematic structure underlying and organizing their dispersed arrangement, however, we will run into problems. For example, it seems reasonable to say that the reference to Blazes Boylan's "bold hand" on the letter to Molly has more dramatic value as a determinant of Bloom's behavior during the course of his day than the pulp novel or the flyer on the model farm. After all, *Ulysses* could be described as a novel of adultery. But the problem is that *Ulysses* fits into a number of generic and thematic categories, none of which completely describes it because of the difficulty in determining the difference between an extrinsic and an intrinsic detail. Each particular image, plot detail, or thematic unit resists assimilation by a general or unitary theme and structure.[14] This is not to say that *Ulysses* has no themes but rather that it has an unaccountable number of them: no single word in the book can account and stand for all the others (not even the word "Ulysses").

What matters in *Ulysses* (as the matter of *Ulysses*) is not the word but the letter of the word — the configuration of letters in an open frame, for each of these letters is like the letter Bloom receives from Milly. Their significance does not lie in the meaning but in the writing, the style. The positive value of Milly's letter equals the negative value of its writing, a value which leads her to remark in the postscript: "Excuse bad writing am in hurry" (4.413).[15] Milly believes that her writing is bad because it fails to conform to a "standard" usage (i.e., the usage of a dominating class that Milly has been taught to regard as a "standard"); but Milly has the unconscious craft of those who lack distinction, the ability to turn a lack of distinction—through a minimal transgression—into a distinction, into a sign of love. Milly has learned this strategy from her father, whose mind is a long chain of clichés, incomplete thoughts, partially remembered names, and hearsay—"dead," insignificant, and devalued language. In reading Bloom's interior monologue, the reader of *Ulysses* undergoes an apprenticeship in the reading of clichés, in the hermeneutics of the exhausted letter transforming Bloom's lack of distinction into a different sort of distinction.

The second act of our drama introduces another letter, this one addressed to Henry Flower in an envelope with a flower in it. This flower, like the one grafted from Bloom's name, can no longer be found in nature, since it circulates from post to post in the symbolic, in the flower-writing of Martha Clifford:

> Dear Henry
>
> I got your last letter to me and thank you very much for it. I am sorry you did not like my last letter. Why did you enclose the stamps? I am awfully angry with you. I do wish I could punish you for that. I called you naughty boy because I do not like that other world. Please tell me what is the real meaning of that word? Are you not happy in your home you poor little naughty boy? I do wish I could do something for you. Please tell me what you think of poor me. I often think of the beautiful name you have. Dear Henry, when will we meet? I think of you so often you have no idea. I have never felt myself so much drawn to a man as you. I feel so bad about. Please write me a long letter and tell me more. Remember if you do not I will punish you. So now you know what I will do to you, you naughty boy, if you do not wrote. O how I long to meet you. Henry dear, do not deny my request before my patience are exhausted. Then I will tell you all. Goodbye now, naughty darling. I have such a bad headache. today. and write *by return* to your longing
>
> Martha
>
> P.S. Do tell me what kind of perfume does your wife use. I want to know.
>
> XXXX   (5.241.59)

Giving this letter a serious reading means giving it a distinction that it may seem to lack in itself. Nevertheless, the style of Martha's writing reminds us that every style has a social function and produces a political effect; every style betokens a relation to value determined by the relations of power that frame it and make themselves concrete within it. In other words, Martha's word is the paradigmatic letter of the word that composes and decomposes the (anti)book *Ulysses*.[16]

What does Martha want? We seem to know what Bloom, the linguistic fetishist, wants: the word in and for itself, detached from the other and invested with imaginary value. Like the men in the novels of Sacher-Masoch, Bloom wants to teach Martha to humiliate and punish him; but unlike such a character, Bloom seems unwilling to go all the way, and the only punishment he has in mind is some verbal abuse. Pinpointing Martha's desire requires more care. Although she is reluctant to engage in the exchange of obscenities through the mail, she is also fascinated by the words Bloom wants her to write, as we read in the celebrated line: "I called you naughty boy because I do not like that other world. Please tell me what is the real meaning of that word?" Martha cannot write what she wants to know more about—the word that Bloom has asked her to write for which she substitutes the words "naughty boy," though she does write what she does not know she wants to know more about—"that other world." That other world is the world of the word she cannot write, the world of desire she cannot admit to having, the world of finalized meanings in which the secrets of desire in words are revealed. From one point of view, Martha's letter is a symptom of the will to knowledge and a counterpart to Stephen's question about the word known to all men; her letter ends with the words "I want to know." Martha agrees to tell Bloom all if he will tell her all—that is, all there is to know about that other world. She wants to know the name of his wife's perfume, her essence, and the real meaning of "that beautiful name": Flower. She wants to know the essence of the other's other, the other of the man whose name is the essence of her desire. But Martha's desire to know something about Molly veils a secret desire to know herself as the other (woman)—not merely a woman's desire but the desire to be a woman, to be what "she" thinks a woman is supposed to be. Her letter is not a symptom of the feminine but of the will to be feminine, to play that part in a sexual masquerade. In the end, ironically, her desire proves to be more readable than Bloom's (though not more readable than Molly's) simply because it is less perverse; for if Martha plays the role of the reluctant sadist who supports Bloom's intermittent masochism, it is only because there is a role to be played.[17]

After reading Martha's letter and destroying the envelope, Bloom thinks: "Henry Flower. You could tear up a cheque for a hundred pounds in the same way. Simple bit of paper" (5.303–4) For Bloom the name Flower is a mask that he puts on and takes off, that he can tear up and throw away or mutilate any number of times and then use again. In the chapter I have been discussing, "Lotuseaters," there are flowers everywhere resonating with the names Flower and Bloom and proliferating beyond the control or consciousness of any individual character. These are the blooms of fantasy and the flowers of speech, imaginary perspectives and rhetorical strategies that individuals employ against the real, against the literal truth of death, contracts and compromises enabling them to live and protecting them from the great nightmare that Stephen Dedalus talks about. Bloom accepts the dispensation of the postal order; he knows that the name Flower does not signify his identity or essence—he knows that the same could be said of his real name. Nevertheless, he makes use of these names as tokens or symbols that anyone can hold or possess for a while. He knows—because his real name is a borrowed name and because his son is dead—that names have temporal limits. The flower as a thing is the symbol of this symbol, of a (proper) name that has negativity and death inscribed within it, of a body whose death in life produces, for a while, a life in death, an imaginary transubstantiation:

> Enjoy a bath now: clean trough of water, cool enamel, the gentle tepid stream. This is my body.
> He foresaw his pale body reclined in it at full, naked, in a womb of warmth, oiled by scented melting soap, softly laved. He saw his trunk and limbs riprippled over and sustained, buoyed lightly upward, lemon-yellow: his navel, bud of flesh: and saw the dark tangled curls of his bush floating, floating hair of the stream around the limp father of thousands, a languid floating flower. (5.565–72)

Ironically, this languid, suspended flower points the way to Hades: the funeral, the cemetery. The transformation of the body into a symbol, a signifier, in the womb of warmth, is also a descent into the tomb. Bloom keeps the flower only for a while or intermittently; he does not remain suspended; he goes to the funeral of Paddy Dignam, where he joins a company of men for whom he is the other, the outsider. No longer a flower or a father, he is an alien, a member of the tribe of Reuben, a reputed cuckold, and the son of a suicide. This is not, however, the hour of Bloom's melancholy (which comes in "Sirens") but rather the hour of his disenchantment, of a disenchanting interior monologue that erupts onto the surface of this masculine society only once and creates a distinct effect:

> Mr Power gazed at the passing houses with rueful apprehension.
> —He had a sudden death, poor fellow, he said.
> —The best death, Mr Bloom said.
> Their wideopen eyes looked at him.
> —No suffering, he said. A moment and all is over. Like dying in sleep.
> No-one spoke. (6.310–15)

What Bloom says is neither profound nor original; but it happens to be the truth in the sense that, from the point of view of this social group, it should not have been spoken. Basically he refuses to mourn, to participate in a general state of mourning, to engage in the ceremony and ritual which attempt to erect the literality of death into a rigid symbolic form. This form, or the monument, has nothing to do with the real dead but with the living dead who want to transform the concrete relation to death — the transitory flower, the limp father — into an eternal erection. Of course, Bloom, like these other men, knows the way to the village Finglas (in French, *fin*, the end, and *glas*, the death knell), where workers dig granite blocks out of the earth and shape them into monumental forms; he thinks, "Mine over there towards Finglas, the plot I bought. Mamma, poor mamma, and little Rudy" (6.862–63). When he hears Tom Kernan praising the language of the funeral service in the Irish church ("*I am the resurrection and the life. That touches a man's inmost heart*" [6.670]), he replies affirmatively. But his interior monologue approaches the question of death differently:

> Your heart perhaps but what price the fellow in the six feet by two with his toes to the daisies? No touching that. Seat of the affections. Broken heart. A pump after all, pumping thousands of gallons of blood every day. One fine day it gets bunged up: and there you are. Lots of them lying around here: lungs, hearts, livers. Old rusty pumps: damn the thing else. The resurrection and the life. Once you are dead you are dead. (6.672–77)

In the gospel according to Bloom, death is death. A man not without feeling for loved ones who have died, Bloom nevertheless tends not to inflate death or to capitalize it. Death is death. It is like the place in the central post office where they keep the letters that remain after the general distribution, at the end of circulation, or almost at the end, since it is difficult to say what happens in death and whether something does not remain in circulation on the other side of life. Even in the graveyard there are possibilities for a recirculation of the letters, giving Bloom the idea of putting gramophones and telephones in every grave. He watches an "obese gray rat" (6.973) wriggle itself in under a plinth and recognizes that even here there are systems of symbolic exchange and distribution: "Underground communication. We learned that from them" (6.991). Perhaps we could say that between life and death there is the letter, which is irreducible to one or the other; for without the letter (or the litter as it is called in *Finnegans Wake*) the opposition between life and death would be absolute, and the other world would be the hell of Christianity, the place where all motion stops, where multidirectional distribution becomes unidirectional retribution: "I do not like that other world she wrote. No more do I" (6.1002–3). Bloom wants to get back to life or the world of the word, of the letter that kills in order to keep up the circulation.

So in turning the page from "Hades" we read the signs of the printing press, the first headline of "Aeolus": "IN THE HEART OF THE HIBERNIAN METROPOLIS" (7.1–2). All the broken hearts of "Hades" are recirculated in and transumed by the heart of the modern city, which, like the human heart itself, is a machine. And through this machine, through the silence of its paralysis in periodic breakdowns, life death continues to speak. The order of the world is never complete; something always remains for a second distribution. When an unknown man in a mackintosh shows up at the Dignam funeral, Hynes discreetly asks Bloom if he can identify the stranger, and from a misunderstanding the character M'Intosh is born (6.891–98), whose name will finally appear in the pink edition of the *Telegraph*, along with the name L. Boom (16.1260). "If we were all suddenly somebody else," remarks Bloom (6.836).

In "Aeolus," he enters his element; no longer merely a post, Bloom is a postman, the one who carries the word from site to site and from master to master, and nowhere is he more mastered by the machine. Still, this is not Joyce's attack on the modern culture industry and its technology, since, while he is not unaware of the potential for violence and exploitation in the instruments of mechanical reproduction, he is also interested in learning to hear and to understand the language they speak.[18] For example, he hears what the printing presses say to Bloom:

> The machines clanked in threefour time. Thump, thump, thump. Now if he got paralysed there and no-one knew how to stop them they'd clank on and on the same, print it over and over and up and back. Monkeydoodle the whole thing. Want a cool head. (7.101–4)

> Sllt. The nethermost deck of the first machine jogged forward its flyboard with sllt the first batch of quirefolded papers. Sllt. Almost human the way it sllt to call attention. Doing its level best to speak. That door too sllt creaking, asking to be shut. Everything speaks in its own way. Sllt. (7.174–77)

The machine speaks of death ("This morning the remains of the late Mr Patrick Dignam. Machines. Smash a man to atoms if they got him caught" [7.80–81]) or of the death principle that runs life. The printing press, a machine within a machine (the social machine), produces and reproduces the discourse of power; it works and makes things work by making work and the worker into a thing. It formulates its own law, its gesture and rhythm, when it shows that the power to create is the same as the power to destroy, that the essence of motion is stasis, the always imminent possibility of the break. In other words, if the machine makes the worker into a machine, it also mimics the worker who, like Bloom, recognizes that the machine's voice, its speech, its writing, is like the human in being a series of repetitions, with pauses, silences, delays; a machine works even in not working, because, when it ceases to repeat and reproduce its law, when its silence is no longer balanced rhythmically against its speech, it merely speaks a different language, a language of the outlaw, of jouissance. Bloom, no less than Stephen, has his subversive pleasure, even though the object of that pleasure is more dispersed than the object of Stephen's. Bloom's jouissance takes the form of play, including the playfulness he injects into performing his daily tasks; it is the silent laughter punctuating the flow of dead language through his mind. Bloom takes life as a sort of farce. In "Aeolus," he works to produce an effect that never gets produced, to make a connection that never gets made. Instead of selling an advertisement, he is snubbed by the pseudointellectuals in the newspaper office, ridiculed by the newspaper boys, and rudely dismissed by Myles Crawford, who tells him to tell Keyes he "can kiss my royal Irish arse" (7.991). Bloom, of course, does not allow himself to be insulted; choosing equanimity over resentment, he simply stands "weighing the point and about to smile" while the senescent Crawford strides away "jerkily" (7.993–94).

The style of farce almost defines *Ulysses* and *Finnegans Wake* and is not isolated to the characterization of Bloom.[19] While it has been argued that Bloom's relation to language is passive, that he lacks control over his discourse as the uncritical receptacle of every word that comes along, it should be said that his passivity is also a way to language, a decision about the value of speech, summed up in this fragment from his interior monologue: "Useless words" (8.477). This "useless" in "Lestrygonians" resonates with the two occurrences of it in "Calypso," where Bloom broods over his inability to save Milly from a problematic sexual initiation or to prevent Molly from going to bed with Blazes Boylan (4.448–50). It also resonates with Joyce's allusion to *Ulysses* in *Finnegans Wake* as the "usylessly unreadable Blue Book of Eccles."[20] The word is not necessarily meant to suggest the impotence of language, its lack of force or function (though it certainly calls the idea of essential force into question); on the contrary, it challenges the speaking subject's ability to master language and all of its effects. Implicitly recognizing constraint in his relation to language (beyond which it may be useless for him to reach but within which it is possible to play a game that subverts the system with its own rules), Bloom capitalizes on the system not only by selling advertisements — that is, by dealing in signifiers — but by selling himself as a signifier. I refer to his slightly surreptitious advertisement in the *Irish Times*, the one with which he captures the attention of Martha Clifford. Passing this newspaper in "Lestrygonians," he thinks:

> There might be other answers lying there. Like to answer them all. Good system for criminals. Code. . . . Wanted, smart lady typist to aid gentleman in literary work. I called you naughty darling because I do not like the other world. Please tell me what is the meaning. Please tell me what perfume does your wife. Tell me who made the world. The way they spring those questions on you. And the other one Lizzie Twigg. My literary efforts have had the good fortune to meet with the approval of the eminent poet A.E. (Mr Geo. Russell). No time to do her hair drinking sloppy tea with a book of poetry. (8.323–33).

Bloom cannot beat the system of words by imposing his individual will on it. He cannot force Irish men to hear him or Irish women to love him. Nevertheless, he finds a use for useless words in farce — a use besides that designated by the given codes. He satirizes the code. In the passage above, for example, his thoughts are stereotyped and even cruel, since like his author (for whom the name A.E. cannot have been a neutral reference) he is animated by resentment and ambivalence, especially toward the feminine. But Bloom's restricted cruelty in what might be described as a fetishism of the cliché resists the general cruelty he sees all around him in "Lestrygonians" and elsewhere, the cruelty of hungry men. He backs away from the masculine world of the Burton restaurant, with the recognition that "Hungry man is an angry man. Working tooth and jaw" (8.662–63). Bloom's perverse language games are the outlets for repressed desire, which in most men translates into ferocious hunger, a violent consumption of the material world that is barely distinguishable from rape and murder: "Eat or be eaten. Kill! Kill!" (8.703). A man consumed by hunger is a desiring machine run amok. Bloom solves this problem by deploying the machine against itself, by transforming hunger into an object of consumption, or taste. He enjoys a simple but pleasant lunch of wine and a Gorgonzola cheese sandwich.

Bloom's correspondence with Martha Clifford involves a similar strategy. The symbolic violence of his letters defuses the physical violence that threatens him from within (and will nearly hurt him from without in "Cyclops"). Although he plays on Martha's desire to know the meaning of the word and of that other world, he also makes that desire his own by suspending it in the space between them. He suspends it in writing, in the word not only as fetish but as toy, something to be played with and shared by more than one person, an object to pass back and forth in symbolic exchange. Bloom wants to play, not to kill. But a letter can follow a different trajectory from that of Bloom's letters to Martha; it can ignore the space between two subjects and violate the other's desire. This is what happens when Mr. Breen, already half mad, receives a postcard in the mail, which has the effect not of suspending desire but of provoking immediate reaction. Mrs. Breen tells Bloom about it:

— Read that, she said. He got it this morning.
— What is it? Mr Bloom asked, taking the card. U.P.?
— U.p: up, she said. Someone taking a rise out of him. It's a great shame
for them whoever he is. (8.256–59)

The letters violate Mr. Breen by capitalizing on the insecurity of his relation to the social symbolic. Just as the origin of the card is uncertain, so is the literal meaning of its message.[21] Unfortunately, Mr. Breen is not the sort of subject who can allow for ambivalence and play; unable to take a joke, he decides to prosecute the sender, whose identity is unknown to him. Mr. Breen's overreaction corresponds inversely to his impotence, his inability to get it up in the sexual sense and his inability to get up in the world, to rise to a position of social prestige and power. Mr. Bloom has his own problems along these lines, as Nosey Flynn reminds him with this question about Molly's upcoming singing tour, "Who's getting it up?" (8.773). These words give Bloom a slight heartburn, but they do not destroy his capacity for distancing and seeing himself in ironic terms.

If Bloom and Breen are doubles they represent two different styles of ressentiment. While Breen runs around Dublin lugging his law books, Bloom retreats into himself; he has a vision in which the imaginary approaches the real as a missed or lost encounter. He recreates himself by *re*collecting another self from another place in another time — on Howth Hill, "under the wild ferns," the rhododendrons, the flowers:

> Ravished over her I lay, full lips full open, kissed her mouth. Yum. Softly she gave me in my mouth the seedcake warm and chewed. Mawkish pulp her mouth had mumbled sweetsour of her spittle. Joy: I ate it: joy. Young life, her lips that gave me pouting. Soft warm sticky gumjelly lips. Flowers her eyes were, take me, willing eyes. (8.906–10)

These flowers return at the end of *Ulysses* in Molly's voice, from her symbolic mouth. We chew these flowers of speech in reading the book.

Loving, eating, joy — everything, every pleasure, is suspended for Bloom, in the chewed seedcake, in the flowers that were her eyes. The words, the letters, resonate in this still moment. But there is a price to be paid for this suspension, this symbolization; the presence of the past suspends and divides the present or Bloom's desire in the here and now, in his relationship with Molly. He would and would not, the *vorrei e non vorrei* from *Don Giovanni* misremembered by Bloom in "Calypso" as *Voglio e mon vorrei* (4.327). I would and would not, I will (want) and would not.[22]

What does Bloom desire? The answer lies somewhere between the "will" and the "would not" on which *Ulysses* is suspended.

Notes

1. As David Hayman notes, Joyce learned of language as gesture not only from Vico: "Perhaps by *A Portrait*, certainly by *Ulysses*, and most emphatically in *Finnegans Wake*, he began to make words serve as gestures, mining language for its expressive potential. The prime question by the time we reach the *Wake* is 'how do words *act*.' Jousse, Richards and perhaps Saussure may have helped him clarify his ideas on language in its two natures (synchronic and diachronic) and thus on language as a figure both for mankind's stability and for historical change" (Hayman, "Language of/as Gesture in Joyce," in *Ulysses: Cinquante Ans Après*, ed. Louis Bonnerot [Paris: Didier, 1974], p. 213).

2. James Joyce, *Ulysses: A Critical and Synoptic Edition*, prepared by Hans Walter Gabler with Wolfhard Steppe and Claus Melchior (New York: Garland, 1984), p. 933. All references to *Ulysses* are to this edition. References to the reading text follow the line numbering by episode common to this and to the new trade editions of *Ulysses*. References to the synoptic text are by page and page-line numbers. The reader should not construe my use of the Gabler edition as a claim to its final authority.

3. Oscar Wilde, *The Picture of Dorian Gray*, ed. Isobel Murray (Oxford: Oxford University Press, 1974), pp. xxxiii–iv; "The Decay of Lying," in *The Artist as Critic: Critical Writings of Oscar Wilde*, ed. Richard Ellmann (New York: Random House, 1968), p. 307.

4. James Joyce, *A Portrait of the Artist as a Young Man: Text, Criticism, and Notes*, ed. Chester G. Anderson (New York: Viking Press, 1968), p. 203.

5. Paul van Caspel, *Bloomers on the Liffey: Eisegetical Readings of Joyce's "Ulysses"* (Baltimore: Johns Hopkins University Press, 1986), p. 43.

6. According to Jacques Aubert, "Proteus" is a text in which "aucune identité n'est assignable *à priori*. . . . A defaut de l'identifier [the light playing on the sea, for example], il faut en comprendre le fonctionnement, un fonctionnement qui lui tient peut-être lieu d'identité, la comprendre comme moyen d'authentification des signes colorés, c'est-à-dire comme moyens de justifier les signatures" (no identity can be assigned *à priori*. . . . Instead of identifying it, it is necessary to understand its operation, an operation which takes the place of identity perhaps, to understand it as a means of rendering authentic the colored signs, that is to say, as a means of justifying the signatures. [Aubert, *Introduction à l'esthétique de James Joyce* (Paris: Didier, 1973), p. 140]).

7. Richard Ellmann, *Ulysses: The Corrected Text*, ed. Hans Walter Gabler with Wolfhard Steppe and Claus Melchior (New York: Random House, 1986), pp. x–xii. As Gabler's synoptic text indicates, the lines in question (418.7–11) are present in the Rosenbach manuscript but absent from the typescript based on a lost working draft. In the textual notes (p. 1738), Gabler explains the omission as a typist's eyeskip. He argues that Joyce must have intended the passage to stand because some of it "is required to carry forward Stephen's argument." I find that Stephen's argument gets along perfectly well without the passage. If it is as crucial to the meaning of the book as Ellmann proclaims it to be, how did Joyce miss it in the proofs?
Suzette Henke offers a different viewpoint in her phenomenological reading of *Ulysses* as an utterance of "the word known to all men" — "the Logos that defines being, engenders sympathy, and identifies the symbol-system of the race" (*Joyce's Moraculous Sindbook: A Study of "Ulysses"* [Columbus: Ohio State University Press, 1978], p. 3).

8. For a discussion of this concept through a rich and complex reading of Freud's *Beyond the Pleasure Principle*, a reading that also explicitly and implicitly explores the relation of Freud to Nietzsche, see Jacques Derrida, "Spéculer — Sur 'Freud' " in *La Carte postale: De Socrate à Freud et au-delà* (Paris: Flammarion, 1980), pp. 277–437.

9. As David Hayman argues, it may be that Stephen experiences an authentic orgasm in the "Proteus" episode by masturbating. But if he does, he also "turns pleasure into punishment, bending under the weight of conscience imposed on him by his early training" (Hayman, "Stephen on the Rocks," *James Joyce Quarterly* 15.1 [1977]: 5–17). Bloom, of course, will masturbate on the same beach later in the day before the vision of a young woman's underdrawers. Ironically, Stephen is a purer version of the fetishist than Bloom, since it takes only the word, the signifier, to arouse him.

10. I am drawing suggestions from Philippe Sollers's discussion of Joyce in *Vision à New York: Entretiens avec David Hayman* (Paris: Bernard Grasset, 1981), pp. 100–134.

11. I owe my specific use of this French term both to Lacan's seminar on feminine sexuality and to Jane Gallop's commentary on the same. Gallop summarizes the meaning of the word in the context of French feminism: " 'Jouissance,' is frequently cited by translators as an untranslatable word, one that will tolerate no mediation but must be present in the text and not displaced into another language's 'equivalent.' It means enjoyment, also orgasm, and tends to be linked to a loss of control, a more primitive experience than the words 'plaisir' (pleasure) and 'orgasme.' . . . You can have one or multiple orgasms; they are quantifiable, delimitable. You cannot have one 'jouissance' and there is no plural." In another passage, she refers to jouissance as an enjoyment, a pleasure, that exceeds exchange and possession: "This opposition of *jouissance* and possession can refer to a legal meaning of *jouissance*, as having

the use of something. Notice the example of usufruct, given in the dictionary under *jouissance*. 'Usufruct' is the right to the *jouissance* but *not the ownership* of something; in other words, you can use it and enjoy it, but you cannot exchange it" (Gallop, *The Daughter's Seduction: Feminism and Psychoanalysis* [Ithaca: Cornell University Press, 1982], pp. 29–30, 50). I would add that for Lacan jouissance is not physiological: "Thought is *jouissance*. What analytic discourse brings out is this fact, which was already intimated in the philosophy of being — that there is a *jouissance* of being" (Jacques Lacan, "God and the *Jouissance* of The Woman," in *Feminine Sexuality: Jacques Lacan and the "Ecole Freudienne*," ed. Juliet Mitchell and Jacqueline Rose, trans. Jacqueline Rose [London: Macmillan, 1982], p. 142; and see Lacan, *Le Séminaire livre xx: Encore*, ed. Jacques-Alain Miller [Paris: Editions du Seuil, 1975]).

12. In his "Paris Notebook," Joyce wrote that "All art . . . is static for the feelings of terror and pity on the one hand and of joy on the other are feelings which arrest us" (*The Critical Writings of James Joyce*, ed. Ellsworth Mason and Richard Ellmann [New York: Viking Press, 1959], p. 144). In *A Portrait of the Artist*, Stephen maintains that the "esthetic emotion is . . . static," arresting and raising the mind "above desire and loathing" (pp. 205, 213). Stephen speaks not of the "joy" that arrests but of something more elusive, less definite: "the silent stasis of esthetic pleasure, a spiritual state very like to that cardiac condition which the Italian physiologist Luigi Galvani . . . called an enchantment of the heart." It seems to me that this metaphor, linking a spiritual state to a physiological condition, suggests that Joyce's aesthetic, by this time, has moved beyond the oppositions between static and kinetic art, between pleasure of the mind and of the body. What is suggested in *A Portrait* (not only by Stephen's words but by the fictive frame through which he speaks them) points toward the scene in *Ulysses* where Stephen is bound to art not only by his indifferent love of the beautiful but by his desire, his ressentiment, and his double bind. What undoes the opposition between the static and the kinetic is jouissance (or, to use the word coined by some of the French Joyceans, *joyance*). We could sum all this up by saying that the God "paring his fingernails" in *A Portrait of the Artist* (p. 215) has become in *Ulysses* what Hélène Cixous calls "le rire du texte pervers," a hysterical God (*Prénoms de personne* [Paris: Editions du Seuil, 1974], p. 244).

13. Margaret C. Solomon argues that Bloom is "a symptom, a metaphor of an unconscious structure which underlies all change and perhaps undergirds the gestalt of characterization in the entire Joycean cannon" ("Character as Linguistic Mode: A New Look at Streams-of-Consciousness in Ulysses," in *"Ulysses": Cinquante ans après*, ed. Louis Bonnerot [Paris: Didier, 1974], p. 124. I would agree that Bloom is an overdetermined symptom of an unconscious structure, but this structure can hardly be a stable whole. If Bloom is a metaphor, he is a metaphor of a sliding metaphoricity — not the whole but the hole; as a fictive representation of what may already be a fiction, he signifies the metonymization of metaphor. He is not a point of unity but a point of dispersion. In fact, he is a point in the Dispersion — a Jew.

14. Even calling *Ulysses* a novel has given rise to controversy, though I consider debates over genre to be less serious than debates over theme because the novel has always been a loosely defined form, if not an antiform, whose boundaries are open, whereas the notion of thematic unity and hierarchy is a concept, not a form, whose authority rests on the authority of Western logocentric ideology. For the best discussion of the genre question, see A. Walton Litz, "The Genre of *Ulysses*," in *The Theory of the Novel: New Essays*, ed. John Halperin (New York: Oxford University Press, 1974), pp. 109–20).

15. Shari Benstock observes, "Perhaps Bloom, looking at the orthography of Milly's note, can determine whether 'bad writing' refers to the message or to careless and hurried handwriting, or both. But the reader cannot distinguish, because he reads print not script." In defense of my own reading of Milly's letter, I would note that orthography accommodates itself to systems of value just as much as usage and style. Benstock's overall thesis finally supports my understanding that the printed letters in *Ulysses* demonstrate the resistance of

language to the attributions of fixed meanings and values. More dramatically than quoted speech, the letters are inherently antimimetic. As she notes, "letters can never be mimetically represented by the printed text. In exploiting the range of possible uses of letters, Joyce has signified . . . the absence of 'epistemological sanctity' in *Ulysses*" (Benstock, "The Printed Letters in *Ulysses*," *James Joyce Quarterly* 19.4 [1982]:417, 426).

16. Martha's letter and the postal drama I describe here should be read along with all those letters and litters running from one end to the other of *Finnegans Wake*. John Paul Riquelme has recently emphasized this function (or I should say, this insistence) of the letter in Joyce's work — a function he reads in light of the encounter between Lacan and Derrida over Poe's "The Purloined Letter": "Lacan's essay and the response to it by Jacques Derrida yield some pertinent perspectives for the reader of *Finnegans Wake*, because both writers stress the place of the letter in our language and literature. These interpreters of Poe see in his use of the letter the functioning of alphabetical characters in a structural play of difference producing meaning, and they perceive the working of the epistle as a primary image for communication. Even more emphatically than Poe, Joyce situates literature and life in relation to letters — alphabetical, typographical, epistolary, and belletristic" (Riquelme, *Teller and Tale*, p. 28). Riquelme, however, is more interested in the letter that Joyce has "purloined" from literary tradition than in the structure of the letter as litter, that is, the irreducible remnant that resists all of our generic, ethical, and aesthetic judgments. And this may account for the fact that he hardly sees the structure of the letter underlying *Ulysses*, where the writing is never so stylized as it is in *Finnegans Wake* and where it is difficult to distinguish the literary letter from the litter of everyday life.

17. The reluctant sadist is a sadist in a scenario written and directed by a masochist. But what about the intermittent masochist? If the masochist, as Gilles Deleuze suggests, works toward the production of a fantasy or a fetish in which he suspends desire, then Bloom would seem to be a second-degree masochist, or one who has suspended the desire to suspend desire. But this way of stating things begs the question if we recognize that the realm of masochism is the realm of second degrees, of masks, and the masquerade, of symbolism. Again, I would refer the reader to Baudrillard's notion of the fetishism of the signifier and the code. In Bloom's case, the limit of the masquerade is the boundary at which the romanticism of the masochist encounters the realism of the sadist. Playing close to the limit, Bloom participates in both positions. For a clarification of the difference between masochism and sadism and a critique of the Freudian concept of sadomasochism, see Gilles Deleuze, *Présentation de Sacher-Masoch: Le Froid et le cruel*, with the complete text of *La Venus à la fourrure*, trans. Aude Willm (Paris: Editions de Minuit, 1967).

18. Not only is Joyce not against the machine; he is eminently the product of the age of mechanical reproduction. His interest in the cinema and his method of writing for the printing press (even to the point of composing directly on galleys and placards) emphasize to what extent his work conforms to this Deleuzian formula: "The modern work of art is anything it may seem: it is even its very property of being whatever we like, of having the overdetermination of whatever we like, from the moment it works: the modern work of art is a machine and functions as such" (Gilles Deleuze, *Proust and Signs*, trans. Richard Howard [New York: George Braziller, 1972], p. 128). See Walter Benjamin, "The Work of Art in the Age of Mechanical Reproduction," in *Illuminations*, trans. Harry Zohn (New York: Schocken Books, 1969), pp. 217–51.

19. The style of farce in *Ulysses* reflects what Vivian Mercier describes as "the archaic, tradition-bound nature of Gaelic literature and culture [that] preserved into modern times something of the ancient, playful attitude to language" (*The Irish Comic Tradition* [Oxford: Oxford University Press, 1962], p. 80). Monika Fludernik argues that the style of "playful narrative" becomes the dominant style of *Ulysses* through a development from "Calypso" to "Sirens." It reflects the character of Leopold Bloom and eventually gives way to the pastiche of the later chapters. Fludernik uses this development to criticize the concept of an "initial style" in the first half of *Ulysses* that is rigorously distinct from the styles of the second half. I agree

with her that "playful narrative" or, as I would have it, farce is present to different degrees throughout. Nevertheless, I still see some value in distinguishing the first from the second half of the book. These are heuristic, even readerly, distinctions that need not be taken as absolute differences. See Monika Fludernik, "Narrative and Its Development in *Ulysses*," *Journal of Narrative Technique* 16, no. 1 (1986):15–40.

20. James Joyce, *Finnegans Wake* (New York: Viking, 1959), p. 179, lines 26–27. All further references, by page and line number, are to this edition.

21. There have been numerous attempts at decoding these letters, although it is usually assumed that they have something to do with urinary and/or sexual impotency. In the French translation of *Ulysses*, "U.P." is replaced by *Fou Tu*, that is, "you're nuts," "you've been screwed," or "it's all up with you" (as translated by R. M. Adams). Robert Byrnes argues that all the characters in the novel appear to know the meaning of the letters; but I rather suspect they each know several meanings—including, for example, the allusion to Irish revolutionary slogans that Ruth Bauerle notes—without knowing exactly "what's up." I have no doubt that readers will continue to find interesting and valid significations for these letters. Each new discovery, however, supports my point about their fundamental illusiveness. As Shari Benstock's reading implies, "U.P." dramatizes the resistance of the letter to erasure by interpretation. For the most exhaustive discussion of the letters, see Robert M. Adams, *Surface and Symbol: The Consistency of James Joyce's "Ulysses"* (New York: Oxford University Press, 1962), pp. 192–93. For more recent discussion, see Ruth Bauerle, "Ambly U.P.ia," *James Joyce Quarterly* 9, no. 1 (1971):117–18; Shari Benstock, "The Printed Letters," pp. 424–25; Robert Byrnes, "U.P.:up' Proofed," *James Joyce Quarterly* 21, no. 2 (1984):175–76; and Bernard Benstock. "Who P's in U," *James Joyce Quarterly* 21, no. 4 (1984):372.

22. As Malcolm Richardson points out, Bloom's *voglio* is not an innocent slip. It signifies his knowledge of Molly's desire for Boylan and the unconscious movement of his own desire. Richardson develops the suggestion of R. M. Adams that the *voglio* alludes to the Leporello aria at the beginning of *Don Giovanni*, which contains the following refrain: "*Voglio far il gentiluomo, / E non voglio piu servir*" (I would like to play the master, / Would no more a servant be). Divided between the desire to be Molly's master and her servant, even her go-between, Bloom combines the traits of Zerlina, the young peasant girl who would and would not submit to Don Giovanni's seduction; Don Giovanni himself, who wants her; and Leporello, who wants to be master and would not be servant. See Malcolm Richardson II, "Joycean Irony and Mozart's *Don Giovanni*," *Comparative Literature Studies* 17, no. 2 (1980):93–101; and Adams, *Surface and Symbol*, p. 71.

INDEX

[Only those critics who are cited in more than one essay are indexed; the others can be traced through the footnotes. Characters are listed by their surnames, where known and appropriate. Book titles are not included, except for James Joyce texts, but can be located under the author's name.]

Gramley Library
Salem College
Winston-Salem, NC 27108